Dollars and Sense
Financial Wisdom in 101 Doses

Gerald W. Perritt

DOW JONES-IRWIN
Homewood, Illinois 60430

©Gerald W. Perritt, 1986
Previously published by Investment Information Services Press

All rights reserved. No part of this publication may be
reproduced, stored in a retrieval system, or transmitted,
in any form or by any means, electronic, mechanical,
photocopying, recording, or otherwise, without the prior
written permission of the copyright holder.

Cartoons by Doug Borgstedt

This publication is designed to provide accurate and
authoritative information in regard to the subject matter
covered. It is sold with the understanding that neither the
author nor the publisher is engaged in rendering legal, accounting,
or other professional service. If legal advice or other expert
assistance is required, the services of a competent
professional person should be sought.

*From a Declaration of Principles jointly adopted by a Committee
of the American Bar Association and a Committee of Publishers.*

Acquisitions editor: Richard A. Luecke
Project editor: Rita McMullen
Production manager: Ann Cassady
Printer: Arcata Graphics/Kingsport

ISBN: 1-55623-082-6

Library of Congress Catalog Card No. 87-51714

Printed in the United States of America.

1 2 3 4 5 6 7 8 9 0 K 5 4 3 2 1 0 9 8

Preface

A few years ago, the management of one's personal finances was a rather simple task. You bought some whole life insurance to protect your family, budgeted your income to meet daily expenses and saved a few dollars each month for retirement. Retirement savings were usually invested in a passbook savings account, stocks, bonds, mutual funds, or perhaps U.S. Savings Bonds. Although some knowledge of economics and finance was needed, financial life was definitely much simpler then.

Today, however, there has been a virtual explosion in the number of financial products and services available. Take the insurance decision for example. Today you can choose from among whole life, term life, universal life and single premium deferred life. Or take the variety of bank accounts available. In addition to passbook savings accounts, banks now offer low denomination certificates of deposit, money market accounts, sweep accounts and checking accounts with lines of credit. How about investment alternatives? In addition to stocks and bonds, you can now invest in Treasury securities of all types, puts and calls, financial futures, bonds of all types and mutual funds. A few years ago, you could select from less than 400 mutual funds which either invested in stocks or bonds. Today, you can select among the more than 2,000 different mutual funds that are each seeking to meet a wide variety of investment objectives. Changes in tax laws have also made a number of different retirement plans available which were formerly reserved for only the *very* rich.

Thus, to be able to compete in today's financial world, an individual should obtain an investment education. Since most individuals, probably like yourself, cannot afford the time to go back to school, they must rely on self-education. But beware when buying these investment books. Many of the finance books written today either attempt to sell a particular investment strategy rather than educate or are extremely dry in their writing style. The result of each scenario is either a one-sided view of the financial markets or a book that you might struggle through rather than enjoy.

Dollars and Sense presents, in layman's terms, a description of numerous financial alternatives, investment strategies and products. My goal in writing this book is to make you a more informed financial consumer.

Gerald W. Perritt

About the Author

Gerald W. Perritt, President of Investment Information Services and Perritt Investments, earned a doctorate degree in finance from the University of Kentucky in 1974. Since then, he has taught, written and lectured on investing. Among the colleges Dr. Perritt has taught at are Babson College in Boston, the University of Miami and DePaul University in Chicago.

Dr. Perritt is the founder and editor of two advisory newsletters—*Investment Horizons*, a small stock advisory, and *The Mutual Fund Letter*, a practical and conservative advisory on mutual fund investing. He also maintains a comprehensive mutual fund data service called *FundProbe*

Other titles by Dr. Perritt include *Small Stocks, Big Profits* and *Mutual Funds And Your Investment Portfolio*. He is also a contributing author to *Barron's* and the *Journal* for the American Association of Individual Investors as well as a trusted and frequently quoted source for *Money, Forbes, Financial World, USA Today, The Wall Street Journal* and others. In addition to his publishing ventures, Dr. Perritt is also a professional money manager for both individual and institutional accounts.

When Dr. Perritt is not writing about or managing money at his office in Chicago, he enjoys a good round of golf, downhill skiing, theatre and a nice vintage wine.

Acknowledgments

After writing *Dollars and Sense*, I realized there would be so many individuals to thank. Let's face it, with 101 chapters covering almost every investment topic, there was a lot of data and information to compile and sources to be checked.

So, to those of you who I or my staff contacted in putting this book together, my sincere appreciation in lending accuracy and timeliness to this book.

Special thanks goes out to Cheryl Pierce, Karen Brask and Dianne Chaykin who worked feverishly in putting the chapters together in record time.

And my appreciation to Arlen Laskinsky of Altschuler, Melvoin & Glasser, who graciously contributed his tax expertise in untangling the "simplified" tax laws.

Finally, thanks to Dick Luecke of Dow Jones-Irwin who has made my life as an author a bit less frantic and a lot more enjoyable. I truly appreciate your efforts.

G.P.

Contents

1	Your Financial Checkup	1
2	Personal Financial Housekeeping	6
3	A Do-It-Yourself Financial Plan	8
4	To Your Health	15
5	What is Your Future Worth?	18
6	REMIC—Wall Street's Latest Debutante	20
7	Your Personal Tax Records	22
8	Old Tax Returns Sold	24
9	Noncash Charitable Donations: Watch Out For The IRS Auditor	25
10	This Party's Not Related	27
11	You, Inc.	28
12	Playing Your (Credit) Cards Right	32
13	Reserving Credit	35
14	Keeping Your Credit Record Clean	41
15	Credit—Don't Leave College Without It	45
16	Is Your Mortgage Worth Saving?	47
17	Adjustable Rate Mortgages—Handle With Care	51
18	A Mortgage Shopping List	57
19	Moving Daze And How To Survive It	60
20	The Cost Of Living: It Depends Where You Live	65
21	Some Tips For The Homeowners	68
22	Energy-Efficient Appliances: A Solution To "Rate Shock"	70
23	To Catch A Thief	73
24	Keeping Your Homeowner's Insurance Up To Date	75

25	Universal Life Insurance Debate	78
26	The New Case For Annuities	84
27	Make Room For Daddy Mac & Grannie Mae	88
28	Keeping Up On Your Social Security Benefits	92
29	A Retirement Savings Worksheet	94
30	Retirement Portfolio Administration	100
31	What To Do With Your Retirement Portfolio Today	104
32	Don't Be Misled By Bank Ads	108
33	The Best Benefits Of An IRA Are Kept For Last	110
34	Interest-Free Loans From Your IRA? No Way!	114
35	A Retirement Plan Better Than A Keogh	115
36	Your Retirement Nest Egg: The Three-Million-Dollar Misunderstanding	117
37	On The Road Again	121
38	It's A Lemon	124
39	The Hard Numbers On College Costs	126
40	College Financial Aid: Sources You May Not Think Of	128
41	High Leverage Mortgages	133
42	Selecting Mutual Funds? Get The Facts First!	135
43	The Mutual Fund Prospectus: Read It Before You Invest	137
44	A Mutual Fund Evaluation Worksheet	144
45	Buying Yesterday's Winners: A Formula For Mediocrity	153
46	Should You Invest In A Mutual Fund Sequel?	155
47	Mutual Fund Investment and Taxation	157
48	A New Trend In The Mutual Fund Industry: Fund Closings	164
49	Investment Advisory Services	168
50	Mutual Fund Recordkeeping	175
51	Keeping Up With The Money Market	177
52	How To Select A Money Market Fund	179
53	The 50 Largest Money Market Mutual Funds	185
54	Shopping By Mail? A Few Things To Keep In Mind...	191
55	How To Interview The Financial Help	192
56	Coping With The Financial Hard Sell	199
57	Will I Get Rich If I Invest In The Stock Market?	204
58	Common Stock Values Depend On What You're After	206
59	Developing An Investment Philosophy: A Lesson From History	211

Contents

60	Investors' Greatest Ills, And Some Cures	213
61	Reading Stock Market Quotations	218
62	The Dow Jones Industrial Average	222
63	Other Measures Of Stock Market Prices	228
64	Measuring Portfolio Performance	230
65	Speculation Is In The Eye Of The Beholder	237
66	Finding The Next Superstock	241
67	The Original "Value Approach To Investing"	243
68	Paying Your Broker, Your Banker, The Candlestick Maker	247
69	Time Is Money	253
70	How Risky *Are* Your Investments?	259
71	The Price You Pay For The Best Investment Returns	266
72	Portfolio Diversification: A Matter Of Time And Assets	269
73	Dollar Cost Averaging: The Ins And Outs Of Playing The Market By Numbers	273
74	Investing By Formula	281
75	The "Dividends" From Common Stock Investments	291
76	Small Investors, Small Stocks, Big Profits	296
77	Investment Strategies and Bear Markets	302
78	Games Money Plays	307
79	The Rule Of 72: Cheaper Than A Calculator	313
80	Investment Games You'd Be Better Off Not Playing	315
81	Taxable Versus Tax-Exempt Returns: What's The Difference?	322
82	An Investment Riddle: When Is A 5% Investment Return A 7.6% Investment Return?	325
83	A Close Look At Ginnie Mae Funds	326
84	Commodity Funds—Future Speculating For The "Little Guy"	332
85	Convertible Bonds: An Alternative Equity Investment	340
86	Bonds That Don't Make Interest Payment—On Purpose	345
87	How Do You Take Your Municipals?	349
88	Investing In U.S. Savings Bonds	355
89	How To Earn Returns On Idle Cash	359
90	Equity CDs—High Yield With A New Twist	362
91	Investing In Gold And Precious Metals	364
92	Keeping Your Broker Honest	373
93	Commodities For The High-Risk Investor	378

94	One-Stop Shopping	380
95	What Is Money? Who Controls It?	381
96	How The Fed Counts Money	385
97	The Federal Dollar: Where It Comes From, Where It Goes	387
98	Uncle Sam's Big IOU	389
99	What Is The Consumer Price Index?	394
100	Why The Fed is Worth Watching	398
101	Who's Protecting Your Money?	401

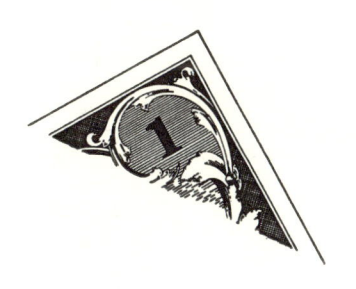

Your Financial Checkup

Most of us are pretty conscientious when it comes to the state of our physical health—we see our doctor, dentist, maybe even our eye doctor or allergist on a regular basis. But when it comes to our financial health, the picture is quite different. We simply ignore the importance of a regular financial checkup. Nonetheless, it's important, in terms of your financial health, to review your status at least once every year.

Determine Your *Net Worth*

Simply stated, this is the value of what you own minus the amount of money you owe—your current level of wealth. If you owe creditors more than the value of your assets, you are technically insolvent. That is not to say that you are bankrupt. As long as your current intake (income plus new debt) exceeds your current cash outgo, you will be able to keep your head above water. However, you are also in a very vulnerable position. If your ability to borrow, or your wage or salary income, is somehow limited, technical insolvency can lead to not-so-technical bankruptcy. Also, the passage of every year shortens your working life. You should be continually increasing your net worth so that your assets will provide the comforts needed when you retire. Figure 1-1 contains a worksheet which can be used to compute personal net worth.

To begin, list the current value of your assets. Use current market values instead of historical costs or current prices. The sofa you bought last year for $500 may be currently selling for $600 in a furniture mart, but yours may only bring $200 if it was sold in a garage sale. To determine the market value of nonfinancial assets like furniture and applicances, check newspaper ads for the current asking price of comparable items. Since final prices are usually less than asking prices, our suggestion is to deduct 10% from these prices to realistically estimate value. A realtor will be able to tell you what

Figure 1-1
Computing Your Net Worth (The Personal Balance Sheet)
Date _____

ASSETS (What you own)		LIABILITIES (What you owe)	
Cash	$_____	Mortgage on residence	$_____
Savings deposits	_____	Other mortgages	_____
Life insurance (cash surrender value)	_____	Notes and loans (including installment debt on auto, credit cards, etc,)	_____
Stocks and bonds (including mutual funds)	_____	Other unpaid bills	_____
Personal residence	_____	Business debts	_____
Personal assets (furniture, jewelry, tools, etc)	_____	Other liabilities	_____
Automobile(s)	_____		_____
Collectibles and precious metals	_____		_____
Rental property	_____		_____
Business assets	_____		
Vested pension fund	_____	Total liabilities	_____
IRA, Keogh accounts	_____		
Other assets	_____	Net worth (Total Assets minus Total Liabilities)	
Total assets	$_____		$_____

comparable residences in your area have recently sold for, and an auto dealer can tell you what he has been paying for used automobiles like yours. The employee benefits officer will be able to supply the current value of your pension benefits if you are eligible for company-sponsored retirement benefits ("vested"). Use recent bank and other credit statements to determine the amount of money that you owe.

Fine-Tuning Your Net Worth

The next step in determining the state of your financial health involves what's been happening to your net worth. Has it been increasing? Decreasing? If the former, is the increase enough to meet both present and future needs?

Figure 1-2 is a worksheet that can be used to measure increases or decreases in net worth over time. In the first part of the worksheet, income from all sources is recorded. The second part is a catalog of monthly and annual expenses. Note that I have included two columns. Estimated income and expenses are actually a one-year financial plan. If you find that you have a deficit after deducting expenses from income, your net worth over the year may actually be declining. As a result, you may want to reduce budgeted expenses or attempt to increase income.

I suggest that before completing your estimates, you examine current levels of income and expenses by recording the amount earned and expended for the current year. To reconstruct the year's financial activities, use pay stubs, bank statements, etc. to record income earned, and use your check register and credit card statements to record expenses. While this process is time-consuming, you should find the final report quite informative. Many people are surprised to find how much (or how little) they spent for various items. In addition, a catalog of past expenses will help you plan for the coming year. Finally, the estimated income statement provides a benchmark with which you can compare actual expenses and the initial plan. If you find discrepancies during the year, consumption patterns can be changed to bring year-end results back in line with the initial plan.

Some Helpful Guidelines

These are no hard-and-fast rules for planning consumption expenditures. In fact, as a percentage of total income, the more you earn, the less you'll spend. The reverse is true as income is reduced. The percentage of income allocated to various expenditures is both a function of income level and personal taste. However, based on national spending patterns for the "average" family and on benchmarks established by lending institutions, I can offer a few guidelines for structuring your consumption patterns. These guidelines apply to families with aftertax income between $20,000 and $40,000. Housing expenditures (including utilities and home repairs) should average approximately 35% of net income (e.g., a family with an annual aftertax income of $25,000 will spend approximately $8,750 per year or $730 per month on housing). Food (groceries, household supplies, and meals eaten out) represent 20% of one's take-home pay. The transportation budget should average 10% and clothing 8% of aftertax income. The average American family saves *approximately* 6% of its take-home pay.

How "healthy" you are financially is largely a function of how well (off) you want to be. Several of the chapters in this book describe financial-planning methods that can help you define goals, both short-term and for your retirement years. Your (at least) annual financial checkup should help you both determine those goals and see how well you're meeting them.

If you want to increase your wealth, you must follow a very carefully prepared financial plan. (More about that later.) While it is easy to find excuses not to plan (I don't have the time; I can't

Dollars and Sense

Figure 1-2
Statement of Income and Expenses

	Current Year (Estimated)		Current Year (Actual)	
	Monthly	Annual	Monthly	Annual
INCOME				
Salary (after income taxes)	_____	_____	_____	_____
Interest	_____	_____	_____	_____
Dividends	_____	_____	_____	_____
Business income (net of expenses)	_____	_____	_____	_____
Rental income (net of expenses)	_____	_____	_____	_____
Other income	_____	_____	_____	_____
Total income	_____	_____	_____	_____
EXPENSES				
Food (groceries, household supplies, meals out)	_____	_____	_____	_____
Rent or mortgage (includes property taxes)	_____	_____	_____	_____
Other taxes (intangible taxes, etc.)	_____	_____	_____	_____
Utilities (gas, electric, water, phone, etc.)	_____	_____	_____	_____
Home repairs	_____	_____	_____	_____
Home furnishings/appliances	_____	_____	_____	_____
Clothing (include laundry)	_____	_____	_____	_____
Auto loan payments	_____	_____	_____	_____
Auto upkeep (gas, oil, and repairs)	_____	_____	_____	_____

Continued

Figure 1-2
Statement of Income and Expenses, *Cont'd*

	Current Year (Estimated)		Current Year (Actual)	
	Monthly	Annual	Monthly	Annual
Other transportation				
Insurance (life, health, home, auto, etc.)				
Medical and dental				
Gifts				
Education				
Entertainment				
Vacations				
Other expenses				
Total expenses				
Income less expenses				

stick to a budget; I always spend everything I make, etc.), a little time and effort spent listing your net worth and income and expenditures may show you how much planning could mean. After all, as an income earner you have the responsibility to derive the greatest satisfaction possible from your efforts. While I admit that "wealth cannot buy happiness", increased wealth will allow you greater freedom to choose a lifestyle consistent with your desires. To put it another way, you owe it to yourself to get the most "bang for your buck."

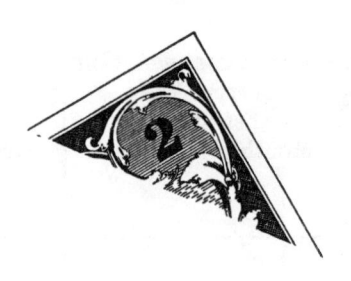

Personal Financial Housekeeping

Long-range financial planning can be a rather complex process. Frequently, individuals find that they must turn to planning professionals (financial planners, accountants, attorneys, etc.) for assistance. While these pros can be quite helpful in the planning process, you must provide the data they need to generate a plan. Professionals will also most likely want to know what planning you have done in the past and what actions you have already taken.

To get the most from your visit with a financial planning professional, I suggest that you first consider the following questions which will most likely be asked during the initial interview. The list is not exhaustive. Rather, the questions relate to general matters to be considered in developing any financial plan and focus on helping you put your financial house in order, especially in the event of an unexpected tragedy—death, impairment, or property loss.

1. Have you reviewed your current financial status?

A good starting point is preparing a statement of assets and liabilities (a *balance sheet*) to determine your net worth. You should prepare such a balance sheet at least annually to determine whether your short- and long-range goals are being realized—particularly your investment and retirement goals. It should encompass all major assets and liabilities, including life insurance. A copy should be put aside for your executor.

2. Do you have a will?

If not, one should be prepared by your attorney in concert with your tax advisers, if for no other reason than to designate an executor, and to name guardians for your children. If you have a will, it should be reviewed and updated periodically, especially in light of the substantial changes in the gift and estate tax laws made in 1981. Your will should be stored in a safe place and your executor should have access to it.

3. Have you considered how title to your property should be held?

In some situations, plans have been thwarted by the way the title to property was held. For example, you may want your property placed in trust for your spouse when you die. But if your husband or wife is already listed as a joint owner of that property, too bad—the property, by operation of law, may automatically pass to your spouse. Spouses jointly holding a substantial amount of property should review these holdings to ensure achieving desired tax and economic results.

4. Have you provided your executor with information concerning your estate?

Your executor should know the location of key documents (such as your will), the names of your attorney and accountant, and should have a good idea of the nature and extent of your assets.

5. Have your personal papers and valuables been properly safeguarded?

A safe deposit box or fireproof home safe is a virtual necessity for most people, not only for the financial security they provide but also because they provide a safe place for personal papers and momentos that are difficult or impossible to replace.

6. Is your homeowner's and auto insurance adequate?

Your home has probably increased markedly in value. You should make sure that your insurance coverage has kept pace. Furthermore, higher prices for precious metals have caused some insurance companies to impose coverage limitations on silverware and other valuable personal effects. You should check your present policy and decide whether you need supplemental coverage. In some cases, increasing the deductible may reduce long-term insurance costs. However, remember that tax deductions for unreimbursed casualty and theft losses are now much harder to come by. Another good idea is to catalog and photograph all your property to help ensure proper settlement of any insurance claims.

7. Is your life insurance coverage adequate?

Inflation may have eroded the value of your coverage. Inflation aside, your coverage should be periodically reviewed in terms of liquidity. As the mix of your assets changes and as your children finish school and become self-sufficient, your need for liquid assets may also change.

8. Do you carry excess liability insurance and disability insurance?

Usually this insurance is fairly inexpensive, and the benefits available if a major accident occurs could be enormous.

Source: "Personal Financial Planning Opportunities" 1985. Deloitte Haskins + Sells.

A Do-It-Yourself Financial Plan

Nearly everybody is in the financial-planning business these days. Some are good, most just want to sell you something. If you're tempted to seek a planner's advice, consider the source.

Even if you feel you need an "expert's" help, it won't come cheap. Figure on anywhere from $25 to $500 for a cheap plan, nothing more than a set of forms cranked through a computer, really, and available from several brokerage houses and big accounting firms. Getting a personalized assessment of your finances from a planner who actually interviews you typically costs $1,000 or more and makes little sense unless you're earning something in the six-figure range.

While few of us fall into that category, most of us could use some help in developing a coordinated strategy for reaching our financial goals. Unfortunately, too many self-appointed experts are rushing to the rescue. On the whole, the advice they dispense is, at best, self-serving and at worst, downright dangerous. Virtually anyone can call himself a financial planner and be one by simply hanging out a shingle. At least 200,000 people in the United States now claim the title. They range from insurance peddlers to brokers, accountants, bankers, and lawyers. By some estimates, they are collectively managing well over $147 billion. Yet the financial-planning industry is totally unregulated. And while it is making a voluntary attempt to standardize planners' qualifications, at present they are all over the map. Some planners have had no training at all. Quite a few base their credentials on having passed a series of exams given by the College for Financial Planning in Denver. At the top end are CPAs and other bona fide planners with an M.B.A. or law degree. All have their biases. Insurance agents and brokers are naturally going to suggest a plan heavy on products and investments that generate commissions for them, while a CPA may focus more on taxes, and an attorney more on estate-planning. Shysters tend to push gold, diamonds and other "collectibles," along with shaky tax shelters, and schemes and scams of all kinds.

Who Can You Trust?

No planner can magically assure your financial security. A good one can make useful suggestions, but will stress that it's your money and you're the one who has to live with decisions. The first order of business will be an analysis of your current situation. So, even if you plan to seek outside advice, it will be helpful to fill in the "Do-It-Yourself Financial Plan" (Figure 3-1) before you consult a pro.

There are basically two types of independent planners, those who take commissions on the investments they "sell," and those who don't. The latter call themselves "fee-only" planners and make their money solely by giving advice. If a fee-only planner recommends an investment—setting up a trust for sending a child to college, or more life insurance—the commissions earned if you follow his advice go to someone else. Supposedly, a fee-only planner can thus be more objective in evaluating your true needs. On the other hand, it's up to you to implement the plan—the planner is only selling you advice. Some planners charge for an initial interview, similar to the consultation fee you would pay to shop for an attorney. After that, fees depend on the level of service you require. A basic plan outlines your long-term financial goals and offers a realistic strategy for getting there. Expect to pay extra, for instance, if you want a planner to fill out your income tax forms or renegotiate the mortgage on your home. Once you have a plan, count on updating it at least annually, more often if there are major changes in your personal situation.

Word of mouth, or asking for suggestions from people you know who have used a planner, is the best way to get names. Two other sources are industry trade groups, the Institute of Certified Financial Planners (2 Denver Highlands, 10065 E. Harvard Ave., Suite 320, Denver, CO 80231-5942) and the International Association of Financial Planners (2 Concourse Parkway, Suite 800, Atlanta, GA 30328). Several brokerage firms have now trained their stockbrokers in the basics of financial planning for middle-income folks, separate from the pricier services they offer wealthy clients. Among them are Sears-Dean Witter, Merrill Lynch, E.F. Hutton, and Prudential-Bache. A computer-generated plan from a brokerage typically costs about $200. One independent company that is strictly in the business of selling such plans is the Consumer Financial Institute (288 Walnut St., Newton, MA 02160). Based on a long questionnaire that you fill out and mail in, the firm will produce a plan for you in three weeks at a cost of $195.

Figure 3-1
Do-It-Yourself Financial Plan

Effective financial planning begins with an assessment of your current assets and liabilities. The worksheet below is designed for this purpose. Column headings in Part A cover the following: *Description and Amount of Assets*—specific stocks, bonds, mutual funds or other investments you currently own and the number of shares, etc.; *Current Yield After Taxes*—the formula for figuring your aftertax yield is based on your tax bracket. Multiply the asset's current yield by a quantity equal to 1.00 minus your tax bracket expressed as a decimal. For example, the aftertax yield of an asset with a current yield of 13% for a person in the 35% bracket is 13.00 × (1.00 − .35), or 13.00 × .65 which equals 8.45%; *Net Annual Income*—the amount of income the asset is providing you yearly; *Current Market Value*—the highest price that the asset would fetch today in the open market; *Percentage of Total Portfolio Value*—the percentage of your portfolio's total current market value that the asset represents; *Percentage Increase or Decrease in Market Value in Last Yr./Last 5 Yrs.*—on paper, this is the percentage gain (loss) in the asset's market value for each time period.

A. Analysis of Your Present Investments

Kinds of Assets	Description and Amount	Current Yield After Taxes	Net Annual Income	Current Market Value	Percentage of Total Portfolio Value	Percentage Increase or Decrease in Market Value in Last Yr./Last 5 Yrs.
I. Cash						
NOW accounts		____ %	$ ____		____	
Other checking accounts					____	
Brokerage accounts						
Subtotal					==== %	

II.	Savings accounts				
	Savings certificates				
	IRA/Keogh accounts				
	Subtotal	$_____	_____	$_____ %	
III.	Life insurance (cash value)				
	Subtotal			$_____ %	
IV.	Common stocks				
	Subtotal	$_____	_____	$_____ %	
V.	Fixed-income securities (corporate bonds, municipal bonds and govt. securities)				
	Subtotal	$_____	_____	$_____ % _____ %/_____ / _____ / _____ / _____	
VI.	Mutual funds				
	Subtotal	$_____	_____	$_____ % _____ / _____ / _____ / _____	
VII.	Other investments				
	Subtotal	$_____	_____	$_____ % _____ / _____ /	
Total Assets		$_____	_____ 100	$_____ %	

Continued

Figure 3-1
Do-It-Yourself Financial Plan, *Cont'd*
B. *Analysis of Your Debts*

Type of Obligation	Maturity Date	Interest Rate*	Aftertax Interest Cost	Monthly Payment	Outstanding Balance
I. Mortgage(s)					
First	_____	____%	____%	$_____	$_____
Second	_____	_____	_____	_____	_____
II. Credit Cards					
#1	_____	_____	_____	_____	_____
2	_____	_____	_____	_____	_____
3	_____	_____	_____	_____	_____
III. Installment Loans					
#1	_____	_____	_____	_____	_____
2	_____	_____	_____	_____	_____
3	_____	_____	_____	_____	_____
IV. Other debts	_____	_____	_____	_____	_____
Totals				$_____	$_____

*Annual Percentage Rate

C. Sharpening Your Financial Strategy

I. Maintain an "emergency fund" equal to three months' income.
II. Keep monthly payments on all debts to less than 20% of monthly aftertax income.
III. Maintain adequate insurance.
IV. Contribute the maximum yearly tax-deductible amount to an IRA/Keogh.
V. Don't invest elsewhere until you have satisfied points I, II, III, and IV.
VI. If you can afford to own your own home, invest first in where you live.
VII. Try to put 15% of your aftertax income (outside of IRA/Keogh contributions) in other investments.
VIII. Spread your investment risk by putting about 80% in assets offering consistent current income and capital growth for the long pull (high-grade common stocks and mutual funds, high-quality bonds) and 20% in assets that are riskier, but have the potential for greater capital growth (more speculative stocks and mutual funds).
IX. In general, avoid using leverage (borrowing) to invest.
X. Make your own investment decisions. Nobody else has the same stake in the outcome.

Who Needs a Pro?

The plain truth is that computer-generated plans don't do anything for you that you can't do on your own. And unless you're wealthy or have complicated tax- or estate-planning needs, you probably don't need professional planning advice. Fill in the worksheet (Figure 3-1). It will "cost" you about 45 minutes, a fraction of the charge for consulting a planner. You should be able to find answers to any questions you still have in the numerous self-help books that are on the market or free at your local library. Two good basic handbooks: John Dorfman's *Family Investment Guide* ($3.50) and *Personal Financial Planning* by G. Victor Hallman and Jerry S. Rosenbloom ($5.95).

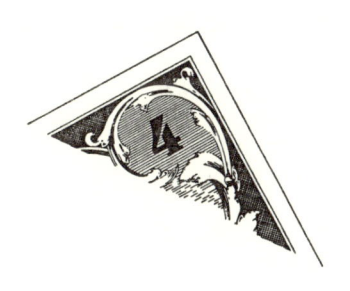

To Your Health

The squeeze is on. Rising medical costs are prompting most large companies and many smaller ones to put the arm on their employees to pay for more of their own health care. That makes the annual decision—which health plan to choose—more important, and probably more confusing, than ever.

With the variety of plans now available, it isn't easy to tote up the pluses and minuses of each. You probably have a traditional group health plan, but it may have new twists (like a deductible). Maybe you can opt for a health maintenance organization (HMO), or the latest thing, a preferred provider organization (PPO), both of which get you discounts on care, but only from participating doctors and hospitals.

Paying a deductible for regular group insurance may be the biggest jolt. Many companies that have never had deductibles are now asking employees to ante up $100 or $200—per year per family member—before receiving benefits. If you've been paying a deductible for a while, expect it to go up, possibly to as much as $500. And don't be surprised if the fine print kindly explains that the company no longer will pay all the bills if you're hospitalized.

No matter which type of plan you choose, more money for nearly all medical expenses is bound to come out of your pocket. Before long, insurance experts say, most employees can expect their share of the family's annual medical bills to run into a few *thousand* dollars, instead of a few hundred. The only good news is that the additional expense may give you a tax deduction (although recent tax changes make the deduction for medical expenses tougher to claim).

There's no getting around poring through the usually dense information on health insurance most companies provide. But once you've read it all, make a list of your questions and go over them with a company benefits counselor before you make your decision. Typically, you can only change plans once a year. So, it's important to assure yourself and your family of good medical care—at a reasonable cost.

Some Qs and As

As you go through the explanation of your healthcare benefits, try to reduce the verbiage to the essentials. Here are some key questions that you need to answer to pick the plan that's best for you:
- *Is there a new or higher deductible?*
 If so, how much you have to pay before coverage begins may be buried in a long description of your "broadened coverage" or added sweeteners, such as a new employee fitness center. Extra coverage may not do you any good if it's for treatment you don't expect to need or exercise equipment you won't use.
 The deductible is typically lower in a PPO—or nonexistent— to encourage you to use doctors and hospitals with a record of being cost-conscious (hence, "preferred providers" because they keep employers' health costs down). Although an HMO usually sells a package deal to a company that includes its own doctors and hospitals, your personal physician may well belong to a PPO in your area.
- *Does the plan cover your family's specific needs?*
 While it's impossible to predict how healthy everyone will stay in the coming year, some expenses are probably at least likely. A good example: orthodontics. Most group insurance plans, even those that include dental coverage, don't cover braces. But many HMO and PPO plans now cover at least part of the cost.
- *Can you choose your own doctor or hospital?*
 Traditional plans usually let you use any physician or hospital you like. But with HMOs and PPOs, you're generally limited to using physicians and hospitals that belong to the company's plan. Get a list of who they are and where they're located. A discount at a "neighborhood clinic" that's a 45-minute drive from where you live won't help much in an emergency.
- *Who pays how much?*
 Your costs are typically spelled out in terms of the deductible and the copayment (what you pay each time you use a health service after coverage begins). Find out if just you, or the entire family, must meet the deductible before your benefits start. Sometimes the trade-off for a higher deductible is lower copayments.
 Choosing a plan with a higher deductible, then, would make sense if someone in the family is in poor health and

requires frequent visits to the doctor. Even though HMOs are essentially prepaid plans, check the fine print: Often, you have to pay a small extra amount for prescription medicine, say, $5 each time you have a prescription filled.
- *Are there reimbursement limits?*
It's almost certain that there are indeed points past which you begin picking up the whole tab. The limits may be different for different illnesses or expressed as a lump-sum daily, yearly, or lifetime amount. By the same token, there should be a limit on the amount *you* are required to pay. Many companies limit employee payments to $1,000 or $2,000 a year.
- *Is your coverage good out of town?*
Most plans will pay for at least some care when you're away from home, but the extent of your coverage may depend on how far away you were when the emergency occurred or whether you were traveling on business. Check HMO and PPO plans in particular for the rules on when they will pay for an "alternate provider" outside of participating doctors and hospitals in your community.

Many plans have other wrinkles, all aimed at keeping the company's costs down. For example, some employers give you the option of paying a lower deductible in return for paying more of your insurance premium. But if your family's health costs are generally less than $1,000 a year, you're probably better off paying the higher deductible.

A few companies will actually pay you to stay healthy. Such plans work like this: You pay a yearly deductible of, say, $175 per person or a maximum of $350 for your family. But as an incentive *not* to use the plan, the company pays you $500, less any benefit. If during the year you have $350 in covered medical bills, the company takes care of the first $175 and 80% of the rest, or $140. You get back $360—$500 minus the $140 benefit.

Almost all companies have raised their deductibles for hospital stays. For instance, it's no longer unusual for employees to be asked to pay the first $100 of every hospital admission and at least 20% of the doctor's hospital bill. Some companies attempt to keep hospitalization to a minimum by paying the full cost of lab tests only if they are performed before a patient is admitted.

Check your plan for waivers on all types of deductibles. Sometimes the deductible for hospitalization, for instance, can be waived by the company's insurance carrier if circumstances are unusual.

If, after going over your plan with a company benefits counselor, you still have questions, insist on talking with a representative of the insurance carrier directly. After all, if you're being asked to shoulder more of the burden for health care, you're entitled to be sure you're getting your money's worth.

What Is Your Future Worth?

We may assign a money value to all sorts of assets—house, car, business equipment. But when it comes to the "value" of a human being, we tend to be more abstract, thinking in terms of moral qualities, not money quantities. However, for many individuals, the ability to earn employment income is their most valuable asset. We call this asset "human capital." It is defined as the present worth of an individual's future employment earnings.

It may sound callous to refer to a human being as an income-producing machine. But that is exactly what most working folks are. We have expended a large sum of money or a long period of time learning skills which, when practiced, generate income. Further, like a machine, age often takes its toll on our ability to continue to generate income. In short, like a machine, we wear out. Unlike most machines, however, we cannot be overhauled. On the other hand, unlike the machine, we can, through proper planning, utilize tangible wealth to supplement and then replace employment income. Thus, one goal of financial planning is to replace worn out human capital with investment capital. *What* we're replacing, however, depends on what we're "worth." This is calculated as the *present* value of our *future* earnings—what we've called human capital.

To compute this value, we must forecast future annual net earnings over our expected remaining income-producing years. To determine the present value of earnings, we apply a capitalization (discount) rate. Calculating this rate is really beyond the scope of this book. Suffice it to say that the rate tells us what future income is worth in terms of the present. It allows us to judge future and present income on a comparable basis. Tables are available that list present value (discount) rates. Figure 5-1 is an example.

Figure 5-1 lists the discount rate that can be applied to current net (aftertax) income to obtain a quick estimate of the present worth of future earnings. For example, suppose that your current

Figure 5-1
Human Capital Multiplier

Remaining Years of Employment	\multicolumn{7}{c}{Estimated Annual Earnings Growth Rate}
	0%	2%	5%	8%	10%	12%	15%
5	3.6	3.8	4.1	4.5	4.7	5.0	5.6
10	5.7	6.1	7.0	8.1	9.0	10.0	11.2
15	6.8	7.6	9.1	11.1	12.8	15.0	18.3
20	7.5	8.5	10.6	13.6	16.4	20.0	26.8
25	7.8	9.1	11.7	15.6	19.5	25.0	36.9
30	8.1	9.4	12.4	17.3	22.4	30.0	47.0
35	8.2	9.6	12.9	18.7	25.0	35.0	60.4
40	8.3	9.8	13.3	19.8	27.4	40.0	75.8

aftertax annual income is $25,000 and that you plan to work for another 10 years. You expect your income to increase by 5% each year over this period. The appropriate discount rate, then, is found at the intersection of the appropriate column (representing remaining employment years) and row (representing the estimated income growth rate). In this case, the appropriate rate is 7.0. Thus, given a current aftertax income of $25,000, the present value of future earnings is 7.0 × $25,000 or $175,000.

In terms of financial planning, the value of human capital is the sum which, when invested at the current rate of interest, will yield an amount that exactly duplicates future wages or salary. In this case, $175,000 invested to earn 9% (the current yield on high-grade corporate bonds).

Why is this question so important? Again, the answer gets down to a question of human worth. Most of us have homeowners and automobile insurance to provide replacement of these assets if they should be destroyed by accident. However, many people fail to adequately insure their human assets. The procedure outlined above can be used to estimate the insurance coverage necessary to "replace" human capital.

REMIC—Wall Street's Latest Debutante

If you like Ginnie Mae, wait until you meet her newest cousin, REMIC.

Not to be confused with the famous actress, REMIC stands for real estate mortgage investment conduit. This new type of mortgage-backed security sweeping Wall Street was made possible by the Tax Reform Act. Experts say the new vehicle could bring with it more mortgage money for home buyers.

Investment firms, which have also begun selling REMICs, predict they will revolutionize the way mortgage pools have traditionally been put together and sold to investors. If all goes well, the securities could open the door for other new kinds of mortgage-related offerings that would be appealing to both issuers and investors, helping to drive down mortgage rates.

The REMIC provisions of the 1986 tax law allow issuers to package mortgages and sell them to the public in a variety of ways. Like Ginnie Maes, REMICs are also bond-like vehicles backed by pools of mortgages, whose cash flows create securities of different maturities. Securities firms are issuing them on their own behalf as well as for clients that range from the Federal National Mortgage Association to banks and other financial-services companies. Therefore, depending on the issuer, default risk varies widely.

Moreover, investors may find even the nomenclature of the new securities confusing. Although they are called REMICs, the securities are sold in the form of trusts titled "collateralized mortgage obligations" or CMOs.

One of the first of these trusts was a $200 million offering in October 1986 by Salomon Brothers, the New York bond firm, for Meritor Financial Group, a Philadelphia-based financial-services conglomerate. The securities, which were backed by 9 1/2% FNMA mortgages, were priced to yield from 7.81% to 10.15%.

Early Repayment Risk

Like Ginnie Maes, however, REMICs will return less than their projected yields to investors if the mortgages they represent are paid off faster than anticipated. Lower interest rates—a boon to the bond market in general—can wreak havoc with mortgage securities.

REMICs, coming at a time when the mortgage market is only just recovering from the wave of refinancing, possess another risk. The market is already bulging at the seams. Having caught the fancy of the general public, the trading volume of Ginnie Maes, or pools of mortgages guaranteed by the Government National Mortgage Association, and similar securities has quadrupled over the last five years. Last year, over $2 trillion of the securities changed hands, outpacing the volume in common stocks.

The activity in mortgages has been so hectic that some experts have compared it to the "go-go" days of the stock market in the late 60s. That period often forced the New York Stock Exchange to close early because it couldn't keep up with orders, while "back office" problems in handling volume forced many small brokerage firms out of business.

REMICS will now give issuers flexibility they've never had, not only to bring even more mortgage-related securities to market, but perhaps riskier ones. Those are likely to include securities backed by commercial mortgages, a variation that first came on the scene a little more than a year ago and almost immediately caused problems. As a result of dealing in the securities, Ticor Mortgage Insurance Co. was forced to default on mortgages it insured. The defaults shook the infant market, raising questions about the creditworthiness of other commercially insured pools.

But even a sterling credit rating won't protect mortgage-security buyers who simply might be intrigued by the new REMICs from further interest rate jolts. Just ask Ginnie Mae investors who learned to their dismay that while the government guarantees that interest and principal will be paid on those securities, that's as far as it goes. Future market value and yield are anybody's guess.

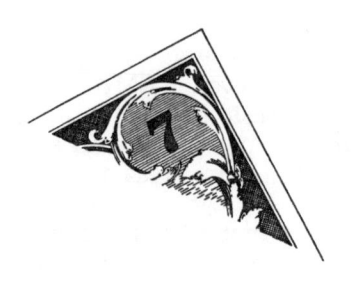

Your Personal Tax Records

Even if you've already gone through the annual headache of filing income tax returns for this year, there is still some additional work to be done. To establish proper documentation should your return be selected for an IRS audit, or simply to provide data for next year's tax returns, you must keep accurate and complete records.

Tax filers are urged to keep their recordkeeping in order. Over the years, Congress has become less tolerant of individuals who understate their income and/or overstate their expenses. Accordingly, there is pressure on the IRS to toughen enforcement rules; this dictates the need for individuals to maintain appropriate and accurate records.

What to Retain

Unless you operate a business, the required record-keeping can be relatively simple. Because the burden of proof rests with the taxpayer, it is to your advantage to retain accurate and complete records, especially for deductions. The IRS generally will disallow deductions that cannot be adequately substantiated; this can often result in a 5% negligence penalty plus additional penalties based upon interest on the underpayment of the liability.

For many years, the primary information returns (IRS forms reporting amounts distributed to taxpayers that by law must be completed by banks, companies, etc.) were those for interest/dividend income (Form 1099) and wages/salaries (W-2 Forms). Since 1983, however, the IRS has been crosschecking additional income sources, such as state and local tax refunds, social security benefits, IRA contributions, and IRA and pension disbursements. And beginning with 1985 returns, the service will computer match information on alimony payments and mortgage interest deductions.

In addition to information returns, certain personal records should be retained, such as cancelled checks, bank statements, and receipts. These records are necessary to substantiate medical expenses, interest and taxes paid, charitable contributions, and other deductible items.

It is also important to maintain information, such as stock brokers' advice and real estate records, showing purchase price, proceeds from sales, and investment-related deductions. If you own securities, it is important to maintain a record of each security owned, including stock splits and stock dividends. You should list certificate numbers, number of shares, and sales prices.

Although Congress has repealed the stringent record-keeping requirement of the 1984 Tax Reform Act relating to business use of automobiles, the IRS still requires substantiation to support deductions. Also, documentation should be retained to support the write-off of a personal computer for business or investment use. Other deductible business expenses should be substantiated as well. Besides receipts, an appointment book—listing meeting places, dates and times, business contacts, and business purpose of the expense—is useful. Remember, for entertainment expenses exceeding $25, the IRS requires receipts.

Regardless of tax requirements, certain personal financial records should always be retained. Bank statements and the cancelled checks returned with them generally should be held in case they are needed to settle any disputes. Receipts for major purchases and any copies of warranties you receive should be kept indefinitely. It is also important to keep good records (including photographs) of your valuables and household effects for insurance purposes.

Where and How Long to Keep Records

Once you know which records to retain, you should store them in the proper place. All valuable or irreplaceable documents should be stored in a fireproof lockbox or safe, file cabinet, or safe-deposit box. Records for insured items should be stored apart from the insured property to prevent the concurrent loss or destruction of both the records and the property.

The law doesn't require you to keep personal records for any specific time. However, a good general rule to follow is that tax returns, bank statements, and cancelled checks should be retained for at least six years. Records supporting the accuracy of your income tax return should be kept for as long as they may be material in determining your tax liability. This is generally three years (the number of years the IRS has to audit a return) after the return is filed. However, a six-year period applies if there has been at least 25% understatement of income. And, if a taxpayer submits a fraudulent return or fails to file a return altogether, there is no limit on how many years the IRS has for assessment.

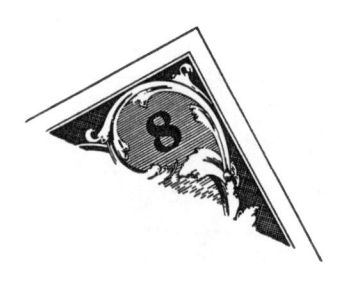

Old Tax Returns Sold

Although when you drop them in the mail (hopefully before April 15) you probably say "good riddance," it's actually a good idea to keep copies of your tax returns. I'm not suggesting them as a souvenir of painful memories. In fact, there are times when back returns come in handy (which means you should store them in a safe place).

When? For one thing, if you sold your home and bought a more expensive one, you could defer some of the taxes on the sale of your old house. But you'd need previous returns to establish the cost basis. Obviously, the information you need is contained in previous returns. Suppose you paid too much last year. You can file an amended return, but you need last year's return to do it.

OK, I've made my case. But what if you haven't kept those precious copies of back tax returns? Fortunately, you can obtain copies of prior tax returns or transcripts of tax account information. Either request can be made on Form 4506, "Request of Copy of Tax Form or Tax Account Information." The charge for photocopies of prior returns is $4.25 per return.

Full payment must accompany all orders. Taxpayers should allow at least 45 days for delivery when requesting photocopies of prior year returns, and at least 30 days when requesting tax account information. To order Form 4506, taxpayers can call their nearest IRS branch office or write to: Internal Revenue Service, Kansas City, MO 64999.

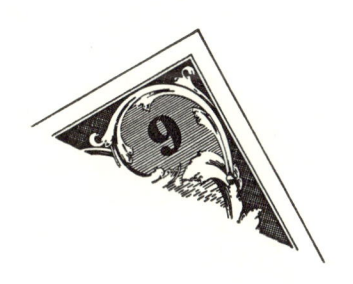

Noncash Charitable Donations: Watch Out for the IRS Auditor

Most of us are in the habit of "giving something to charity" each year. Normally, that "something" is cash, and we simply deduct it from our taxes. The situation becomes more tricky when we donate property—whether it's used furniture to the Salvation Army or a signed Picasso to a local museum—because a value must be assigned before we take the deduction. Gifts of art are particularly tricky because worth is so hard to determine. The IRS, which refers questionable donations to its Art Advisory Panel, claims the average rate of overvaluation in recent cases the panel reviewed was a whopping 600%. As a result, the IRS has adopted new reporting requirements for gifts of art and stiffened the penalties for getting carried away in evaluating those donations. The new rules make it more important than ever to follow instructions for making these gifts to avoid being audited or having the deduction disallowed.

A provision of the 1984 tax act now requires that a deduction for any kind of donated property (except publicly traded stock) valued at more than $5,000 must be accompanied by a formal, detailed appraisal. (Another recent change is a new tax form—8283—which must be used to claim deductions for noncash donations of more than $500.) The appraisal must include a description of the item, its fair market value, and how that value was determined. Appraisers must list their qualifications and supply their signatures and Social Security numbers. The same requirements apply if you make several smaller gifts that add up to more than $5,000.

If the IRS disagrees with an appraisal, it will cost you plenty. An appraisal that the IRS considers at least 150% too high will now result in penalties ranging from 10%–30%. Another new rule requires a charity to file a report with the IRS if it sells an art-work within two years of the donation. The report must include the donor's name and the amount the item was sold for. If the item sells for a lot less than the appraised value, expect the IRS to get in

Dollars and Sense

touch with you. If you give art to a charity that intends to resell the item immediately, lop off 40% of its appreciated value before taking a deduction. Given the new reporting rules, it's a good idea to stash a copy of the gift's appraisal in your safe-deposit box.

The best safeguard against being assessed IRS penalties is to use a reputable appraiser, one who has been in business for years and will stand behind you in case there are problems later. If you are unsure about an appraiser's credentials, check further. Most of the leading ones belong to the Appraisers Association of America, an industry trade group. If you are planning to make a gift of art or other valuables, give yourself plenty of time to find a good appraiser and get the necessary paperwork completed before year-end. One bright spot: the appraisal fee is tax deductible subject to the limitation for miscellaneous deductions.

This Party's Not Related

You were right about your mother-in-law. She's no kith nor kin of yours, and the IRS will back you up on that. In a recent ruling, the IRS found that a real estate sale involving a man and his mother-in-law qualified for the same tax treatment accorded a sale between strangers. The mother-in-law wasn't a "related party."

You, Inc.

Most self-employed people at least consider the idea of incorporating at some time or another. Despite a gaggle of recent changes in the tax rules, the advantages for many professionals and owners of one- or two-person businesses still hold. What's more, many families can enjoy the same tax breaks. A mom-and-pop corporation, with the kids as some of the shareholders, can save taxes on income-producing assets like real estate. It can also let families accumulate savings for college with pretax dollars, and down the road, save on estate taxes.

Of course, it costs money to set up a corporation. *Informed advice from an accountant or attorney who keeps abreast of the latest tax decisions in this often murky field is a must.* The tax rules are still intricate, and there are plenty of pitfalls for small-business owners and professionals who fail to abide by the numerous corporate formalities. For example, you must file corporate papers, keep careful records, make contributions to Social Security and unemployment taxes, pay legal fees, and conduct stockholders' meetings.

Despite the bragging often heard at cocktail parties, incorporating isn't a panacea for all tax ills. But you may be surprised at some of the ways it can be used to reach a variety of long-term family goals.

Mixed Bag of Tax Changes and More to Come

Recent changes in the tax laws have had a major impact on small-business owners in general and on self-employed professionals who incorporate largely for tax purposes. These laws lowered the taxes on income under $50,000 to 15%. For taxable income of between $50,000 and $75,000, the maximum rate is now 25%.

Congress also made the so-called Subchapter S corporation a more attractive financial-planning device. The name comes from the section of the federal tax code that authorizes unusual tax treatment for this type of corporation. These closely held companies don't pay federal corporate tax. Instead, each stockholder pays income taxes on his or her share of the corporation's profits at the stockholder's individual rate.

The 1982 tax act decreed that S corporations can now have an unlimited amount of "passive income" from interest and dividends, rents, royalties, and the like. Moreover, it widened the allowable number of stockholders to 35.

Incorporated professionals, on the other hand, lost a nifty tax-deferral scheme that let them stash away more retirement savings than they could put into a Keogh plan. Previously, professionals who incorporated could, in effect, deduct a significant amount of their pretax income, funnel it into a pension plan, and allow it to accumulate tax-free until they retired. Under the old rules, an incorporated doctor making $182,000 could set aside 25% of income, or $45,475 each year. The new rules limit the same doctor's annual pension contributions to $30,000, the ceiling on Keoghs.

One incentive for a husband and wife to set up a mom-and-pop business as an S corporation was diluted by changes affecting fringe benefits. Owners used to be able to provide group medical and life insurance tax-free to themselves and their employees. While these fringe benefits are still deductible to the corporation, they are treated as taxable income to shareholders who own more than 2% of the S corporation's stock.

On the whole, however, the two principal advantages of incorporating remain:

Limited Liability As long as a corporation abides by the rules, its owner's personal assets can't normally be used to satisfy company debts or any legal judgments against the company. (Note: This doesn't mean that professionals, say, a doctor or dentist, can limit their professional liability by incorporating; the rule only applies to *creditor* liability.)

Lower Taxes Most of the recent cutbacks in the tax advantages of incorporating have been aimed at professional corporations formed by doctors, lawyers, accountants, and other "professionals." These corporations were formerly considered little more than a federal tax subsidy for the rich and famous. Nonetheless, certain tax advantages of incorporating still remain:
1. *Tax deferral.* Corporations (except S companies) can define their own "fiscal year"—12-month accounting period. If this is different from the calendar year used by the government for tax purposes, you can shift income and expenses between fiscal years to gain tax advantages.
2. *Income splitting.* Putting family members on the payroll can spread the tax bite by shifting income to children in lower income tax brackets. It can also qualify relatives for social security benefits.

Dollars and Sense

3. *Tax-advantage loans.* Your corporation can make loans to you out of earnings which are taxed at the lower corporate rates. Such loans have to be made properly; they are sure to be scrutinized by the IRS. Professional corporations also allow owner-employees to borrow from their pension plans, a benefit private plans like Keoghs don't permit.
4. *Tax-free dividends.* The dividends your company earns on investments are not taxed. Domestic corporations do not pay taxes on 80% of the dividends they earn from stocks they own in other domestic corporations. Thus, if You, Inc. owns stock which pays, say, $10,000 in annual dividends, only $2,000 is taxable (20% of $10,000).
5. *Swap expenses.* You can use differences between your personal income and your corporation's income to obtain tax advantages. For example, say you want to buy a computer. If your personal income is greater than your company's, you might buy the computer to give yourself the deduction and lease it back to the firm. Or, if it's more advantageous, You, Inc. might buy the computer and lease it to you.

A related lesser-known tax benefit of incorporating a small business is referred to as "1244 stock." It works like this: Stock is considered a capital asset. So, when you sell stock, you realize either a capital gain or a capital loss. If you, as a private taxpayer, realize a loss, the amount of the loss you can deduct from taxes is limited. If your capital losses are more than your capital gains, the most you can deduct in any one year is $3,000. Section 1244 of the Internal Revenue Code, however, lets a small business corporation deduct a capital loss of up to $100,000 if you file a joint tax return with your spouse, $50,000 if you file a single return. The only limit is that the loss can't be more than you paid for the stock in the first place.

Inc. Your Portfolio

The same kind of creativity is behind the growing popularity of using an S corporation to shelter a certain amount of taxable income by giving it to family members in lower tax brackets. A family would be able to reduce its overall taxes, for instance, by putting income-producing investments into an S corporation with children (who are at least 14 years old) in lower tax brackets as shareholders. Your Family, Inc.'s dividends from stock it owns or perhaps the rental income from real estate investments would become corporate earnings taxed at the childrens' lower rate. One of the problems with this sort of income-splitting is having to transfer *actual* property, such as real estate, to give a child the income. Setting up a trust is one answer. But wealthy parents can run into gift-tax problems if the amount exceeds the $20,000 that married couples can give each child tax-free yearly. A solution could be a gift of S corporation stock to transfer, say, a 5% interest in a condominimum. One possible drawback, however, is that a child owns whatever is put into the S corporation, so long as the corporation continues to exist. Parents, however, can keep permanent control of the company by giving children non-voting shares.

The legal details of incorporating vary by state, but the general procedure is the same. If you use an attorney, plan on at least two sessions. The first will involve obtaining the information the attorney needs to draw up your articles of incorporation and bylaws; the second will involve going over those papers and holding the first corporate meeting of stockholders. Between sessions, your attorney will ask the state to issue a certificate of incorporation and to confirm that no other company has already taken the name you hope to use.

You or your lawyer must also apply for state and federal identification numbers and order a "corporate kit"—a binder containing stock certification and a stock transfer ledger with room for minutes of corporate meetings. Expect the legalities to take about six weeks.

The clerical chores, however, continue. As a taxpayer, You, Inc. must file state and federal income tax returns. If the company shows a profit, quarterly estimated taxes will be due. The company must also withhold employees' income and social security taxes and account for those with another quarterly form. At the beginning of the year, you must issue W-2 forms for the prior year and send copies to both state and federal tax offices. If your company provides worker's compensation, paperwork is involved.

Be sure you know what you're getting into. The popularity of incorporating as a way to save taxes has spawned a slew of books on the subject, some of which make outlandish claims. Check the titles in the business section of your local library and bookstores. Anything published more than a year ago won't be up to date on the latest tax changes.

Playing Your (Credit) Cards Right

Interest rates on almost everything have fallen from their high mark of the early '80s. Even credit card issuers are lowering the rates they charge on unpaid balances. Wells Fargo Bank in California, for example, lowered the interest rate on its Visa and MasterCard accounts from 20% to 17%. But like most "good things," there is a catch—several, in fact. For one thing, fixed mortgage rates have fallen to around 11% and banks are charging a mere 8% prime rate on loans to their best corporate customers. So the credit card reduction isn't quite as generous as it first appeared.

And that's not all. While Wells Fargo deserves credit for at least giving its customers a tiny break, the new lower rate applies only to cardholders who have had accounts at the bank for at least five years.

Expect other banks to follow suit. If they lower interest rates on bank charge cards, there will be strings attached. For example, some banks may lower the interest rate on credit-card balances, but raise the annual fee they charge for the card. Other banks may determine your new credit-card rate according to the number of other accounts you have with them: 20% if you only have a credit card, 18% if you have a card and a mortgage, 16% if you have a card, a mortgage, and an auto loan, and so on.

Compare Terms and Benefits

All the hubbub makes this a good time to take stock of your credit cards and, if you're like most people, to throw some away. But which to hold and which to fold? Base your decision on the card's credit terms, such as the following:
- *Is there a grace period?* This is the amount of time you're allowed before you're charged interest. In some cases, interest begins to be compounded virtually the second you make

a purchase. Other cards give you up to 30 days free to pay before interest is charged.
- *How is your balance figured*? Three methods are commonly used. With the *adjusted-balance* and *average-daily-balance* methods, interest is charged on your balance during the current billing period. With the *previous-balance method,* on the other hand, current payments aren't subtracted before interest is calculated. If you rarely pay the entire amount you owe on a credit card, it doesn't matter much which method is used. But if you tend to pay the balance in full, say every six months, and your card doesn't have a grace period, you'll pay significantly more if the previous-balance method is used. There's little reason to even own a bank card if you pay the balance in full every month. You'd probably be better off with a so-called travel and entertainment (T&E) card, such as American Express, Carte Blanche, or Diners Club especially if the "extras" they offer like premiums or discounts at certain hotel chains/restaurants, would be useful to you. These cards involve an annual fee, but charge no interest if you pay the full amount you owe each month. The highest fee is charged by American Express for its Gold Card—$65. (The green card is somewhat less.) Carte Blanche's fee is $40, while Diners Club charges $45. Although T&E cards aren't credit cards per se, since you're expected to make full payment monthly, most of them now offer a credit option you can use if you run short of cash.
- *Are bank cards accepted at more places than T&E cards*? Yes. For example, most retailers only accept bank cards. But issuers of bank cards have obviously felt the competition from T&E cards. The result: the "premium" Visa and MasterCard which charge the same interest rate, but offer higher credit lines—as well as higher annual fees—than the "plain vanilla" variety. If you have a premium card, ask yourself how many of the extra services—such as travel insurance or discounts on various types of merchandise—you really use. Are the extra services worth the higher annual fee?
- *What about interest rates*? All bank card issuers are free to set their own interest rates, grace periods, and annual fees—contingent on the laws in the state where the card is issued. Currently, the national average for all bank cards is running close to 18.3%, but if you look beyond banks in your home state, you can definitely do better than the average. The best deal may be available from an out-of-state bank able to sell across state lines. One that accepts applications nationally is Simmons First National Bank in Pine Bluff, Arkansas. Simmons currently charges 11% on bank-card purchases and gives you a 25-day grace period before the interest clock

Dollars and Sense

starts running. It also charges an annual fee of $25.00. Not far away, Union National Bank in Little Rock is charging 14.7% and interest is added from the date you make a purchase. Union's annual fee is $20.

An up-to-date list of other banks that have low credit card rates and sell nationally is available for $12 from Bank Card Holders of America (333 Pennsylvania Ave. S.E., Washington, D.C. 20003), a consumer organization. The BHA also maintains a list of banks that don't charge annual fees.

Reserving Credit

Most commercial banks and some savings institutions will let you reserve up to $50,000 in a personal credit line that can be tapped for almost any purpose. If your finances are in good shape, a line of credit is as easy to get as a credit card and as simple to use as writing a check.

Bankers continue to keep their focus squarely on consumers. One reason: They continue to enjoy healthy profit margins on all types of personal credit. Buoyed by surveys showing that consumer confidence remains high, banks have lowered the interest rates they charge to finance a new car, boat, or home. But these rates haven't fallen as low as the rates banks pay to raise money. Although the prime interest rate (the interest rate banks charge their most creditworthy customers) has plunged from 13% to 9% during 1985 and 1986, the average rate charged on outstanding credit card balances remained close to its all time average high of 19%.

But when it comes to personal lines of credit—variable-rate, unsecured loans activated by writing a check—a curious anomaly developed. Most commercial banks were offering these accounts, in amounts of from $1,000 to as much as $50,000 unsecured, at rates well below the interest they charged on credit card balances or personal installment loans.

Moreover, most banks don't assess an annual fee on personal credit lines until you use them. Not so with the credit lines attached to pricey plastic, such as American Express Gold Cards, Gold Mastercards, and Premier Visas. Annual fees for those cards are about $18 to $25 for cards with credit lines of $500 to $3,500, and between $30 and $50 for those with lines of $5,000 to $50,000.

With most consumers already packing a fistful of plastic, banks—and many brokerage firms—began pushing several types of personal credit lines in several varieties. These currently range from simple overdraft protection in the form of a credit line attached to your checking account, to a draw on the equity you have in your home or the value of your investment portfolio to available cash secured by nothing more than your good name. Once you've returned an application for a credit line, a lender notifies you when it has been approved and for what amount. If the line isn't attached to your regular checking account, you'll receive special checks. Any fees are usually deducted from the amount borrowed.

Nobody, of course, likes to be in debt. But leverage (using credit to make a purchase) can be a springboard to increasing your wealth if you use it wisely. The popular catchphrase for it is building wealth with OPM—other people's money—including lines of credit. Here's a rundown on what banks around the country are currently offering in the way of these loans, what you can expect to pay for them, and how to apply.

Instant Cash in Your Checking Account

The term "overdraft protection" is an accurate enough description for a credit line linked to your checking account; the bank will cover checks for more than you actually have on hand—up to your credit limit. But these lines, often called "ready reserves," are more than that. They are available cash for any purpose.

Ready reserves are typically no trick to get. They are often easier to obtain, in fact, than a personal loan. The application you fill out for a ready reserve is similar to an application for a personal loan. In reality, a ready reserve is a preapproved loan for a certain amount. The difference is that the interest rate "clock" doesn't start ticking until you use the funds. Therefore, banks seldom ask why you want the "loan".

Generally, banks have only two requirements for maintaining a ready reserve. One is that you must have, or open, a checking account in the bank. The other is that you must keep that checking account until any cash you've been advanced on your ready reserve has been repaid. One caveat: If you close a checking account while you still are on your ready reserve, the bank is likely to demand immediate repayment in full.

Terms of Payment

Once you use your line of credit you are subject to two charges as well as repayment of the money you used. One is the monthly fee, which can range anywhere from 1% to as much as 5% on the outstanding balance. You must also pay interest on the loan. The size of the loan may determine the interest rate. As a rule of thumb, you can probably qualify for a line of credit equal to half your monthly gross income. This also depends on your credit history. First National Bank of Chicago, for example, uses this guideline and applies the interest rate on a sliding scale according to the amount of the credit line. On lines of more than $25,000, the rate is 0.5% over the prime rate; on less than $25,000, it's 1% over prime, and on less than $15,000, 1.5% above prime. California's Security Pacific charges a straight 2.5% over prime for credit lines up to $50,000. Note, too, that many of these accounts charge *Variable* notes: The interest you pay may change over the life of the loan with changes in the rate—such as the prime rate—it's based on.

Shop terms carefully. Be clear on how the interest rate is determined. Not all banks peg the rate on personal credit lines to the prime rate. Watch out, too, for hidden costs. Wells Fargo, for example, is one of the few banks that charges credit line borrowers a "membership fee"—a hefty $45 annually. To qualify for its Capital Advantage line of up to $50,000, applicants must have a minimum yearly income of $30,000, an "acceptable" level of debt, at least $2,500 in liquid assets, and a minimum net worth of $50,000. Crocker Bank not only assesses its Prime Line customers a $24 annual fee, but also charges a new account fee of $125.

Some banks automatically deduct monthly payments on an outstanding credit line balance from your checking account or may give you that option. If you can handle the payments, there's nothing to prevent you from opening checking accounts—and obtaining ready reserve cash—at several banks. One legitimate tactic would be to apply for several credit lines at the same time. That way, you can truthfully say on each application that you currently have no other lines outstanding.

Using Your "Ready"

Why load up on ready reserve cash at several banks? Say you have the chance to buy a tidy little apartment building that would provide you with some tax write-offs and a bit of extra income besides. You can probably get a mortgage, but coming up with the down payment is a definite problem. Enter your ready reserves. Although one account might not be sufficient to cover the down payment on the building, several might well be. All you would have to do is write the checks. Just remember, those loans must be paid back starting one month from the date you signed the checks.

Many banks offer credit lines that aren't attached to checking accounts. But without the checking account, fees are typically higher. For instance, the rate for non-checking credit line customers at First Chicago is automatically 2% above prime. However, First Chicago's going rate on unsecured personal loans is 18.75% (versus a prime rate of 9%), up to a maximum loan of $7,500 which must be repaid over three years or less.

Crediting Your Home

Home equity credit lines have sprouted up everywhere in the past few years. Practically all banks of any size, as well as many brokerage firms, now offer them. The accounts let you use your equity—the market value of your house or condominium minus the unpaid balance on your mortgage—as collateral for the loans. But although home equity accounts are less expensive than second mortgages, they're also more risky.

These accounts are essentially variable-rate overdraft checking accounts secured by up to 75% of the equity in your house. Unlike second mortgages, home equity accounts are typically restricted to primary, owner-occupied residences. Closing costs and other fees totaling anywhere from $300 to as much as $4,000 are paid when the account is opened.

Most home equity account lenders require that you pay only interest during the first five years of the loan. After that, you can generally either retire the principal with a lump sum payment or refinance and choose a repayment schedule of as long as 20 years.

A few of these accounts, however, are *balloon loans*—initial payments cover a portion of the loan but the final payment, covering the remainder, is substantial. For instance, Chicago's Harris Trust gives its customers the option of paying interest only for five years, but then requires the balance in full. It will lend a maximum of 70% of equity and charges interest at the rate of 0.5% over prime. This may still be a saving in that the rate was considerably below Harris' existing rate on second mortgages—12-5/8%, plus fees equal to 2.5% of the loan. Customers of Wells Fargo's Equity Advantage Account recently paid 11.27% plus a $450 loan fee to borrow up to $10,000, compared with the bank's personal loan rate of 17.75%.

Because the initial terms of home equity accounts are enticing, financial advisers say they are best suited for cash-on-demand expenses, such as home improvements and college tuition. The reason: It's tempting to take out more money than you can realistically repay, thereby running the risk of putting your home in jeopardy.

May Not Be So Perfect

Ironically, the popularity of both personal credit lines and home equity accounts has created a drawback for consumers. While having a good "banking relationship" (several accounts at the same bank) can often get you a lower rate on a personal loan, credit lines are more like credit cards—no deals. Big banks and brokerage firms typically offer them as packaged products, take them or leave them. Applications themselves resemble those used for major credit cards. Security Pacific, among other banks, advertises its credit lines in the financial section of major newspapers. The ads include a tollfree number to call to request an application by mail.

Although credit line rates and terms are typically not negotiable at big banks, you might find a smaller bank willing to haggle. Unlike a large lender, a small bank in your hometown knows you and may see extending you a line of credit exactly the same as giving you any other kind of loan. It's worth a personal visit to your regular banker to discuss it, particularly if you have, say, your IRA as well as a certificate of deposit or two at the bank.

What To Do with All That Money

Borrowing, as a key element in building your personal wealth, is a popular subject just now. Using OPM—other people's money—to leverage your way to riches is the topic of everything from seminars and TV shows which extoll the virtues of buying real estate with " no money down" (at least none of yours) to scads of do-it-yourself guides in bookstores, most of them inexpensive paperbacks. While many of these books have rather sensational titles, they are a good source of ideas if you are looking for an investment or thinking of buying or starting a business. On a more basic level, you may discover borrowing power you didn't know you had or ways you might be using leverage more effectively. Here are a few of the more popular titles.

How to Borrow Everything You Need to Build a Great Personal Fortune, by Herbert F. Holtje and John Stockwell, $4.95, Prentice-Hall.

How to Borrow Your Way to a Great Fortune, by Tyler G. Hicks, $4.95, Prentice-Hall.

Leveraged Finance: How to Raise and Invest Cash, by Mark Stevens, $5.95, Prentice-Hall.

How to Use Leverage to Make Money in Local Real Estate, by George Bookl, $4.95, Prentice-Hall

How to Pyramid Small Business Ventures into a Personal Fortune, by Mark Stevens, $4.95, Prentice-Hall

Business Capital Sources, Second Edition, Tyler G. Hicks, $15, IWS, Inc.

Tax Guide for Buying and Selling a Business, Fifth Edition, by Stanley Hagendorf, $39.95, Prentice-Hall

Other Sources of "Reserved" Credit

Credit lines, of course, are just one of several possible loan options available to you. Relatives and friends, for instance, might be willing partners in a business venture. A doting uncle might well make a loan that need not be secured by collateral. To avoid running afoul of the Internal Revenue Service, however, draw up a promissory note using forms available at many stationers. The agreement should include a repayment schedule and an annual interest rate high enough to compensate the lender for foregone interest income.

Here's a quick review of other sources.

Whole Life Insurance   One of the best ways to raise cash at bargain rates is to borrow against the cash value of an old policy. Veterans who continued their GI insurance, for instance, can borrow at just 5% interest. The amount available to you from any whole life policy depends on the number of years you've had it, your age when it was issued, and the size of the policy's death benefit. Besides being inexpensive, this kind of borrowing has three other big advantages: There's no credit check, you don't have to disclose your reasons for the loan, and you can determine how—or whether—you pay back the loan. (After all, it was your money in the first place.)

Company Savings Plans   A growing number of company-sponsored savings and profit-sharing plans now let vested employees borrow against their balances. Such loans are typically at below-market rates and repayment is usually made by payroll deductions. Federal pension laws limit the maximum you can borrow to $50,000, or half your vested benefits. While terms on these loans range from 10 to 25 years, you must repay within five years if the money is used for purposes other than buying, building, or refurbishing your house.

Credit Unions   Rates offered by even the big credit unions are not as competitive with those offered by conventional lenders as they used to be, but worth investigating. Few credit unions, however, make unsecured personal loans for more than $5,000.

Margin and Asset Accounts   Many large banks, as well as brokerage firms, now offer borrowing on margin to customers who pledge a portion of their investment portfolios as collateral. Contrary to what many people believe, margin borrowing can be used to finance more than just stocks and bonds. To get a $10,000 personal loan, you must satisfy margin requirements ranging from $12,000 worth of U.S. Treasury notes to $20,000 in stock. Asset management-type accounts—which combine a margin account with a credit card and other features—also let you borrow against your portfolio. Initial deposit requirements, however, typically range from $50,000 to $25,000.

Mail-Order Loans   Borrowing by mail is an option to consider if, like many people, you find loan interviews an ordeal. Leading business magazines and newspapers carry ads for numerous reliable companies that make unsecured personal loans based on very detailed questionnaires. Their rates are competitive with those of conventional lenders. These companies are often an excellent source of capital for a speculative business.

Keeping Your Credit Record Clean

Credit bureaus don't know as much about you as you might think. Understanding how credit-reporting works can help you protect your borrowing power even when your bills get out of hand. A triple-A credit rating, as Mother used to say, is as good as money in the bank. But what happens when, despite the best intentions, the bills pile up and you can't pay everybody? It might cause some sleepless nights, but a blip in your credit history needn't haunt you forever.

Contrary to what many people believe, the computers whirring away at national credit bureaus aren't recording every detail about your private life and selling that information to others. These firms merely keep track of data provided by their customers —your creditors. But some creditors are more diligent than others in reporting delinquencies, others don't report at all. By knowing which is which, you can decide whom to pay first, whom to let slip, and still preserve your pristine credit rating.

Among the quickest to report late-pays are major banks, finance companies, and national retailers. Most of them notify credit bureaus the minute your bill is 30 days past due. That means it isn't wise to skip a monthly payment to Visa or MasterCard, which can also cost you interest and a late charge. American Express, on the other hand, doesn't report a missing payment, or assess interest or penalties. However, American Express has said it intends to begin notifying credit bureaus about customers whose cards have been revoked and whose accounts have been turned over to a collection agency. Smaller retailers, doctors, and hospitals don't usually report until your account is several months in arrears, or it has been referred for collection. Major oil companies, utilities, and credit unions typically don't share any information with credit bureaus. The same is true of mortgage lenders. Instead, your mortgage credit usually is examined only when you are buying other property, when lenders contact each other directly. House payments may represent the biggest chunk of your debt load, but mortgage makers assume you'll protect your largest investment.

How Do You Rate?

Despite these exceptions, credit bureaus still wield tremendous control over your buying and borrowing, while your power over them is minimal. Thanks to the passage of the Consumer Credit Protection Act in 1968 and the addition of the Fair Credit Reporting Act in 1970, you have the legal right to see your report, review it for errors, and insert your own explanation of any past problems. However, your rights are limited. A credit bureau must show you your report, but it isn't required by federal law to give you a copy. Luckily, the more responsible agencies supply copies for a fee of $10 or so. It's a different story if you have been denied credit based on information in your report. In that case, federal law requires the reporting agency to provide you a duplicate without charge. You must, however, contact the agency within 30 days of the credit denial.

Unfortunately, being denied credit is the easiest way to find out who has your records. That's because you have no say as to which bureau handles your file, only your creditors do. Moreover, the credit bureau has limited responsibility for the accuracy of the information your creditors give. If the local branch of a national department store incorrectly reports you as a deadbeat, it's not up to the agency to verify it. You must straighten things out with the merchant. While horror stories about the credit-reporting industry have lessened since the enactment of the consumer laws, it's a good idea to review your report about once a year. One of the best ways to find out which bureau your creditors use is to ask the creditors themselves, or ask at a local bank. TRW Credit Data and Trans Union are two of the largest reporting agencies. But in most areas, one or two local bureaus will have most of your information.

Keep in mind that a credit bureau doesn't actually assign you a credit rating. It merely records fairly detailed information about credit activity in your various accounts. When you apply for additional credit, potential lenders use the raw data in your report to decide whether you fit their particular profile of a good risk. Most lenders determine that using a system of credit scoring. Essentially, you get points for the various items on most kinds of credit applications. While lenders keep their scoring systems secret, knowing what kinds of information tend to count heavily with most lenders can help you answer at least some questions in a way that is truthful, but also boosts your total score.

Crediting What You Say

A typical credit application, of course, asks you to fill in dozens of blanks, requiring practically everything but a certified set of your fingerprints. Out of all these questions, however, only 6 to 12 figure in your score. (A potential lender, however, may well match your entire application with your credit report, both to check your honesty and get a more accurate picture of all your outstanding debts.) The questions that count are based on the lender's past experience with its own credit customers. Therefore, the way you are evaluated can vary from lender to lender, from city to city, even from one neighborhood branch of a bank or retail store to another in the same town. As a rule, the most heavily scored questions are items that lenders have traditionally viewed as indicators of "stability." Here are some of those categories, how various types of lenders usually judge your answers, and some tips for improving your score:

Occupation—Most credit-scoring systems award points on a sliding scale for categories ranging from professional through clerical to semiskilled and unskilled. Jobs that earn the most points are those that suggest responsibility. While federal law prohibits lenders from discriminating on the basis of race or sex, unfair biases exist. For instance, the woman who describes herself as an executive assistant is likely to get more points than she will listing her occupation as secretary.

Length of time at your present job and address—Whether you have put down roots means the most to lenders in rural areas and medium-sized cities. It's usually less important to lenders in urban centers, where job hopping is more common and the population more transient. Generally, how long you've lived in the same place counts most when you're applying for an installment loan.

Other types of credit you have—Potential lenders typically award the most points for travel-and-entertainment cards such as American Express and Diners Club, slightly fewer points for bank cards such as Visa and MasterCard. Least likely to impress lenders are department stores charge cards. Having a loan from a finance company could actually hurt. Many of these companies advertise that they'll lend money to almost anybody.

Income—The old saying that it's easy to borrow money if you have money is true. The higher your income, the more points you'll score. So besides salary, list any income from other sources, such as alimony or child support, as well as dividends and interest from investments.

Debts—If you're applying for a mortgage or installment loan, your level of income isn't as important as the percentage of it you're paying out each month to meet existing obligations. Some bank credit card issuers are also beginning to look more closely at that ratio. An acceptable debt loan is typically in the range of 35% to 40% of monthly gross income, including your rent or mortgage payment.

Checking Your Credit Report

After tallying up your score on your application, most lenders will add or subtract points based on other information in your report. Even if your application scores a home run, a poor bill-paying history can still put you out of the ball game. But take heart. A creditor who turns you down must tell you specifically why. There's always the chance that a reasonable explanation or additional information will change the lender's mind. If not, that particular strike against you may not matter to a lender down the street. The time to review your credit report is before you need credit. Because errors are common, it's wise to do it annually. Find out from your current creditors, such as your local bank or mortgage holder, where information about you is being kept by bureau(s) in your area. Call and ask whether you can order a copy. If you can, write a letter giving your name, any other names you've had credit in, address (plus previous addresses if you've moved in the past five years), Social Security number(s), and a check for the fee. Keep a photocopy of the letter. Most credit reporting agencies say they process requests in a day or two, but a reply has been known to take as long as three months. If your report doesn't arrive within about 10 days, send a separate copy of your request letter and write in big red letters across the front "NOT RECEIVED." Keep badgering the bureau until it responds. If your bureau doesn't sell copies of its reports, you will probably have to make an appointment to go in and look at your file in person.

Because credit reports are written in computerese, it can be difficult to detect errors. However, the key to decoding your report is on the back. There you will find a list of initials used to describe various kinds of financial transactions. The report will list your payment history with each creditor that has supplied information to the bureau. If you and your spouse hold some accounts jointly, the payment record for those accounts should be contained in both partners' reports.

If there's an error in your report, the credit bureau is required by federal law to delete the inaccurate information. Keep in mind, however, that you must notify the creditor who supplied the bad data yourself, provide proof of the mistake, and demand a correction. Under the Equal Credit Opportunity Act, creditors have 90 days to comply. Recheck your report to verify that the change has been made.

Most information in your report doesn't stay there as long as you might expect. Potential lenders are typically interested in your payment history over just the past year or two. So credit bureaus purge their files about that often. Debts written off by creditors as uncollectible, however, can stay on your record for 7 years and a bankruptcy can remain for 10 years.

Credit—Don't Leave College Without It

Why does a college student need a credit card? Believe it or not, most young people are better off establishing credit while they are still in school—and will probably have an easier time doing it than they will after graduation.

Credit card issuers are becoming increasingly interested in the college market. Sort of the old "get 'em early," idea, yes, but fortunate for youngsters who can now begin establishing credit before they get out in the working world and need a credit history to buy a car, for example, or rent an apartment.

The College Credit Card Corporation, which represents a variety of credit card issuers, annually visits more than 500 college campuses. At each school, it distributes special student credit applications to juniors, seniors, and graduate students. More than 300,000 students fill them out each year. The company then forwards the applications to its clients—among them, banks, gas companies, and national and regional retailers. College Credit claims that between 85% and 90% of its young applicants receive credit. No cosigner is required, but most credit card issuers impose relatively low credit ceilings: usually $500 to $700 on bank cards and $300 to $500 on cards from retail stores. If the company doesn't visit your child's school, your son or daughter can write directly to College Credit Card Corporation, 1819 Kennedy Blvd., Philadelphia, PA 19103.

Establishing Credit

Bankcard Holders of America—a nonprofit organization that advises consumers on their credit rights—recommends that students establish credit in stages. For example, open a checking or savings account at a bank, then apply for credit at a local retail store. Retailers in the community usually have less stringent stan-

Dollars and Sense

dards than do issuers of the big-league cards. With successful payment records on those accounts and prompt payment of gas bills, a student can then move up to the majors. For more tips on student credit, send a stamped, self-addressed envelope to Bankcard Holders of America, 2025 Eye St. NW, Suite 1022, Washington, DC 20006.

Is Your Mortgage Worth Saving?

The equity you have in your home isn't the emergency nest egg it used to be. House prices doubled and even tripled in some places over the past decade. But with the onset of mortgage rates so high as to shut out many buyers, appreciation hit the brakes. As a result, the average market value of existing single-family homes increased just a tiny 3% in 1984 and by only 4% in 1985.

Given the current low rate of return on your investment in a home you've owned for years, you may reason that you are sitting on cash—accumulated equity—that could work harder elsewhere. Refinancing—if it means giving up an old, low-interest mortgage — rarely pays. But borrowing against home equity does make sense for some people, either to invest the cash more profitably or perhaps to save for their children's education. If you can make more with money you take out of your house than you have to pay in mortgage interest, refinancing can be a route to increasing your net worth. But you have to gauge the costs and the risks carefully. Whether equity borrowing is right for you hinges on how much extra you can afford in monthly payments on a new mortgage, your tax bracket, and the long-term return you could expect to get on another investment.

What You Pay for Leverage

Refinancing can be surprisingly expensive. For example, say you have a $50,000 mortgage at 11% and can refinance it with a $100,000 loan at 13%, just two percentage points higher. Not bad, but the lender will also charge you a loan-origination fee on the deal, probably three "points"—3% of the new loan amount. That changes the picture considerably. Since you probably also paid three points to borrow the original $50,000, borrowing an additional $50,000 actually costs you six points. That means that the effective carrying cost of the new loan is closer to 15%, not 13%, which may change your mind. Over the life of the loan, you will pay thousands of dollars more in interest.

One wrinkle here is taxes. Because the interest on your mortgage is tax deductible, it actually costs you something less than the loan's stated interest rate. There is a relatively simple formula for figuring that aftertax cost: Multiply your mortgage rate by 1 minus your tax bracket, expressed as a decimal. For example, the aftertax cost of a 13% mortgage for a person in the 27% bracket is

$$13.00\% \times (1.00 - .27)$$

which is an "effective" rate of 9.49%. In order to make refinancing pay, this homeowner would have to put the cash into an investment yielding at least 9.49% after taxes.

Suppose for example, that 30-year tax free municipal bonds were yielding about 10% or so when that mortgage rate was 13%. A homeowner in the 27% tax bracket, then, could borrow at 9.5% and invest at 10% for a positive 0.5% annual return. These numbers indicate that in this instance, it would not be worth the trouble to refinance and reinvest the proceeds.

Swap It for a Shorter-Term Loan

There are, of course, other mortgage refinancing alternatives. If you took out a fixed-rate, 30-year loan within the past few years, it might pay to exchange it for a new, 15-year mortgage. Typically, there are no prepayment penalties in the exchange. While monthly payments on the 15-year mortgage would be from 12% to 15% more than the payments on a 30-year loan at the same interest rate, because you pay off a 15-year mortgage in half the time, the interest-cost savings is huge. For example, the monthly payments on a 30-year, $75,000 loan at a fixed rate of 13% would be $830. If you kept the loan to maturity, you would pay a total of $223,674 in interest. Compare that with the same mortgage for 15 years. The monthly payments would be about $949. But the total interest costs would be just $95,807, a savings of $127,867. However, the difference in monthly payments on a 15-year loan might not be as great as you'd expect. And as interest rates rise, that difference narrows, as Figure 16-1 shows.

Or ... Mortgages You Pay Every Week or Two

Another refinancing alternative—although it's relatively new and uncommon—is mortgages with weekly and biweekly payments. These arrangements originated in Canada in the early 1980s and are spreading to the United States. The medium-sized City Savings Bank of Meriden, CT, began offering them in 1984 and dozens of other lenders have followed suit.

Is Your Mortgage Worth Saving?

Figure 16-1
Shortening the Payback

The monthly payments on a 15-year mortgage are higher than they are on a 30-year mortgage at the same interest rate. But the higher interest rates go, the smaller the difference becomes because the shorter loan repays principal faster.

Loan Amount: $50,000

Interest Rate	Monthly Payment 15-Year Mortgage	Monthly Payment 30-Year Mortgage	Variance
8%	$478	$367	$111
10	537	439	98
12	600	514	86
14	666	592	74

These loans are simple to understand. Payments are either one-fourth (weekly) or one-half (biweekly) the monthly payment on a conventional, 30-year loan at the same interest rate. But there are a couple of catches. One is that lenders don't want to process all those checks. So borrowers are typically required to have a checking or savings account with the lender from which payments are automatically deducted. The other wrinkle is that you pay more yearly than you would with a conventional mortgage. If you're paying $400 a month on a conventional loan, you're paying $4,800 a year ($400 × 12 months). If you made a $100 mortgage payment weekly, you'd pay $5,200 a year ($100 × 52 weeks).

Figure 16-2
Paying More Often

Making mortgage payments weekly or biweekly is another way to reduce principal faster. While the payments are a bit higher, the borrower saves a whopping amount of interest over the life of the loan. The table shows what the interest savings would be on a $50,000 loan at three different interest rates.

Interest Rate	Payment Frequency	Term of Loan	Each Payment	Total Interest Cost of Loan
11%	Monthly	30 yrs.	$476.16	$121,422.38
	Biweekly	19.9 yrs.	238.08	72,927.02
	Weekly	19.8 yrs.	119.04	72,464.78
12%	Monthly	30 yrs.	$514.31	$135,138.60
	Biweekly	18.9 yrs.	257.16	76,189.04
	Weekly	18.8 yrs.	128.58	75,643.87
15%	Monthly	30 yrs.	$632.22	$177,613.21
	Biweekly	16.1 yrs.	316.11	82,444.70
	Weekly	16.0 yrs.	158.06	81,643.21

If you can afford the extra bite, over the long run these fast-pay loans can save you from one third to one half in interest costs. With weekly or biweekly payments, a conventional mortgage is paid off in about 19 years. The higher the loan's interest rate, the less time it takes to accumulate equity and own your home outright. Figure 16-2 illustrates how that works. Will fast-pay loans become widespread in the United States? They have become popular in Canada partly because interest on home mortgages isn't tax deductible there. But many American homebuyers would welcome the opportunity to avoid paying a lot of mortgage interest, especially since recent tax reductions have made the deduction of interest payments less appealing to many individuals. As a result, many first-time homebuyers are looking at their purchase as a place to live rather than as a real estate investment.

Adjustable Rate Mortgages—Handle with Care

Your home is probably the biggest investment you'll ever make. How you finance it is the biggest part of that investment decision.

A house used to be a simple investment. You picked it out, got a mortgage with a monthly payment you could handle—usually with a little grunting and sweating—and then settled back to enjoy your home while its market value moved steadily upward. But what was a good deal for borrowers was a bad deal for banks. The inflation that pushed house prices upward also cut the value of the fixed monthly mortgage payments they received. Meanwhile, Congress was deregulating interest rates on deposits, squeezing banks between fixed income and rising costs.

Enter the adjustable rate mortgage. More than half the mortgages being written today allow the bank to raise the interest rate if the general level of rates goes up. This increases the borrower's monthly payments, giving the bank a cushion between its costs and its mortgage income. If interest rates drop, the bank reduces the mortgage rate and monthly payments accordingly. This new arrangement has made it possible for banks to keep lending to would-be homeowners despite the ups and downs of interest rates. But it makes buying a home a much more uncertain bargain.

Here's the Deal

In theory, adjustable rate mortgages are not too complicated. The loan agreement has three main features:
1. *The index rate.* This is the interest rate that will determine changes in your mortgage payments. The rate chosen is usually one that is well publicized: the interest rate on Treasury bonds, for instance, or the mortgage index published by the Federal Home Loan Bank Board.
2. *The margin or spread.* Your mortgage rate is not set at the index rate, but at some constant number of

Dollars and Sense

Figure 17-1
Comparison of Terms on Four ARMs

Term of Review	Current Rate*	Cap	Index	Spread
One year	10.25%	None	1-yr. Treasury bond	2%
One year	10.75%	2% each review 17.5% max. rate	1-yr. Treasury bond	2.5
Three years	12.25%	None	3-yr. Treasury bond	2
Five years	12.875%	2.5% of each review 17% max. rate	5-yr. Treasury bond	1.75

* Plus a change of 2 points, or 2% of the mortgage amount.

percentage points over it. Obviously, if two banks use the same index rate, but one has a spread of 2% and the other uses 3%, the first is a better bargain.
3. *The term of review.* This is how often the bank can adjust your rate. Some but not all adjustable mortgages set "caps" on the increase permitted at each review, or on the increase possible over the life of the mortgage, or both.

Figure 17-1 shows the indexes, spreads, and terms on four different adjustable rate mortgages offered by one savings and loan.

Confusion over "Teasers"

Choosing an adjustable rate mortgage is made more complicated by the way they are marketed. To get borrowers in the door, banks are offering "teaser" (discount) rates below their own index-plus-spread formulas. The one-year, no-cap mortgage in the figure, for instance, is being offered at a current rate of 10.25%. But its index, the one-year Treasury bond rate, stood at 11.19% when the deal was offered. Adding the 2% spread shown in the table, the bank "should" have been charging borrowers 13.19%. The 10.25% teaser is almost three full percentage points lower.

On a 30-year, $75,000 mortgage, the teaser rate would yield a monthly payment of $672—*for the first year.* But on the first review date, even if the index rate does not rise at all, the mortgage rate would jump to 13.19% and the monthly payment would rise to $843, an increase of 25% or $171 per month.

Especially on adjustable mortgages that are reviewed after one year, it is the rate after the teaser expires that indicates how affordable the loan is for you. If you feel sure you can handle the higher payment, the initial teaser is a real saving. If you can't, the teaser is a trap.

All four of the sample mortgages in the figure include teasers. The then current index-plus-spread rate on the three-year review would be 14.26% rather than 12.25%, and 14.4% would apply on the five-year review rather than the 12.875% listed. With three or five years before review, of course, the total savings from the teaser rate is much larger than with a 1-year review. Moreover, the average American family moves every five years. If you know that you will be selling your home in a few years—if college-age children will be leaving home, for instance, or a company transfer is a near-certainty—the lower current rate is attractive. But remember that your plans may change, leaving you stuck with the higher rates you thought you wouldn't be around to see.

Interest Rate Risk

The loss of the teaser discount is not the only factor that can change your mortgage. If index rates move sharply higher by your first review date, you will be hit with a double whammy: no more teaser and a higher base.

Suppose, for instance, that the one-year Treasury rate on our sample $75,000 mortgage rose over the next 12 months by 2.2 percentage points. This new rate would result in a monthly payment of $973, up 45% or $301 from the original payment. Few family budgets can take that kind of strain.

Some index rates move up and down more than others. In general, the shorter the term of the index, the more volatile it will be. Thus, one-year Treasury rates can head through the roof—they peaked at 16% in early 1981—but they drop just as sharply—18 months later they were hovering around 8%. However, if your review date occurred when rates were at their worst, you could have been stuck for a year with monthly payments based on an 18% interest rate.

Keep your eye out for loans which include negative *amortization*. This is a fancy way of saying that despite your monthly payment, the total debt you owe the bank is going up, not down. This can happen with *some* adjustable rate mortgages if the caps just delay, instead of eliminating, interest rate increases.

It works this way: the mortgage guarantees that your rate or your monthly payment will not increase by more than a certain amount at each review date. But if the index-plus-spread formula calls for increases above the cap, these mortgages add the difference back to your loan. Then, at regular intervals, the whole mortgage is recalculated on the new, higher loan amount, raising your payment anyway. Most of the banks we surveyed back in 1985 did not offer mortgages that permitted negative amortization, but a minority did. Be sure you ask whether the mortgage you're considering does or does not permit it.

Dollars and Sense

Which is the Best Deal?

The homebuyer should be looking for two things in a mortgage: he or she must be able to afford the monthly payments—not just as they stand today, but as they might increase in the future—and the prospective buyer should pay as little as possible in interest costs over the time the mortgage is outstanding. While there is no end to the potential changes in monthly payments with an adjustable rate mortgage, you can check these two points by working out just two possibilities. Ask your bank for two amortization schedules on the mortgage you are considering. (The amortization schedule shows your payments for each month until the mortgage is paid off, broken down into interest cost and repayment of the loan principal.)

The first schedule should show the worst case. Assume that at each review date interest moves up by the full amount of the cap. For instance, the five-year review mortgage in our table could rise by its 2.5% cap at the first review, to 15.37%. At the second review, 10 years from now, the rate could theoretically go higher than 17%, but this is the lifetime cap of the mortgage. After that, a worst case schedule would keep the rate at 17% for the life of the mortgage. (Note that this calculation cannot be performed for a mortgage with no caps.)

The second schedule should show the average case, that is, it makes no assumptions about future interest rate changes, but just holds the index rate at its current level. At the first review, the payment would rise to allow for the loss of the teaser rate; after that, there would be no change. (Holding the rate steady represents an "average" in that neither potential increases nor decreases—which would result if the index rate declines—are projected.)

Your first concern is whether any of the possible monthly payments are too high for you. Your second concern is the total interest you may have to pay on the various alternatives you consider. Add the cumulative interest on one-, three- and five-year review agreements. The worst-case figures will probably show huge savings if you pay more now for the longer review period. Assuming that rates stay where they are now will make the shorter review mortgage look better. Of course, if rates should drop steadily in the future, the shortest review period looks best of all. But in that case, borrowers with longer review terms could comfort themselves with the knowledge that they will eventually benefit, although somewhat less, when their own review dates roll around.

Be Stubborn

As you compare mortgages, don't hesitate to insist on complete information on all these points, including the amortization schedules. In our survey we found that some bank employees are

Dollars and Sense

not yet fully at home with adjustable rate terms. We had to repeat and rephrase questions, and sometimes send bank officers scurrying to their superiors for answers. But banks that really want to offer good service—and that's most banks—will take the time to get you the information you need. And it would be foolish to commit yourself to what might be a 30-year debt without first knowing exactly what you're in for. To help you "shop," we've included a handy checklist—see Dose 18.

A Mortgage Shopping List

Shopping for mortgage money has become much more complicated than it used to be. A decade or two ago, most lenders offered only fixed-rate mortgages with fairly standard maturity periods. These days, the maturities on fixed-rate mortgages vary all over the lot. So do loan origination fees and charges, as well as interest rates and payment provisions. Mortgage lenders now offer ARMs (adjustable-rate mortgages), adjustable-mortgage loans (AMLs) or variable-rate mortgages (VRMs). These variable interest loans come with or without interest balloons and conversion features. In addition, the periods over which interest adjustments can be made vary from one to five years.

Instead of a simple loan so you can buy a house, a mortgage has become a mind-boggling exercise in shopping for the best deal. Fortunately for the consumer, federal law requires the lender to give you information when you apply for a mortgage. You should get a written summary of important terms and costs of the loan. This information should include the circumstances under which the rate could increase, what the effects of an increase would be, and any limitations on the increase. A brief glossary of mortgage terms is listed in Figure 18-1. ARMs are discussed in more detail in Dose 17—"Adjustable Rate Mortgages—Handle with Care." In addition, the following worksheet (Figure 18-2) can be quite useful for comparing the terms and conditions of variable interest rate loans. Our advice is to shop several lenders, compare terms, and then select the deal which best fits your pocketbook and personal needs.

Figure 18-1
Key Terms in Variable Rates Mortgages

Annual percentage rate (APR)
The cost of credit expressed as a yearly basis. It includes interest as well as other charges. Because all lenders follow the same rules

Dollars and Sense

Figure 18-1
Key Terms in Variable Rates Mortgages, *Cont'd*

in quoting the annual percentage rate, it is a good basis for comparing the cost of loans.

ARM (adjustable-rate mortgage)
A mortgage with a fluctuating interest rate. You may also see ARMs referred to as AMLs (adjustable-mortgage loans) or VRMs (variable-rate mortgages).

Cap
A limit on how much the interest rate or the monthly payment on an ARM can change, either periodically or during the life of the mortgage. ARMS may contain one or more types of caps. Payment caps don't limit the amount of interest the lender is earning, so they may cause *negative amortization*.

Discount
Some lenders offer ARMs at a slightly lower than usual rate for a fixed period (most often, the first year of the mortgage). After this discount period, the ARM rate will probably go up depending on the index rate.

Index
The index is the base interest rate used to adjust ARM payments. Quite often, the prime rate is used for this purpose. No one can be sure when an index rate will go up or down. You should ask the lender what index they use to determine the loan's interest rate, how the index for any ARM you are considering has changed in recent years, and where the index is reported.

Margin
The number of percentage points the lender adds to the index rate to calculate the ARM interest rate at each adjustment.

Negative Amortization
With a fixed-interest mortgage, each payment covers a portion of the loan principal as well as interest. The amount of the loan is *amortized* over the life of the mortgage. The case is different with ARMs because interest rates change. As a result, monthly payments may not cover even the interest, let alone the principal. In such a case, the unpaid interest is added back to the principal, actually *raising* the unpaid balance. This is called negative amortization.

Points
Lenders frequently charge "points" on both fixed-rate and adjustable-rate mortgages in order to increase the yield on the mortgage and to cover the costs associated with arranging the loan (closing costs). A point is equal to 1% of the principal amount of your mortgage. For example, if you obtain a mortgage for $80,000, one point equals $800. These points may be paid by the borrower or the home seller, or may be split between them. They are usually collected when the loan is *closed (finalized)*.

A Mortgage Shopping List

Figure 18-2
MORTGAGE CHECKLIST
(Ask your lender to help fill this out.)

	Mortgage A	Mortgage B
Mortgage amount	$_____	$_____
Basic Features		
Fixed annual percentage rate	_____	_____
(The cost of your credit as a yearly rate which includes both interest and other charges)		
ARM annual percentage rate	_____	_____
Adjustment period	_____	_____
Index used and current rate	_____	_____
Margin	_____	_____
Initial payment without discount	_____	_____
Initial payment with discount (if any)	_____	_____
How long will discount last?	_____	_____
Interest rate caps: periodic	_____	_____
overall	_____	_____
Payment caps	_____	_____
Negative amortization	_____	_____
Convertibility or prepayment privilege	_____	_____
Initial fees and charges	_____	_____
Monthly Payment Amounts		
What will my monthly payment be after 12 months if the index rate—stays the same?	_____	_____
goes up 2%?	_____	_____
goes down 2%?	_____	_____
What will my monthly payment be after 3 years if the index rate—stays the same?	_____	_____
goes up 2% per year?	_____	_____
goes down 2% per year?	_____	_____
Take into account any caps on your mortgage.		

Source: *Consumer Handbook on Adjustable Rate Mortgages.* Federal Reserve Board, Federal Home Loan Bank Board.

Moving Daze and How to Survive It

Few things, aside from the death of a loved one or a divorce, put more stress on a family than moving. But in the anguish-provoking process of dismantling a nest in one place and building a new one, it is important not to overlook how relocating may affect your financial planning.

Now that mortgage rates have come down out of the stratosphere, companies are again transferring large numbers of employees and recruiting new employees with offers of relocation. The good news is that these companies are going much farther than they used to toward making a major move palatable. For example, in the aftermath of high interest rates that slowed corporate relocations to almost half a few years ago, certain benefits are now practically fixtures of any job change that requires a move. Accept a switch these days and virtually any large company will at least give you some help in selling your present home and in buying a new one. Most will also offer to help a spouse find a job in the new location and provide "curtain money" (often the equivalent of a month's pay) to help cover the miscellaneous expenses of settling into a new home.

But making a successful move, particularly to a new state, calls for sizing up the impact that relocating may have on other aspects of your personal finances. Not the least of these considerations is taxes. Remember that it is state, not federal, law that determines most income and estate taxes. And since state and local taxes are currently deductible from gross income, they affect your federal income taxes as well. All this requires doing some arithmetic ahead of time to avoid any financial surprises.

Most important, you will want to time the selling of your old house and the buying of the new one carefully so you are not taxed as a resident of two states. If you get stuck owning both homes for more than 183 days—roughly half the year—you could run into real trouble proving which one is your "principal residence" in the eyes of the law.

Fortunately, there are steps you can take if you find yourself in that situation. Get a certificate of domicile from the state you are moving to, if you can. (Not all states issue them.) Then change your automobile registration, as well as your plates and license, notify your insurance company, and get a new driver's license. You will also want to open new checking and savings accounts and register to vote in your new state.

Get a Head Start

The move will go most smoothly if you negotiate well with your employer from the beginning. More money, of course, is a prime consideration. But how much more? Housing and transportation are the two biggest variables in comparing the cost of living in one area versus another. To give you an idea of the spread, see Dose 20—"The Cost of Living: It Depends Where You Live." The Figure in this Dose shows how much income you would need to get $50,000 of actual buying power in selected cities around the country according to recent government statistics.

If you anticipate trouble selling your old home—or simply don't want to worry about what vandals might do to the empty place when you're gone—most large corporations will take it off your hands by turning it over to a home-buying company. You aren't required, of course, to accept the home-buying company's appraisal. But if the offer is in the ballpark, you will probably come out ahead financially by taking it, rather than leaving the family behind, possibly for months, in the hope that a better bid comes along.

Mortgage subsidies are something that you should negotiate up front. Many large companies arrange mortgages for transferees or new employees at below-market interest rates. Others subsidize the relocated family for the first few years in their new home.

Nearly all corporations pay for shipping your household goods and one or two house-hunting trips for the employee and his or her spouse. About 25% of companies will also pay for children's expenses on such trips. In addition, companies usually pay closing costs on home purchases, and some will also pay the realtor's commission on the sale of your old home.

If a company really wants you—or wants to keep you—practically anything may be negotiable. Don't be afraid to ask for anything that might make the move easier or keep you intact financially—say, help with higher tuition at a special school for a handicapped or a gifted child. To avoid problems, just be sure the terms of your deal with your employer are clear. The safest way to prevent misunderstanding is to get everything in writing well ahead of time.

Doing It Alone

Relocating without the help of a big corporate employer is, of course, more expensive. How expensive? Consider this: The Employee Relocation Council, an association of 1,000 major corporations and 8,000 relocation-service firms, estimated that the average cost of moving a home-owning employee in 1984 was $33,348; the average cost for a renter was $8,900. Even with the decline in interest rates since then, many moves, even in highly efficient companies, still cost more than $50,000.

One of the biggest headaches in relocating yourself is having to pick a mover. Most corporate employers make those arrangements and insure your goods for their full replacement value. They naturally rely on movers who have good track records, and the movers usually do all they can to protect that business. But if you're on your own, a little planning can help you avoid the biggest dangers of moving: overpricing, delayed pickup or delivery, and lost or damaged goods.

Even if you are only making a local move, start by reading the Interstate Commerce Commission's free pamphlet "When You Move: Your Rights and Responsibilities," which you can get from nearly any moving and storage company. Ask friends or relatives who have moved recently which companies provided reliable service. You might also get recommendations from your real estate agent.

If you are moving within the same city or state, the firm you choose should be authorized by the appropriate state regulatory agency, usually the Public Utilities Commission. A company typically has to conform to certain standards to keep its authorization. However, it's still a good idea to ask the agency if any complaints have been filed against a mover you plan to use and, if so, what kind of complaints.

If you are relocating to another state, you will want a carrier that is certified by the Interstate Commerce Commission (ICC). The ICC also keeps a record of complaints about any company with recurring problems. Check the reputation of a major carrier's local agent, because that is the person you will be dealing with. To avoid the potential hassle of going to small-claims court in a dispute over lost or damaged goods, hire a mover that participates in the American Arbitration Association. Once you have decided on a mover, have the agent estimate—in writing—what you will be charged for the move. The base price usually depends both on the weight of your shipment and the distance involved, but movers give two kinds of estimates on interstate moves: nonbinding and binding.

A nonbinding estimate is the agent's educated guess as to the total weight of your shipment. The final cost, however, won't be tallied up until your goods are loaded on his truck and weighed. If the agent's estimate was low, you will owe him the difference. If you were overcharged, you will get a refund. By contrast, a binding estimate is definite: You pay that rate even if the shipment proves to be heavier than the mover thought.

The cost of a move within the same city and sometimes within the same state is figured on an hourly rate. Fees in most metropolitan areas range anywhere from about $40 per hour to as much as $120 in New York or Los Angeles.

Watch Those "Extras"

A mover's basic fee covers only the cost of loading your goods onto the van, transporting them to your new dwelling, and unloading them. Everything else, like packing and disconnecting a washer and dryer you want to take, is extra. Figure on paying extra for bulky items, such as a piano, or if movers have to use an elevator or service entrance.

While certified movers must provide minimum liability coverage, you will want to purchase additional insurance on expensive furniture and other items that might be broken during a long-distance move. (Note: Before you buy this additional insurance, check your homeowner's policy, which may protect your goods when you move.)

The amount of insurance on your goods will be stipulated in the mover's contract for service or *bill of lading*. Read it carefully before you sign. Among other items that should be included are the total cost of the move, an inventory of goods to be shipped, and the pickup and delivery dates you and the mover have agreed on.

On moving day, you should supervise closely with your signed contract in hand, along with the inventory list including a description of the contents of every box or crate. Don't leave until everything is loaded onto the van. When your goods arrive at your new home, unpack valuables and expensive breakables such as china right away. Describe the damage on your inventory list before you sign it and give a copy to the driver of the van. If you later find more damage or that items are missing after everything has been unpacked, get a damage claim from the mover and submit it for settlement. Damage claims can be filed up to nine months after delivery.

If you aren't satisfied with the mover's offer to repair or replace damaged or missing items, you can appeal in writing to the American Arbitration Association. Address the letter to: The American Movers Conference, Attn: Dispute Settlement Program,

400 Army-Navy Dr., Arlington, VA 22202. Your other choice is to file suit in small claims court.

What's Deductible and What's Not

When you're moving to a new job location it's important that you keep careful track of all your moving expenses, both direct and indirect. Many of these items are fully, or at least partly, tax deductible if the following criteria are satisfied. First, your new job must be at least 35 miles farther from your old home than your old job was. Second, you must remain, full-time, in the general location of your new job for at least 39 weeks after the move.

Direct moving expenses are fully deductible and include the following: Cost to transport you and your household members to the new home; cost to transport your family's household goods and other belongings; and the cost of meals and lodging during the move.

Indirect expenses have an upper deduction limit of $3,000. However, you may only deduct $1,500 for costs of house-hunting trips and temporary living expenses. Indirect costs include the following: One month (maximum) living expense at your new location and the cost of traveling to and from your new location to look for a new residence.

Unpacking Your Papers

Resettling in a new state inevitably requires finding a new lawyer anyway. As soon as you can dig out your will, have it redrawn by a local lawyer in your new state. Due to differences in state laws, the old one may no longer be valid.

A major move, with or without a helping hand from an employer, affects a family in so many ways that it is bound to produce at least a few anxiety attacks. But if you are as prepared as you can be, abandoning one shelter for another needn't leave any lasting scars either emotionally or financially.

The Cost of Living: It Depends Where You Live

How much has inflation/deflation affected the cost of living in your area? A Rochester, Wisconsin-based management consulting firm, Runzheimer International, analyzes total annual living costs including housing, taxes, transportation and goods & services. It sells the data to companies that use it for employee relocation, recruiting new employees, site selection analysis and to figure pay differentials for employees based in different parts of the country.

The Runzheimer analysis shows the great disparity among living communities nationwide. The high cost areas on the East Coast (Boston, New York and Washington, DC, for example) and on the West Coast (Los Angeles, San Diego and San Francisco, for example) create a real challenge for companies that relocate employees into these areas from less costly locales.

"Resistance from employees to move to higher cost locations is rising," according to Runzheimer, "because the difference in the cost of living between high and low cost locations is widening. As a result, the financial impact felt by employees moving to these areas is more severe and apparent."

Compounding the problem are areas such as Houston and Oklahoma City where the depressed oil industry has actually caused home market values to decline over the last year.

As an example, an employee transferred from Houston to New York in 1980 would have spent 37% more to purchase a home in the New York suburbs versus the Houston suburbs. In 1987, to relocate from the Texas location to New York, an employee would have to pay 161% more.

As a yardstick for making its comparisons, Runzheimer totes up how much of a $50,000 salary a family of four would have to spend living in what it dubs "Standard City, U.S.A."

The Standard City family resides in a 2,400-square-foot home with a three-year-old mortgage and owns two cars—a late-model driven 14,000 miles per year and a four-year-old driven 6,000 miles

Dollars and Sense

Figure 20-1
Annual Living Costs

City	Total Outlay 1980	1987
New York	$45,077	$65,629
Los Angeles	47,039	58,794
Chicago	43,381	56,118
Philadelphia	39,443	54,444
Dallas	35,688	51,617
Atlanta	35,626	51,392
STANDARD CITY, U.S.A.	36,041	50,000
Wilmington	32,752	48,781

per year. Car expenses include both fixed and operating costs. The family also pays federal, state, and local income taxes, plus Social Security. They also pay sales taxes and purchase goods and services typical for a family in their income bracket at their location and set aside a certain amount for investment and savings.

According to Runzheimer, this average family is now spending 39% more to maintain its standard of living than it was five years ago. Figure 20-1 reveals similar increases in most areas. In addition, New York City has replaced Los Angeles as the most expensive place in the country to live.

Some Tips for Homeowners

Maybe instead of buying a new home, you're thinking about doing some remodeling of your current home. Well, you have plenty of company. *Remodeling,* in its annual report on "Remodeling Cost vs. Value," reported that an estimated $90 billion will be spent in 1987 on a wide range of home improvements—from luxury items such as swimming pools to more practical projects like double-pane insulating glass doors and windows.

There are two reasons for the boom in home remodeling. First, take-home pay for the average American was up more sharply in recent years than it has been in the past. After surviving the pocketbook squeeze triggered by the last recession, consumers are now undertaking projects that they had postponed until times got better. And, while the prices of existing houses in desirable neighborhoods have risen steadily over the past few years, the cost of building materials has remained about level. In many cases, therefore, it has become more economical to remodel an existing house than to trade up to another one.

Cost vs. Rewards

But not all remodeling projects are created equal. That is, some projects will add a great deal to the market value of your home, while others may add very little. It is very important to determine how much a project will add to the resale value of your home before you commit any dollars to the project. According to *Remodeling's* "1986 Cost vs. Value" study, if you plan to sell within five years, the smaller home improvement investments tend to give higher returns. In other words, it will take some time for the cost of massive remodeling to be reflected in the price of your home. So you're probably better off avoiding major improvements, which have longer payback periods, and sticking with smaller projects, whose costs may be nearly fully recovered after a short time. Figure 21-1 provides

Figure 21-1
The Costs (and Rewards) of Home Improvements

	Cost Range	Average Cost	Short-term Recovery (percent)
Room Addition	$23,000–$32,500	$28,000	65%– 70%
Swimming Pool	$14,000–$30,000	$19,000	30%– 35%
New Kitchen	$ 7,800–$27,000	$18,000	70%– 90%
Solar Greenhouse	$ 8,500–$17,000	$13,500	90%–110%
Second Bathroom	$ 4,900–$11,600	$ 7,300	100%–130%
Deck	$ 3,000–$ 7,000	$ 4,800	65%– 75%
Fireplace	$ 2,600–$ 3,900	$ 3,250	125%–130%

Data: *Remodeling Contractor*, "Cost vs. Value" Annual Report, July 1986

the cost ranges, average costs, and short-term recoveries from a variety of home improvements. The latter is the percentage of your original investment you can expect to recoup if you sell your house within five years of making the improvement. As you can see, one of the best short-term improvements that you can make on your house is the addition of an energy-efficient fireplace. A $3,250 fireplace installed today may add $4,000-4,200 to the resale value of your house in five years. On the other hand, some high-priced items such as swimming pools or hot tubs may add very little to the value of your home.

To maximize the potential recovery of any project, it's also important to identify the kinds of improvements that are popular in your area of the country. Talking to several realtors can serve as a guide. Nationally, some trends are emerging today: replacing the old family room with a high-tech entertainment center, using extra space as an exercise room, and turning the den into a home office. Aside from these higher-ticket items, other national trends include replacing wall-to-wall carpeting with bleached oak or parquet floors, for example. Skylights and double-pane windows have also become quite popular.

In 1987 it is estimated that consumers will remodel more than 4 million bathrooms at an average cost of $6,500, 3 million kitchens at an average cost of $19,500, and buy $10 billion in window and door replacements. With record numbers of dollars being pumped into the professional remodeling business, you can bet that the best contractors in your area are booking up pretty quickly. So if you've decided that remodeling is the route for you to go, now is the time to get started.

But before you do, you might want to contact *Remodeling* for their "Cost vs. Value" annual report at 655 15th Street, NW, Washington, DC 20005 or call (202)737-0717.

Energy-Efficient Appliances: A Solution to "Rate Shock"

If you cringe each month when the electric bill arrives, don't be too hasty to put all of the blame on your utility company. Part of the problem may lie with the energy-guzzling appliances you own.

It all adds up—month in and month out. Each load of dirty clothes laundered, every batch of dishes washed, and each meal cooked sets the wheels on the utility meter spinning furiously. Energy is no longer inexpensive, as it was in the 1960s and 1970s, and utility costs can definitely wear a sizeable hole in your pockets.

In fact, the Washington (D.C.)-based American Council for an Energy-Efficient Economy (ACEEE) estimates that today the average American family spends between $500 and $1,000 per year operating major household appliances. That same family, in 1970, spent between $200 and $600. This marked increase is due to the fact that residential electricity rates in the U.S. have more than tripled during the past 15 years—an increase that's considerably greater than the general inflation rate.

Even now that oil and natural gas prices have stabilized somewhat, electricity rates will most assuredly continue their rise as costly new power plants are completed. These projects cause the sudden jolt in utility prices commonly known as "rate shock." The best, and probably only, way consumers can effectively combat this "rate shock" is by purchasing energy-efficient appliances and using them wisely. The secret is knowing what you're paying for and taking the time to shop around.

The Real Price

Paying for an appliance doesn't merely consist of writing the check or signing the charge slip—that's only the beginning. Next comes the cost of running that appliance. And, in the case of most major household appliances, the *operating* cost is far more than the *purchasing* price. For example, running a standard model refrigerator for 15-20 years costs three times as much as the purchase price.

Hence, the first consideration when buying an appliance is finding an energy-efficient model that will minimize the yearly operating cost. Because the energy cost for large appliances varies greatly from one model to another, federal law requires that Energy Guide Labels be placed on all new refrigerators, freezers, dishwashers, clothes washers, water heaters, and room air conditioners. These labels contain information such as the manufacturer's name, model number, capacity, and a yearly cost table with which to calculate the annual cost of operating the appliance. For specific cost information on items that do not carry labels, ask the salesperson for the manufacturer's fact sheet.

If you know what you are currently paying per kilowatt-hour of electricity (which you can obtain from your monthly electric bill), the yearly cost table on the Energy Guide Label will tell you what it will cost to run that appliance each year. For dishwashers, clothes washers, and other items that are only used periodically and do not draw constant electricity, you will also need to estimate how many hours per year you use these appliances in order to determine the yearly operating cost.

More important to consumers than the annual operating cost is what it costs to own and operate an appliance over its lifetime. This is called the lifecycle cost and is calculated as follows.

$$\text{Purchase Cost} + \text{(Yearly Energy Cost} \times \text{Estimated Lifetime} \times \text{Discount Factor)} = \text{Lifecycle Cost}$$

Now, suppose that Mr. and Mrs. N. R. Gee are in the market for a new room air conditioner and have decided to conduct a lifecycle cost analysis to compare two different models. The Gees are currently paying $.10/kilowatt-hour of electricity and, because they live in the Midwest, estimate that they will most likely only operate the unit for about 750 hours during the year. Given these two factors, the Gees read the Energy Guide Label on each model and find that the yearly energy cost for Models A and B are $117 and $90, respectively. Air conditioner A is a standard model and sells for $300, while model B costs $375 and is advertised as being highly energy efficient.

Using the above information and the estimated lifetime and discount factor data provided in Figure 22-1, the Gees apply the lifecycle cost formula:

Model A $300 + ($117 × 15 yrs. × 0.81) = $1721.55
Model B $375 + ($ 90 × 15 yrs. × 0.81) = $1468.50

The lifecycle cost comparison clearly indicates that the Gees will save slightly more than $250 in operating costs over the life of

Figure 22-1
Characteristics of Appliances for Lifecycle Cost Comparisons

Appliance	Average Lifetime (years)	Discount Factor*
Air Conditioner (central)	12	0.84
Air Conditioner (room)	15	0.81
Clothes Washer	13	0.83
Clothes Dryer	18	0.78
Dishwasher	12	0.84
Freezer	20	0.76
Range/Oven	18	0.78
Refrigerator/Freezer	20	0.76
Water Heater (electric)	13	0.83
Water Heater (gas)	13	0.83

* Based on a 5% real discount rate and an energy price escalation rate of 2%/year above inflation.
Source: Saving Energy and Money with Home Appliances
American Council for an Energy-Efficient Economy
Washington, D.C.

the appliance by purchasing the more energy-efficient air conditioner (Model B).

As this example illustrates, consumers do not have to cut their energy consumption in order to attain a smaller utility bill. If there's any doubt that energy-efficient appliances significantly reduce utility costs, consider this: Usage studies conducted by the ACEEE conclude that if every U.S. household owned the most efficient refrigerator available, electricity use would drop by the equivalent of the output of 12 large nuclear power plants. That translates into fewer dollars that consumers would have to dole out to their utility companies each month.

To obtain a copy of The Most Efficient Appliances, which provides specific listings of the top-rated models for all major appliances, send $2.00 to: ACEEE, 1001 Connecticut Ave. NW, Suite 535, Washington, D.C. 20036.

To Catch a Thief

High-tech gadgetry to thwart housebreakers is expensive and some of it doesn't even work. The simpler an alarm system, the better.

Fear of crime has made home security very big business. If you want to, you can spend several thousand dollars for complete systems that use pressure mats and photoelectric beams, as well as ultrasonic, microwave, and other detection devices.

Besides being costly, fancy security systems are a nuisance to live with. You have to remember to turn them on and off. Kids and pets inevitably trip delicate sensors setting off false alarms.

Yet most burglars, seeing a house is "wired," will pass it up. The vast majority are amateurs looking for an easier mark. Although your local police can tell you which kinds of systems work best in your area, there are some general considerations to keep in mind.

Quite a few do-it-yourself systems are on the market, costing from as little as $50 to several hundred dollars. They come in a kit, requiring assembly and installation. If you're relatively handy, check them out.

By contrast, professionally installed systems typically start at $1,000. A good installer will thoroughly test the equipment and instruct you on how to use it. The reputable companies also generally prefer to lease, rather than sell, the more elaborate equipment. Since the contract may run for as long as five years, be sure you know what you're getting into. The annual cost of leasing a central reporting system monitored by an alarm company can be as much as $4,000.

Direct hookups to local police cost less and, since they cut reaction time, improve chances of collaring the crook and recovering any stolen property. Some systems link you to both the police and fire departments. Be wary, however, of systems that use automatic dialers. Police and fire fighters in some cities have refused to respond to these nonhuman dialers because of excessive numbers of false alarms.

Check on other local ordinances that may relate to home-security systems before you buy. You may need a permit to install security equipment or there may be restrictions on the kind of equipment allowed. Some local laws rule out sirens or any kind of audible outdoor alarm altogether, or prohibit them if you live near a hospital or other "quiet zone."

The best system will protect the perimeter of your house—doors and windows—all the time, and the interior of the house when you're away. Most perimeter systems also include smoke and heat detectors. Expensive systems may also feature temperature and moisture detectors to prevent frozen water pipes.

Keeping Your Homeowner's Insurance Up to Date

Your home may not be appreciating as rapidly as it once was, but it has almost certainly increased in value since you bought it. Spring cleaning ought to include dusting off your homeowner's insurance policy to make sure your coverage is still adequate. Most homeowner's policies are written with a replacement cost provision that applies to the house and sometimes to its contents, as well. But you need to carry enough insurance to get the full benefit. Normally, that means buying insurance equal to about 80% of what it would cost to replace your house and any valuables new.

How Do You Figure That Cost?

Your insurance agent can probably help by recommending the proper amount of coverage based on current information on construction costs and housing values. In most states you can also buy a special *inflation guard endorsement* on your homeowner's policy. This device automatically increases your coverage limits by small periodic amounts. Still, an inflation endorsement doesn't necessarily mean your coverage is keeping pace with your needs. Check your policy for the coverage limitations on valuables, such as silverware and jewelry. These and other items may have climbed in value with rising prices for precious metals. Another thing to watch for are smaller restrictions, called "sublimits," that apply to certain kinds of property in many homeowner's policies—including securities, artwork, stamps, coins, boats, and guns.

More Insurance . . .

You may need extra insurance to protect some property. For example, say you have $50,000 of insurance on your house. You also own a coin collection worth about $3,000 and you recently bought a fur coat worth about $2,000. The coverage limit on your coin collec-

Dollars and Sense

tion is probably $100, while the policy's theft coverage on your fur coat is probably limited to $500. In this situation, you might want to insure the coins and the coat on an "all risk" basis to get full coverage. Other kinds of property that often need to be separately insured in this way include jewelry, art, stamps, cameras, watches, musical instruments, golf clubs, silverware, gold-plated items, and pewterware.

Universal Life Insurance Debate

Life insurance policies combining protection with investment vehicles for high yields—so-called "universal life policies"—seemed like such a good idea, hardly anyone bothered to look at what's behind those yields. Better late than never.

Few new financial products have ever received the kind of uncritical reception accorded universal life insurance when it was first introduced a few years ago. "At Last—an Almost Ideal Policy," trumpeted *Money* magazine in July 1981. Both the *New York Times* and *The Wall Street Journal* chimed in, praising universal life as "New, Improved Life Insurance...that offers higher interest rates on tax-deferred savings" and saying "New Life-Insurance Policies Are Better Deal; They Offer Decent Returns Besides Protection." Only *Consumer Reports* dared to wonder aloud, "Is it really as good as it sounds?"

The answer, as has become clear, is "not really," and financial writers have begun doing some backtracking. *The Wall Street Journal* discussed the problem with these policies under the headline, "Return on Universal Life Insurance Can Be a Lot Less Than Expected" and said that "Unfortunately, there's a lot less to the quoted rates on universal life than some consumers might think."

What practically everybody missed about universal life the first time is that quoted interest rates on the savings portion of policies some companies are offering don't reflect charges for sales commissions and administrative expenses. Those charges can significantly reduce the savings yield, just as the difference in the level of costs that mutual funds pass on to their investors makes some funds better deals than others.

That makes it nearly impossible to compare universal policies by merely looking at current rates. Further, all three factors that affect the growth of the savings component—the rate, the insurance charges, and other expenses—can vary over time. Some companies adjust the interest rate as often as monthly.

All this is not to say that universal life is bad. Even though advertised rates overstate the yields on these policies, they are a vast improvement over traditional "whole life" insurance. Whole life policies, a staple of the industry for decades, typically pay a dismal rate of return, in the neighborhood of just 6%—that much only if the policy is held 20 years or so. But to understand universal life, you need to know about whole life, as well as the other basic product the industry offers, term insurance.

Whole Life Versus Term Insurance

Traditional whole life combines protection with a savings feature, though the low rate makes it an unattractive investment vehicle. The annual premium doesn't change, but you actually pay more than necessary to cover the risk of death in the early years of the policy and less than necessary to cover the risk of death in the later years.

The annual premium for a policy with a *face amount* of $100,000 on a 30-year-old man would typically be about $1,200 a year. Some of that goes toward savings. If you surrender a whole life policy before it matures, you get back a *cash value,* which is set by a predetermined schedule written into the policy. That cash value tends to build at a snail's pace in the early years, somewhat faster later. But unless you live to be around 100, the cash value remains less than the face amount of the policy. In other words, you don't get back the full $100,000 unless you die!

Adding insult to injury, most whole life policies give buyers no way to tell the rate of return, no control over how much of each premium goes toward savings or how that money is invested. Policyholders pay the fixed annual premium and are never told what portion goes to pay the protection, what is contributed to savings, and how much is taken out for commissions and other fees.

While millions of dollars worth of whole life is still sold every year, it isn't the best buy for most people. The exceptions, says the Consumers Union, which publishes *Consumer Reports* and has probably made the most objective study of the industry over the years, fall into three categories: 1) people in high tax brackets, who may benefit from its tax-shelter aspect; 2) people who genuinely need a "forced savings" and have no better one available; and 3) people who know they will need insurance after retirement age. As a rule, however, both the Consumers Union and most financial advisers recommend term insurance over whole life and investing the big difference between premiums yourself.

Term insurance provides death protection only. If you die while the policy is in force, your beneficiary gets the specified face amount of the policy. Since your chances of dying when you're young are relatively small, the modest annual premium of perhaps $250 for a 30-year-old man makes term insurance attractive for young families who are most likely to need a lot of life insurance. As you get older, the premium rises every year or every few years. Past retirement age, term insurance becomes quite expensive.

In bringing out universal life, the insurance companies' idea was to combine term insurance with a savings feature that offered a better return than whole life. On the surface, universal policies are also more straightforward than whole life policies: the amount of protection provided and the savings elements are both clearly identified. Things start to get fuzzy, however, when it comes to those high yields that most companies emphasize in their ads.

How Universal Life Works

Many variations on the theme of mixing insurance and investing are now being marketed by a wide range of companies. They got their start in the mid-1970s, when owners of whole life cashed in their policies at a record rate to put the money into higher-paying investments such as money market mutual funds.

That led insurers to develop more interest-sensitive, investment-oriented policies. The first, called *variable life,* was introduced by Equitable in 1976, with Securities and Exchange Commission approval. It allowed the savings portion to be used for investments; the policyholder had a guaranteed death benefit, but not a guaranteed cash value. In return for the investment risk, variable life offered the potential for a substantially higher yield than whole life provided.

The SEC's decision to allow insurance companies to offer investments and the subsequent deregulation of the financial industry paved the way for a variety of financial institutions to sell insurance. In 1979, E.F. Hutton & Company, the brokerage firm, introduced universal life, sharpening the focus on investment still more.

The money you put into a universal life policy goes into a fund from which the company makes two major deductions. The first is for plain protection—in effect, term insurance. The other is for the company's expenses, plus profits. The amount of your money that remains after those deductions—the savings portion—earns interest at a rate that depends on how it is invested. Some companies invest it entirely at their discretion, others invest it according to an agreed-upon financial index or give you the option of putting the cash into any of several investment vehicles such as stock, bond, or money market mutual funds.

The flexibility of universal life, both in the amount of insurance you can elect to purchase and in the annual premium—called a "contribution" because you can vary it within limits—is a real plus. With traditional whole life, the insurance protection, the face amount, is fixed when you buy the policy. Although a company may let you lower the face amount, you normally can't raise it. If you decide you want more insurance, you usually have to take another medical exam and buy a new policy.

With universal life, it's rarely a problem to add more protection to the same policy, although you may still have to take another medical exam. Several universal life policies also have cost-of-living-increase options, which most traditional policies don't permit.

Universal life lets you pay whatever annual premium you wish (within limits), so in a year when you can afford it, you can elect to put more money into a policy and hasten the buildup of cash value. When your personal finances are tight, you can skip a yearly premium altogether. In that case, the charge for the insurance protection is taken out of the accumulated cash value, assuming you have enough there. An insuring company charges for protection depending on their experience with the mortality rate of policyholders.

Both whole life and universal life offer the advantage that you can get at the cash value of a policy if you need it. With whole life, the two usual ways to put your hands on that money are to take out a policy loan, or to surrender your policy and withdraw the entire cash value. Universal life goes further, allowing you to make partial withdrawals from the cash-value investment funds, often with no penalty or at most a modest fee of $25 or so. Thus, the savings portion of universal life is akin to owning shares in a garden variety mutual fund. But—here's the nub of it—you have to analyze universal life as you would any other investment.

Do You Want the Coverage?

A universal life policy only makes more sense than simply buying term insurance if you want protection and savings in the same package. Moreover, you have to go beyond comparing yields of various universal policies with the same features to find the best deal. The better yardstick is to look at the policies' projected cash values after different intervals, but even those are subject to change.

Companies that sell universal life stress the value of the policies as a tax shelter. If you put the savings portion into investments that perform well, you can quickly increase the value of the policy while accumulating tax-sheltered appreciation and earnings. The fact is, however, that tax-conscious investors can, for example, earn the same 10% available from universal life on tax-exempt municipal bonds.

Life insurance has generally enjoyed special tax status. Conventional whole life is tax sheltered in three respects. First, the cash value buildup isn't taxed as it accumulates. Second, death benefits normally aren't subject to income tax. Third, if you cash in a policy, you pay tax only on the amount by which the cash value exceeds the premiums you've paid over the years (less any dividends you've received.)

Both whole life and universal life have been effected by the Tax Reform Act of 1986. Instead of allowing life insurance interest to accumulate tax-free, the total amount of interest received each year from proceeds from insurance companies is included in your gross income. Prior law allowed an exclusion of $1,000 annually.

Universal Life II

The latest wrinkle in insurance-investment products is to offer policyholders still more control over investment decisions. Two companies, Acacia and Prudential, brought out something called "Universal Life II" and at least eight other companies are expected to bring out similar policies.

Like universal life and variable life, Universal Life II combines death protection with an investment account. Until now, however, only universal life permitted you to vary which portion of the premium went to investments and insurance, or to skip a premium and use the accumulated cash to cover just the insurance. Meanwhile, only variable life allowed you to switch the savings portion among the family of mutual funds—say, out of stocks and into bonds—as you desired. Now, Universal Life II unites the flexible-premium and fund-switching features of both its predecessors in the same policy.

Other companies are making the borrowing feature of universal life still more attractive. Merrill Lynch, for example, now offers "Prime Plan 4," a high-ticket policy with a minimum investment of $10,000. It allows the investor to choose among such investment vehicles as a money market account, stock or bond mutual funds, or a zero-coupon bond; insurance premiums are paid from earnings on the investment. The brokerage firm charges a commission annually of about 1% of the yield.

Prime Plan 4 policyholders can borrow up to 75% of their money in the first three years of the policy, up to 90% after that, and at almost no cost. The annual interest rate on loans against the policy is 5.25%. But because loans are made from the investor's account, the policyholder is still earning 4.5% interest. Thus, the net cost of borrowing from it is just 0.75%.

Look Down the Road

The powerful insurance industry wields considerable influence as a lobbying group. Assuming it is successful in retaining the tax-deferred status of life insurance, I strongly suggest you still regard the newer variations of these products with a critical eye. As investments, universal life and its clones should only be purchased for the long haul. Because of the policies' high sales charges, it often takes up to 10 years for the tax-sheltered earnings to achieve the projected rate of return.

While the past is no guide to the future, you should ask insurance agents peddling these investment products for recent fund performance reports. Since these policies are indeed investment instruments that must be registered with the SEC, agents who sell them must be licensed by the National Association of Securities Dealers and operate under the supervision of a registered broker-dealer. Further, buy these products only from companies that have consistently gotten top marks from A. M. Best, which rates the financial strength of insurance sellers.

If you don't intend to hold an insurance-investment product for at least 10 years, you'll come out ahead buying term insurance—to get just the death benefit—and investing the difference on your own.

The New Case for Annuities

If you're looking for a long-term retirement investment with current tax advantages, annuities are no longer a discouraging word. In the early 1980s, tax-deferred annuities were some of the hottest products on Wall Street. Then Baldwin-United, one of the biggest issuers of these policies, went bust. But annuities are back and, despite recent tax changes, worth another look.

In 1983, it was hard to beat the return available on single-premium deferred annuities. Sold through brokerage firms, they combined interest rates as high as 14% with deferral of taxes, and investors gobbled them up. With the bankruptcy of giant Baldwin-United Corp., however, 165,000 annuity investors have had to settle for far less than the return they were promised, while the insurance industry scrambled to clean up its act.

Congress has helped repair the tarnished image of annuities by largely leaving them alone. Although the 1984 tax law effected withdrawals prior to age 59-1/2 and changed certain beneficiary rights, the damage was minimal. However, the additional tax on early withdrawals from deferred annuity contracts was increased from 5% to 10% effective for taxable years beginning after December 31, 1986. This does not apply if an individual began receiving benefits as of March 1, 1986 under a written election designating a specific schedule of benefit payments.

Many policies without sales charges (no-load) are now paying about 8.5% guaranteed for 10 years, with the choice of three- or five-year policies paying slightly less. While those rates are comparable to currrent rates on bank CDs, shopping for an annuity is a bit more complicated.

The Annuity Advantage

The typical annuity investor is a) between the ages of about 40 and 70 or b) has accumulated wealth that puts him or her in a high marginal tax bracket. If that fits your description, you might consider an annuity both to ease your tax burden now and to save for retirement, when your tax bracket will probably be lower. It would also give you guaranteed returns from this portion of your portfolio.

An annuity also solves the two basic problems with an Individual Retirement Account (IRA):
- You can only defer taxes on interest accumulations you earn on the $2,000 you put in every year.
- You have to pay taxes on those savings dollars when you begin making withdrawals.

However, the money you put into an IRA is, in most cases, sheltered—an advantage that annuities can't claim. While annuities may not be replacements for IRAs, as a companion of one of these plans, an annuity can let you put aside—tax-deferred—much more of your savings.

How much of a boon the tax deferral is, of course, depends on your tax bracket. But at current bracket rates, assuming the same 10% interest on $50,000 invested in either a bank CD or a deferred annuity, the annuity is the better choice if you're in a high income bracket. Here's why:

Say you have $50,000 to invest, that you're 50 now and looking forward to retiring at age 65. If you roll over your annuity which pays 10% every year for the next 15 years, by the end of that time your savings will have grown to $208,862. If you then withdraw the entire amount—paying taxes of $60,368 on the earned interest—you'll be left with $148,494.

But look what would happen if you put the $50,000 into a CD instead. Each year, taxes are due on 12 months of interest. Since money that goes for taxes each year could otherwise be earning for you, too, it cuts the "effective interest rate" on the CD to 6.2%. And at that rate over 15 years, you accumulate just $123,264.

Moreover, annuities have payout options that let you defer taxes well into retirement. Instead of taking a lump sum at age 65, for instance, you can elect to receive the money in monthly payments, either for a certain number of years or for life.

How They Work

Annuities fall into two basic categories. Although you can buy annuities and begin receiving payments right away (immediate-pay annuities), we're concentrating here on *deferred annuities*. These policies, which don't start payments until some years after purchase—usually when you retire—also come in several varieties.

The different classes of deferred annuities are defined by the various ways you can invest in them. You can put the money in all at once (single-premium annuity), in fixed installments over some period of time (fixed-premium annuity), or in varying amounts whenever you like (variable-premium annuity). In all cases, when you buy a deferred annuity you're essentially loaning the issuing insurance company your money for a defined period of time. Like any lender, you expect to be paid interest sometime down the road.

Single-premium annuities are the most popular. Although a few policies have an initial investment of as little as $1,500, the more usual minimum is $5,000 or $10,000. There's no ceiling on how much you can invest and you can use an annuity as collateral for a bank loan.

Generally, the more complicated the payout option you select, the higher your premiums will be. Some annuities provide monthly income for a fixed period, say, 10 years. Others make payments while you live (lifetime annuities) and then stop. Still others will pay you during your lifetime, then continue making payments for the life of a beneficiary (generally a spouse).

For planning purposes, it's important to note the difference between fixed-dollar annuities and variable annuities. A fixed-dollar annuity tells you at the onset exactly how much your monthly payout will be, whereas a variable annuity does not give you that assurance.

Instead, buying a variable annuity is similar to buying shares of a mutual fund—you purchase "units" of the annuity, along with other investors, and the insurance company invests those premium proceeds in stocks or other securities. Thus, the value of your units may fluctuate quite a bit from month to month or year to year, depending on the company's investment policy and how successfully it manages the annuity's portfolio.

Since the majority of deferred annuities now on the market are variable, the company's investment acumen is key. Most companies offering these policies guarantee certain minimum benefits, but advertise "estimated benefits" based on their track record. As with a mutual fund, the past may be no guide to the future.

Features and Fees

In wake of the Baldwin-United debacle, safety and security have to be the annuity investor's foremost concerns. Only certain insurance companies can offer single-premium deferred annuities, though they often sell their products both directly to the public and through brokerage firms.

If you're interested in purchasing an annuity, check on the insurance company's financial position to be sure it's solid. The best source for that information is the A.M. Best Report, available at many public libraries and in brokerage offices.

When you're comparing policies, scrutinize both the annuity's declared interest rate and the length of time you're guaranteed a return at that rate. A policy that pays a high rate guaranteed for only one year may not be the best choice; the company could lower the rate the next year. You might be better off with an annuity from a company whose current rate is a bit less than others are currently paying, but guarantees its rate longer.

Compare minimum guaranteed benefits closely. Pick several "target" years, when you might want to withdraw the money, and find out what the value of your annuity would be after, say, 2, 10, and 20 years (both as a lump sum and as monthly payouts over a certain period).

Sales charges and/or management fees obviously affect an annuity's rate of return. Although most annuities don't have sales charges, a few nick you for as much as 7% of your initial investment. Pick a no-load policy, so that all the money you put into a policy goes to work for you immediately.

But even no-loads have a catch: Check your withdrawal rights and watch for other insurance-related fees. With no-loads, you usually have to pay a surrender charge of 4 or 5% if you withdraw all your funds. However, some companies drop the surrender charge after you've held your annuity for 5 or 10 years and a few have no surrender charge at all.

Planning Ahead

If you're in good health, but worried that your other savings and investments won't provide enough capital when you retire, you might consider buying an annuity. The advantage, if you come from hearty stock that tends to survive to a ripe old age, is that you'll never outlive your income.

The drawback is that once you begin receiving payments, that income is fixed and won't rise with inflation. So, although an annuity can be useful as part of a retirement program that also includes an IRA, Keogh, and other investments, it's not the place to put all of your savings.

For more information on evaluating and buying annuities, the American Institute for Economic Research offers an excellent 32-page booklet entitled *Annuities From the Buyer's Point of View*. You may order a copy by sending a $3.00 check to the American Institute for Economic Research, Great Barrington, MA 01230.

Make Room for Daddy Mac & Grannie Mae

Instead of loaning your kids money to buy a house, consider buying one together. After you retire, they might return the favor and buy yours. It's become an all-too-familiar refrain: Inflation is making it all but impossible for even two-career young couples to buy a home. Equally disturbing is the flip side of this dilemma, something you don't hear as much about. It is the plight of older homeowners, many of whom own their homes free and clear, but find themselves struggling on fixed incomes just to make ends meet. At first glance, these two groups wouldn't seem to have much in common. But both need help. And two newer types of mortgages can provide it.

The barriers to home ownership faced by many young people are well known. Often young couples either don't have the cash required to put down on the home of their choice, or they don't have enough income to handle the monthly payments. Older homeowners also get into a fix at the opposite end. In many cases, the equity these seniors have built up in their homes over the years is their biggest asset. But unless they are willing to sell—and most don't want to—that equity is a frozen asset that can't put food on the table or pay medical bills. Moreover, the ranks of elderly homeowners likely to become trapped in this distressing situation are growing. An estimated 25 million Americans are over 65 years of age. Another 5,000 turn 65 every day. At that rate, their numbers should swell to 36 million by the year 2000. Mortgage bankers say that of those who are already 65, about 70% are homeowners and half own their homes outright. The combined equity they are sitting on is put at anywhere from $600 billion to as much as $1 trillion.

Keeping It in the Family

The answer—both for young people trying to accumulate equity and for older folks needing to free it up—may be closer than they think. It could well lie in two newer types of loans, the shared-equity mortgage (SEM) and the reverse-annuity mortgage, that parents and children can use to help each other. Some sizable tax breaks give these loans an extra fillip that can make them attractive even to outside investors.

Both SEMs and reverse-annuity mortgages have been around for about six years. While some California banks offered them for a time, they never really caught on. Such transactions can be complex, and most banks simply didn't want the bother of having to structure agreements that satisfied all parties and the Internal Revenue Service besides. Enter the middleman—an economics professor who heads the University of California School of Real Estate and Urban Economics at Berkeley. In June 1984, Kenneth Rosen formed the for-profit Family Backed Mortgage Association, Inc. and devised two programs to make intrafamily loans simpler for both borrowers and lenders.

The first of Rosen's programs, Daddy Mac, is intended to help young couples. It works like this: Parents and children split the ownership of a house (typically 50-50, although other proportions could be used). Each pays half of the downpayment, along with half the monthly mortgage, taxes, and insurance. To avoid trouble from the IRS, the offspring must pay rent for their use of the parent's share of the house—and at the going market rate. Still, their monthly outlay is likely to be anywhere from 25% to 30% less than it would cost them to buy the same house alone. Since home mortgage interest is tax deductible, the exact savings depends on the youngsters' tax bracket.

What's in it for parents? Besides a small cash flow in the form of rent payments, a tidy tax shelter: annual depreciation deductions for owning half of an investment property. Other deductions—for property taxes and mortage interest—are split evenly. Likewise, parents and children share any capital gains when the house is sold.

Ideally, the parents' tax deductions from a SEM will be great enough to offset their annual cash outlay (except for any contribution toward the downpayment). Because the value of the parents' depreciation deductions gradually declines, however, an agreement might call for the children to buy out the folks' interest in the fifth or sixth year. Depending on interest rates, the children could do that either with a second mortgage or a completely new loan. Parents could also decide to give their share of the house to the kids. If so, they will owe their portion of any capital gains on the market-value appreciation of the property (after the depreciation already claimed). Making the parents' share of the house a gift is not subject to gift taxes if the amount is no more than $10,000 per parent for each child.

Dot All the i's, Cross All the t's

In addition to the loan agreement, parents and children who elect to use a SEM should have a separate legal contract that specifies all the details of the arrangement. It should spell out, for example, what happens if parent or child defaults, whether the child can sublet the house to someone else, and under what circumstances the house can be sold. While your lawyer can draft such a contract, this is the role that companies like Family Backed Mortgage have stepped in to fill. For a small fee, Professor Rosen's company analyzes the sale-leaseback that a family is contemplating, determines the borrowers' financial qualifications, prepares the necessary legal paperwork, and refers the applicant to a willing lender. In return for the referral, Rosen collects 1.5% of the loan amount at closing from the lender. So far, he claims to have lined up more than 125 lenders nationwide who are willing to make these mortgages.

Indeed, equity sharing seems to be taking hold. Home developers in Virginia are now using equity sharing in their marketing programs. A company doing condominium conversions in the Washington D.C. area is offering to match up residents who can't afford to buy their units alone with a syndicate of outside investors. In Shawnee Mission, KA, Electronic Realty Associates uses a computer to pair cash-short buyers with investors across the country. Although interest in SEMs is growing, potential investors should be wary of self-styled "equity-sharing consultants"—real estate agents, investment advisers, and others who may not know all the intricacies of these transactions. Not the least of these are IRS guidelines that the plans must meet.

The idea of nonrelatives participating in a SEM parallels the concept behind shared-appreciation mortgages (SAMs) that were popular mostly on the West Coast a few years back. Born at the height of the inflation-driven, house-appreciation boom, SAMs faded as the increase in house prices slowed or even flattened.

The Golden Retirement Annuity Mortgage

So far we've looked at special arrangements that meet the needs of young people struggling to purchase a first home. But what about those caught at the other end—older homeowners? Rosen's other program, Grannie Mae, isn't as jazzy, but should also help fill an important need. The formal name is the Golden Retirement Annuity Mortgage Association. Like Daddy Mac for the youngsters, Grannie Mae is a sale-leaseback—but in this case, parents sell their own houses to their children, investing the proceeds in an annuity. They then lease the house back from the kids for the remainder of their lives. It works for elderly homeowners who have at least an 80% equity position in their homes.

The idea would seem to be appealing for children who want to ease their parents' financial burden—and who can use the tax shelter besides. If an older couple has no children or prefers not to involve them in a sale-leaseback, Rosen can help them contact outsiders who might be interested. The couple's annuity payments will vary, depending on the value of the house, the age of the younger spouse, and the lease payment (again, it must be the fair-market charge).

Two examples: A couple, both age 65, with a house valued at $100,000 and no mortgage, would net $8,600 a year after paying rent. A 75-year-old widow living in a $150,000 house without a mortgage, on the other hand, would net nearly $18,000 annually. Furthermore, nobody pays a commission to a real estate broker to handle the sale. And if the seniors have lived in the house for five of the last eight years, $125,000 of the sale is tax-free. However, the children could wind up paying some estate and income taxes because of the sale-leaseback, and might even have a negative cash flow paying in more than they get out. Nonetheless, the arrangement is something to consider. And it keeps the mortgage all in the family.

Keeping Up On Your Social Security Benefits

Your employer is responsible for reporting your earnings and contributions to the Social Security Administration. It's also a good idea to monitor your contributions yourself to be sure that everything you are entitled to is being properly credited.

The form you need to do that (Request For Statement of Earnings Form, SSA-7004) can be obtained from any Social Security office. In return, the Social Security Administration will send you a computer tally of the data it has on you. Expect to wait at least six weeks for a reply.

A sample of the report you will get back is shown in Figure 28-1. The report breaks out your annual earnings subject to Social Security tax for the most recent three years. Wages covered by Social Security before that are likely to be lumped together and may span as much as 20 years. So, it's best to check your account every three years.

The U.S. Department of Health and Human Services, of which the Social Security Administration is a part, publishes a series of free booklets covering various aspects of Social Security. You

Figure 28-1
Sample Summary Statement of Earnings Covered by Social Security

Years	Covered Earnings
1938 thru 1951	None
1952 thru 1983	$ 94,042.13
1984	30,568.33
1985	29,700.00
1986	32,400.00
1987 (not yet completed)	38,836.50
Total Earnings	$225,546.96

can get them by writing or calling any Social Security Office. The following is a partial list of what's available:

"Your Social Security"

"How You Earn Social Security Credits"

"Thinking about Retiring?"

"A Brief Explanation of Medicare"

"Your Social Security Checks - While You are Outside the United States"

"Estimating Your Social Security Retirement Check—Using the Indexing Method"

In addition, the department publishes the "Social Security Handbook" (SSA publication 05-10135). The guide provides a detailed explanation of retirement insurance, survivors insurance, disability insurance, health insurance, supplemental security income, etc. The guide costs $9.00, and is available from the Superintendent of Documents, U.S. Government Printing Office, Washington, D.C. 20402.

A Retirement Savings Worksheet

You've probably tried to do it a dozen times. You sit down with your pencil, pad, calculator, and maybe some old tax returns, mutual fund prospectuses, and brochures on retirement real estate. And you try to work out how much you have to put away between now and then to finance a comfortable retirement. Several hours later, you're exhausted, mired in paper, and not much wiser.

The usual problem is that there are too many possibilities. In every year between now and when you retire, your income will change, the rate of inflation will change, and so will the returns available on the whole host of investment options. Switches in government policies will alter the amount you can expect from Washington in the form of Social Security benefits and the amounts you'll have to send to Washington in taxes.

If you try to follow each one of these threads, you'll never arrive at a conclusion, and you'll drive yourself crazy in the process. But if you settle for a quick-and-dirty calculation on the back of an envelope, you won't trust the result (at best) and (at worst) you could be badly misled by it.

What you can do is to steer a middle course. The accompanying worksheet (Figure 29-1) and Figures 29-2 and 29-3 will help you organize a likely projection of your retirement needs, under today's conditions, and expressed in today's dollars. You can then get your saving and investment plan under way. As time passes, you can keep your program up to date by recalculating the figures when inflation, investment returns, and your income change.

Filling in the Sheet

Item 1 is easy—how much you made, before taxes last year. By basing your calculations on this number, you adopt the goal of maintaining your current standard of living in retirement. If, in the future, your rate of total pay moves up faster or slower than infla-

A Retirement Savings Worksheet

Figure 29-1
Retirement Saving Worksheet

---

(1) Current Pretax Income $_____
(2) Pretax Retirement Income as % of Line 1   _____%
(3) Percent Current Income to be Replaced
     By Social Security _____
     By Employer's Plan _____
     By Contributory Plans _____
     Total All Plans   _____%
(4) Line 2 − Line 3, Percent from Own Savings   _____%
(5) Line 1 × Line 4, Goal in 1986 Dollars $_____
(6) Capital Needed (1986 $) to Earn Line 5 (from Figure 29-4) $_____
(7) Value of One 1986 Dollar, Invested Each Year Until Retirement (from Figure 29-5) $_____
(8) Line 6 − Line 7, Required Annual Savings $_____

---

tion, thus raising or lowering your living standard (and your saving capacity), you may want to refigure your retirement goal.

Item 2 takes some thought, some consulation with your spouse if you have one, and some figuring. You can live much more cheaply in retirement, without giving up any of the pleasures of life, but how much more cheaply depends on the specific ways your expenses and your day-to-day life will change—and you're the best judge of that. Here are some key points to consider:

- Working costs will disappear from your budget: commuting, meals away from home, and work clothes, for instance. Child-related expenses will be past, especially education costs, from school clothes and supplies to college fees. Savings will no longer be a budget item (although you'll still be managing your investments).
- Your housing costs will probably be lower. If you're making mortgage payments now, that's an additional savings program that prepays retirement housing expenses. You may want to add to your budget for some retirement expenses—extra travel, for instance. And an extra allowance for medical costs is wise.
- Finally, since you'll have a lower dollar income, your income tax bracket will be lower, so the dollar amount of your taxes will fall by a larger percent than your income. The fact that you won't be paying Social Security taxes any longer will also make a big difference for most workers; moreover, Social Security benefits are not taxable except for retirees with additional incomes over $25,000 (single) and $32,000 (married couple).

Figure 29-2

Current Pretax Income	Percent Needed in Retirement
Up to $25,000	70%–75%
$25,000–$50,000	60 –65
$50,000–$75,000	55 –60
Over $75,000	50 –55

There are rules of thumb for figuring out the percent of current income you'll need in retirement. They're shown in Figure 29-2 for you to use in a test run of the worksheet, but we urge you not to rely on them. You'll get much more accurate results, and feel safer about using them, if you work up a personal retirement budget based on your actual living expenses.

Item 3 is the most difficult blank to fill in. It shows the share of your retirement income needs that will be covered by sources other than your personally managed savings. Social Security is the toughest of all. We hope everyone is aware by now that there is no legal guarantee that you will get any Social Security benefits at all. Congress has the right to decide who gets how much, and to change the amounts as they wish. For lack of better information, we've included the current Social Security ratios for various preretirement income levels in Figure 29-3. When you fill in the worksheet, you can work from the percentages in the table, or perhaps reduce them a little to allow for some future cuts. You should certainly not increase them.

Social Security taxes are paid on income up to a maximum amount. If you earn more than this, you no longer pay Social Security. In turn, however, benefits are also paid only up to the maximum. As a result, if your income prior to retirement exceeds the Social Security maximum, the benefits you receive will represent a smaller percentage of your preretirement income. In our example, the maximum taxable income is $31,271 and the maximum replacement rate (the maximum amount that Social Security covers your preretirement income) is 27%. So, for instance, if you earn $42,000, a reasonable replacement rate to use would be 20% (27% of the $31,271 maximum, or $8,443, divided by $42,000). These figures are based on the benefit paid to a single worker. If your nonworking spouse is also old enough to be eligible for benefits, the amount is increased by 50%.

Figure 29-3

Income Level	Replaced Percent by Social Security
Low Income ($8,022)	54%
Average Income ($15,887)	41
Maximum S.S. Amount ($31,271)	27

You'll probably find it easier to fill in the next blank, figures for pension and other plans that are sponsored by your employer. Your employee benefits office or the company's financial department may be able to give you a number or a range to plug in the worksheet. You can also enter on the next line expected benefits from employer-sponsored savings plans that you fund with your own contributions. Here, too, your employer may be able to help you estimate how much retirement income you might build up for yourself with any given level of savings put into the plan. You can also omit this line, and then decide how much of the required savings amount on the worksheet's bottom line you want to put into your employer's contributory plan.

The worksheet gets easier from here on. Item 4, the difference between the retirement income you want and what will come from other sources, tells you how much of the job is on your shoulders. Item 5 multiplies your personal retirement goal by your current income. The answer shows, in 1986 dollars, how much annual income your personal investment should provide in retirement.

To fill in Item 6, look at Figure 29-4. It tells you how much money you would have to accumulate, again in 1986 dollars, to get the desired pretax income in Item 5, assuming various returns on investment. (You can find numbers that fall between rows easily. For instance, if your savings earned 4%, a $7,500 income goal would require $187,500, halfway between the amounts of $5,000 and $10,000.) Naturally, you'll subtract from this number any savings you have already built up.

The returns on investment used in the table include an adjustment for inflation. For instance, using the 4% return column means you expect your retirement savings to earn a rate 4 percentage points higher than the rate of inflation. In retirement, you would leave all your returns invested, except that 4%, to preserve the purchasing power of your nest egg. The 4% is pretty reasonable. A 6-8% return in excess of inflation might be available if you put all your savings in a well-diversified common stock portfolio—but that's also riskier than many other investments. A 10% return above inflation is extremely high, and would entail a lot of risk.

Figure 29-4
Retirement Nest Egg Needed, in 1986 Dollars

Desired Income from Savings	\multicolumn{5}{c}{Real Return on Retirement Investments}
	2%	4%	6%	8%	10%
$ 5,000	$ 250,000	$125,000	$ 83,333	$ 62,500	$ 50,000
10,000	500,000	250,000	166,666	125,000	100,000
15,000	750,000	375,000	250,000	187,000	150,000
20,000	1,000,000	500,000	333,333	250,000	200,000
30,000	1,500,000	750,000	500,000	375,000	300,000

Figure 29-5
Value of Annual Investment of One 1986 Dollar, In 1986 Dollars

Your Present Age	Years to Retirement	2%	4%	6%	8%	10%
25	40	$61.61	$98.83	$164.05	$279.78	$486.85
30	35	50.99	76.60	118.12	186.10	298.13
35	30	41.38	58.33	83.80	122.35	180.94
40	25	32.67	43.31	58.16	78.95	108.18
45	20	24.78	30.97	38.99	49.42	63.00
50	15	17.64	20.82	24.67	29.32	34.95
55	10	11.17	12.49	13.97	15.65	17.53

(Aftertax Real Return on Savings)

Item 7 is also worked out after inflation. Using Figure 29-5, you can see how much you would have, when you retire, if you put away $1 every year at various rates of return on your savings. For example, if there were no inflation, and savings earned 6% per year after taxes, a 35-year-old worker could put away $1 each year until he retired and accumulate $83.80. Using your own age and the returns you expect, above inflation, in your own savings program, you can fill in Item 7.

The bottom line is the amount that you would have to save each year, in dollars of 1986 purchasing power, to reach your savings goal. Divide Line 6 by Line 7 and you'll have Item 8, a reasonable estimate of your annual required savings.

It's An Ongoing Job

Staying on track with your retirement savings isn't a one-time job. First of all, the tables show results excluding inflation, but we don't live in a world without inflation. As the years go by, you'll have to boost your annual saving figure from Item 8 by the percentage that the cost of living rises. So, if your annual savings goal today is $1,200, or $100 a month, and inflation is 5% next year, you'll then have to squirrel away $105 each month . . . and so on, making a new adjustment each year as you see what inflation does to your budget. Second, you have to keep checking your investment returns. Last year, your IRA could easily have earned 6% more than inflation in a money market account. Next year, it may be no more than 4%. In that case, you have choices to make. You might change your investment, taking on greater risks in exchange for a chance at higher returns. You might raise your annual savings, reducing your present spending in order to have more to spend in retirement. Or you might lower your targeted living standard in retirement.

Finally, you need to estimate how taxes, both immediate and deferred, will alter your results. For instance, if you invested your

A Retirement Savings Worksheet

retirement nest egg in common stocks with a good record of raising their dividends as fast as inflation, their total market value would probably rise with inflation over time. But unless you sold the stocks, you would not owe any capital gains tax on that increase in value. On the other hand, if you bought bonds that yielded an interest rate equal to inflation plus 4%, you would have to pay income taxes, not only on the 4%, but on the rest of the interest return as well.

Retirement Portfolio Administration

Despite some changes in the tax laws, IRAs are a hot topic. The government provided the incentive: invest up to $2,000 annually in an IRA and pay no taxes on your earnings until you retire. Taxpayers have rushed in droves, eager to reap the benefits of one more tax break. It all looks good on paper—all those tax benefits *and* IRA-invested dollars pumping the economy. But where exactly are all those IRA dollars going? Growth in total assets in the typical IRA portfolio and the proliferation of investment vehicles available to IRA investors have complicated most investors' decisions. Advisers of all types have given their prescriptions for what constitutes a "good" IRA investment —not to mention advice concerning trading versus buy and hold, fixed-income securities versus equities, the relationship of assets in the IRA to those in other accounts, etc.

Managing an IRA has become a complex issue. Investors must decide about how many different funds should be included in the IRA, how to go about investing each year's contribution, whether they should use mutual funds in their IRAs or invest in stocks and bonds directly, the kind of records they should keep, and how to change their IRA portfolios over time.

Diversification

As I indicate throughout this book, the best way to avoid investment disasters is to diversify. Basic diversification means holding at least 10 different common stocks along with some cash that can be used for buying additional stock. Given today's average stock price, this requires a portfolio of approximately $40,000. Thus, my recommendation is to invest IRA contributions in mutual funds, which provide adequate diversification benefits. When the total value of the mutual fund portfolio has reached the minimum amount, you can begin to invest on your own. Favorable experiences with mutual fund investments may lead many investors to continue using them even after the portfolio reaches that amount.

The number of different mutual funds you should hold depends on the total value of your IRA portfolio. The number will also be determined by the minimum investment requirements set by many funds and by annual administrative charges which will consume part of your total investment. As the value of your IRA portfolio increases, more mutual funds can be included.

Most funds set a minimum requirement for you to buy in initially—on average, $500 or $1,000. The minimum for subsequent investments is about $100. This means that, if you're just beginning your IRA programs, the first year's contribution can be spread over a maximum of three funds.

The annual administrative charge for most mutual funds is modest—from $5 to $15 annually—these charges can pile up if you expand the number of mutual funds in your IRA. For example, an investor with $2,000 in an IRA spread over four funds can pay up to $60 in annual maintenance fees. This is 3% of his total investment which, we believe, is excessive.

Finally, more funds mean more paperwork and more time spent on analysis and performance evaluation. If time is money, more time and more money can be saved by including fewer funds in your IRA portfolio. Given these considerations, Figure 30-1 lists a few guidelines regarding the number of funds and fund families to include in your IRA portfolio. (A fund "family" is a variety of different types of funds offered by the same management.)

Compare Returns

Very few of us know how our investment portfolio has been performing. We are aware of whether we made or lost money, but

Figure 30-1
Portfolio Maintenance Guidelines
How Many Funds?

Portfolio Value	Maximum Number of Funds	Type of Funds
0–$4,000	2	One money fund and one stock or bond fund (use one fund family)
$4,001–$10,000	4	One money fund and two or three stock or bond funds (use one or two fund families)
$10,001–$30,000	6	One money fund and three to five stock or bond funds (use no more than three families)
above $30,000	8	Two or three money funds and four to six stock or bond funds (use one money fund for each fund family)

few of us sit down and figure out whether the return is adequate. Investors should monitor their overall returns at least once each year, particularly from IRAs since these are usually held for relatively long periods, which can compound the effect of poor performance.

My suggestion is to compare the return from your IRA portfolio with the performance of similar investments. For example, if your IRA dollars are invested in liquid assets (bank CDs, money market mutual funds, etc.) compare your portfolio's performance with T-bill yields. If you have been investing in common stocks, compare returns with the S&P 500 stock index. If you invested in a combination of liquid assets and common stocks, compare your portfolio returns with the average return from T-bills and S&P 500 stocks, weighting the average toward the vehicle you hold more of.

At this point, it may seem appealing to simply keep your IRA in mutual funds. But remember that for most of us, an IRA is a long-term investment program. The objective is to obtain the greatest possible value when the portfolio is liquidated, while keeping risk at an acceptable level. And historically, the highest yields from long-term investments have come from common stocks. Besides, investors who gradually build their stock portfolios and hold on for long-term appreciation take far less investment risk than those who continually dip in and dart out of the market. Thus, my recommendation is to gradually build up the stock portion of your overall portfolio to a desired percentage. New cash should be gradually invested in additional stocks over time.

Building an Equity-Oriented IRA Portfolio

Make each contribution as close to the beginning of the year as possible. This gives you the fullest possible benefit from the tax deferment. Invest in a money fund immediately each year and then gradually shift into common stock funds to obtain the benefits of dollar cost averaging, explained in Dose 73. If you are not currently in the stock market, shift 20% of your liquid asset investments to common stocks *now* and then shift a dollar amount equal to approximately 4% of the value of your total portfolio every quarter. (As the value of your portfolio grows, so will the dollar amount you invest periodically in stocks.) Figure 30-2 gives some guidelines for gradually building your equity (stock) portfolio. Your goal should be to establish a ratio between the proportions of stocks and liquid assets in your portfolio. (This ratio is somewhat arbitrary and depends on your risk preferences.) Once your portfolio reaches the desired proportions, future investments should maintain the ratio.

Conclusion

As the number of assets you hold increases, so do the management and administrative decisions you must make. Although

Figure 30-2
A Program for Easing into the Stock Market

Begin by investing 20% of your portfolio in stock (equity) funds and 80% in money market funds.

THEN:

Portfolio Value	Action
$0–$4,000	Invest $100/quarter in equity funds
4,001– 5,000	Invest $200/quarter in equity funds
5,001– 8,000	Invest $300/quarter in equity funds
8,001–10,000	Invest $400/quarter in equity funds
10,001–20,000	Invest $500/quarter in equity funds
20,001–40,000	Invest $1000/every 6 months in equity funds
above 40,001	Invest $2000 annually in equity funds

your IRA portfolio may currently represent only a small fraction of your overall investment portfolio, it is important to develop good administrative and management habits now. The payoff will be a more comfortable retirement lifestyle.

What to do With Your Retirement Portfolio Today

In Dose 30 we looked at an overall investment strategy for building a retirement portfolio. But as everyone knows, there's no limit to the kinds of vehicles you can use to build such a retirement account. As a result, individual investors with different risk preferences and at different times in their lives may choose to go different routes. Where to invest your retirement dollars used to be an easy decision—most of us chose money market accounts or bank certificates of deposit (CDs) to take advantage of the high interest rates prevailing during the early 1980s. But times have changed, and investors should now consider some other alternatives to get the most out of their retirement accounts.

Back in 1982 when, given the tax incentives, many of us initially opened Individual Retirement Accounts (IRAs), annual rates of return on "money markets" and CDs ranged from 11% to 13%. Some banks were even offering premium rates as high as 15% to first-time IRA investors. Today, interest rates are much lower and common stock prices have skyrocketed. What formerly seemed like an easy decision has become a virtual nightmare for many investors. Our guess is that many will choose not to carefully analyze answers to the question, "What should I do now?" Instead, out of confusion, they will merely repeat what they have done in previous years. And for many, this de facto decision could lead to less-than-optimal investment results.

First-time investors generally tend to make two mistakes. They are not usually aware of their investment options and the possible outcomes of various investment strategies. And many novice investors want the highest return possible. But return is only half the investment equation. The other half is risk. The higher the possible return, the greater the risk it involves.

Rates of Return

Figure 31-1 shows the annual compound rates of return from various possible investments over different periods. The investments

Figure 31-1
Fifty Years of Returns 1937–1986

	Annual Compound Returns		
	Ten Years 1977–1986	Twenty Years 1967–1986	Fifty Years 1937–1986
Common stocks	13.8%	10.2%	10.4%
Long-Term corporate bonds	10.0	7.6	4.6
Long-Term government bonds	9.7	6.9	4.2
T-bills	9.1	7.4	3.8
Inflation	6.6	6.2	4.2

Source: *Stocks, Bonds, Bills, and Inflation: 1987 Yearbook.* Chicago: Ibbotson Associates, 1987.

are listed in descending order of risk. Common stocks (represented by returns from the Standard & Poor's Index) have the greatest risk while Treasury bills involve nearly no investment risk at all. As you can see, the riskiest investments also had the highest returns. And, equally important, of the four investments listed, only common stocks have consistently generated investment returns that were higher than the rate of inflation. Remember that the goal of investing is not an increase in *dollars;* it is an increase in *wealth,* or real purchasing power. Inflation, as you probably know all too well, makes dollars "cheaper"—a dollar simply buys less. So, if the return from your investment is 5%, but so is the rate of inflation, while you may have more dollars, your wealth hasn't increased because your purchasing power is the same. For example, over the period 1977-86, if you had invested in Treasury bills (or short-term money market accounts) your portfolio value would have increased by 9.1% each year. But consumer prices during this period were also expanding at an annual rate of 6.6%, so your actual wealth would only have increased by 2.5% per year. On the other hand, over the same period, holding a widely diversified portfolio of common stocks (of average risk) would have increased your *wealth* by 7.2% per year.

Figure 31-2 illustrates the value of three alternative investment portfolios over the period 1978-84. Money market mutual funds represent a low-risk investment portfolio, long-term government bonds a moderate risk, and common stocks a high-risk portfolio. Note that relative to money market investments, the increase in value of the common stock portfolio was 19% greater in value after seven years. It is also noteworthy that even though the government bond portfolio produced whopping returns in 1982 and 1984, the overall value of this portfolio after seven years was nearly 25% less than the overall value of the money fund portfolio. The lesson learned is clear. If you want to expand your investment wealth over the long term, the preferred investments are equity instruments like common stocks or stock mutual funds.

Figure 31-2
Compound Growth of $1,000: 1978–84
(Assumes reinvestment of interest and dividends)

	Money Market Funds	Long-Term Government Bonds	Common Stocks
	$1,000	$1,000	$1,000
1978	1,072	989	1,065
1979	1,191	980	1,262
1980	1,343	951	1,672
1981	1,569	955	1,589
1982	1,761	1,358	1,932
1983	1,912	1,388	2,366
1984	2,103	1,579	2,513

As I mentioned earlier, a portfolio should also contain a proportion of liquid assets, such as money market funds, which can easily be *converted* into cash. As can be seen in Figure 31-2, shorter maturity liquid assets (in this case, money markets) provide a better yield than longer-term vehicles. In fact, the best mix of assets appears to be common stocks and short-term debt securities. However, the greater your need for safety, the greater should be the percentage of money instruments in your overall portfolio.

Some General Investment Guidelines

Based on this, I have developed a set of guidelines for creating a retirement portfolio. The guidelines vary by the age of the investor. I've assumed that younger investors look for long-term investment results and, thus, can be more aggressive than older investors who may be cashing in their investment portfolios in the near future and therefore must be more conservative. Of course, for some investors these assumptions may be incorrect. Thus, each individual must modify the guidelines to suit his or her retirement goals and attitude toward risk.

Generally, the younger you are, and the longer the time until distributions are made, the higher the proportion of common stocks in your portfolio should be. Regardless of your age, a certain proportion of your portfolio should be held in debt-type instruments. T-bills, money market instruments, short-term bank CDs, and high-grade corporate bond funds with maturities of from three to eight years are appropriate. The proportion can range from 20% to 50%, depending on your age and risk preference. These assets offer both liquidity and current income in the form of interest.

Up to Age 40 (Aggressive Investors) A diversified portfolio of common stocks or equity-oriented mutual funds is recommended for individuals in this age bracket. This will allow for asset growth and generation of current returns. For investors in this group, a "growth" or "aggressive growth" mutual fund is probably the best vehicle. The optimum portfolio here would return roughly two-thirds from growth in share price and one-third from dividend income. Avoid income-oriented mutual funds which offer little prospect for growth, since inflation will most likely outstrip income earned from these investments. Finally, avoid bonds and preferred stocks, since the long-term growth prospect for these securities is zero.

Age 40 to Age 50 (Moderately Aggressive Investors) The guidelines for this age group are generally the same as for the group above. However, if you begin receiving distributions from your retirement portfolio within 10 years, some of the funds should be shifted out of common stocks and into assets that will generate current income. Portfolio composition should range from 100% equity investments to 80% equity and 20% debt-type instruments.

Age 50 to Age 60 (Moderately Conservative Investors) Since many individuals in this age bracket are nearing retirement, a shift even more toward debt-type securities should be made. This shift reduces risk and generates current income, since distributions will be made in cash. The relative portions of income-producing assets and common stocks in your portfolio will depend on your age and when you expect to begin "cashing in" your retirement portfolio.

Age 60 Plus (Conservative Investors) For older people, a large percentage of retirement portfolios should produce current income. However, some equity investments should also be included to provide a "hedge" against increasing consumer prices. In other words, instead of a fixed income, you *still* want some investments that keep pace with inflation. To provide both income and "protection," 30% to 40% of your portfolio should probably be invested in short-term money market instruments, and 30% to 40% in corporate or U.S. government bonds, bond mutual funds, or bank CDs with maturities of from three to five years. The balance of the account should be invested in a widely diversified portfolio of common stocks. Generally, common stocks (or common stock mutual funds) that regularly pay cash dividends are preferred.

Regardless of age or attitude toward risk, however, everyone should begin to build a retirement portfolio. The best time to begin is now.

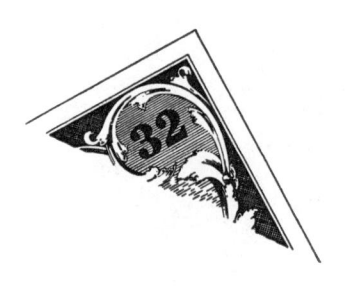

Don't Be Misled By Bank Ads

The record level of dollars that poured into Individual Retirement Accounts (IRAs) during the last couple of years has spurred even greater competition among commercial banks that have been vying for your retirement funds. Of course, competition is good for the consumer when rivals try to outdo each other by offering more attractive packages in an effort to bring in more accounts. However, competition sometimes encourages creative advertising, which is often misleading.

If you take a look in the business section of your local newspaper or in many of the mass-market financial publications, you'll find plenty of examples of the bank advertising that is drawing criticism from investors and legislators alike. Several legislators feel that because banks can quote rates in nearly any way they choose, to make the rates attractive, investors are being misled. So our elected officials have been working to pass legislation requiring banks to clearly disclose what an investor can *really* earn on each type of account. But only a few states have enacted legislation regulating advertised rates.

The problem arises when investors try to compare rates offered by different banks because these rates are not quoted on a comparable basis. For example, one bank recently advertised a 20% return on IRAs. It turned out to be a "teaser" that was in effect for only the first two or three months of the IRA. Another bank offered a 12.5% return on IRAs, compounded annually. Yet another advertises a rate of 12.25%, compounded daily. What the difference in interest rates and compounding periods can mean is summarized in Figure 32-1.

To illustrate the importance of comparing investments on the same basis, consider the implications of the rates quoted above. Bank A promises a 12.5% rate on a five-year certificate of deposit, compounded annually. At the end of five years, an initial deposit of

Figure 32-1
Effective Annual Yields

The difference in interest rates and compounding periods have a surprisingly big effect on your actual return. The table below shows effective annual yields under different rates and compounding schedules for a five-year period.

Interest Rates	Compounded Daily	Compounded Monthly	Compounded Quarterly	Compounded Annually
8.5%	8.87%	8.84%	8.77%	8.5%
9.0	9.42	9.38	9.31	9.0
9.5	9.96	9.92	9.84	9.5
10.0	11.63	11.57	11.46	10.0

$2,000 at Bank A would grow to $3,604. Bank B promises a 12.25% rate on a five-year certificate of deposit, compounded daily. At the end of five years, an initial $2,000 at Bank B would grow to $3,690. While at first glance it would appear that Bank A is offering a better rate, in fact, Bank B's offer is significantly better. The big difference between the two offers involves more than just the quoted interest rate. How often interest is compounded affects the final value of the investment, as well. The more often the compounding, the better the return. In order to compare two alternative investments with different interest rates and different compounding periods, you need to know the "effective annual yield" of each. In the above example, Bank A's offer has an effective annual yield of 12.5% while Bank B's effective annual yield is 13.0%.

When you are shopping for rates on any bank investment, be it on your IRAs or certificates of deposit, be sure to check the effective yield of each. The higher the effective yield, the higher your actual return will be. It's up to you as a consumer to specifically ask for the figures yourself.

The Best Benefits of an IRA are Kept for Last

What goes into an Individual Retirement Account (IRA) must come out some day. But with a little advance planning, you can stay financially flexible as you approach and enter retirement. Better still, a new law lets more of your tax-sheltered nest egg grow for a longer time—at least for now.

The millions of Americans who rushed into IRAs with dollar signs in their eyes eventually will have to make some serious decisions. If you are contributing annually to an IRA and can take advantage of the tax break, the law says you *may* begin withdrawing some of those savings when you turn 59-1/2, and you *must* begin making withdrawals at age 70-1/2. Fortunately, you also get a nice span of time—11 years—which gives you more room than usual to tailor your withdrawals to your needs. If you tend to procrastinate, as most of us do, that break comes just when you will probably need it most. But *what* to do with your IRA benefits—short of a 6-month round-the-world tour—is the salient question.

During those 11 years, you may make any withdrawals from an IRA that you care to, without having to pay the tax penalty that applies to younger savers. The tax penalties for IRA withdrawals before age 59-1/2 may not be prohibitive, depending on how long you've been sheltering investment income in your IRA. But the IRS does sock you twice for early withdrawals. First, if you dip into your account before the "magic age", you pay the penalty tax of 10% on the amount withdrawn. On top of that, the money you take out is immediately taxed as ordinary income.) You will pay income tax, though, on any funds you withdraw even if you're 59-1/2 or above. Whatever you leave in your account continues to pile up tax-free investment income. And, as before, you are allowed to invest the funds, or change where the funds are invested, as you see fit.

When Safety Matters Most

When you are between ages 59-1/2 and 70-1/2 and retired, flexibility in your IRA investments may be less important than safety of principal. If an IRA is your main source of personal retirement income, your risk tolerance may be quite low. If that's the case, stocks, bonds, and mutual funds may seem less attractive than a bank certificate or an insurance annuity. But you still have some choices to make. Some banks and some insurance products offer IRA investors more flexibility than others. For instance, banks and savings institutions are legally free to determine their own penalties on early withdrawals from certificates of deposit. They can, for example, waive penalties for customers who have reached age 59-1/2, but not all of them do. Some forego the charge only if you intend to redeposit the money in another, higher-paying account at the same bank. Others allow you one free switch or a one-charge withdrawal. Keep in mind that nearly all interest rates and terms on bank certificates are negotiable. If the sum involved is substantial, sit down and talk with a bank officer. You might be able to use free withdrawals as a bargaining chip. For instance, you might offer to forego them in exchange for a higher rate or for a guaranteed favorable rate for a longer time.

Remember, too, that a financial institution has the right to charge an early-withdrawal penalty only if you invade your IRA principal. You can withdraw the accumulated interest at any time. (This is true of any kind of saving certificate.) So, if interest rates rise and you are "stuck" with perhaps an old, lower-paying certificate of deposit (CD) that hasn't matured or a low-yielding money market fund, withdraw the interest and start a new IRA (if you're under 70-1/2) with the proceeds. Use the interest to buy a new CD at the higher rate. You can also stipulate that future interest on your old IRA be paid to the new retirement account. Most banks do not charge any fee for transferring interest on one account to another.

Annuities are Predictable

You can also use your IRA proceeds to buy an insurance annuity, which provides annual guaranteed payments. The yearly income from an annuity is based on average life-expectancy as well as on the type of investments purchased with the premiums. Annuity payments may be fixed or variable. Fixed-rate annuities are popular with conservative investors because the monthly payments they receive from this investment will never change. If you are concerned that your annuity income will be eroded by inflation, you might want to leave a portion of your IRA income in an account that will keep growing. An example of how this would work is given in Figure 33-1.

Be aware, too, of the important differences between the four basic types of annuities. A "life-only" contract pays you until your death; heirs get nothing. A "life and period certain" annuity pays you or an heir for a guaranteed time, typically 10 years. An "installment refund" annuity agrees to pay either you or your heir at

Figure 33-1
Cashing Out of an IRA

Your tax-sheltered savings can continue to grow even after you begin taking money out. A man and wife who retire at ages 65 and 60 respectively can extend their payouts over at least 25 years. Here is how their accumulated savings of $100,000 would be distributed, assuming the balance in their account keeps growing at 12% a year.

Year	Annual Payout	Earnings on Account Balance	Cash Value (end of year)	Cumulative Distribution
1	$ 4,270	$12,445	$108,175	$ 4,270
5	6,884	16,793	145,336	27,495
10	12,506	23,078	198,023	77,446
15	22,719	28,429	239,832	168,192
20	41,274	27,127	217,851	333,049
25	74,983	4,738	0	632,545

Source: E.F. Hutton, Inc.

least the full amount that you put in. Finally, "joint-life" annuities involve various options and guarantees. For instance, the payments, based on two life expectancies, might be made first to both persons then to the survivor. See Dose 26 for more on annuities.

Your IRA Won't Go Before You Do

Up until the tax law was changed in 1984, reserving at least part of your IRA for an annuity was indeed good insurance against the possibility that you would live longer than IRS withdrawals allowed for. That's because, under the old rules, the maximum withdrawals required each year were based on life expectancies that were fixed at the time of your retirement. This meant, for instance, that a man age 70-1/2 had to withdraw his entire savings in an IRA before his 82nd birthday, which was his maximum life expectancy—too bad if he made it to 96! If he was married to a woman who was, say, 10 years younger, the couple could combine their joint life expectancies and just about double the payout period. But if the poor fellow were single or a widower, he was out of luck if he lived to be 83. Blessedly, that's no longer true.

Under the new, more sensible rules for taking payouts, you can keep recalculating your life expectancy as you grow older. Suppose, for instance, our 70-year-old lives to age 75. According to the experts, he can then expect to live another 10 years—to age 85. Now the IRS will let him extend his IRA payouts almost to age 85. If the old fellow makes it to 90, the payouts stretch to age 94, and so on. Joint life expectancies can be refigured this way, too. Because of these recalculations, the 1984 tax law also reduces the minimum amount you have to withdraw each year. Previously, the required withdrawals increased annually, because the payout was figured by subtracting a full year from your original, fixed life expectancy. Now payouts are on actual changes in life expectancy, which are less than full years. For instance, the joint life expectancy of a married couple, both age 62, is 24.4 years. At age 63, the same couple has a joint life expectancy of 24.1 years, just 0.3 of a year less.

And You Can Leave More to Your Heirs

Since, given these provisions, you can shelter more of your savings in an IRA for a longer time, the investment continues to grow faster because of the income earned on the higher balance. When you die, any money left in your account is included in your estate. Most often, the beneficiary of an IRA is a surviving spouse. Estate taxes are not levied in this case, and a spouse doesn't get any special income-tax breaks on what he or she gains from the remainder in an IRA.

Still, there are ways to defer income taxes. For one, the survivor can leave the assets in the existing IRA and, by simply changing the name on the new account, become the new owner. Then payouts could start at the normal age, anywhere between 59-1/2 and 70-1/2, when IRAs indeed offer more than at any other time.

Interest-Free Loans From Your IRA? No Way!

One notion that has been going the rounds lately is that you can get a "free" 60-day loan by taking money out of your IRA. This is because the law allows you 60 days each year to "roll over" the funds in your IRA account—reinvesting them in the same or different vehicles. The assumption is that you can use the funds for the 60-day rollover period and then quickly put them back into a new IRA on day 60.

I believe that this is a *very* bad move. In this, as in all things, there ain't no free lunch. For one thing, while the money is out of your IRA, you lose out on tax-sheltered income. And, even though you're "loaning" yourself the money, you aren't paying interest on this personal loan—remember interest is tax deductible.

You could actually lose money using this strategy. Suppose you started your IRA in 1982 and have contributed $2,000 per year. By now, with superior investment results, you might have as much as $12,000 of market value in your account. I checked with my favorite bank and found that an unsecured 60-day loan of $12,000 would cost you about $240 in pre-tax interest. If you're in the 35% tax bracket, using your IRA instead of taking a loan saves $156 after taxes. But you don't earn 60 days worth of return in your IRA. The lost investment return might well come to $180, on which no tax would be due until you retire.

What's more, if anything—a car accident, an illness, forgetfulness—causes you to keep your IRA money one day over the 60-day limit, you will instantly owe $4,200 in taxes on the $12,000 and $1,200 more in tax penalties for the period the funds were invested in the (no longer) tax-exempt IRA. Some bargain loan.

A Retirement Plan Better than a Keogh

If you have income from self-employment—say, a part-time business you run from home—there is a retirement plan you might not be familiar with that can significantly reduce the federal income taxes you pay on those earnings. It's called a Simplified Employee Pension, or SEP.

A SEP is actually a hybrid of two other, better-known retirement plans: a Keogh, which is also for self-employment income, and an Individual Retirement Account (IRA). In general, any self-employment income that qualifies for a Keogh also qualifies for a SEP. Besides a part-time business, that could include income from freelance or consulting fees, as well as directors' fees if you serve on any corporate boards. The limit on tax-deductible annual contributions to a SEP is also the same as it is for a Keogh. Like both Keoghs and IRAs, SEPs let you accumulate tax-free earnings on your contributions until you pay yourself a pension after age 59-1/2. But a SEP offers more tax-planning flexibility than the other alternatives. For example, the deadline for a tax deduction with a Keogh or a corporate-sponsored plan is December 31. However, you still have until April 15 of the following year to establish a SEP plan. The later deadline means you can wait to see how your tax picture for the entire year shapes up before deciding whether to shelter any income for that particular year—and, if so, how much income. It also lets you base the decision on where to invest that money on more current market conditions—say, on which way interest rates appear to be headed, compared with where they were the previous December.

Moreover, the Internal Revenue Service now requires the owners of Keogh and corporate-sponsored plans to submit a five-page annual report detailing the current status of those plans. With a SEP, on the other hand, there are no IRS reporting requirements. Nearly every financial institution that offers IRAs and Keoghs also can advise you on the mechanics of opening a SEP.

Dollars and Sense

Be sure you choose a bank, brokerage firm, insurance company, or mutual fund group that lets you move your money around without charging penalties for early withdrawal of the invested funds. Such penalties are commonly charged by banks, for example, for cashing in certificates of deposit before they mature.

You can also change custodians, or the financial institution where you keep a SEP, as often as you like. And you can split up your yearly contribution to a SEP among several investments. For instance, you might want to put some of the cash in money market funds if rates are currently attractive, put some of your money in stocks, and stash the rest in long-term bonds with a fixed return.

Your Retirement Nest Egg:
The Three-Million-Dollar Misunderstanding

Recently a friend related the following story. She had received a brochure that was supposed to help her figure out how much money she would need "to enjoy her retirement years." She followed the directions faithfully and worked out her retirement goal—it came to $3 million!!! In a panic, she cut her assumed monthly income requirement from $1,700 to $1,000. Result: $1.8 million. Maybe she could make do with $800 a month? That would involve a mere $1.4 million.

Intrigued, we asked her to send us the brochure. As we had expected, its figures were arithmetically correct, but totally misleading. The calculation outlined took assumed income needs in today's dollars and projected them, over the years until retirement, at a forecast inflation rate of 8% per year. In the 30 years that will pass before our friend retires, a household budget of $1,700 a month in 1986 purchasing power would become $17,102, or an annual outlay of $205,224 in the dollars of the year 2016. The worksheet then required her to multiply this by an expected post-retirement lifetime of 15 years. Abracadabra! A cool three mil.

It's not just the inflation adjustment that made these figures so alarming. The calculations also answered the "wrong" question. The brochure's bottom line was not, as our friend had thought, the amount of capital she would have to *accumulate* by the day of her retirement party. The question it really answered was: What might her total *outlays* be, for all living expenses over a 15-year period, expressed in dollars worth about $0.08 in today's currency?

Asking The Right Question

If the question she asked was, "How big a nest egg do I need?" the answer would be less alarming because most retirees have sources of income other than their savings. So to determine what you really need to sock away you should subtract what you expect from Social Security and any pension and profit-sharing plans financed by your employer from what you need to live on once you retire. All you have to worry about is the remainder.

If our friend was aged 35 in 1986, and built up a fairly steady work history at companies with employer-financed retirement plans, she might well find that an amount equal to 40-50% of her preretirement income is covered by Social Security benefits and company pensions, even though Social Security will become less generous in the future. Thus, if she needs $1,700 to live on she could conservatively aim to provide no more than $100 (in 1986 dollars) herself.

Any calculation of future income and spending depends on assumptions about unpredictable variables. The inflation rate is the shakiest of them. Economists have trouble predicting it from year to year; any 30-year forecast is hogwash. The solution is to do your calculation entirely in today's dollars. Start with the income you'd need to provide yourself if you retired today. Work out the amount of invested capital you'd need to produce that income annually, using *real* rates of return. That is, rather than assuming that your savings will pay you 9% or 12% or 15%—all rates that investors have experienced in the recent past—use rates of return adjusted for inflation. Historically, these have been 2-4% for bond investments, 6-8% for common stock investments. If the past is a reasonable guide, securities should continue to return rates close to these.

An annual income of $12,000 can be produced by a portfolio worth $240,000 yielding 5% ($12,000 divided by .05). To provide this income from her own resources, our friend would need to accumulate $24,000 of investable funds, in terms of today's purchasing power. Of course, by the time the year 2016 arrives, that portfolio would look much bigger. But divested of inflation fluff, its worth would still be just under a quarter-million in 1986 dollars, and the income would be $12,000 in 1986 purchasing power.

Can It be Done?

Individual investors can accomplish that kind of saving, but it's no piece of cake. The toughest part is to find and stick with investment vehicles that, over the long pull, yield returns far enough above inflation—without taking on an unacceptable degree of risk. One of the biggest barriers to success is the fact that investment income, including realized capital gains, is taxed—even if it fails to cover inflation and thus is not a real return at all. Thus, a big contributor to success in retirement investment is the growing number of tax-sheltered saving plans for the individual, from the universal Individual Retirement Account (IRA) to plans sponsored by employers. To accumulate the amount you need to retire, you also have to keep adjusting your year-to-year financial plans as the fluctuating inflation rate alters a) the acceptable rate of return, b) the dollar amount of savings required, c) and your rate of pay.

According to stockbrokers we've talked with, monitoring rates of return seems to be the worst stumbling block. Many of their best clients, they say, couldn't tell you what rates of return their investments earned in the past, with or without inflation, or what they expected for the future. Needless to say, you can't go anywhere with an investment plan if you don't bother to keep track of where you've been.

To return to our example, over 30 years, our friend could achieve her goal by putting an average of 12% of her income in investments that produced a 7% real return. (It is reasonable to shoot for higher returns during your working life, while expecting somewhat lower returns on more conservative investments after retirement.) Her required monthly savings for retirement came to just over $200 in 1986, and would be increased thereafter in line with inflation. In her income bracket, that is no small sum. Like most people, she will probably have a lower savings rate in her younger years, while setting up a household and raising a family, and a higher one when these responsibilities are past. But it's worth stretching to save in the earlier years. Early savings have decades to grow, and can compound to amazing sums.

Suppose, for instance, that instead of starting from zero at age 35, she had saved only $50 a month (in 1986 purchasing power) for the 10 years between age 25 and 35. By the time she reached 65, the expected value of that money would take care of about one-third of her $240,000 investment goal, and drop her required monthly savings in her last 30 working years from $200+ to less than $150.

All our calculations have assumed that our friend would get through retirement without spending any of her nest egg, living just on its income. That's a good goal to shoot for—first, because if you have to draw on your capital after you retire, you may exhaust your principal and be left with nothing, and second, because it provides an estate for your heirs. But if our friend were willing to spend her savings (and she didn't live past age 90), she could safely settle for an investment goal of about $170,000. This, too, would reduce her required monthly saving beginning at age 35 to about $150 per month.

Working It Out

After taking the "Retirement Shock Test" (no kidding—that's what the brochure was called) our friend reported that she was going to abandon all hope of a comfortable retirement and spend every extra penny immediately on white-water raft trips down the Colorado River. Once she had worked through the numbers correctly, though, she had both the information and the motivation to undertake some serious investing.

To work out your own saving plan, you'll need to plug in precise figures about your circumstances. Your employer can provide in-

Dollars and Sense

formation on company retirement plans and income replacement in retirement. Then you'll need to figure out how much, saved regularly, will get you to your investment goal by retirement. Take all the help you can get from investment professionals. But be sure you do the numbers yourself or at least understand how they were arrived at. The explanation and retirement savings worksheet discussed in Dose 29 will help you plug in the numbers. And if the bottom line is $3 million, start over.

On The Road Again

There's no sure-fire way to keep from losing travel documents or to safeguard them from thieves. However, there's more you can probably do to protect yourself in advance.

You've seen the commercials a thousand times: The unfortunate couple on vacation, penniless and morose because they've lost their travelers' checks. Suddenly, a smooth-talker taps them on the shoulder. "No problem!" he says, "There's a conveniently located office just around the corner where you can get a refund."

But what if you find yourself in a more complicated situation? In these days of terrorist threats, you probably consider yourself an unusually wary traveler, especially on trips outside the U.S. But a masterful pickpocket could still rob you—in the blink of an eye and without you knowing it—of your travelers' checks, cash, credit cards, airline tickets, and passport.

Too many people carry everything with them, rather than leaving tickets or their passport back in the hotel room, because they're afraid the room will be rifled by thieves while they're out. Then, when a pickpocket or purse-snatcher strikes, all is lost.

Instead of toting your travel documents while you're sightseeing, have them locked in the hotel safe. Take along several large, self-addressed envelopes for this purpose and seal up anything you won't need in each city you visit—your passport, tickets, extra cash or travelers' checks, and other valuables.

Make Several Copies

By planning ahead, there are several other things you can do to protect yourself. Before you leave, make several photocopies of your passport, tickets, credit cards you'll be taking along, driver's license or other identification, and the first and last travelers' checks in the batch you purchased. Take one copy with you and leave another at home with a relative or friend.

If you've had new passport pictures taken, get four copies instead of the usual two. The spares will speed things up if your passport is lost or stolen and a new one has to be issued.

Replacing Your Passport

Having proof of citizenship and adequate identification is essential to getting a lost or stolen passport replaced quickly. If yours is stolen, report it immediately to the local police. You may be referred to the nearest Interpol office, which tries to control trafficking in the lucrative business of illegal passports.

Get a copy of your report to the authorities and take it to the nearest U.S. embassy or consulate. These offices tend to observe business hours of the host country. They also close on weekends and observe both local and U.S. holidays, but a duty officer is supposed to be on hand for emergencies at all times.

With the copies you brought along of your old passport and driver's license or other identification, you shouldn't have to wait long for a limited passport that will let you continue your travels or return home. If there's any question about your identity, however, you'll probably have to wait 24 hours or more while the embassy or consulate cables Washington to search for your passport record.

Refunds

Airline Tickets Because airline tickets are as negotiable as cash, getting a refund for lost or stolen airline tickets is more of a problem. You aren't likely to get a duplicate free.

Instead, you'll probably have to buy a new ticket—and perhaps pay a higher fare than the SuperSaver or other bargain you set out with—and then file a refund application. Expect to wait as long as several months to be reimbursed, minus the cost of processing your application. The fee is anywhere from $5 to $20, depending on the airline.

Travelers' Checks Virtually all travelers' checks can be replaced abroad—assuming you have a copy of the check numbers—but you can get full refunds on some faster than others. Visa checks and checks issued by some large banks typically can only be replaced during banking hours. Both American Express and Thomas Cook have 24-hour "emergency" arrangements with rental car companies. If your checks are lost or stolen outside office hours, the rental car companies will advance you $100 or $200 to tide you over.

Credit Cards If your credit cards disappear, call the bank or card company. The number, which you wrote down at the beginning of your trip, is often on the reverse side of a card. In most cases, your liability is limited to $50 if you report the loss right away. If you can't call yourself, telephone a friend back in the U.S. willing to cancel your cards and order replacements. Don't be surprised if the new cards beat you home.

Nothing can guarantee that your documents will never be lost or stolen, but these precautionary measures will help get you back on the road again with the least amount of inconvenience.

It's a Lemon

The problems start the day you drive your shiny new car off the lot—and keep coming. What can you do? Use the law to put the squeeze on the manufacturer.

Unfortunately, few new-car buyers take the time to give their cars a really thorough going-over when they take delivery. The car should conform perfectly to all the specifications set out in the written contract. If it doesn't, you have the right to leave it with the dealer until it does.

But even if the car seems perfect when you leave the showroom, it could still turn out to be a lemon. According to the lemon laws in the 39 states that have them, that's a car or light truck that a) you've had in the shop at least four times in unsuccessful attempts to repair the same serious defect or b) has been out of service for at least 30 days during the warranty period.

Generally, lemon laws cover cars and light trucks for one year from purchase, or until the warranty runs out. They say if the problem can't be fixed, you're entitled to a new car or your money back. Sounds good, but there's a catch. In most states, you can't take your gripe directly to court. First, you have to go through the arbitration or grievance program specified in the manufacturer's warranty. The procedure can be lengthy and the cards are stacked against you since the manufacturer runs the show.

The "Big Three" U.S. automakers each operate their arbitration programs a little differently. Chrysler's panels review only problems under warranty, while Ford's program includes all lemon-law complaints, regardless of a car's age or mileage. General Motors' arbitration program is handled by local Better Business Bureaus. The BBBs hear lemon-law claims and complaints about certain older cars, as specified in a settlement reached between GM and the Federal Trade Commission several years ago.

All of these programs are governed by federal arbitration law that says you're entitled to a verdict within 40 days of the date you file. In practice, you could wait months. If you go on to court, the case could drag on for years.

How do you protect yourself? If you suspect you may have a lemon, keep careful records of repairs. Each time you take the car back to the dealer, give the service manager a written list of the problems and keep a copy. Go over the dealer's head by contacting the manufacturer's regional or zone office. If that doesn't help, send a certified letter setting out your complaint to the consumer-relations folks at the manufacturer's national headquarters. All of this will help document your arbitration case.

If you don't like the arbitrator's decision and decide to go to court, hire a lawyer who specializes in lemon-law cases. The Center for Auto Safety in Washington, D.C., should be able to refer you to an attorney in your area.

The Hard Numbers on College Costs

The piano bangs out "Pomp and Circumstance." Suzy Jones, resplendent in cap and gown, steps up to receive her high school diploma. And there, front row center, are the proud parents. But wait a minute—something's wrong with this picture! Instead of a tear, that's a twitch in the proud mother's eye. And Father Jones hasn't stopped biting his nails since the ceremony began. What's their problem? Maybe it's the fact that, come September, Suzy will be starting college. But isn't that good news? Not if you look at the figures published by the American Council on Education. According to the Council, the 1987-88 academic year cost parents $5,870 at publicly supported universities, and $11,791 at private institutions. And tuition and fees are expected not only to rise, but to increase faster than inflation—an estimated 6-7% per year in 1988.

I pushed some numbers on this point, to see just how much saving it will take to put your child through college. We assumed that after a couple of years at 6%, the rate of increase in tuition and fees would move back down toward, and eventually reach, the overall level of inflation, which we took to be 5%. For a child who is now 15, the first year at a publicly supported college will cost $7,271, and the whole four years will cost $31,341. If your child is now 10 years old, costs will be up to $9,281 by his or her freshman year and the 4-year total will be $40,002. For today's five-year-old, figures are $11,845 and $51,053.

How much will you have to save to make it? The approximate required monthly savings are shown in Figure 39-1. The outcome depends, of course, on what rate of interest or return you get on your savings (we assumed pretax investment returns of 6%, 10%, and 14% per year), and how much of that return is taxed away. In the ranges shown, $243 to $345 a month is needed to cover the whole cost at a public institution for today's 10-year-old. If you expect loans or scholarships to cover, say, half the cost, the monthly figures can be halved. On the other hand, if you want to send your

Figure 39-1
Required Monthly Savings for Education at a Publicly Supported College or University

Current age of child:	5			10			15		
Pretax rate of return on investment:	6%	10%	14%	6%	10%	14%	6%	10%	14%
Parents' tax rate									
15%	$227	$177	$136	$331	$284	$243	$788	$738	$692
28	240	195	157	343	301	264	800	756	716
33	242	202	166	345	308	274	801	769	726

child to a typical private university, and pay for all of it yourself, the figures would nearly double. Small wonder mother and father looked nervous—they have two children still to go.

College Financial Aid: Sources You May Not Think Of

Pssst—does your college-bound daughter happen to be a licensed helicopter pilot? Is your youngster a former golf caddy? Do your child's career plans include wine making, professional paperhanging, or funeral direction? If so, a scholarship may be waiting.

The National Commission on Student Financial Assistance estimates that $6 billion in private scholarships, grants, and low-interest loans goes begging each year. And by no means is it all based on esoteric criteria. There are scholarships for kids from many different ethnic groups, for children of parents in all sorts of occupations, and for children whose parents are members of unions and trade associations; who belong to certain civic organizations, lodges and clubs; or have particular religious and political beliefs.

Don't expect to find a "free ride," a full-tuition grant for all four years. Few of those are offered anymore. The reason? The same staggering cost of higher education worrying all but the wealthiest of families. As of 1987, tuition and room and board at the most expensive private colleges and universities cost up to $15,000 a year, and even at state schools the yearly tab can run well over $4,000. (See Figure 40-1)

Most private gift givers prefer to spread their generosity around. Their grants tend to range from a one-time present of a few hundred dollars to renewable awards or loans of several thousand. Studies show the average gift is about $900 per student. Some of the money comes with strings attached, most often that a student major in a specific subject, attend a certain school, or join an organization. And there are contests that involve writing an essay, giving a speech, or displaying a talent.

Don't assume family income rules out a scholarship. Private aid is rich with possibilities even if your child has been turned down

Figure 40-1
Sampling of College Costs—1986-1987

Privately Supported Schools	Tuition and Fees	Room and Board	Total
Harvard	$11,370	$3,730	$15,100
Massachusetts Institute of Technology	11,000	4,230	15,230
Northwestern University	10,380	3,908	14,288
Princeton University	10,960	4,058	15,018
Stanford University	10,476	4,414	14,890

Publicly Supported Schools	Resident	Tuition and Fees Out-of-State Student	Room and Board	Total
University of Arizona	$ 990	$3,844	$2,400	$3,390
Florida State University	900	1,600	2,550	3,450
University of Illinois	1,844	4,472	3,100	4,944
Iowa State University	1,304	3,830	1,918	3,222
University of Michigan	2,180	7,268	2,910	5,090

for the evermore restrictive federal grants and loans. Apply whether you have any hope of qualifying or not. Some private scholarships actually require proof that a student is not eligible for federal aid.

Cheered? Just a bit of standard advice: Of course your child should consult high school conselors and college financial aid offices. Find out if money is available from your employer. Bring up scholarships at parties (your old college buddy or an alum of another school your child is interested in could have helpful connections). But there are lots more places to look. Business and private sources now sponsor $15 billion in student aid, or 35% of the total educational support in the United States. Here's how to launch a scholarship search and be sure you have left no stone unturned.

Where to Start

Begin your search by drawing up a personal profile of your youngster, similar to a resume. Start with the basics: your child's academic and athletic achievements, talents and hobbies, career plans, and choice of schools. Don't limit your youngster's choice of colleges because of cost. Some of the most expensive schools offer the most in the way of student aid, albeit in odd ways. Harvard has scholarships (endowed in the 1600s) for students whose last names are Murphy, Anderson, Baxendale, Borden, Bright, Downers, Haven, or Pennoyer. Wellesley aids young women aged 26 and under who want to study in Europe, but they must vow to stay single while doing so.

At least some private money, however, is open to all students. One source is United Student Aid Funds, a New York company that offers low-interest loans (no interest while attending school), up to a maximum of $25,000. Undergraduates and vocational students in any field may apply.

Career Preferences

But your child's career choice probably offers the widest field of private aid possibilities. Industry trade groups that offer scholarships span the alphabet, from the American Institute of Certified Public Accountants to the American Society of Zoologists. Also check on co-op programs. These work-study grants not only help pay college expenses, but can also give your child's career a head start. Co-op programs are listed in *Undergraduate Programs of Cooperative Education in the U.S. and Canada* (free from the National Commission for Cooperative Education, P.O. Box 0775, Boston, MA 02115) and *Cooperative Education Opportunities Offered by the Federal Government* ($2 from Octameron Associates, P.O. Box 3437, Alexandria, VA 22302).

Your child's resume should also list all of his or her extracurricular activities, present and past. The Boy Scouts of America is affiliated with 31 different scholarships. Amounts vary and most are for specific schools, though they range from Rose Hulman Institute of Technology in Terre Haute, IN, to Wesleyan University in Middletown, CT and Stanford University. (The Girl Scouts of America offers just one award: $1,000 for young women majoring in horticulture at Temple University in Ambler, PA.) But you may be in luck if your daughter is an aviatrix. The International Women Helicopter Pilots gives two $4,000 "Whirly Girl" scholarships yearly. Recipients must already be licensed to pilot either private helicopters or commercial airplanes. Both male and female excaddies are now eligible for Chick Evans Scholarships that include tuition plus housing at 15 different colleges and universities. Among them: the University of Illinois, Michigan State, Purdue, and Marquette University. Where you live is important. Many scholarship donors designate their gifts for local kids. There is money for Illinois students studying agriculture, for Texas students who want to live and study in Sweden, and for kids from Rhode Island majoring in Italian.

Birthrights

Numerous ethnic and religious organizations provide for their own. To name but a few of these awards there are scholarships for children whose ancestry is Irish, Italian, Portuguese, Danish, Russian, or Ukrainian. Other groups offering help include the Sons of Poland, Daughters of Penelope (Greek), and Children of Jewish War Veterans. There are also scholarships for the great-grandchildren of Confederate soldiers and children of glassblowers or professional paperhangers. Children of families who belong to the National Campers and Hikers Association are eligible for eight grants a year of from $250 to $2,000 to study forestry or wildlife.

With an idea of the variety of scholarships available, head for the local library. The best scholarship directories cross-reference grants by several categories and briefly outline requirements. Here are some catalogs to check:

- *The Scholarship Book: Complete Guide to Private-Sector Scholarships, Grants & Loans for Undergraduates* (Prentice-Hall)
- *Student Aid Annual* (Chronicle Guidance Publications)
- *Financing a College Education* (Harper & Row)

Computer Matchmakers

A scholarship research service can also be helpful. All of them require the same sort of personal profile you and your youngster should use to scout on your own. Fees run from $35 to $50, but offer the chance to tap into a vast database of as many as 250,000 sources. A word of caution: shysters have entered the search business who may provide little more information than you could find in the library. Before you send them money, find out how long they have been in business and exactly what they will do for you. The good ones guarantee to provide a minimum of currently available sources of aid. Their listings are also specific enough to be truly useful (scholarships for students planning a career in aerospace, for example, not just aid in the broad field of engineering).

Two of the biggest services with track records are Scholarship Search Service (407 State St., Santa Barbara, CA 93101) and National Scholarship Research Service (Box 2516, San Rafael, CA 94912). Once you submit your child's resume, it takes about three weeks to get a printout listing scholarships for which the youngster qualifies. There are also tips on how to apply: write (don't call) sources you are interested in; be creative in filling out an application—emphasize ambitions, motivations, and what makes your child different from everyone else applying for the same money; include a photo if it seems appropriate; and after applying, stay in touch. Finally, if your child is turned down the first time, apply next year. Persistence often pays.

The good news is that median family income is keeping pace with rising college costs. Still, those costs (including tuition, room and board) are inflating at an average 7% yearly. At that rate, Figure 40-2 shows what four years of college could soon cost.

Dollars and Sense

Figure 40-2
Projected costs of a College Education (four-year average)

Year	Public College or University	Private College or University
1988	$19,601	$ 53,902
1990	22,441	62,712
1995	31,474	86,555
2000	44,145	121,397
2005	61,915	170,266
2010	86,839	238,807

High Leverage Mortgages

For any mortgage, especially a high leverage mortgage, the borrower's credit report can be a main stumbling block to qualification. It is never too early to start cleaning up your credit.

Clean Up Your Credit. If your credit report shows slow or missed payments on any item that a lender would question, then you should write a letter to your lending institution or loan processor and explain the item(s) in question. Have your letter of explanation ready at the time your loan application is given to the processing agent.

Remember, too, that the bank that takes your loan application may not be the actual lender or investor, but instead may be the mortgage broker. Thus, your loan "originator" can only project which documentation will be needed and only after the actual investor sees the loan package will you know what other documentation will be required. If you can anticipate any requests, you will be that much closer to approval.

Prepare Your Income Records. Ninety-five percent mortgages require stiffer income qualifications than do smaller mortgages. For an 80% or 90% loan, generally your total house payment should not exceed 28% of your gross monthly income, and your house payment plus any other debts should not exceed 36% of gross income. These ratios may vary from investor to investor, but most 95% loan applications must work within 25% (total house payment-to-income) and 33% (total debt-to-income) ratios based on gross income.

You should discuss your mortgage with your employer or whoever will be completing the Verification of Employment (VOE) sent to your employer by the bank. Perhaps an upcoming salary increase could be reflected on the VOE and any other benefits such as company car should be mentioned. Bonuses and overtime, if they are likely to continue, can be included as income. Alimony, child support, part-time employment, and rental income can be reported also.

Avoid Financing Purchases on Your Credit Card. If you must use credit, try to use only one card and pay it off every month. Some investors will consider a recurring credit card balance as a monthly debt, and this may raise your debt-to-income ratio above the qualification limit.

Avoid Financing Large Purchases. In fact, do not even inquire about financing a car, furniture, boat, appliance, etc. Your credit report may list these inquiries, and the investor will assume that immediately after your mortgage has been approved you'll proceed to finance more.

Know Your Source for Downpayment. How can you minimize the funds needed to pay the downpayment, closing costs, and points? Depending on the loan program you choose, these costs can run 10% or more of the loan amount. The lender will require, on a 95% loan, that the borrower cover at least half of these costs with his own funds. Two other sources—the seller and gifts from an acquaintance or relative—are acceptable for paying closing costs.

Gifts can be used by the borrower as long as the money is actually a gift and not borrowed. This must be verified by both donor and recipient, and the donor must put in writing that he or she does not expect to be repaid. The amount of the gift cannot exceed the borrower's own funds used.

Other tips to minimize closing costs are to choose a loan program with as few points as possible, close your loan on the last day of the month, and request to receive the benefit of simultaneous title issue on your mortgage title policy.

Learn About Mortgage Insurance. Any mortgage exceeding 80% loan-to-value requires mortgage insurance. In these cases, not only must the actual lender approve the borrower, but the mortgage insurance (MI) firm must review and approve the loan also. Mortgage insurance insures the lender against default by the borrower and is paid by the borrower. There is an up-front charge (between 1%-2% of the loan amount on 95% loans) and also a monthly assessment added to the mortgage payment. If the lender seems hesitant to approve your loan, request that it wait for the MI firm to grant approval. This should lessen the investor's concern and thus expedite his approval as well.

Once the necessary documentation is compiled, your loan package is ready to be submitted for approval. The loan package should consist of your verification of employment and deposit, appraisal, credit report, any letters of explanation, sales contract, mortgage or rental verification, and balance statements from any creditors. If there has been a questionable item on any of these, be ready to explain this also. And remember, at current interest rates, every extra $1,000 you add to your downpayment, decreases your monthly payment by *only* $10.

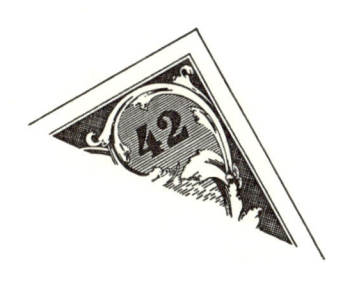

Selecting Mutual Funds? Get The Facts First!

"They're sold, not bought." You usually hear that line about life insurance policies, but all too often it's true of mutual funds, as well. With more than 1,100 mutual funds on the market, it's obviously impossible to check them all out. So a lot of people end up looking only at those that are shoved under their noses by brokers.

That's bad strategy. It means you learn only about *load funds*—which have a sales charge tacked on to compensate the broker. It also means you only check out a few funds. And it means that *your* needs and objectives are the last thing cranked into the selection process.

Fortunately, there's an efficient way to sort through the whole universe of mutual funds, and do it in a reasonable amount of time. The Wiesenberger Investment Companies Service, available in most public libraries, provides the two things you need: all the relevant information on each fund and summary statistics that let you narrow your options before you start digging. (*Investment companies*, by the way, is the legal term for mutual funds.)

We'd have trouble coming up with a question about any fund that Wiesenberger doesn't answer. The information ranges from a fund's investment objective to its toll-free telephone number. Despite this wealth of information, for the job of fund selection, we think the following items are the most useful:

1. *Investment Objectives.* Wiesenberger recognizes several types of objectives. Among them: maximum capital gain, growth, income, safety of principal, and tax-free income. The funds are grouped by combinations of these goals: maximum capital gains (MCG), long-term growth/income secondary (LTG), growth and current income (G + I), balanced funds (B), and income (I).

2. *Portfolio Mix.* The types of securities used, such as common stocks, bonds, and short-term, interest-earning cash balances.

Dollars and Sense

    3. *Turnover.* This is the percentage of the portfolio holdings that the fund manager chooses to replace over a 12-month period.

    4. *Fund Services.* Funds may offer a variety of services, such as IRA accounts, Keogh plans, regular withdrawal programs, and so forth.

    5. *Load* or Sales charges or other fees, if any.

    6. *Dividend History and Policy.*

    7. *Investment Results over 10 Years.* Year-by-year results are shown for the preceding 10 years, as are several calculations for the entire period.

    Best of all, many of these items are included in Wiesenberger's "Mutual Fund Panorama," a summary of information on all the funds. The panorama lets you spot likely candidates without plowing through the manual, fund by fund.

    For more information on the Wiesenberger Investment Companies Service, see Dose 44 and 49.

The Mutual Fund Prospectus: Read It Before You Invest

"Investigate before you invest." This motto, adopted by the Better Business Bureau, often goes unheeded by many stock, bond, and mutual fund investors. While there is an abundance of information regarding potential investments, many investors believe they don't have the time or the expertise to obtain and evaluate such data. This is silly. If you don't evaluate an investment before you put your money in, you may as well "invest" in slot machines—you're gambling in both cases. This doesn't mean that a careful examination will protect you from any and all loss. But it will better your odds and insure that you invest in a vehicle that meets your risk requirements and financial needs. Actually, evaluating a relatively straightforward investment like a mutual fund is not at all complex.

When you evaluate any investment alternative, you should start with a basic question: Is this investment "right" for me? If you're evaluating a mutual fund, the answer lies in the goals and objectives of the fund and in the fund management's ability to carry out those objectives. You should also evaluate the services provided by the fund and the costs of these services. This information is contained in the fund's prospectus which, by law, must be sent to all potential investors before the fund can accept your purchase application. The problem is that many investors simply don't read the prospectus before they put their money in. And then they're surprised when they incur service charges, or don't get some services, or don't get the returns they expected.

Here are just a few examples of the things that can happen if you don't take the time to read the fund's prospectus before you invest. Many investors in the 44 Wall Street Fund were shocked when their fund shares took a nosedive even though changes in the stock market were moderate. Many of these people were surprised to learn that fund management was using leverage to manage the portfolio. They were also shocked to find that the fund isn't diversified and held fewer than a dozen stocks in its portfolio at the time of the price plunge. This information, of course, was spelled out in the fund's prospectus. But these investors ignored this document in an attempt to rush into a fund which had previously been at the top of the performance ladder.

Investors have argued with fund management over unexpected fees, have been dismayed to learn that they had to wait 30 days to switch their investment from one fund to another in the family, and were dumbfounded when they received a large (fully taxable) distribution shortly after they made a purchase. These investors all had one thing in common: they hadn't read the fund's prospectus.

What's Important

Before making an investment in any fund, investors should first request and read the following documents: annual report, latest quarterly or semiannual report, the simplified prospectus, and the Form B prospectus (called the Statement of Additional Information). Here's what to look for.

The fund's prospectus contains three sections that spell out what management will do with your money. To evaluate a fund as a prospective investment, begin by reading the statement of *"Investment Objectives and Policies."* In this section, the fund spells out its investment objectives and the strategies used to pursue these goals. Some funds merely tell you that they are going to invest to emphasize current income, capital growth, or both. Others are quite specific regarding their investment philosophy. Our advice is to consider only those funds which are quite specific in spelling out their investment goals, philosophy, and portfolio management strategies. (An example is illustrated in Figure 43-1.)

Next, look at the statement of *"Risk Factors."* A fundamental axiom of investing is that return and risk are related. The greater the anticipated returns from an investment, the greater will be the risks assumed by an investor. While this is a basic tenet of the investment world, some investors want the largest return possible but forget that the assets involved can be quite risky. These people often select mutual funds solely on the basis of recent performance. Since many of these individuals don't look at how these short-term returns were earned, they are often perplexed when the funds perform below expectations. (An example of one fund's statement of risk factors is illustrated in Figure 43-2.)

Next, turn to the listing of the fund's *investment restrictions,* which are determined by the Investment Company Act of 1940. Many funds voluntarily place additional restrictions on their investments. (One fund's summary is reproduced in Figure 43-3.) Once

> **Figure 43-1**
> **Investment Objective**
>
> The Fund invests with the objective of capital growth. Although income is considered in the selection of securities, the Fund is not designed for investors seeking primarily income rather than capital appreciation.
>
> The Fund seeks out areas of the economy that it believes will benefit from favorable trends for a number of years. The areas of emphasis change from time to time; the dominant area at this time is the information group, with other areas of emphasis in specific industries including banks and real estate. The Fund examines and invests in companies within the identified areas. It particularly seeks smaller companies which it regards as having superior potential, although they are not yet widely recognized as growth companies; strategic position in specialized markets, because of technological, marketing or managerial skills; and adequate capitalization, affording financial strength and stability.
>
> The Fund invests primarily in common stocks and in securities convertible into common stocks. The Fund may also invest in preferred stocks and in obligations, such as bonds, debentures and notes, that in the opinion of management are depressed in price and are believed to present opportunities for capital appreciation. It may invest in corporate or government obligations or hold cash or cash equivalents if a defensive position is considered advisable.

you have found out what fund management *intends* to do with your money, check to see how well it has met these objectives in the past. A brief review of the summary of *"Income and Capital Changes,"* contained in the prospectus, should provide this information.

How much you earn on your shares depends on two aspects of the fund's structure—income and expenses. *Income* is the dividends and interest income earned on the fund's investments. Expenses are the pro rated share of the costs of managing the fund which are covered by shareholders. Expenses include investment advisory fees and the costs of holding board meetings and preparing and distributing shareholder reports. Net investment income is distributed on a basis per-share and is taxed at ordinary income tax rates. *Open-end* funds (which have no limit on the number of shares they sell) *must* distribute at least 90% of all net investment income. In addi-

> **Figure 43-2**
> **Risk Factors**
>
> In seeking capital appreciation, the Fund will often purchase common stocks of small and medium size companies which may be unseasoned and often fluctuate in price more than common stocks of larger, more mature companies, such as many of those included in the Dow Jones Industrial Average. Therefore, during the history of the Fund, its price per share has often been more volatile, in both "up" and "down" markets than most of the popular stock averages.

> Figure 43-3
> **Investment Restrictions**
>
> 1. The Fund will not purchase securities on margin, participate in a joint trading account, sell securities short, or act as an underwriter or distributor of securities other than its own capital stock.
> 2. The Fund will not purchase or sell real estate or interests in real estate, commodities or commodity futures. The Fund may invest in the securities of real estate investment trusts, but not more than 10% in value of the Fund's total assets will be so invested. Less than 5% of the Fund's total net assets were at risk in the securities of real estate investment trusts in the past year. The Fund does not currently intend to place at risk more than 5% of its total net assets in such investments in the foreseeable future.
> 3. The Fund may make temporary bank borrowings (not in excess of 5% of the lower of cost or market value of the Fund's total assets) for emergency or extraordinary purposes.
> 4. Not more than 5% of the total assets of the Fund, taken at market value, will be invested in the securities of any one issuer (not including United States Government securities).
> 5. Not more than 25% of the Fund's total assets will be concentrated in companies of any one industry or group of related industries.

tion, if the fund realizes a net capital gain, it must distribute at least 90% of the gain to shareholders. This is reported as "distributions from realized gains." If the fund experiences a net loss, this is carried forward against future realized gains.

Net asset value is the per-share value of the fund's portfolio of assets less liabilities. For no-load funds (which don't involve a sales charge, fees), net asset value is the same as share price.

The *portfolio turnover rate* is a measure of fund trading activity. A fund with a turnover ratio of 50% is turning over its entire portfolio, on average, once every two years.

Evaluation

When evaluating management's ability to carry out its stated investment objectives, here's what to look for. First, measure the historical net current yield of the fund. To calculate net current yield, divide the distribution from net investment income by average per share net asset value. An estimated average net asset value can be obtained by adding the net asset value (NAV) at the beginning of the year to year-end NAV and dividing by 2. Do this calculation for the last three to five years. (For example, the net current yields of the fund illustrated in Figure 43-4 have been 2.4%, 2.6%, and 2.9% for the past three years. Compare these current yields to the yields from a broad index of overall stock market performance like the S&P 500 Index. A fund oriented toward capital gains should yield less than the market average, while an income fund or a

Figure 43-4
Per Share Income and Capital Changes
(For a share outstanding throughout the year)

	Year Ended March 31				
	1985	1984	1983	1982	1981
Income and Expenses:					
Income	$.76	$.88	$.84	$.81	$.67
Expenses	.16	.22	.16	.18	.17
Net investment income	.62	.66	.68	.63	.50
Dividends from net investment income	(.64)	(.64)	(.62)	(.52)	(.39)
Capital Changes:					
Net asset value at beginning of year	24.47	25.08	17.04	19.51	12.12
Net realized and unrealized gains or (losses) on securities	6.37	.44	8.99	(1.74)	7.28
Distribution from realized gains	(1.58)	(1.07)	(1.01)	(.84)	—
Net asset value at end of year	$29.24	$24.47	$25.08	$17.04	$19.51
Ratio of operating expenses to average net assets	.82%	.87%	.95%	1.03%	1.06%
Ratio of net investment income to average net assets	3.24%	2.69%	4.05%	3.54%	3.06%
Portfolio turnover rate	13.8%	22.2%	30.5%	45.1%	51.6%
Number of shares outstanding at end of year (to nearest thousand)	10,568	6,268	5,029	3,319	2,929

growth and income fund should provide higher annual current yields.

Next examine the fund's portfolio turnover rates for the last several years. A low rate indicates a long-term holding posture, while an extremely high ratio indicates an aggressive trading strategy. As a benchmark, the annual turnover ratio for the average mutual fund is approximately 80%.

Finally, compare the annual rates of return earned by the fund each year for the past several years with those provided by the major stock market averages. Annual return can be approximated by using the following formula.

$$\frac{\text{NAV (year-end)} + \text{All distributions} - \text{NAV (beginning of year)}}{\text{NAV (beginning of year)}}$$

For example, over the period of April 1, 1984 through March 31, 1985, the fund illustrated in Figure 43-4 provided a total return of approximately 28.6%.

$$(29.24 + 1.58 + .64 - 24.47)/24.47 = 6.99/24.47 = 28.6\%$$

These rates of return should be computed for at least the past five years. Check to see whether these returns are more or less variable than those of the general market. More variability means more investment risk.

Remember to compare the results of these analyses to the objectives stated in the prospectus. There should be general agreement between historical results and policy statements. If widespread discrepancies become apparent (e.g., a fund with a buy-and-hold objective has an experience of high turnover ratios, or an aggressive growth fund has an abnormally high current yield), take a pass on that fund and look for another whose investment actions and results agree with policy statements.

Consider Costs

When investing in mutual funds, or in any asset for that matter, you must consider the cost of obtaining, maintaining, and eventually liquidating the investment. Transaction and portfolio maintenance costs reduce investment returns and should be considered and weighed against potential returns. Again, for mutual funds, the prospectus contains the data needed to make cost evaluations. Costs borne by mutual fund investors fall into three categories: sales commissions, management fees, and general operating expenses. First check the section entitled "Purchase and Redemption of Capital Stock." For *front-end load funds* which charge a sales fee when you buy shares, this section lists the commission schedule and payment terms. Also look for fees charged on reinvestment of distributions and for fees charged for redemptions. Generally, 12(b)-1 fees, fees charged current shareholders for marketing the fund's shares to new investors are listed under "Marketing Expenses" or in the section describing the activities and compensation of the investment adviser. Many funds include the specifics of these charges in the "Statement of Additional Information." Remember, this is a separate document. Since more and more funds have chosen to pass along marketing expenses to their shareholders, careful reading is necessary. The "Investment Adviser" section of the prospectus describes the contract between the fund and the person making its investment decisions. This section lists the compensation aid to the investment adviser along with a listing of operating expenses borne by the adviser and those which are assumed by fund shareholders. The history of these charges is summarized in the "Statement of Income and Capital Changes." (See Figure 43-4.)

The expense ratio is the total of management fees, transfer fees, and general operating expenses paid by shareholders divided by the fund's average total assets. The average expense ratio for common stock funds is slightly below 1.00%. My suggestion is to avoid those funds whose management fees exceed 0.75% annually and those for which the total expense ratio exceeds 1.25%.

Services

Before buying a fund, we suggest that you list the services you require. These may include any or all of the following: retirement accounts, automatic dividend reinvestment, withdrawal plans, etc. Next, refer to each relevant section of the prospectus and list the services provided by the fund, the terms and conditions, and note any costs associated with services provided.

Finally, refer to the "Dividend and Federal Tax Status" section of the prospectus. Note how often distributions are made and approximate distribution dates. (If a fund does not include approximate distribution dates in its prospectus, you may have to call for the information.) Tax status might involve tax losses carried forward, disputes with taxing authorities, and/or special tax rules applied to the fund.

A mutual fund prospectus is meant to provide potential investors with information. Unfortunately, it is often written in legal jargon and may be somewhat difficult to follow. But careful reading is a requisite to long-term investment success. We've pointed out the sections that are essential reading, which may make the job easier. The prospectus doesn't tell you the specific return you will earn. It does point out the fund's return potential along with the associated risks that you will be assuming. The prospectus is mandatory reading for all investors who want to increase the probability of earning acceptable long-term investment returns. To assist you in evaluating mutual funds, "A Mutual Fund Evaluation Worksheet," along with further explanation, is included in Dose 44.

A Mutual Fund Evaluation Worksheet

Suppose you wanted to pick a mutual fund. How would you go about it? Figure 44-1 lays out most of the information listed in Wiesenberger's Investment Company Service for a dozen funds. The funds were picked because they are representative of the whole group, not because they are all superior performers.

Note that the information is divided into three categories: Suitability, Risk, and Return. These let you make the best choice for your own purposes, without spending all your spare time on the project. You will be able to rule out most funds on grounds of suitability. Then you can cut the list further by risk category. Make a final cut by looking at the measure of investment return.

Suitability

You probably already have an investment objective in mind. If you're saving for retirement and have quite a few years left before retiring, maximum capital gain might be your goal. If you're using investment income to live on or are close to retirement and want to be a little more cautious, the income end of the scale might look better.

A fund's investment objective is its goal. Its investment philosophy is the route taken to reach that goal. Wiesenberger is a little uneven on this point. For some funds, it gives some information on how investments are chosen. For instance, Fund 4 selects stocks on the basis of the earnings and dividends growth of the issuing companies; Fund 7 tries to forecast the economy; Fund 6, which looks for low-priced shares, does not attempt to predict the stock market.

For other funds, only the objective is mentioned. But even then, you can make some deductions using other information that Wiesenberger provides. Fund 1, for instance, has an objective of maximum capital gains. It had a portfolio turnover rate above 100%

last year (that is, it traded virtually its entire portfolio at least once over the last 12 months). It has gained more than the average fund in rising markets and lost less than average in declining markets. (This is indicated by the Volatility figure, which is explained below.) Finally, it had only 49% of its assets in common stocks when the latest edition of the Wiesenberger manual was published.

Our best guess is that Fund 1 is a market timer, trying to predict the overall direction of the stock market and move its money in and out before major bull and bear markets. So we've entered "market timing" under philosophy. Of course, before you actually invest in a fund, you should study its prospectus and reports to confirm your conclusion about its philosophy.

It's best to pick a fund with a philosophy that seems reasonable to you: a philosophy you might use yourself, if you were the expert running the portfolio. You're more likely to feel comfortable with such a fund, and trust its overall strategy through market fluctuations. In addition, you'll get some feel for how well and how strictly the fund applies its philosophy over time.

Turnover is often regarded as a measure of investment risk. However, studies done to prove this have had contradictory results. We use the turnover ratio only as an indicator of investment philosophy, as in the example above. Portfolio mix tells you what kind of securities the fund invests in. If you already have money invested in short- and long-term fixed-income holdings, you might want a 100% stock fund. In contrast, a balanced fund holds all three types of securities and is intended to be a complete securities investment program.

Volatility measures the swings in a fund's share prices. Since the whole stock market is moving all the time, a mutual fund's volatility is usually calculated in terms of overall shifts in the market—Wiesenberger uses a market index—the New York Stock Exchange (NYSE) Composite—to reflect these shifts. One of the manual's most valuable summaries shows how volatile each fund's shares have been in the last four rising markets and in the last four falling markets, covering a period of about six-and-a-half years.

To keep the worksheet manageable, we've picked two of these volatility numbers for each fund: The *best* performance in a rising market and the *worst* in a falling market. For example, Fund 1's ratio of 1.96 means that its increase in value was 96% higher than the increase for the NYSE Composite in one of the four rising markets. The worst it did was a drop in price only 85% of the fall in the NYSE Composite in one declining market. (That is, it did 15% better than the market as a whole, although its price did drop.) The increase for Fund 5, in comparison, was only 11% more than the rise in the overall market in its best period, and the fund dropped 23% more than the composite index in its worst period.

You're the only authority on how much volatility you can stand. Many an investor has panicked and sold out a good fund at

Figure 44-1
Fund Evaluation Sample Worksheet

Fund No:	1	2	3	4	5	6	7	8
I. Suitability								
Fund Objective	MCG	MCG	LTG	LTG	G+I	G+I	B	I
Philosophy	Market Timing	Growth Co's		Earn's Div. Gr.	Large Co's	Share Value	Econ. Cycle	Max. Inc.
Portfolio Mix	CS	CS	CS	CS	CS	CS	CS/B/C	B
Volatility								
Best, Rising Market	1.96	2.09	1.47	1.62	1.11	1.32	0.88	0.41
Worst, Falling Market	0.85	1.64	1.52	1.58	1.23	0.99	1.07	1.49
Yield	2.4%	2.5%	2.1%	6.0%	4.7%	4.0%	5.4%	12.9%
Portfolio Turnover	113%	35%	218%	50%	11%	25%	10%	45%
II. Risk Measures								
Volatility	2CT	CT						(2CT)
Best, Rising Market	1.96	2.09	1.47	1.62	1.11	1.32	0.88	0.41
Worst, Falling Market	0.85	1.64	1.52	1.58	1.23	0.99	1.07	1.49
% of Return from Capital Gains	91%	85%	64%	63%	20%	69%	19%	280%
Size of Fund (Mil. $)	72	876	106	961	1.015	1.026	141	148

III. Return Measures

Fund Objective	MCG	MCG	LTG	LTG	G+I	G+I	B	I
Volatility								
Best, Rising Market	1.96	2.09	1.47	1.62	1.11	1.32	0.88	0.41
Worst, Falling Market	0.85	1.64	1.52	1.58	1.23	0.99	1.07	1.49
Ten-Year Record								
Total Return	250%	80%	69%	200%	56%	197%	88%	40%
Avg. Ann. Return	13.4%	6.1%	5.4%	11.6%	4.5%	11.5%	6.5%	3.4%
Expense Ratio	1.07%	0.53%	0.61%	0.63%	0.45%	0.66%	0.67%	0.77%
Load	8.5%	None	8.5%	None	7.25%	8.5%	8.0%	8.5%

IV. Comments

Key: MCG—Maximum Capital Gains
LTG—Long-term Growth/Income Secondary
G+I—Growth and Current Income
B—Balanced Funds
I—Income

147

the bottom of a decline, or as soon as it returned to its purchase price, only to kick himself for it when performance turned around. In choosing a fund, you should also consider how soon you may need the money you invest. If your twin sons start college in three years, you may not be able to wait out a bad market.

If you have a minimum income target, meet it with dividends as far as possible, rather than by selling shares. The share price may be depressed just when you need the money. But if you plan to reinvest your whole return and leave your shares to grow, dividends may be worth less to you than capital gains, because dividends are taxed right away. While, you pay no tax on capital gains until you realize them. Most of the items used to measure Suitability are summarized in the Wiesenberger manual, either in the Mutual Fund Panorama or under Price Volatility. As a first cut, you should select a dozen or more funds on the basis of suitability, and then weed them out with the next step.

Risk

The statistical experts have done a lot of fancy work in defining investment risk, but to the typical investor, risk can mean either of two possibilities. First, that the value of the investment will swing wildly up and down. If it does, there's a good chance that it will be down and not up when the investor wants to take his money out. Second, risk may mean that the fund's management will simply fail to achieve its objective. While similar funds are performing as expected, this investment will be the one that lags behind. The Risk section of the worksheet will help you scan fund data for indications of the first problem, not the second.

Volatility, as explained, shows the fund's price gyrations in the past, compared to the *total* stock market. The figure is bound to change over the years—history never repeats itself exactly. But if a fund is investing according to a systematic philosophy, its volatility is not likely to change radically. The price of Fund 5, for instance, will probably remain more stable in price than Fund 2's.

Several funds have "CT" or "2CT" listed under Volatility in the Risk section. "CT" stands for "counter trend." This means that in one or two of the four declining markets covered by Wiesenberger, the prices of these funds actually rose, moving against the market index. Fund 8's "(2CT)" indicates that it lost value during two rising markets.

Volatility refers to changes in a fund's share price. But the total value of an investor's holding is also affected by the dividends received. These are cash-in-hand returns, nailed down for good regardless of future share prices. For that reason, funds that pay high dividends are likely to provide the investor with a smoother flow of returns than those that shoot for high capital gains with stocks that pay low or no dividends. This does not mean that high-dividend funds are likely to generate higher total returns than funds that focus on price appreciation. But a steady stream of dividends can help even out price swings.

In the worksheet, we've shown the percent of each fund's return that came from capital gains. The remainder, of course, came from dividends. The higher this number on the worksheet, the higher the fund's risk of sharp swings in total return.

Finally, fund size may be a guide to risk. Large, diversified funds like Nos. 5 and 6 are too big to put significant shares of their assets in a few risky small companies. Instead, they can easily invest in big companies that tend to be more stable in price.

Return

With rates of return, we get down to the nitty-gritty. Once you've found a set of funds that meet your needs and whose risk you can tolerate, you wish you could predict which one will produce the highest return in the future. You want to avoid those that will turn in below-average results.

Over a period of many years, diversified, high-risk portfolios tended to turn in higher returns than low-risk funds. If you can bide your time, it will probably be worth your while to choose funds like those toward the left of the worksheet. But even in our small sample, several funds that apparently took only moderate risks had excellent returns, while some higher-risk funds had poorer results.

And so we come to the knottiest problem in mutual fund selection: how much attention to give past investment results. It is against the law for a broker or fund sponsor to say to you or even imply that the past results of the fund indicate its future results. If anyone does tell you that, *do business elsewhere!* Not because this is completely unreasonable, but because someone who breaks one securities law will probably bust through several more before finishing with you.

But law or no law, we all know that investors consider past results. This isn't surprising. If a man bets you he can jump over a five-foot wall, you'll feel one way about the bet if you've seen him jump it once or twice, and another way if you've seen him try and fall flat on his face. The trouble is that investors use information on past performance badly. Money floods into funds with good recent results and bleeds out of funds that lag behind for any length of time. But when you think about it, this reverses the old stock market maxim—buy low, sell high: These investors are "buying high" and "selling low."

Any investment strategy needs time to work out. The 10-year period covered by Wiesenberger is the absolute minimum for evaluating past performance: 15 or 20 years would probably be better. The 1960s were so different from the 1970s that many top funds of the first decade "tanked" in the second, and vice versa. But a fund that, basically, did well for the whole 20-year period would have weathered all kinds of stock markets. Going back to the worksheet, if you used recent performance as a criteria, you would get into Fund 2 right after it rose 109% more than the market, and just in time to lose 64% more than average on the downswing.

Then how should you use past investment results? Mainly as confirming or contradictory evidence of your ideas about a fund's objective, the value of its philosophy, its stance toward risk, and its ability to work consistently within these boundaries. If a fund appears just right for your needs, but its 10-year results are worse than others in its class, the next move is not to write it off as a bad fund, but to look into it further.

Send for the prospectus and past fund reports. Management's discussions of the funds's results will give you their version of its performance. Inspect the portfolio holdings, checking for consistency from year to year and with the fund's philosophy and objective. You just might find yourself a fund that's temporarily down, but has excellent prospects as a long-term investment.

You can't quarrel with good results, but you should do a little thinking about them. For instance, Fund 1's shares rose by 250% over 10 years, with dividends reinvested. Great. But a few other funds did significantly better, and without taking the risk of a market-timing, low-dividend strategy. (Fund 1, by the way, is one that's pushed hard by stockbrokers. If you don't do your own digging, in Wiesenberger or elsewhere, you could hear Fund 1's success story, but never learn that Funds 2, 5, or 7 existed.)

A final consideration is fund expenses and sales charges, which reduce your rate of return. Expenses tend to absorb a smaller percentage in the larger funds; like any overhead cost, they are a smaller burden when spread over larger volume. They are charged annually, so they can be compared with the average annual rate of return figures on the worksheet (which are calculated after deducting expenses). An initial sales charge or load can reduce your return by a lot or a little, depending on how long you hold your shares. Over a 10-year period, an 8.5% load (which is common) will knock about 1% per year off your average annual rate of return. Spread over 20 years, an 8.5% load cuts the annual return by half a percentage point. If you sold out after just 12 months, of course, your return would drop by the full 8.5%. Wiesenberger calculates returns without taking loads into account, so you must subtract them before comparing funds.

The blank worksheet (Figure 44-2) gives you a format for choosing the right fund for you. It differs slightly from Figure 44-1. There are three lines each for objectives and philosophy: one for entries from Wiesenberger or any other reference work on mutual funds, one for the objective and philosophy expressed in the fund's reports and prospectus, and finally, one for your own assessment.

Figure 44-2
Worksheet for Mutual Fund Evaluation
Fund Names:

SUITABILITY:				
Objective				
Reference Source				
Fund Documents				
Self				
Philosophy				
Reference Source				
Fund Documents				
Self				
Portfolio Mix....................				
Volatility				
Best, Rising Market...........				
Worst, Falling Market.........				
Yield				
Portfolio Turnover...............				
Fund Services				
COMMENTS:				
RISK MEASURES:				
Volatility				
Best, Rising Market...........				
Worst, Falling Market.........				
% Return from Capital Gains				
Size of Fund				
COMMENTS:				

Continued

Figure 44-2
Worksheet for Mutual Fund Evaluation, *Continued*
Fund Names:

RETURN MEASURES:			
Objective			
Reference Source			
Fund Documents			
Self			
Volatility			
Best, Rising Market...........			
Worst, Falling Market.........			
Ten-Year Record			
Total Return..................			
Avg. Ann. Return.............			
Expense Ratio...................			
Load			
COMMENTS:			

These will often be identical, but not always. The "Self" line leaves you some room to express your own preferences. For instance, I automatically assign market-timing and stock-trading funds to the riskiest class of funds. That's one of my personal prejudices— you probably have some of your own. Finally, there is a line for "Fund Services." Check it if a fund offers all the services, such as IRAs and regular withdrawal plans, you might reasonably expect to use if you stay with the fund for a long period.

There's no ignoring the fact that this is work. Altogether, picking a fund or a group of funds will probably take you several two- or three-hour sessions at the desk, with time in between when you send away for reports and prospectuses. But once the choice is made, your only job will be keeping up with the quarterly reports your fund sends you, to make sure it continues to operate along the lines that first made you choose it. In terms of peace of mind as well as of investment returns, these may be the highest-paid hours you ever worked.

Buying Yesterday's Winners: A Formula For Mediocrity

We all know that if you want superior returns from your mutual fund, you have to pick this year's star performer. However, there's just one small catch. To do this, you must select the year's best performing funds *before* the year begins. In lieu of using a crystal ball, most investors try to pick this year's best performing funds by buying last year's star. Of course, this is based on the assumption that history will conveniently repeat itself. But will it?

Most financial and business publications report on the best-performing mutual funds for a given year. Frequently, these reports glamorize the managers of these top funds. While they are entertaining, the articles tend to imply in their adulation of yesterday's winners that the same funds will be tomorrow's winners as well. The fact is, these reports are merely historical scorecards. Instead of taking these articles as recommendations, investors would actually do much better choosing their funds by throwing darts at a list of all funds available. So much for history repeating!

Recently I examined the returns for the top ten funds in each of the years from 1981 through 1985. Here's a bit of what I found.

First, this wasn't a very exclusive group. Of the 50 funds that made the top 10 in that period, only 5 made repeat performances. Any fund in the top 10 one year apparently found it quite difficult to duplicate that feat in a subsequent year.

Second, not only was it difficult for a fund to repeat its superior performance two years in a row, it was even difficult for last year's star to earn a return greater than Standard & Poor's 500 stock index—it didn't even "beat the market" in most cases! Figure 45-1 compares the performance of "last year's stars" and of mutual funds in general. Of the 10 best performing funds in 1981, 6 managed to beat the market the next year. Of the 10 best 1982 performers, only 3 beat the market in 1983. And so it went. Over the four

Figure 45-1
The Ability of Last Year's Top Performers
To Beat the Market Next Year

Year	Percentage of Previous Year's Top 10 Funds Which Beat the Market*	Percent of all Funds Which Beat the Market
1982	60%	68%
1983	30	49
1984	40	66
1985	10	45
Average	35	57

* Market defined as the total return on S&P 500 stock index.

years 1982-1985 taken together, only 14 funds bested the return on the S&P 500 stock index the year after stardom. This represents a dismal 35% success rate, especially when compared to the fact that more than half of all mutual funds, on average, managed to beat the market during the 1982-85 period. Even if you look at average returns over the entire period, one year's star performer tended to underperform the market for most of the five years.

What we may be looking at is the law of gravity at work. In statistical terms, this is *gravitation toward the mean*. What it means is that, like apples falling from a tree, if you deal with an average set of numbers (remember the Bell curves they used to grade your *paper* in school?), the highs over time and lows tend to fall towards the middle. (The difference is that the low numbers fall "up".) So, if you follow an average—like mutual fund returns—for a while, the highs and lows will move towards the middle.

And this is what actually happened. When the average rate of return for the 10 best and 10 worst performing funds in a given year is taken during the next year, the average rate of return for the best performers is lower than it was during the previous year and the average rate of return for last year's worst performers is better during the subsequent year. For the years 1981-1984, the return for the 10 best performing funds averaged 41.0% annually. The average annual rate of return for these funds during 1982-1985 dropped to 17.2%. The average return for the lowest performing funds during their worst years was minus 14.8%. The average rate of return for these groups during the subsequent year rose to +12.6%. The average annual rate of return for the S&P 500 stock index over this period was 20.2%. Thus, in the year following a particularly good or bad year, a fund's return tends to approach the average for all funds rather than to remain extremely high or low. What's the bottom line of all this for you as an investor? If nothing else, if you want better than average returns over the long run, last year's star is *not* the way to go.

Should You Invest in a Mutual Fund Sequel?

The notion of a sequel, as we all know, was born in Hollywood when certain big producers decided that if you had a good idea, you'd better milk it for all it was worth—after all, you may never have another good idea again. We credit Sylvester Stallone with perfecting this method, which we have dubbed the "coattail effect." First he brought us "Rocky." Then came "Rocky II," "Rocky III," and "Rocky IV". Of course, Sly is not the only coattails culprit. Other producers have subjected us to "Airplane II," several sequels of the "Star Trek" movie, "Halloween II," "III," and ... how many are there now?—ad nauseum. All these sequels relied on the successes of the original movies to draw in their audiences. The consensus of viewers after seeing a sequel is generally that the original was better.

But what does Hollywood have to do with Wall Street, and more specifically, mutual funds? Plenty, because just when you thought it was safe to invest your money in trusted, well-known mutual funds whose names are nearly household words, enter the mutual fund sequel. When two of Wall Street's popular mutual funds were closed to new money, "sequels" to these funds were opened. Where once there was only the Vanguard Explorer Fund, now there is Explorer II. The huge Windsor Fund is also off-limits now, but the Vanguard Group has brought us Windsor II. Many other funds have jumped on the sequel bandwagon, with some, such as Pioneer, already on a third.

Investors are drawn to these sequel funds primarily because of the associations with the original fund. But here is where the problem lies. While the new funds generally have the same objectives as their predecessors, the similarities often end there. Investors may not realize that sequel funds often have different portfolio managers and research staffs than the original fund. This is an extremely important point, because the portfolio manager is the fund's primary decision maker. Even having the same objectives is not necessarily a ticket to success for the newcomers because today's stock market is a far different environment than the stock market of 1967 (when the Explorer Fund began) or of 1958 (the Windsor Fund's first year). However, clever mutual fund marketers certainly could not let such details interfere with the opportunity to make the most of the "coattail effect," and fund sequels continue to pour into the market.

When considering whether or not to invest in a mutual fund sequel, raise the following questions—and get some answers. Whose interest is really being served here—yours or the fund promoters? What other reason is there to close a successful fund and then "clone" it if it's not to create a certain aura of intrigue, thereby luring even more investors, and their dollars, to the fund's family? Why don't the promoters simply create new funds? Do they have to rely on the names of the successful funds to draw in new accounts? Are fund promoters actually running out of original ideas? Tune in next week . . . .

Mutual Fund Investment and Taxation

Mutual funds have achieved an unprecedented degree of popularity. Where once country club gossip may have centered on which stock was offering a particularly good buying opportunity, today's country club denizen is probably discussing which Fidelity sector fund looks most attractive. The advantages of mutual funds are many, with professional management of your investment dollars among the largest. Yet, few investors truly understand *what* a mutual fund is and *how* a mutual fund investment differs from a stock investment.

An open-end investment company that pays out at least 90% of its realized income during the tax year is considered a conduit, or pipeline, between its shareholders and the corporations whose securities the fund holds. Thus, all distributions paid by such funds create potential tax liabilities for shareholders. It is this conduit treatment and the fact that mutual funds pay *distributions* rather than *dividends* to shareholders which usually confuses mutual fund investors and, in some instances, results in the payment of federal income taxes which otherwise could be avoided. The goal of this chapter is to clear up this confusion and perhaps save investors a few tax dollars.

Income From Mutual Funds

A mutual fund earns income over its tax year by investing in a portfolio of securities and obtaining investment income in the form of cash dividends and interest paid to the fund by the security issuers. The mutual fund can also earn capital gain income resulting from price changes of the securities held in its portfolio. Such capital gain (loss) income may be either realized (if the fund has disposed of the securities during the tax year) or unrealized (if the securities continue to be held by the fund at the end of the tax year). Increases (decreases) in fund income, whether realized or not, are instantaneously transmitted to fund shareholders through increases (decreases) in the value of total assets and, thus, in the fund's per share net asset value.

Shareholders may sell fund shares at any time. At the time of sale, any gains or losses in per share net asset value are realized by the individual shareholder less any deferred sales charges (back-end loads) that may apply to the particular fund.

Mutual fund shareholders may also realize investment income from the distributions paid by the fund. (Remember that the fund *must* distribute 90% of all net investment income and net realized capital gains in order to be considered a conduit by the Internal Revenue Service and that funds pay *distributions* not *dividends*.) Payments made to shareholders by mutual funds are actually distributions of realized income from realized capital gains, interest and dividends. On the ex-distribution date, the per share net asset value of the fund will fall by the amount of the distribution. Thus, the income received from the distribution is offset exactly by the decrease in per share net asset value. Since the income distribution to shareholders is realized by them and is taxed accordingly, the fund must indicate the source of the components of all distributions paid during the year. The various components and their tax treatments are discussed below.

Investment Income This is the income earned by the fund from cash dividends and the interest payments it receives. This income is considered to be ordinary income and is taxed at the particular taxpayer's marginal tax rate.

Capital Gains Income In trading securities, the fund may realize capital gains and losses. The gains and losses are netted, and the excess realized capital gains are paid out to fund shareholders. If the combination of realized capital gains and losses results in an overall loss, the fund is allowed to carry the loss forward for up to eight years. These capital losses can be used to offset net realized capital gains in future periods. Due to the changes in the tax law, this distinction between capital gains income and investment income loses some of its significance. Under the current tax law, capital gains will be taxed at the same rate as ordinary income.

Buying Wisely Since mutual fund cash distributions result in an immediate decline in per share net asset value equal to the per share distribution, individuals who purchase mutual fund shares immediately before the ex-distribution date effectively have a portion of their investment capital returned to them. The distribution is considered a taxable event and even though the distribution equals the decrease in net asset value, the investor is left worse off by the amount of the tax he must pay on the distribution. Therefore, *under* *normal circumstances,* taxpaying investors should wait and make their fund purchases immediately after the ex-distribution date (unless of course these investors enjoy paying unnecessary income taxes on their investments).

The Tax Advantage of Losses

Since mutual funds can carry forward net realized capital losses, it is possible for new investors to "buy" the tax advantage of losses suffered by others and "avoid" paying taxes on some of their capital gains. First, we must point out the fact that, whenever possible, mutual fund managers try not to distribute capital gains to shareholders without endangering their conduit status. They recognize the fact that gains in per share net asset value are more desired by shareholders since unrealized capital appreciation goes untaxed while with capital gains distributions the shareholder is subject to federal income taxes in the year the capital gains are distributed. Thus, as year-end approaches, managers with net realized capital gain positions use up realized capital losses carried forward from prior periods and begin to sell off assets which have declined in value until total realized losses equal total realized gains. This gimmick preserves the value of fund shares while eliminating bothersome taxable capital distributions. The advantage of buying a fund with realized capital losses being carried forward can be seen from the following example.

Suppose two mutual funds currently own exactly the same assets. Both are no-load funds with per share net asset values equal to $10. Fund X purchased its portfolio of securities at about one-half of today's market value, and thus, the fund has a net unrealized capital gain position. Fund Y acquired the securities in its portfolio recently after liquidating assets which had declined in value over the preceding year, and thus, the fund has net realized capital losses which it is carrying forward. Since both funds hold exactly the same securities, Fund Y is a more desirable investment than is Fund X. To see why, consider what would happen if the assets held by both funds rise in price. If Fund Y sells some of its holdings, it can utilize the losses being carried forward to offset the realized gains. If Fund X sells off some of its securities, a distribution of capital gains must be made since the fund is left with a net realized capital gain position. The fund's shares will fall in price in an amount equal to the distribution, but shareholders are at a disadvantage compared to those holding Fund Y's shares by the amount of personal income taxes paid on the distribution.

Identifying Gains and Losses

As previously indicated, it is very important that mutual fund investors maintain adequate records of all share purchases, including shares purchased through reinvestment of distributions and redemptions. In addition to a summary report of fund purchase and sale transactions, investors should retain all statements from the fund which document specific purchases and sales.

When fund shares are sold (redeemed), a profit (or loss) may be realized by the investor. The amount of profit (loss) is determined by the difference between the price at redemption and the mutual fund investor's acquisition cost. If poor, or no, records of prior purchases exist, it may be virtually impossible to determine or substantiate the magnitude of gain or loss.

FIFO and the Identifiable Cost Method For income tax purposes, the cost of mutual fund shares which have subsequently been sold can be determined by either the "first in, first out" (FIFO) method or by the identifiable cost method. The FIFO method assumes that the shares sold were the first ones acquired. The identifiable cost method requires that the shares sold be specifically identified as the ones acquired on a specific date at a specific acquisition cost. The differences between the two methods can have an impact on an investor's tax bill, so the distinction is important.

Using the identifiable cost method can help save tax dollars. For example, suppose that you purchased 100 shares of a mutual fund on January 1st at $20 per share. A market advance increases the net asset value of the fund to $25 per share on January 15th, which is when you decide to buy another 100 shares of the fund. On January 30th, when the net asset value of the fund reaches $30 per share, you decide to sell 100 shares. Under the FIFO method, it would be assumed that the 100 shares that you sold would be the first 100 shares that you bought. Since you receive $30 per share and paid $20 per share, your capital gain amounts to $1,000 ($30 - $20 = $10; $10 x 100 shares = $1,000), which is taxable.

However, under the identifiable cost method, you can specify which 100 shares you sell. By "choosing" to sell the 100 shares which were purchased on January 15th at $25 per share rather than the 100 shares purchased on January 1st at $20 per share, you can trim your taxable capital gains to $500 ($30 - $25 = $5; $5 x 100 shares = $500). Of course, under either method, your overall position *before taxes* is still the same.

When using the identifiable cost method of accounting for share costs the IRS places the burden of proof on the taxpayer. That is, you must be able to trace a sale to specific shares. The easiest method for doing this is to periodically request that your fund send you stock certificates which represent your holdings. When a sale is made, record the certificate number(s) and the date of acquisition along with the original cost and proceeds received. If you leave your shares on deposit with the funds (as most fund investors do), use a form similar to the following illustration to keep a record of each purchase. When a sale is made, write to the fund and instruct it to sell a specific block of shares acquired on a specific date. Request that the fund verify the sale in writing.

Remember also that when liquidating holdings some of the shares may have been acquired through automatic reinvestment of prior distributions. Thus, the cost basis for these shares is the per share net asset value at time of reinvestment. Since the income tax liability on these shares may be partially satisfied in prior years, ignoring the cost of shares acquired this way could *result in an overpayment of income taxes.* For example, suppose that you invested $2,000 in Fund XYZ two years ago. Since the per share net asset value at that time was $10, you acquired 200 shares. Recently, you liquidated your holdings in this fund and received $3,000. It might appear in this instance that you must pay taxes on $1,000 of realized capital gains. However, suppose that the fund made two distributions during this period totaling $600. Since these distributions have been previously subject to taxation, the investment income subject to taxation at the time of liquidation is $400 not $1,000. Thus, we cannot understate the need to maintain good mutual fund accounting records.

The Tax Reform Act of 1986 and Mutual Fund Taxation

Since mutual funds invest in stocks and bonds, the Tax Reform Act of 1986 affects fund investors in the same manner as those who invest in stocks and bonds directly (with one or two notable exceptions). That means that taxable bond funds, growth and income funds (or balanced funds) and high yielding common stock growth funds should benefit from the new tax legislation. Sector funds will

---

Mutual Fund Investment Record Keeping

Name of Fund: _____
Telephone Number: _____
Account Number: _____
Address: _____

Date	Transaction	Amount	Share Price	Shares	Balance
2/8/84	Initial Purch.	$1,000	10.00	100	100
3/9/87	Purchase	$1,000	20.00	50	150

be impacted to the same degree as the industry in which they concentrate their investments.

Mutual fund investors, like stock and bond investors, will get clipped by one of the changes in the tax law. Under prior law, investment expenses such as fees paid for investment seminars or subscriptions to business/financial publications were fully deductible for tax purposes. However, under the current tax law, Section 212 expense deductions, which include investment advisory fees, will *not* be deductible unless they exceed 2% of adjusted gross income. Since all mutual funds employ investment advisors who charge a fee which ranges from 0.4% to 2.0% of the assets under management annually, mutual fund investors will receive a boost in income that is subject to taxes without realizing an increase in the actual distributions received from the fund.

For example, suppose that an individual invests $10,000 in a fund which charges a 0.75% annual management fee. Suppose that this fund earns a current annual return of 4% on its investments. Under the old tax law, the fund would deduct the $75 management fee from its investment income ($400) and distribute the balance ($325) which would be reported as taxable income. However, since the advisory fee is no longer deductible under the new tax law, the fund would still distribute $325 but the fund investor would have to report the entire $400 as taxable income (provided that total advisory fees do not exceed 2% of the investor's adjusted gross income). The mutual fund industry is lobbying hard to have this so-called phantom income tax repealed in how it pertains to mutual fund investors. At the time this book went to press, a bill was introduced in the Senate which, if passed, would cause phantom income tax to disappear. The final outcome of this battle remains to be seen.

Another change under the new tax law is the treatment of capital gains. Previously, only 40% of net long-term capital gains was includable in an individual taxpayer's income. With the long-term capital gains tax break gone, mutual funds with high portfolio turnovers look a little more attractive under the new bill. Because short- and long-term capital gains are now taxed at the same rate, investors may find these funds more palatable.

Finally, all regulated investment companies, which includes all mutual funds, are now required to adopt a calendar tax year. Thus, funds which earn investment income during the year are required to make such distributions in the year in which the income was actually received. Thus, fund investors lose the benefit of earning income during one year, but not being taxed on such income until it is distributed by the fund during the next year.

Mutual Fund Investment and Taxation

Understanding your investments is important to long-run investment success. All too often, investors have been lured into risky investments, such as oil and gas limited partnerships, that they did not understand and were subsequently burned. While an understanding of mutual funds will not guarantee that every investment you make in that area will be a winner, it can help save you tax dollars and improve your investment odds.

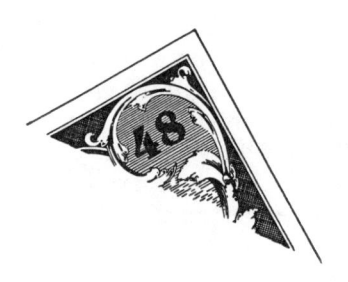

A New Trend in the Mutual Fund Industry: Fund Closings

According to the Investment Company Institute, a mutual fund trade group, 1986 was a record-smashing year for mutual fund sponsors. By the end of the year, the assets of stock, bond, and fixed-income funds topped $400 billion for the first time ever.

While this is certainly great news for mutual fund managers who earn their living by taking a percentage of total assets under management each year, what does it mean to those who recommend mutual funds to their clients?

For these individuals, the news is a mixed bag. On the one hand, more funds are coming to market each day, many offering investment opportunities that were not previously available. On the other hand, some funds have been deluged with so much money that fund managers have cut off sales to new investors. This is especially true of those funds that have lured investors by their high rankings on the performance ladder over the last three years.

Figure 48-1 lists some of the funds that closed. These 10 funds shut their doors to outsiders for a variety of reasons, as the table shows. Kurt Lindner, portfolio manager for the Lindner and Lindner Dividend Funds, reported that both of the firm's funds currently have high cash positions and, due to market conditions, he has been unable to find appropriate investments. Penn Mutual, which was initially capped when total assets reached $200 million, reopened its doors for a limit of either 60 days or until it sold $25 million in new shares. Management of the MFS High Yield Municipal Bond Trust closed its doors because its rapid growth in total assets outstripped its ability to find suitable investments in the "junk" bond market.

More to Come

Given the popularity of mutual funds among individual investors these days, one thing is for sure: More fund closings are on the

Figure 48-1
Mutual Fund Closings

Fund Name	Date Closed	Total Assets at Closing ($ millions)	Reason
Horace Mann Growth	2/83	$ 70.5	Went private
Ivy Institutional	3/85	80.0	Grew too rapidly
Lindner Fund	1/84	315.2	Too large
Lindner Dividend	5/85	68.4	Market conditions
MFS High Yield Muni Bond	6/85	139.1	Grew too rapidly
Penn Mutual	10/84	200.0	Grew too rapidly
Sequoia Fund	12/82	248.6	Reached size objective
Vanguard Explorer	5/85	362.0	Too large for objective
Vanguard Q Div I	1/85	152.0	Reached size objective
Vanguard Windsor	5/85	3616.3	Too large

way. This is especially true for funds with good numbers in the recent past. I suspect that coverage of future top performers in the financial press will attract a flood of new money to these funds. As a result of rapid growth in total assets along with limited investment opportunities, many of these funds will also be forced to terminate sales to new investors.

While there are many reasons a fund might stop selling shares, most often it is because management believes that increased growth will interfere with carrying out its investment strategy (i.e., hamper management's ability to produce superior investment returns).

Investment theorists and practitioners have long suspected that mutual funds with smaller assets tend to outperform the giants of the industry. First, smaller funds tend to be more flexible than larger funds. They can dip and dart in and out of individual stocks and the stock market itself more easily than larger funds. For example, a fund with $40 million in total assets needs to sell only $12 million of its common stock holdings to move from being 100% invested to 70% invested. A $1 billion fund, on the other hand, must liquidate $300 million of its holdings to achieve a similar cash position.

Second, smaller funds tend to hold more concentrated portfolios of common stocks than do larger funds. For example, a $40 million fund can hold fewer than 42 stocks without committing more than $1 million to any single issue. On the other hand, $1 billion funds tend to hold hundreds of different stock issues. The vast number of holdings of larger funds virtually places them in the position of having "bought the market." And as I have said many times: You can't beat the market if you own it. Smaller mutual funds also tend to hold (and trade) smaller blocks of stocks. Since smaller block trades have less of an effect on prices than large block smaller block trades have less of an effect on prices than large block trades, smaller funds tend to obtain better prices when buying or selling common stocks. This also results in savings in transactions costs. which gives small funds a decided edge in the performance game.

Finally, mutual funds that steadily receive relatively large injections of new money from shareholders tend to outperform those that don't. A few million dollars injected into a tiny fund can be substantial, but it is a rather insignificant amount to a billion dollar giant. For example, a $6 million cash injection represents a 15% rate of growth in total assets to a $40 million fund, but only a 0.6% rate of total asset growth to a $1 billion dollar fund. Therefore, a small fund is more likely to receive relatively large cash injections and obtain favorable investment performance.

Here's How It Works

I put these theories to a test by selecting a group of 70 common stock mutual funds. I obtained fund size and investment returns for the years 1979 through 1984 and then compared investment returns for subgroups of funds of varying size. A summary of the total annual rates of return earned by these funds when ranked according to size is illustrated in Figure 48-2.

As can be seen, the annual rates of return earned by the smallest funds greatly exceeded the returns provided by the largest funds. Furthermore, the average annual rate of return for funds with total assets below $181 million (groups 1 through 4) was 20.3% versus 9.9% for those funds which had more than $181 in total assets (group 5). Over the six-year period covered by this study, the average annual rate of return of the stock market (as measured by the total return of the S&P 500 Common Stock Index) was 15.9%. Thus, the average annual rate of return for funds in all but group 5 (the largest funds) matched or beat the market's rate of return.

These findings underscore the basic reason funds close their doors to new shareholders. Namely, having large amounts of assets makes a fund manager's job more difficult and reduces the proba-

Figure 48-2
Mutual Fund Size and Investment Returns: 1979-1984

Fund Size	Median Fund Size	Range ($ Million)	Investment Returns (%) Mean	Median
1 (Smallest Funds)	$ 12.8	$ 3.4 to $ 19.8	24.2%	25.2%
2	30.5	19.9 to 37.7	21.7	21.3
3	49.5	38.0 to 72.8	18.1	21.0
4	112.0	74.1 to 180.5	17.2	14.7
5 (Largest Funds)	290.5	182.2 to 1665.9	9.9	13.1

bility of superior investment returns. As a result, given the great wave of investor dollars flooding the mutual fund industry these days, you can rest assured that more fund closings are on the way.

I am not saying that a fund with large assets will *not* perform well. Instead, these large funds will most likely return less to investors than smaller funds which can accept modest amounts of new money. The importance of new money was demonstrated several years ago by Alan Pope, a long-time student of mutual fund investing. He concluded that funds which constantly received injections of new cash outperformed those that did not. Since closing a fund cuts off new money, could it be that the future performance of closed funds will suffer? I believe so.

Alternatives

Fund managers are caught on the horns of a dilemma. Should they do what's best for themselves (allow the fund to increase, thereby increasing management revenues) or do what's best for their shareholders (close the fund *before* it becomes too large)? The Penn Mutual fund opted for compromise. Management closed this fund before it grew too large, but plans to periodically open it up again to new shareholders for brief periods. In this way, management believes it can control the growth in total assets. The objective is to reach a balance between optimal size and injections of new capital.

If you find that you are not sure what to do when a fund announces that it is closing its doors to new investors, here are a few rules which simplify the decision process. Invest in those funds with smaller amounts of money under management. Second, never rush into buying a fund rumored to be closing its doors to new investors; a better strategy would be to pass on that fund and look instead for another one with similar investment objectives and investment strategies. Third, investors should sell those funds that close their doors and eventually become abnormally large (i.e., when total assets exceed $300 million for an aggressive growth fund and $500 million for a growth fund). Finally, continue to evaluate new investment alternatives on the basis of their own merit and not on the expectation that a "hot" fund might soon close its doors to new investors.

Investment Advisory Services

Along the way, we've mentioned that it's a wise investor who seeks information from the experts. The list below includes many reliable sources, as well as an indication of what they provide.

Donoghue's Money Fund Report
Box 540
Holliston, MA 01746

Weekly, $595

Current news regarding money funds and analysis of stock market. Rates best-performing funds by return on investment. Updates IRS information. Interviews with portfolio managers. Lists the best short-term investments in regard to interest.

Donoghue's Money Letter
(see address above)

Semimonthly, $99

Follows fund families that allow switching between money market and other funds. Recommendations on portfolio composition according to risk attitude and how to switch.

The Fund Exchange Report
1200 Westlake Ave., N.
Seattle, WA 98109

Monthly, $125

Follows three fund groups: equity, bond, and gold. Uses market timing to suggest appropriate investments in the groups. Subscribers can find out suggestions by telephone. Eight investment portfolios include models of margins and indicate risk level and volatility.

Reviews market performance and emphasizes which elements will influence future performance.

Fundline
Box 663
Woodland Hills, CA 91365

Semimonthly, $127

On monthly basis, lists the best funds to invest in. Uses technical analysis for its predictions. Lists fund groups that provide telephone switching.

FundProbe℠
Investment Information Services
205 W. Wacker Drive
Chicago, IL 60606

Monthly, $249

Mutual fund performance reports covering approximately 700 mutual funds. Reports include risk, return, and portfolio composition information. Quarterly and Annual Supplements included.

Growth Fund Guide
Box 6600
Rapid City, SD 57709

Monthly, $85

Focuses on long-term growth. Extensive evaluation of the 30-35 funds with the best growth potential.

Income and Safety
Institute for Econometric Research
3471 N. Federal Hwy.
Ft. Lauderdale, FL 33306

Monthly, $49

Safety ratings on all major money funds based on portfolio compositions, diversification, average maturity, and yield volatility.

Mutual Fund Forecaster
(see address above)

Monthly, $100

Features "best buy" investment recommendations, switch recommendations, market forecasts based on econometric models, tax advantages, continuous follow-ups, and "funds to avoid." Each issue includes a directory of over 200 funds, both load and no-load as well as closed-end funds.

THE Mutual Fund Letter
Investment Information Services
205 W. Wacker Drive
Chicago, IL 60606

Monthly, $115

Published by Gerald W. Perritt, author of this book. Provides in-depth evaluation of funds in five investment/risk categories and recommends funds with potential for best performance. Also includes economic and market updates, Model portfolios, data-based special reports on investment opportunities and spotlights on recommended funds. New subscribers receive bonus book, *Mutual Funds and Your Investment Portfolio* and personal mutual fund portfolio review.

Mutual Fund Management Systems
P.O. Box 13161
Pittsburgh, PA 15243

Monthly, $100

Follows a few funds for which it recommends market timing—all growth funds and one gold fund.

Mutual Fund Monitor
Newgate Management Corp.
P.O. Box 628
Northampton, MA 01061

Monthly, $125

Evaluates and recommends no-load and low-load mutual funds. Mutual fund portfolios for investment, IRA/Keogh and Trader accounts are updated and their performance tracked in every issue.

The Mutual Fund Specialist
Royal R. Lemier & Co.
Box 1025
Eau Claire, WI 54702

Monthly, $95

Strategies and advice for operating in current economy and market climate. Top performers on a variety of bases. Load and no-load funds.

Investment Advisory Services

The Mutual Fund Strategist
Progressive Investing
P.O. Box 446
Burlington, VT 05402

Monthly, $127

Follows the market and recommends buy, sell, and hold based on its COMPUVEST timing indicator and other timing models. Follows sentiment of other mutual fund advisory newsletters.

No-Load Fund Investor
Box 283
Hastings-on-Hudson, NY 10706

Monthly, $79

Brief news about stock market. Lists 20 best-performing funds, over 400 funds from various investment categories and reports performance. Gives a current cash position for selected funds; recommends funds.

**No-Load Fund*x
235 Montgomery St.
San Francisco, CA 94104

Monthly, $95

Lists all well-performing growth funds in six classes and identifies best performers in each. Addresses subjects of general interest regarding funds. In each issue, one fund is carefully analyzed.

Performance Guide Publications
P.O. Box 2604
Palos Verdes Peninsula, CA 90274

Monthly, $70

Follows nearly 500 load and no-load funds, giving past year's performance data. Recommends investing only in top 30 funds. Extensive commentary on stock market and economy.

The Peter Dag Investment Letter
65 Lakefront Dr.
Akron, OH 44319

17 issues, $250

Updates investment field by analyzing current situation in: stocks, economy, short-term interest rates, inflation, bonds, gold, U.S. dollar, change in investment strategy. Recommends portfolio that suits conditions.

Prime Investment Alert
Prime Financial Associates
Box 701
Bangor, ME 04401

Semimonthly, $70

Advises no-load investors using technical and timing indicators. Comments on economy, legal issues.

Risk-Adjusted Mutual Fund Performance Review
Computer Directions Advisors
11501 Georgia Ave.
Silver Spring, MD 20902

Monthly, $675

Reports current net asset value and total assets, presents risk-analysis figures, ranks best performers by various criteria for various periods and market cycles. Rates investment advisers on equity investment performance. Covers all mutual funds listed by financial media.

Stock Guide
Standard & Poor's Corp.
25 Broadway
New York, NY 10004

Monthly, $88

Gives the following: net asset value, initial minimum investment, maximum sales charge, price record, and yield from investment income.

Switch Fund Advisory
8943 Shady Grove Ct.
Gaithersburg, MD 20877

Monthly, $135

Updates stock market news and gives forecasts. Lists funds it favors for new subscribers. Gives combined fundamental and technical analysis for recommended investment sectors. Ranks fund performance by objectives, gives current information on switching within no-load fund families.

Systems and Forecasts
150 Great Neck Rd.
Great Neck, NY 11021

Semimonthly, $160

Advises movement of money between stock and money market funds as situations indicate. Focuses on about 40 highly speculative funds. Offers 24-hour telephone hotline; gives advice via tape.

Telephone Switch Newsletter
P.O. Box 2538
Huntington Beach, CA 92647

Monthly, $117

Aimed at risk-oriented investors; advice on moving in and out of 35 of the most volatile stock funds following major market ups and downs.

Time Your Switch
6 Pioneer Circle
Andover, MA 01810

Semimonthly, $89

Using charting techniques, shows percentage change in 33 fund portfolios. Updates components of portfolio frequently with aid of six market indicators.

United Mutual Fund Selector
Babson-United Investment Advisors
210 Newbury St.
Boston, MA 02116

Semimonthly, $110

Statistical information on over 400 mutual funds; also contains commentary on mutual fund industry and specific recommendations.

Weber's Fund Advisor
P.O. Box 92
Bellerose, NY 11426

Monthly, $79

Recommends investment positions for 88 funds it follows regularly. Uses both dollar-cost averaging and upgrading approaches.

Wellington's Worry-Free Investing
Euler Enterprises
4853 Cordell Avenue
Penthouse 11
Bethesda, MD 20814

Monthly, $129

Uses technical analysis and line charts to thoroughly cover performance of high yield funds. Commentary on market and economy analysis; recommends funds and buy, sell, or hold.

Wiesenberger Investment Companies Service
Warren, Gorham & Lamont, Inc.
210 South St.
Boston, MA 02111

Four publications: 1) *Annual yearbook* reports on over 1,600 investment companies including 700 mutual funds (not available separately); 2) *Management Results* (quarterly, $100) performance of over 460 mutual funds and 51 closed-end companies; 3) *Panorama* ($18) a quick mutual fund reference; 4) *Current Performance & Dividend Records* (monthly, $150). Four report package, $295; services 2, 3, & 4 available as package for $225.

Mutual Fund Recordkeeping

The mutual fund, by law, is obligated to send you periodic statements of the shareholder's account activity, the fund's investment and earnings during a period, proxy statements, and an updated prospectus. Each fund is also required to submit an audited semiannual and annual report to shareholders. Some funds voluntarily send unaudited quarterly investment and earnings reports, as well. These documents specify the fund's investment portfolio, the returns earned during the period, and a statement of the fund's operating expenses. Investors must receive a prospectus before the fund can accept initial share purchases and should expect to receive another prospectus when the purchase is made and a new prospectus each year thereafter. It is important that the latest prospectus be kept on file so that future purchases and/or redemptions can be made in accordance with the fund's latest business procedures.

It is important that you retain all confirmation statements detailing purchases and redemptions made. At year-end, the fund will send you a summary of the yearly account activity. These statements provide the backup documentation necessary for income tax filings. I suggest that you also keep an account activity summary form similar to the one illustrated on page 176. It lists the date of purchases and sales, how they were made, the dollar value of each transaction (broken down by the number of shares transacted and the appropriate share price), and a running total of the share balance. One document should be maintained for each fund currently owned. The reasons for keeping detailed records for each fund owned is to make tax computations easier *and* to assist in minimizing federal and state income taxes paid on mutual fund investment profits. Attach the latest prospectus and all confirmation slips to this summary report.

Mutual Fund Personal Recordsheet

Name of Fund _____ Minimum Initial Investment _____
Telephone Number _____ Subsequent Investment _____
Account Number _____ Approximate Distribution Dates _____

Fees:

Front-end Load _____ Redemption Fee _____ IRA Maintenance Fee _____

	Purchases and Reinvestments			Sales			
Date	$ Amount	Share Price	Shares	$ Amount	Share Price	Share	Share Balance	Memo

Source: FundProbe®
Monthly Mutual Fund
Performance Reports covering
approximately 800 mutual funds.
Investment Information Services
Chicago, IL (312)750-9300

Keeping Up With The Money Market

Most investors are familiar with money market funds, where an individual can get a piece of the money market action with as little as $500 to invest. Money market funds have made the old passbook savings account all but obsolete. Traditional bank checking accounts, and even better-yielding NOW accounts, have lost a great deal of ground, as well, to the higher yielding and more flexible money market account.

The money market is actually a group of markets which deal in low risk, short-term credit instruments such as Treasury bills, commercial paper, bankers' acceptances, negotiable certificates of deposit (CDs), repurchase agreements, and federal funds. In other words, the money market is a market of high quality IOUs.

These IOUs are not all exactly alike in terms of yield and safety. And because most money market funds invest in combinations of these securities, their yields may deviate slightly. Look in the financial pages on any given day, and you will find that some funds are yielding up to one half of one percent higher or lower than the average yield for all funds.

Money Market Investments

Treasury bills, or T-bills, represent a major portion of the total marketable securities issued by the U.S. Treasury. They are issued with maturities of less than one year, usually 13, 26, or 52 weeks. T-bills are sold at a discount from (less than) face value and are redeemed for full face value by the Treasury at maturity. The amount of the discount, therefore, is what a T-bill investor earns as his return. The smallest T-bill denomination is $10,000.

In terms of safety, Treasury bills are considered "risk-free" because they are backed by the authority of the U.S. government. Therefore, the interest payments and return of principal are fully guaranteed. But because in the investment world, low risk means low return, T-bills provide a slightly lower yield than other money market securities.

The Federal Reserve publishes an informative booklet on buying Treasury securities which you may order at no charge by calling your nearest Federal Reserve bank at (804) 643-1250 or by writing to the Federal Reserve Bank of Richmond, Public Services Dept., P.O. Box 27622, Richmond, VA 23261.

Other than money fund accounts themselves, Treasury bills are the money market instruments most widely held by individual investors. The majority of the remaining instruments require minimum investments that are too large for all but the wealthiest individuals to consider. These investments are geared toward the institutional investor with millions of dollars under management. (Your money fund is an example of such an institution.)

Commercial paper makes up a very large chunk of the money market. It is no more than a short-term IOU issued by a corporation. Commercial paper is unsecured, which means the issuer pledges no assets as a guarantee of repayment. Therefore, commercial paper issued by an established firm would be considered safer than paper issued by a firm with lower credit ratings. Of course, the lower-rated firm would have to offer a higher yield to entice buyers.

Banker's acceptances (BA), another component of the money market, arise primarily in the world of international trade. The bank issuing the acceptance acts as the intermediary between the buyer and seller. A BA has the credit strength of a bank behind it, and is considered quite safe in terms of investment. BAs generally offer a slightly lower yield than commercial paper.

Negotiable *certificates of deposit* (CD) are widely held by individuals as well as institutional investors. The holder of a CD agrees to deposit a specific amount of money for a specified time. In return, he or she receives a stipulated amount of interest. Eurodollar CDs are similar to domestic CDs except that they are a liability of a London branch of a domestic, or foreign, bank.

A *repurchase agreement* (Repo) is an agreement between a seller and a buyer (usually of U.S. Treasury securities). The seller promises to repurchase the securities at an agreed upon price and time. The main attraction of a Repo is the flexibility of maturities which makes them an ideal place to invest funds over short time periods.

Because money funds may invest in any or all of these securities, it is worthwhile to look at the holdings of a fund when reading its prospectus. The safest funds invest only in treasury securities, but also provide the lowest yields. Funds holding other types of money market securities entail only a slightly higher degree of risk, but their better yields often make them a better investment.

How To Select A Money Market Fund

Especially during the rampant inflation experienced in the last decade, money market funds became a popular investment vehicle. These funds invest in a variety of short-term assets—bank certificates of deposit (CDs), treasury bills, and the like—which reflect the going "cost" of money, that is, how much a borrower has to "pay" for a loan. Yield from most funds was above the inflation rate, and the investment involved relatively little risk. But appealing as money markets are, if you don't pick your money market fund carefully, you can end up with hassle rather than convenience. Fortunately, most of the work has already been done for you. You just have to know where to look.

Americans have invested over $200 billion in money market funds in the past few years. That's a lot of money to throw around casually. But to most of us, all money market funds look alike. We're inclined to settle for the first one that comes along. An advertisement, a recommendation from a broker or a brother-in-law—and the choice is made.

In fact, the funds differ a good deal in the services they offer, and in their value in meeting various investment needs. It's these differences that explain most of the variation in the interest rates they pay. There's also a range (though much narrower) in the risk the funds entail.

Luckily, there are statistical services that review all the funds regularly, covering each of these points. *Donoghue's Mutual Fund Almanac* has established itself as the basic source of information on the subject—many newspapers get their data on fund yields from Donoghue. Wiesenberger's Investment Companies Services covers the same ground. It makes no sense to pick a fund from a field of three or four, when spending a little time with these publications will let you screen every single prospect.

Service First, Yield Afterward

Before you even look at yields, you'll want to screen the funds for those best suited to your purpose. You may be planning to use your fund as a high-yielding checking account, as a place to accumulate funds for future investment, or as a permanent investment that involves relatively little risk. These will determine which services matter and which don't.

Figure 52-1 shows part of a listing from Donoghue's Almanac. Among the points to consider are:

Minimum initial and subsequent investment. Some funds will let you get started with any amount; others require as much as $10,000 to start and will take additional funds only in $1,000 increments.

Checking fees and policies. Withdrawals may be limited in number and amount, and service fees may apply to some withdrawals. If you plan to pay bills with your account, you'll need one type of fund; if you're accumulating or investing, another.

Exchange privileges. Firms offering money market vehicles often offer a variety of other investment vehicles, as well as the possibilities of switching between these investments at little or no cost. As a result, one of the chief uses of money market funds is as part of an investment program within a fund family. If that's your plan, the details of the money market member of the fund family are your least important considerations. Find a family with fixed-income and/or equity funds well suited to your needs; their money fund is probably your best bet, too.

Yield Competition: A Neck-and-Neck Race

Yields on money market funds cluster close together; most are within a single percentage point of each other. One percent of additional return isn't to be sneezed at, but the extra income has a price tag on it. Nearly all of the higher yielding funds get their edge by taking on additional risk. Compared to other types of investment, it isn't much risk, but it can affect your final results.

Credit Risk Most funds concentrate their investments in bank certificates of deposits, bankers' acceptances, commercial paper, 1and repurchase agreements.[1] You don't need to know how these basic money fund holdings work, only that their safety depends on the credit worthiness of the banks, companies, and securities dealers who issue them. Some of these investments carry various kinds of private or industry insurance against default. The historical record is even more assuring: no one has ever lost money in funds that confined their holdings to these short-term

---

[1] Discussed in Dose 51–"Keeping Up With the Money Market"

Figure 52-1

	Date Organized	Minimum Purchase $ or Shares Initial or Subsequent		Total Assets (million $) 1985 1984		Checking Service	Minimum Check	Checks Returned	Wire Redempt	Wire Fee	Exchange Privilege	Plans IRA	Keogh
Fidelity U.S. Gov't Res. Fidelity Investments Corp.	11/81	$1,000	$250	$408.9	$368.2	Yes	$500	MO	Yes	$5	Yes	X	X
Financial Daily Income Shares Financial Programs Inc.	3/76	250	50	216.7	240	Yes	500	NR	Yes	None	Yes	X	X
Vanguard 1	6/75	1,000	100	1693.3	1,542.9	Yes	250	MO	Yes	*	Yes	X	X

Reprinted by permission. Donoghue's Mutual Fund Almanac, Box 411, Holliston, MA 01746 (617) 429-5930.
Figures have been updated.
MO-Monthly
NR-Not Returned
* over 5000–None
1000–5000–$5

obligations. So while in theory it's possible for money market funds to lose money if an issuer defaults, it's highly unlikely.

You can find funds with holdings that are either more or less conservative than these "plain vanilla" investments. On the conservative side, some funds buy only Treasury or other U.S. government obligations. Their yields are usually at the low end of the industry range, but their investors avoid all credit risk.

More aggressive money funds go beyond CDs and commercial paper issued by U.S. banks and companies. About one third of all funds purchase Eurodollar CDs (dollars on deposit in banks abroad), which are generally considered riskier, but offer higher returns. Other funds buy the conventional type of investment, but from issuers whose credit ratings are less than top rank. These issuers pay higher interest rates, but expose the lender to more credit risk. Both the Donoghue and Wiesenberger services summarize fund holdings by percentage in each type of investment. To learn which funds hold only top-rated investments, and which accept lower quality, you'll have to inspect the portfolio listings in each fund's prospectus.

Maturity Risk and Rewards Yields on a money fund's holdings also tend to rise with the length to maturity of the fund's assets. The longer the maturity—the time until the fund's holdings can be redeemed by the issuer—the higher the yield, generally speaking. This is because two aspects are involved: the *face value* (price) of the asset itself and the interest the asset pays on a regular basis. The longer the time to maturity, the more interest the asset will pay. For example, if an investment that pays quarterly interest has one year to maturity, it will pay interest four times before it matures. An investment that matures in three months will pay interest only once. In addition, as interest rates change, an investment may be traded at a price above or below its face value, depending on how its interest rate compares to those on other investments. But, as an investment nears maturity, interest becomes less important because less interest will be paid. Both aspects lower the value of an investment as it nears maturity.

If the portfolio manager is willing to buy paper maturing in six months or a year, he can get higher interest rates than by investing for a few weeks or months. There's also a drawback to longer maturities. If interest rates rise, a fund already invested for the next six months is stuck with the old, lower yields, while funds with shorter-term holdings will soon be able to reinvest their money at the higher current rates. This also works in reverse, of course. If rates fall, the longer-maturity fund has "locked in" higher rates. In 1986, the average holding of most money market funds matured in a bit over one month. Portfolio

"HOLD IT, ED! THIS ISN'T THE FUND FOR YOU-!"
XYZ MONEY MARKET FUND
BAD TURNOVER RECORD
POOR PORTFOLIO MIX
SLOPPY DIVIDEND HISTORY
LIMITED SERVICES
DOUG BORGSTEDT

managers in general are not going far out on a limb in exposing their shareholders (and themselves) to changes in current rates.

In theory, swings in interest rates should cause the price of your money fund shares to rise and fall, just as bond prices do. But the swings are so small for very short-term holdings that they never exceed the interest earned on the fund's investments. Changes in interest and price are all combined in the daily returns, and fund prices hold steady.

When money funds were new, some bought longer-term notes—well over a year in maturity. Their prices swung so sharply that investors did experience small losses. But if the prospectus makes clear that your fund invests only in short-term vehicles that really involve the money market, not bonds, this risk doesn't apply.

Once you find the services you want, in a fund that meets your risk requirements, it's time to think of yield. It's unlikely that there will be a great difference in the yields from the group of funds you're considering. However, it is possible for a fund manager to squeeze a little bit extra percent out of the market. Wiesenberger and Donoghue can tell you which funds achieved this feat in the recent past.

The 50 Largest Money Market Mutual Funds

Whether bigger is better is up to you—the investor—to decide. We've provided some clues along the way, and more to come. But the following list will at least give you a feeling for what "big" is, in terms of money market mutual funds. Herewith the 50 largest in terms of assets. (In descending order.)

The 50 Largest Money Market Mutual Funds

Name	Address/Phone	Net Assets (As of 7/17/86 $ millions)
1. Phoenix Money Market Series	One America Row Hartford, CT 06115 (203) 278-8050	$ 4,7523.3
2. CMA Money Fund	633 Third Avenue New York, NY 10017 (212) 692-2929	18,459.1
3. Merrill Lynch Ready Assets Trust	633 Third Avenue New York, NY 10017 (212) 692-2929	11,989.0
4. Dreyfus Liquid Assets, Inc.	600 Madison Avenue New York, NY 10022 (212) 895-1206 (800) 645-6561	7,876.8
5. Temporary Investment Fund (Temp Fund)	Suite 204 Webster Building Concord Plaza 3411 Silverside Road Wilmington, DE 19810 (302) 478-6945 (800) 441-7450	7,646.1

The 50 Largest Money Market Mutual Funds, *Continued*

Name	Address/Phone	Net Assets (As of 7/17/86 $ millions)
6. CMA Tax-Exempt Fund	633 Third Avenue New York, NY 10017 (212) 692-2929	7,550.2
7. Dean Witter/Sears Liquid Assets Fund, Inc.	One World Trade Center New York, NY 10048 (212) 938-4554 (800) 221-2685	6,903.9
8. Trust for Short-Term U.S. Government Securities	421 Seventh Avenue Pittsburgh, PA 15219 (412) 288-1900 (800) 245-0242	5,898.6
9. Cash Equivalent Fund—Money Market Portfolio	120 South LaSalle Street Chicago, IL 60603 (312) 332-6472	5,344.9
10. Kemper Money Market Fund, Inc.	120 South LaSalle Street Chicago, IL 60603 (312) 781-1121	4,675.1
11. Fidelity Cash Reserves	82 Devonshire Street Boston, MA 02109 (617) 523-1919 (800) 544-6666	4,586.6
12. Trust for U.S. Treasury Obligations	421 Seventh Avenue Pittsburgh, PA 15219 (412) 288-1900 (800) 245-0242	4,243.7
13. Paine Webber Cash Fund, Inc.	1120 20th Street N.W., Washington, DC 20006 (212) 713-2152	4,177.8
14. Federated Tax-Free Trust	421 Seventh Avenue Pittsburgh, PA 15219 (412) 288-1900 (800) 245-4270	4,033.9
15. Cash Reserve Management, Inc.	One Battery Plaza New York, NY 10004 (212) 742-6003	4,017.6

The 50 Largest Money Market Mutual Funds, *Continued*

Name	Address/Phone	Net Assets (As of 7/17/86 $ millions)
16. Prudential Bache Government Securities Trust— Money Market Series	One Seaport Plaza New York, NY 10292 (212) 214-1234 (800) 221-7123	3,922.4
17. Fidelity Tax-Exempt Money Market Fund	82 Devonshire Street Boston, MA 02109 (617) 523-1919 (800) 544-6666	3,895.3
18. Shearson Daily Dividend Inc.	2 World Trade Center New York, NY 10048 (212) 577-5794	3,725.2
19. Federated Master Trust	421 Seventh Avenue Pittsburgh, PA 15219 (412) 288-1900 (800) 245-0242	2,963.1
20. T. Rowe Price Prime Reserve Fund, Inc.	100 East Pratt Street Baltimore, MD 21202 (301) 547-2308 (800) 638-5660	2,908.0
21. Dreyfus Tax Exempt Money Market Fund, Inc.	600 Madison Avenue New York, NY 10022 (212) 223-0303 (800) 223-5525	2,630.9
22. Daily Cash Accumulation Fund, Inc.	3410 South Galena Street Denver, CO 80231 (303) 671-3200	2,576.1
23. Merrill Lynch Retirement Reserves Money Fund	633 Third Avenue New York, NY 10017 (212) 692-2929	2,558.5
24. Fidelity Daily Income Trust	82 Devonshire Street Boston, MA 02109 (617) 523-1919 (800) 544-6666	2,509.1
25. Nuveen Tax-Exempt Money Market Fund	333 W. Wacker Drive Chicago, IL 60606 (312) 917-7700	2,351.0

Dollars and Sense

The 50 Largest Money Market Mutual Funds, *Continued*

Name	Address/Phone	Net Assets (As of 7/17/86 $ millions)
26. Active Assets Money Trust	One World Trade Center New York, NY 10048 (212) 524-5000 (800) 222-3326	2,324.5
27. Trust Funds Liquid Assets Trust—Treasury Portfolio	28 State Street Boston, MA 02109 (617) 742-4000	2,099.4
28. Trust For Short-Term Federal Securities—Fed Fund	Suite 204 Webster Building Concord Plaza 3411 Silverside Road Wilmington, DE 19810 (302) 478-6945 (800) 441-7450	2,041.8
29. Hutton AMA Cash Fund	One Battery Plaza New York, NY 10004 (212) 422-0214 (800) 334-4636	2,026.8
30. Municipal Fund for Temporary Investment, Inc.	Suite 204 Webster Building Concord Plaza 3411 Silverside Road Wilmington, DE 19810 (212) 323-7712 (800) 441-7450	2,024.9
31. Vanguard Money Market Trust	Vanguard Financial Center Valley Forge, PA 19482 (215) 648-6000 (800) 523-7025	1,979.4
32. Liberty U.S. Government Securities Fund	One Bankers Trust Plaza New York, NY 10006 (212) 432-4000	1,916.7
33. Thomson McKinnon National Money Market Fund	One New York Plaza New York, NY 10004 (800) 223-2413	1,899.7

The 50 Largest Money Market Mutual Funds, *Continued*

Name	Address/Phone	Net Assets (As of 7/17/86 $ millions)
34. Money Market Trust	421 Seventh Avenue Pittsburgh, PA 15219 (412) 288-1900 (800) 245-0242	1,897.4
35. Paine Webber RMA Money Fund, Inc.	1285 Avenue of the Americas New York, NY 10019 (800) RMA-1000	1,815.8
36. Capital Preservation Fund, Inc.	755 Page Mill Road Palo Alto, CA 94304 (415) 858-2400 (800) 227-8380	1,794.2
37. Merrill Lynch Government Fund	125 High Street Boston, MA 02110 (617) 357-1460 (800) 225-1576	1,769.8
38. Shearson Government and Agencies Inc.	2 World Trade Center New York, NY 10048 (212) 577-5794	1,663.5
39. Automated Government Money Trust	421 Seventh Avenue Pittsburgh, PA 15219 (412) 288-1900 (800) 245-0242	1,646.9
40. Webster Cash Reserve Fund, Inc.	20 Exchange Plaza New York, NY 10005 (212) 510-5000	1,565.0
41. DBL Cash Fund—Money Market Portfolio	60 Broad Street New York, NY 10004 (212) 480-4155	1,557.8
42. Trust For Short-Term Federal Securities—T-Fund	Suite 204 Webster Building Concord Plaza 3411 Silverside Road Wilmington, DE 19810 (302) 478-6945 (800) 441-7450	1,556.6

The 50 Largest Money Market Mutual Funds, *Continued*

Name	Address/Phone	Net Assets (As of 7/17/86 $ millions)
43. Trust Funds Liquid Assets Trust— Prime Obligations Portfolio	28 State Street Boston, MA 02109 (617) 742-4000	1,521.5
44. Tax-Exempt Money Market Fund, Inc.	120 S. LaSalle Street Chicago, IL 60603 (312) 332-6472	1,393.9
45. Daily Tax Free Fund	100 Park Avenue New York, NY 10017 (212) 370-1240	1,314.0
46. Tax-Free Instruments Trust	421 Seventh Avenue Pittsburgh, PA 15219 (412) 288-1900 (800) 245-4270	1,305.0
47. Fidelity Money Market Trust— Domestic Portfolio	82 Devonshire Street Boston, MA 02109 (617) 523-1919 (800) 544-6666	1,263.8
48. National Liquid Reserves, Inc.— NLR Cash Portfolio	1345 Avenue of the Americas New York, NY 10105 (212) 613-2631	1,258.6
49. Delaware Cash Reserves	Ten Penn Center Plaza Philadelphia, PA 19103 (215) 988-1333 (800) 523-4640	1,238.6
50. Alliance Capital Reserves	140 Broadway New York, NY 10005 (800) 221-5672	1,231.7

Shopping By Mail?
A Few Things To Keep In Mind...

Yes, Virginia, there is a Santa Claus—but now he may be foregoing the crowded stores and loading up his sleigh with goodies through catalogs, instead. That's because catalog merchandise is back again, and this time with more momentum than ever before. Statistics from 1984 show that mail order sales exceeded $44 billion. Hundreds of new catalogs have sprung up in the past few years, and the Direct Marketing Association (DMA) estimated that nearly seven billion catalogs (that's about 80 per household) were mailed during 1983.

You may be wondering about some of the new catalogs that have tumbled out of your mailbox this year. If you would like to order merchandise from a company that is unfamiliar to you, you may want to check with the Direct Marketing Association first. The DMA publishes an annual guide that provides information on more than 800 catalogs. The cost of the guide is $2.00 plus postage and handling, and it can be ordered by writing to the Direct Marketing Association, 6 East 43rd Street, New York, NY 10017 or calling (212) 689-4977.

There are a few things you should keep in mind when catalog shopping. First, because you can't physically examine catalog merchandise before you buy, be sure the company offers a satisfactory return and refund policy. Most catalog companies have liberal policies, but the ones that don't (ones that offer only a credit for another purchase, for example) should be avoided. Second, it's a good idea to take advantage of mail-order houses' toll-free telephone numbers when placing orders—this speeds up the overall process (which is a real blessing for those of us who procrastinate) and eliminates many problems that can arise if the order is handwritten. And finally, remember that if the merchandise you ordered is delivered in a state where the company doesn't have a store, you are exempt from state and local sales taxes.

How To Interview The Financial Help

Talk isn't always cheap. If you interview a prospective financial planner, insurance agent, or stockbroker in the right way, your initial chat can form the basis of a profitable relationship. If you do it badly, you can buy yourself a lot of trouble.

Unless you own your own business or occupy a pretty high position at the company you work for, you probably don't think of yourself as an employer. But every time you use a financial product more complicated than a dollar bill, you're actually hiring some help. You're buying the services of the financial professional who provides that product.

It's a complicated relationship. You're the boss—or you should be—but you look to the professional for help and advice about his or her specialty, be it insurance, mutual funds, securities, or anything else. You'll never have any trouble finding candidates for these positions; they're out looking for you. But what should you ask to select the right one? And what are the right answers to your questions? Here are some pointers on conducting that all-important interview which will let you say yes or no to a financial adviser.

Don't Waste Your Time or Theirs—Prescreen

You can't interview a hundred stockbrokers, planners, etc. before you pick one to work with. Somehow you have to narrow the possibilities before using up your time and the adviser's in detailed talk. After a careful first cut, you can spend plenty of time with a few of them and still get the job done faster than if you'd tried to see everyone.

First, ask other experts for referrals. Your family lawyer, your accountant, and any bank officer you deal with regularly will probably know quite a number of financial professionals and be willing to recommend some of them to you. If you ask all these people, you should be able to get a good starting list. Any name mentioned by more than one person is an especially likely prospect. Asking friends and neighbors can turn up some leads, but be careful. Few individual investors ever deal with large numbers of financial professionals, so their ability to compare may be limited. And there's a natural desire to believe that one's own adviser is tops, until proven otherwise.

Also, remember that good past results for a single customer prove very little. The guy who sold last week's winning lottery ticket is not a financial genius. If you ask friends for referrals, try to get some idea of how past results were achieved, and whether there's any reason to think they'll be repeated. Then telephone those on the list who you think are your best bets, considering things like your trust in the referring person, whether the type of firm sounds like what you want, convenience of location, and so forth.

Let Yourself Be Screened, Too

One purpose of these calls is to let some advisers screen you out, too. If the first person you call is a reputable professional, but isn't the right one to help you, he or she will say so.

State as clearly and as briefly as you can:
1. What services you want or think you need.
2. How much money is under consideration (as, "I have decided to invest $10,000 in stocks," or "My income has gone from $X to $Y, and I need more life insurance than my employer provides.")
3. That "so-and-so recommended you"—it doesn't hurt to have it known that you come from a possible source of future referrals, and will likely report back to that person on how you're treated.
4. That you would like further information on the person you are speaking to and his or her personal qualifications, as well as on the company and the services they provide.

By placing these basic facts on the table, you avoid getting into somebody's office only to find that you couldn't do business under any circumstances. You might learn, for instance, that you were misinformed about the services available. You may also learn that the person you call deals only with accounts larger than yours. Don't be offended if that's the case—long-established professionals often restrict their business to larger accounts. You've just saved yourself a needless office visit. (The opposite problem, being turned away because your account is too big, is rare.)

Information Is A Two-Way Street

Step 4 above leads to the next stage. Get as much factual information as you can in written form, and take time to review it.

It makes no sense to waste time in an interview asking questions and writing down answers that are already printed somewhere in the firm's sales packet. Moreover, looking through a company's printed matter in advance can give you further clues for making your ultimate choice. If, for instance, you need a comprehensive financial plan, you could look for breadth of coverage in the printed material sent to you by a planning firm—discussions of multiple products and of the wide expertise of the firm's staff. On the other hand, if you want insurance and only insurance, you might look for depth—extra details on insurance and insurance issues, and a staff specialized in that area.

Once you've narrowed your choice down to a few people and made appointments to see them, write down, at some length, your ultimate goals for the financial services you're investigating. An example might be:
- a complete, lifetime investment program;
- income protection for your family until your children are grown;
- a fixed sum of money by a certain date;
- a combination of such goals.

Don't assume that you know what you want just because you got around to setting up some appointments. I've talked with successful business executives who already had fairly complicated financial holdings, but who realized in the course of our conversation that they were pursuing contradictory goals. Sometimes they even held investments that were working against them. A session at the desk writing a report to yourself on the subject will tell you things you didn't know about yourself.

Once you begin interviewing financial advisers, you may learn that your needs are not quite what you thought they were, or that there are opportunities you didn't know about. Don't close your mind to these new ideas. But whenever one of them turns up that carries you away from your original list of needs, you'll have to do some rethinking. Don't put money into any financial product until you can see clearly how it fits in with your revised list of needs.

The Day(s) of Judgment

These preparations completed, you can begin meeting with prospective advisers. For an intelligent discussion, the adviser will need to know just what your situation is. Such an interview is confidential. If you've taken the trouble to narrow the field to a few respected professionals, you can give them information on your income, savings and investments without worrying. So don't try to play it cagey. If you withhold information, the adviser can't show you what he or she can do. Moreover, you're setting up a relationship of distrust. If you later decide to "hire" this particular person, you're off on the wrong foot right at the start.

Your list of goals is a vital part of this information. As you talk them over with your prospective "employee," be flexible enough to benefit from his or her expert comments. But don't let yourself be talked out of aiming at something you really want, whether it's high prospective returns or extra safety. You also need to be frank about any limitations in your financial situation. If you can't manage insurance premiums above some amount, say, or settle for investment income below a certain sum, or absorb losses higher than a given level, make sure you say so, up front. If the amounts you'll be able to save and invest are unpredictable, say that, too. Quite a few financial products are now being designed to give you the maximum possible flexibility. But that's no good for you until the adviser is aware of your range of needs and resources.

The Behavior Sample: Core of the Interview

All these preliminaries serve only one purpose: to give you the best chance of seeing how a financial expert really works, and would really work for you. Get the information swapping out of the way as briefly as possible. Most of your interview time should be spent letting the expert strut his stuff.

Part of an adviser's job, of course, is to absorb what you say about your situation. Interest in getting this information, and in some detail, is a good sign. Lack of interest is a bad one, unless it's accompanied by an explanation of why a certain piece of data isn't relevant to the decisions you want the adviser to help with.

Once you've got your goals across, ask for ideas about how to reach them. Don't hesitate to ask questions if there's something you don't understand, but hold your comments and criticisms. Let your job candidate paint the whole picture with as few interruptions as possible. What you're looking for, as you rate each interviewee, is an actual demonstration of future on-the-job performance. Here are a few points to consider:

Alternatives There are few financial goals that can be reached by only one route. In helping you solve your problem, your potential adviser will be juggling risk, benefits (such as investment return or level of insurance coverage), cost, and convenience, to name a few variables. Top marks on this test go to advisers who can come up with more than one way of meeting your goal, and explain the trade-offs among the possibilities in terms of the kind of variables mentioned above. Poor marks go to those who don't lay out the options well, or who are fuzzy on the relative pros and cons of each item they suggest. Flunk anybody who gives you only one response and is reluctant to discuss other possibilities.

Goal-Matching Anybody who's been on the job a week can describe quite a few different financial products. What you're looking for is someone who'll focus on what you need to buy, not what he or she has to sell. Good performance on this count indicates both understanding of your goals and willingness to focus all services around them. Top marks go to any adviser who takes your listed goals as the focal point of the discussion, bringing up specific products entirely in that context. Give extra points for a good discussion of ways in which you might want to reconsider some of your original goals.

Give poor marks for a clearly product-centered response, tying your goals against the company's stock in trade to look for a fit. Theoretically, this process should be just as good as the goal-centered one; in fact, it suggests that the product line may not be full enough or completely appropriate for your needs. Give a zero to any adviser who trots out an inappropriate product and offers huge investments returns as an incentive for abandoning your goal list.

Completeness While your financial program doesn't have to be absolutely perfect, it's impossible to solve half the problem and forget the rest. If your start-up investment account is in great shape but you have no insurance when you're hit by a bus, your estate will be in less-than-great shape. It's natural for any adviser to want to focus on what he or she can do. Most of the interview will be spent on these areas. But it's still your job to be sure that nothing important to you falls between the cracks.

Give top marks to an adviser who covers all the bases thoroughly, and has something to offer on most points. That doesn't mean being able to do everything you need. Extra credit if the adviser points out where he or she can't help you and double-extra for volunteering at least two names of other experts who could fill the gaps. (If you get just one, check it out before raising the score. It might be a brother-in-law.)

The grade drops as attention to the whole picture blurs, and the adviser skims over goals where either the needed product line or expertise is weak. Again, a bad sign is recommendations of his or her own products that fail to take into account your goals in other areas. Lowest marks go to those who simply ignore their inability to help you reach a goal or—worse—don't seem to realize that they're doing this.

Clearness While you will be making the final decisions, you will have to depend heavily on what you learn from the adviser you ultimately hire. He or she has to be able to select the information you need, get it across to you clearly and (usually) briefly, answer your questions, and back up all recommendations with logical arguments.

Top marks go to those who get through the whole interview without missing any of the above steps on any major point under discussion. Since customers' degrees of knowledge vary, your first interview will probably provide some information you already had, and make you ask questions on other points. But you shouldn't feel either completely at sea, or bored by the repetition of the obvious. One touchstone of a good communicator is his or her responses to your questions. Don't focus on the content of the answers; try to get a feel for the adviser's goal in answering. Does he or she stop when you seem satisfied with the answer or, rather, try to find out—maybe by questioning you—whether you really got the point?

You're entitled to give poor marks on a purely subjective basis: do you feel that you found out everything you wanted to know? It doesn't matter if your confusion stems from your own lack of knowledge; you need an adviser who can, and wants to, deal with you, given your present understanding. Worst case: you get someone who tells you not to worry about how the product works—he'll take care of that—you can just hand over the money. Stop taking notes. Leave as soon as you courteously can, or sooner.

Compatibility You'll be interviewing several people. Human nature being what it is, you are probably going to meet at least one that you just don't like. It doesn't matter if your reaction is irrational; it doesn't matter if this person is otherwise a great prospect. If you aren't happy talking to this prospect on the phone and in the office, it will mess up your decision making. Keep looking. On the other hand, don't overemphasize compatibility. You aren't going to marry this person. Ferreting out good qualifications on the first four items is more important than making a new buddy. In fact, if you find a successful financial adviser who aces the interview, but is ugly as sin and has the disposition of a rhinoceros with a toothache, you've probably found a winner. As a final check, ask for references. Get the names of at least two present customers from each person you interview. (You may have to wait for these while the adviser gets permission from clients to use their names. Most should be able to refer you to people who have already OK'd this.)

And the Winner Is . . .

When you've seen all the people you selected for interviews, you're nearly ready to make a decision. First, go over your notes on those who are still in the running. Rethink your impressions and the performance of each candidate. By comparing them on the various points above, you should be able to narrow the choice still further. Second, follow up on referrals. You aren't looking for bad reports (though if you get one, it's a very bad sign). The adviser will have sent you to the two people most likely to convince you that he or she can handle a client like you. Usually, they'll do a good job. But if they seem to be very different from you in situation, goals, or risk tolerance, you may conclude that the adviser hasn't really identified your range.

Another useful move is to ask the customers you're referred to if they can give you the names of others who have dealt with the adviser you're investigating. This takes you to people who were not hand picked by your job candidates, giving you an even better shot at an impartial assessment. A final test: wait to see which of your prospective employees follows up in a reasonable manner. No follow-up suggests lack of interest in your account. An attempt to make a quick sale is also bad news. But with luck, one or more of your candidates will be back on the phone in a week or so, with an offer of further information or a report on a product that would accomplish one of your goals, then you'll know you've found your way to the office of a pro.

Coping With The Financial Hard Sell

The scene: your study. You're at your desk. The phone rings. You answer, and hear an unfamiliar voice saying, "Mr. Smith? This is Weatherford Goodfellow of Grubby Securities. Mr. Smith, I'm calling because I know you'll be eager to take advantage of the news from Docuchip Decisions Conglomerated—the stock price has dropped 50% in the past month but our analyst has just learned that the company will introduce a major new product at the industry trade show in May, and he expects a significant rebound. If you buy 100 shares—we're only talking about $8,000—I can take your order right now if you'll just give me a few minor details about yourself."

You think I made that up, don't you? Wrong. I got that call a few months ago and heard the whole pitch because Weatherford Goodfellow was talking so fast I couldn't get into the conversation long enough to say "Shut up." (I have reluctantly disguised the names of both salesperson and firm, thus protecting the guilty from shame and myself from a lawsuit.)

Everyone has been the victim of a high-pressure sales pitch at one time or another. Whether it's a car, a new suit, or a financial product you're buying, there is always a chance—mercifully small—that the salesperson you deal with will be a bad apple. The best defense is to know ahead of time how to counter the hard-sell ploys.

The common theme of all hard-sell strategies is an attempt to override your judgment and stampede you into doing something that is not in your best interest. This can be done in several ways: with an appeal to your emotions, especially those you don't like to acknowledge, such as guilt or greed; with an attempt to confuse you, so that you give up your role as decision maker and let the salesperson decide; or with a "speed trap"—an artificial limit on the time you have to make up your mind.

Unfortunately, financial products and services lend themselves to all of these strategies. There are few issues that carry a heavier

DAILY LIQUIDITY
HIGH YIELDS
NO LOAD
DIVERSIFICATION
TAX EXEMPT
FREE CHECK WRITING
DOUG BORGSTEDT

freight of emotions than accumulating and using money. The newly deregulated financial industries are undergoing rapid change, and some of the choices you have to make are indeed complex and difficult. Finding the time to study a prospective purchase or investment seems to get harder all the time.

Guilt Trips and Other Psychological Traps

Dr. Roderic Hodgins, a Cambridge psychologist and consultant, explains how the hard-sell specialist uses your emotions against you. Dr. Hodgins likes to think of the transaction in reward-and-punishment terms. An unscrupulous salesperson might dangle an "irresistible" reward in front of your nose—so irresistible that you don't stop to consider whether the promise is reasonable. Or, more subtly, he or she might make you feel uncomfortable about not buying, with the prospect of relief from this discomfort as a "reward" if you buy.

For example, many an investor has been backed into putting too much money into a financial vehicle, or into accepting too much risk, because the direct way out—'I can't afford it" or "I'm afraid to"—was just too painful to confess. By pretending to assume that you can easily part with a large sum, a prosperous-looking salesperson makes it easier (emotionally) for you to go along with the proposed investment than to make explicit the reason you can't. (We think Weatherford Goodfellow may have been trying this with his "only $8,000." Anybody who refers to 8,000 of our dollars as "only" gets ruled out right there.)

Dr. Hodgins also points out that high-pressure salespeople often use your own courtesy against you. Most people feel bound by the same rules of polite speech and conduct in business meetings as on social occasions. The hard-sell specialist can ask personal questions you'd rather not answer, use your response to play on your emotions, and use any one of a number of ways to pressure you into buying before you are goaded into saying "rude" things like, "it's none of your business", or "I don't believe it".

The Tower of Babel Approach

A friend recounted how she learned about some of the ploys used to sell investments. While she was studying investment management in graduate school, one of her professors gave the class a stock prospectus for a huge conglomerate company. This legal document, which government regulators require from any company that sells new stock, was 150 pages long. Most of the students were up all night, plowing through it. Next morning, the professor asked for a show of hands—how many had read the whole prospectus? Most hands went up. The professor grinned and shouted, "You turkeys!" Then he explained that the prospectus was far more detailed than it had to be. Most of those 150 pages were thrown in to discourage readers and to distract those who did read them from the few key tables that gave away the company's shabby financial condition.

This kind of deliberate confusion is a standard tactic in high pressure sales. By dumping piles of random information on the helpless customer, the salesperson hopes not to inform but to confuse. You may be left feeling that here is the opportunity of a lifetime, perfectly clear to this intelligent salesperson, but you're going to miss out on it because you can't follow the explanation.

Often, your confusion becomes part of an emotional trap as well: you're meant to feel ashamed of not understanding and reluctant to persist in questioning until you can understand the explanation. Alternatively, the complexity of the investment or financial product can be touted as part of its attraction. You've probably heard this one: "Good grief, even I don't get all the ins and outs of it, but our research boys (or our legal department, or our accountants) know all the gimmicks, so you can get the maximum possible gain." This pitch is frequently used in selling tax shelters—"the boys" know how to thread their way through every loophole in the Internal Revenue Code, and the fact that the product is incomprehensible just proves what a sharp tax shelter it is.

The Speed Trap

This is the hard-sell approach most likely to be used in schemes that are actually fraudulent. For that reason, it is also the clearest danger signal. When you are told that you must commit yourself immediately—especially if you have to produce cash right away—you should almost never do so.

Of course, some investment opportunities really are time limited. An example is bond trusts. Once the original issue is sold out, shares may not be easily available. But while a specific trust may sell out quickly, new ones are being created and marketed all the time. The investor can take time to learn how such a vehicle works, figure out whether it is right for him or her, and decide to buy the next available issue that meets his needs. When the time comes, the investor's quick action won't be based on an uninformed decision. The same applies to buying "opportunities" in specific stocks. A value-oriented investor is looking for stocks that are priced low relative to the value of the business issuing them—because the price of these securities will almost surely rise. This investor has to be ready to pounce when a stock he or she likes becomes available at an attractive price. But "being ready" means doing careful research beforehand and taking your time over it.

Softening Up the Hard Sell

The best way to defeat the high pressure sales brigade is to beat them to the punch. One of the wisest financial professionals we know maintains that the biggest mistake people make is that they wait to be sold. Instead, he says, you should take the initiative, go looking for referrals to experienced and reliable insurance agents, brokers, financial planners, and so forth, and assemble a team of experts. Using their input, you can put in place a saving and investment plan that will make you almost invulnerable to hard-sell pitches and impulse investing.

But just suppose that you get a call or a letter from a high-pressure type, and through the flak you think you perceive something of investment interest to you. How can you get a chance to investigate it on your own terms? Here are a few tips:

1. Demand paper. Refuse to discuss the matter at any length until the salesperson has documented the recommendation. Ask for sales material on the product or service offered. For example, if Weatherford Goodfellow's little company had had any interest for us, we could have asked for his firm's research reports on it, as well as the company's annual report and other financial statements.
2. Demand explanations. When you've looked over the documentation, discuss your questions with the salesperson. This should give you a good estimate of his or her understanding of the issues—which tells you a lot about the value of the salesperson's advice.
3. Demand time. After you've had both written and spoken comments on the product or service offered, take time to think. "I'm not ready to decide yet" or "I want to talk this over with my wife/husband" are perfectly legitimate responses.

Watch out for salespeople who are reluctant to cooperate in any of these steps or try the "speed trap" ploy to short-circuit them. You'll do best dealing with those who appreciate careful and informed clients. (Within reason, of course—if it takes you six months to talk something over with your wife, even the most patient salesperson is bound to get a little antsy.) Only a small percentage of financial salespeople stoop to high pressure tactics. But that's cold comfort if you happen to be the one who succumbs to a Super Salesperson. It's worth your while to take a little trouble, seek out the real professionals, and minimize your contacts with the others.

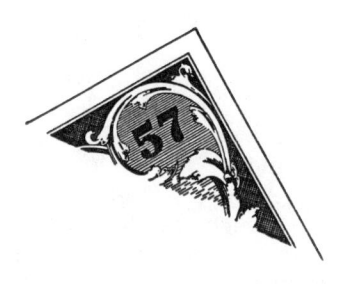

Will I Get Rich If I Invest In The Stock Market?

If you had bought 100 shares of IBM at 44-1/2 in 1913, those shares (through stock dividends and stock splits) would have become 296,000 shares worth $44.4 million by year-end 1985. While the prospect is pleasing it is very unlikely that a novice investor would have been able to "discover" IBM in 1913. By "discover," I mean have the insight to see what the company was going to become. Certainly, people invested in IBM in 1913, and many of them earned significant investment returns. But my guess is that few estates still hold the original 100 shares that someone purchased in 1913—so much for *that* profit.

While it is possible to amass a great fortune with a limited investment, very few investors actually accomplish this. The odds against earning astronomical investment returns are too great. History tells us that most investors earn from 8% to 10% a year from their stock investments over the long run, and that is before brokerage commissions and income taxes are taken into account. Aggressive stock investors can earn an average of from 10% to 12% a year on their portfolios. Aggressive stock pickers with exceptional ability may earn an annual average rate of return of from 12% to 16% on their portfolios. Few if any investors can earn substantially more than a 16% rate of return year after year.

While a few investors will earn substantially more than 16% annually over the long run, the "luck of the draw" probably accounts for much of the excess return. Thus, a reasonable investment goal is to be in the top group of stock pickers—to earn from 12% to 15% annually over the long run. To expect significantly more than these rates of return is to expect too much from the investment "game." To some, these numbers may be disappointing since they appear to be very small. However, if you compound investment returns over time, small improvements in annual returns result in substantial increases over the long run. For example, suppose that you invest $5,000 each year over a 15-year period. The return earned is the historical market average (10% per year). At the end of the 15-year period, the investment would be worth $158,860—$75,000 of capital you invested and $83,860 of compound returns. Now suppose that a second investor also invests $5,000 each year over the same period. However, this investor earns a 14% compound annual rate of return. The result is a portfolio valued at $219,210—an improvement of over $60,000 even though the increase in the rate of return was "only" 4 percentage points. These increases become even more significant if the investments are held for longer periods. Many readers may dream of finding another IBM. But you will be surprised to learn that $4,450 (the amount we "invested" in IBM at the start of the chapter) would have grown to $51.7 million by 1985 if, in 1913, it was invested in *any* portfolio earning 14% a year! In comparison, the investment in IBM "only" earned 13.5%.

What are the implications for today's investor? For one thing, the S&P 500 stock index returned the compound annual rate of 9.8% over the 55-year period 1926-1985. During the same period, small firms listed on the New York Stock Exchange returned 12.6%. (Remember the "small-firm" effect? See "Small Investors, Small Stocks, Big Profits"—Dose 76). So it may be easier to "find" an IBM than you might think. That "find" may well be a diversified common stock portfolio consisting of small firms held for long-term appreciation.

What does all this mean? First, "superior" investment returns are not astronomical (12% to 15%). Second, these returns are obtained by moderately aggressive investors who are willing and able to "stay" with the investment over the long run. This doesn't mean that investors wed common stocks "for better or for worse, in sickness and in health" (theirs not yours). However, many investors use short term tactics which minimize the probability of both earning superior returns and of staying in the game over the longer run. Most notably, concern with short-run performance and excessive portfolio turnover tend to lessen total returns (due to increased transaction costs) and to the increased bite taken by the IRS.

It is worth noting that if you *had* bought 100 shares of IBM in 1913 and never sold, you would have paid no taxes on the 296,000 shares you now hold. In addition, if you turn over (trade) a portfolio only once each year, investment returns will be reduced from 2% to 8% due to transaction costs. As a result, investors should periodically check their average portfolio holding period. Look back over the last five years. If you find that on average you held your common stocks for less than two years, you are trading too much. You are most likely decreasing your overall compound annual rate of return and thus preventing yourself from reaching the superior performance level (i.e., from 12% to 15% annually).

Common Stock Values Depend On What You're After

The calculations investors perform in trying to assign a value to common stocks are endless. Investment services abound that provide, for a fee, any figures you want for any stock(s) you choose—or, heaven forbid, all possible figures for all stocks.

Before you plunge into this sea of numbers, you can spare yourself confusion if you know what you're after. All attempts to figure a "reasonable" value for a given stock fall into one of three categories: current price compared to past prices, or to the current prices of other stocks; current price compared to the value of the issuing company, dead; or current price compared to the value of the issuing company, alive (fundamental analysis).

All three approaches assume two things: 1) that there is an intrinsic value for each stock that is the "correct" price at any given time and 2) that over some period, whether weeks or years, stock prices will move from their current levels toward that "correct" value. The three approaches differ only in terms of the best way to estimate intrinsic value.

Price-to-Price Comparisons

Investors who study stock prices minutely are usually concerned with near-term results. This is a polite way of saying that they are trying to beat the market by accurately forecasting where a stock is "going." The underlying notion is that past movements of the stock's price indicate a reasonable range for its intrinsic value, and that deviations from that range suggest the direction in which the stock price is likely to move soon. But as you might expect, investors have worked out two completely contradictory ways to interpret this information.

The Contrarian school says, "Buy a stock only when everybody else hates it" and the price has been driven to an unreasonably low level compared to its history. That way you get it cheap, and later, when the crowd has eased, it will move up to a higher price. Thus, *Forbes* magazine contained an article listing 89 stocks with low price/earnings (P/E) ratios. (The price/earnings ratio shows the relationship between the price of a stock and the earnings of the company issuing the equity instrument. The ratio was used because it compensates for differences in the size of issuing companies and in the number of shares outstanding so that a variety of companies can be compared.) In terms of all the stocks available to the public, the stocks with lowest P/E ratios are now the cheapest.

Some, no doubt, are cheap for good reason. As the *Forbes* article remarked, "If profit projections are wrong and earnings decline, these shares could disappear into the jungle." But investor psychology always plays a part, too. Many of these stocks are simply neglected by investors: They may be too small for the big institutional investors like insurance companies and pension funds, or in industries too pedestrian to excite the speculator. If the companies that issued them grow at even an average rate in the future, then in theory these stocks should not stay ultracheap. Their prices should rise faster than the average stock—that is, they'll beat the market until they catch up.

The measures of "cheapness" are many. Among the simpler quantitative yardsticks are current versus past stock price; current versus past price/earnings ratio; and P/E versus the average stock's P/E, usually as measured by a large stock index like Standard & Poor's 500, which shows changes in value for an overall market portfolio of 500 stocks. Qualitative indicators include persistent unpopularity with the investment media, lack of research coverage by major retail brokerage firms, and/or little ownership of the stock by large institutional investors.

"Momentum followers" constitute the alternative school in attempting to interpret stock price. Their motto is, "Buy the stock only if enough other people love it." This group of investors believes that a move in stock prices, once begun, tends to persist. (Chartists, who plot graphs of stock price movements, looking for patterns, and who are known to viewers of TV's "Wall Street Week" as "The Elves," belong to this group.) Once a stock gets rolling—which can be determined by looking at past prices, readily available information involving no uncertainty at all—these buyers try to get aboard for the ride.

When momentum fails, they get off. In theory, that is, since momentum is based on the trend of past prices, sagging momentum means that the bloom is already off the rose. Every boom market generates excellent momentum for its participants just before it crumbles. The early-1980s bull market in technology issues is merely the most recent case in point.

Asset-Value Investing

Those who don't feel shrewd enough to contradict the market, or nimble enough to hop on and off at the turns, can seek out accounting values instead. This involves comparing the price of a company's stock to what the company actually owns: factories and machines, land, warehouses full of goods, and just plain cash in the bank. This requires some knowledge of how to read financial statements, and a good deal of patient desk work sorting out companies whose stock prices are near, or better yet below, the value of the tangible assets they own. These companies would be worth more "dead"—that is, sold off asset by asset—than investors are currently willing to pay for them "alive," as going concerns. As long as he or she believes that they are indeed going concerns, the asset-oriented investor considers their present stock prices to be irrationally low because sooner or later, investor attention should push the stock's price at least to a reasonable approximation of the company's asset value.

Assuming that the investor can analyze the financial figures correctly, this is a low-risk approach. If worst came to worst, and the company went under, the sale of its assets would recoup his investment. In the meantime, solid asset values offer some defense (though no guarantee) against further sharp declines in stock price. However, that "meantime" until the market recognizes the stock's value can turn out to be years. Asset-value investing requires patience as well as analytical ability.

Both skill and skepticism are needed to correctly value a stock in terms of company assets. In the sheer animal spirits of a roaring bull market, even professional analysts have been known to come up with some strange asset-value estimates. Just before the oil stocks headed for the pit in 1981, market experts were "proving," with barrels-per-share calculations, that oil stocks "deserved" to sell at prices well above their final, astronomical peaks.

Fundamental Value

The toughest but most realistic approach to valuation is to compare stock prices with the estimated intrinsic values of the issuing companies as going concerns. After all, a company invests in a factory or buys a machine, not to resell it for its cost, but to turn out goods or services worth more than the investment and the other inputs needed to produce the goods. That excess, vulgarly known as profit, creates fundamental value.

The key concern of fundamental analysis is return on investment. Corporations show this figure for past periods, in various forms, in their reports to shareholders. The trick is to forecast, from the company's history and from its present competitive situation, what profits it can earn in the future and what return that will generate for those who buy its shares today. A fundamental value approach doesn't confine the investor to rapidly growing companies or to a low-risk strategy. Any firm, no matter how mediocre in profits or prospects, can look like a good fundamental investment if the price is reasonable.

One well-known institutional money manager carried this idea to even greater extremes during the last recession. He bought for his clients shares in a wide range of bankrupt or near-bankrupt companies. To qualify, the companies had to be not just in bad shape, but in real danger of going belly-up. These stocks were selling, naturally, at giveaway prices. The manager reasoned that he would lose his clients' entire investment in a few of his choices (he did), but that when the business climate improved again, most would be pronounced out of danger, and their stocks would skyrocket. This time, he was right. If the year had been 1931 instead of 1981, he would now be washing dishes for a living.

Living With the Method You Choose

Each of these three ways of looking at stock valuation has its special requirements and pitfalls.

Short-term analysis is practiced by people who follow the market very closely indeed. They tend to be obsessive about it. We're told, for example, that professional stock price chartists disdain amateurs who update their charts daily; with today's computer capacity, hourly or continuous charting informs the big-time Elf. The individual investor who wants to compete is up against heavy odds.

It should also be noted that most academic studies of stock market prices show that statistical methods of predicting future price moves from past price patterns are virtually useless. This does not seem to faze the professional investment houses who use these technical methods.

Asset-value investing is for the very patient. Aside from the work involved, the investor must be willing to wait for his return until the general market catches up with his private revelation of value. Most companies selling at low prices relative to their tangible asset value are not producing much in the way of earnings or dividend growth, so the jackpot, if it comes, will come with a rush at the end of the investor's holding period. Moreover, asset-value investors can get as lonely as the Maytag repairman during bull markets, when other investors are racking up large gains, but asset bargains are scarce.

Fundamental value seekers have an ongoing job, like the statisticians, and frequently suffer long delays before they realize their capital-gains returns, like bargain hunters. They do have the consolation of watching their companies grow, develop their earnings power, and pay dividends.

Dollars and Sense

In spite of the differences, nearly any rational valuation approach "works," in two senses. First, if it is applied to all the stocks on the market at any given time, it will produce satisfactory returns if all qualified stocks are bought and sold as the method demands. However, this is clearly impractical for real-life investing. Another way of applying any valuation method broadly is to use it consistently for a long period of time, even if only a relatively small number of stocks are valued. Over an investment lifetime, any rational method should yield good results, even though the investor has to choose what to buy or sell from a huge universe of qualified stocks. The only method of valuation that has consistently been a loser is inconsistency.

Developing An Investment Philosophy: A Lesson From History

So you want to select and monitor a personal portfolio of common stocks? Well, you're in for some heavy labor. But if you're really serious, you can start with a little amusement: an autobiographical pamphlet called "Developing An Investment Philosophy" by Philip A. Fisher, one of the most successful professional investors of the century.

All right, it doesn't sound amusing. But if you have a taste for the old Horatio Alger stories—rags to riches, a promising young man makes it big—here's the real life equivalent. While Philip Fisher didn't exactly start in rags, his first year in business as an investment adviser (1931) netted him exactly $35.88. And that was after he had correctly predicted the Great Crash while working for a stockbroker in 1929! One reason for the slow start was that in 1931 few people had heard of the professional independent "investment adviser." Fisher was one of the pioneers.

By the end of his career, though, company managements were vying for his approval and recommendation, and being known as "one of Phil Fisher's companies" was a little like being called "the next Xerox."

What brought about the change was just plain smarts (plus the usual quota of luck). Fisher's methods of analyzing companies and their investment merits turned up much more gold than gravel. The pamphlet takes you through his development of these methods, stock by stock. At the end, there's a three-page list of his investment criteria.

Just as useful (if not more so), Fisher details, mistake by mistake, the times when he fouled up. He should be awarded a medal for admitting that after he had predicted the coming 1929 crash, he turned right around and put his own money into three stocks that he thought were still "underpriced". He lost nearly every penny—what they call "a learning experience" these days.

Copies of "Developing An Investment Philosophy" can be obtained from Professional Book Distributors, P.O. Box 100120, Roswell, GA 30077 or call 1-800-848-0773.

Investors' Greatest Ills, and Some Cures

Over the years I have noticed a pattern of grievous investment mistakes made by many individuals when they begin their lifetime investment programs. Avoiding these errors from the beginning can lead to a significant increase in wealth over an investment lifetime. Listed below are the five most common mistakes made by novice investors. Included are prescriptions which, if taken in the prescribed doses, should turn a "novice" investor into a "pro" in short order.

Too-small Portfolio

The first mistake is made by people who only have a few dollars to invest—so they buy only one or two stocks. Frequently, these people suffer large losses on their investments even though stock prices in general have been rising. Many of these investors shrug off the losses by claiming that on this particular occasion they were just unlucky. Next time, they vow, they will invest in the "right" stocks and avoid such losses. These investors have embarked on an investment strategy that can be described as "financial suicide."

The cardinal rule of successful investing is *diversification*. The rich often get richer from their investments not because they are smarter or luckier than the average or novice investor but because they are able to diversify. For example, the investor who holds a portfolio of 15 to 20 common stocks (or the average common stock mutual fund investor) is exposed to less than half the risk faced by someone who holds only one or two common stocks. Besides, although diversification reduces your risk, it doesn't reduce your portfolio's return potential one bit.

What about a small investor who simply can't afford to buy the 15 to 30 common stocks needed for true diversification. The solution? Instead of investing in common stocks directly, invest in a common stock mutual fund which holds dozens of stocks in its portfolio.

Direct Investment

Some investors avoid mutual funds, and opt instead for direct investment because they don't understand how mutual funds operate. Others ignore mutual funds because they believe the returns are less than adequate. This is a second mistake.

Over the period 1976-85, 426 common stock mutual funds provided their shareholders with an average total return of 426%. And of the mutual funds in existence over that period, every one (739 in all) provided shareholders with an average return of more than 358%. During the latest bull market (June 1982 through July 1987), the 50 best-performing mutual funds provided their shareholders with a return in excess of 298% with the top performer yielding a return of 509%.

Investors who are not familiar with investment in mutual funds should educate themselves. Today, the cost of this education is quite reasonable. In the past five years, several books have been published that explain how mutual funds work and how they are purchased. Every one of these books is intended for the ordinary investor. The most popular mutual fund manuals are listed in Figure 60-1. My suggestion is to buy one or two of these manuals and study them carefully. In addition, subscribe to one or two mutual fund advisory newsletters. (A current list of mutual fund advisory newsletter services is contained in Dose 49.) While it is folly to blindly follow the recommendations made by these services, most provide detailed descriptions and analyses of numerous funds. Thus, investors can obtain additional information on which to base their fund selection decisions.

Past Performance as a Guide

Some investors (and many mutual fund investors in particular) are lured into investing in last year's star performer. Part of the reason is that many financial publications highlight the top-performing funds and fund managers on a regular basis. Investors often take this as an investment recommendation. But assumption can be harmful to your financial health.

Yesterday's top performers are rarely tomorrow's big winners. For example, the 10 best-performing mutual funds during 1983 provided their shareholders with a 47.7% average rate of return that year. During 1984, none of these funds were ranked among the top 25 best performers and these funds actually provided their shareholders with an average loss of 2.3%.

To avoid committing this error, don't make an investment merely because it has provided generous returns in the recent past. Instead, try to figure out why the asset yielded better than average

Figure 60-1
Mutual Fund Manuals

Name	*The Individual Investor's Guide to No-Load Mutual Funds*
Author	American Association of Individual Investors
Publisher	International Publishing Corporation
	612 N. Michigan Avenue
	Chicago, IL 60611
Price	$19.95

Name	*The Handbook for No-Load Mutual Fund Investors*
Author	Sheldon Jacobs
Publisher	The No-Load Mutual Fund Investor, Inc.
	P.O. Box 283
	Hastings-on-Hudson, NY 10706
Price	$36.00

Name	*Donoghue's Mutual Funds Almanac*
Author	William E. Donoghue
Publisher	The Donoghue Organization
	Box 411
	Holliston, MA 01746
Price	$23.00

Name	*Successful Investing in No-Load Funds*
Author	Alan Pope
Publisher	John Wiley & Sons
	605 Third Avenue
	New York, NY 10158
Price	$19.95

Name	*The Dow Jones-Irwin Guide to Mutual Funds*
Authors	Donald D. Rugg
	Norman B. Hale
Publisher	Dow Jones-Irwin
	1818 Ridge Rd.
	Homewood, IL 60430
Price	$25.00

returns. Look at the risks involved and compare them with your personal inclination and ability to assume risk.

You should also avoid investments that are being heavily touted at the moment. Investors in gold, gold stocks, and gold mutual funds during the early 1980s know the folly of being lured into an investment because of current hype. Instead, look for investments that are not getting a great deal of attention in the financial press. Do your own homework. Seek advice, but be prepared to make the final decision on whether or not to invest yourself. If you're looking for a mutual fund, use the "mutual fund evaluation worksheet," Dose 44, to help you in your decision making.

Advice

Many people buy mutual funds or unit investment trusts that were recommended by a financial planner or a stock broker. While this is not a serious mistake, this approach to asset selection can reduce your net investment returns.

Many recommended mutual funds pay large sales commissions to the adviser who sells them. The resulting loads (sales charges) can be expensive. For example, if you pay an 8.5% sales commission, this means that only $915 of every $1,000 payment is actually invested in fund shares. This is a stiff price to pay a broker for one-time investment advice. To recoup an 8.5% fee, you'd have to earn 9.3% on your investment—just to break even. Over the long run, these fees can make quite a dent in personal wealth. For example, an investor using load funds in an IRA program can lose $10,700 or more over a 20-year investment program.

This error can be avoided if you use different sources for financial advice and to actually make your purchases. While your broker or other financial salesperson may have only the best of intentions, remember that these people earn their living from commissions on the sales they make. Using an independent source of investment advice will eliminate any doubt about a potential conflict between your interests and those of the salesperson. If you're buying mutual funds, don't pay a broker a commission for recommending a fund. Buy only no-load or low-load mutual funds and deal directly with the fund sponsor. Several mutual fund advisory newsletters provide useful information that can help with fund selection and ongoing portfolio management. (See Dose 49.)

Too Much Trading

Many people seem to believe that the only way to make money in the stock market is by frequently dipping and darting in and out of stocks. Along with lack of diversification, this is the most common error made by unseasoned investors.

Too-frequent traders tend to use so-called "technical" methods to help them decide when the time is right to buy or sell a stock. The idea is to "beat the market" by accurately forecasting price moves. But trading involves transactions costs and tax payments. The more often you trade, the higher these costs. Ultimately, they erode investment profits. Some advisers who rely solely on "trend following" and "stock market timing" claim that their investments outperform the market. But most report their investment results without considering transactions costs or income taxes. If truth be told, over the long run, the returns obtained by these advisers (when adjusted for excessive risks and trading costs) are far below those achieved by passive investment—simply buying and holding a portfolio with no trading. The problem is compounded by the fact that many firms mutual fund "families"—those offering several different kinds of funds investments—make it easy for investors to switch from one fund to another. Even in the case of no-load mutual funds, this can significantly increase tax payments. It also presents the temptation of a risky all-or-nothing approach, investing everything at once to "make a killing." This is exactly opposite the strategy of wealth building through long-term investment.

What, then, should you do? First, take a long-term approach to managing your portfolio. Don't make a purchase unless you can hold on to the asset for at least three years. Second, monitor your trading. If, over the long run, you find that you are turning over (trading) the assets in your portfolio more than once every two years, you are trading too much. Finally, never take an all-or-nothing approach to investing, especially in the stock market. To me, you are fully invested if you hold 20% of your portfolio in cash. Being out of the market means holding at least 20% of investible funds in common stocks or common stock mutual funds.

Avoid the mistakes listed and you will increase your net investment returns and your personal wealth by significant amounts.

Reading Stock Market Quotations

A brief look at stock quotations in the daily paper may leave you feeling like you're drowning in a sea of esoterica. Daily trading activity on the New York Stock Exchange (NYSE)—the nation's largest securities exchange—is reported in every major newspaper. Many papers also list trading on regional U.S. exchanges, foreign exchanges, and in the over-the-counter (OTC) market. These reports contain summaries of the trading activities for each stock traded on the exchange the previous day along with a few pertinent financial statistics. At first glance, the numbers appear to be incomprehensible, but with a little practice even the novice investor can decipher the information given.

For one thing, the custom is to quote stock prices in terms of points. One point equals one dollar. Thus, a stock which sold for 20-1/2 actually sold for $20.50 per share. For most stocks traded on the major stock exchanges, the minimum price fluctuation is 1/8 point or 12.5 cents. To make it easy on the reader, the table below converts fractional points to fractional dollar equivalents. Most stocks are also traded in *round lots*—blocks of 100 shares.

Equivalents	
Fraction	Dollar
1/8	= $0.125
1/4	= 0.25
3/8	= 0.375
1/2	= 0.50
5/8	= 0.625
3/4	= 0.75
7/8	= 0.875

To get a feel for what these mean, take a look at Figure 61-1 which is a portion of a summary of the NYSE reported in *The Wall Street Journal*.

Figure 61-1

52 Weeks				Yld	P-E	Sales				Net
High	Low	Stock	Div.	%	Ratio	100s	High	Low	Close	Chg.
24¼	18½	ACMR n	.15e	.7	16	455	21¾	21¼	21¼	−½
9¼	4¼	ACentC		...	...	42	5¼	5	5⅛	+⅛
79	48⅝	ACyan	1.90	2.6	26	3971	74¼	71⅝	73	−1⅝
28¾	19⅞	AElPw	2.26	8.1	12	8101u	29⅛	28	28	−⅝
70⅛	40⅜	AmExp	1.36	2.3	14	13342	58¾	57½	57⅞	−1⅛
34⅞	16⅛	AFaml s	.40	1.2	22	872	34⅛	33	33⅝	−⅜
44⅜	27¼	AGnCp	1.12	2.8	11	1797	41⅜	40¼	40¼	−¾
23	10¼	AGnl wt		...	...	198	20½	19⅝	19¾	−1
44⅛	32⅛	AHerit	1.32	3.2	15	1	41¾	41¾	41¾	−⅛
13⅜	7⅝	AHoist		...	...	66	8⅛	8	8	−⅜
25¼	19¼	AHoist pf	1.95	9.1	...	3	21½	21½	21½	...
92⅜	54¾	AHome	3.10	3.6	18	5988	86¾	85⅝	85⅞	−⅞
137⅝	86¾	Amrtch	7.08	5.4	12	1724	132½	131	131¼	−½
141	81¾	AInGrp	.44	.4	20	1436	125¼	120½	121	−2⅝
226	137½	AIGp pf	5.85	2.9	...	1	202	202	202	−3
28⅝	15⅞	AMI	.72	4.2	...	2810	17⅜	16¾	17	−½
5	2¼	AmMot		...	...	1186	4¼	4	4	−⅛
25⅝	13⅞	APresd	.50	2.1	26	179	24⅜	23⅝	24	−½
52	51¼	APrsd pf	3.50	6.7	...	31	52	51⅞	52	...
15⅝	5¾	ASLFla		...	...	240	13¾	13⅜	13⅝	−⅛
22	13¾	ASLFl pf	2.19	10.4	...	5	21	20⅞	21	...
15⅝	9⅞	AShip	.80	7.5	8	99	11	10⅝	10⅝	−⅜
46⅞	27	AmStd	1.60	4.1	29	1175	39¾	38¾	39¼	+¼
71¼	53⅛	AmStor	.84	1.3	15	839	67	64½	64½	−2½
81	66	AStr pfA	4.38	5.8	...	42	76¾	76	76	−¼
61½	54¾	AStr pfB	6.80	11.5	...	11	59¼	59	59¼	+¼
26	19⅞	AT&T	1.20	4.9	16	23691	24⅜	24	24¼	−⅛
50	37⅞	AT&T pf	3.64	7.6	...	347	47⅞	47⅝	47¾	−⅛
50½	39	AT&T pf	3.74	7.7	...	221	48⅞	48¾	48¾	−⅜
39	21¾	AmWtr	1.12	3.3	10	281	34	33	33½	−½
95¼	57½	AWat pf	1.43	1.7	...	z100	85	85	85	−7½
22⅜	9¼	AmHotl		...	...	111	10½	9¾	9¾	−⅝
79	66	ATr pr	5.92	7.5	...	10	78⅝	77⅞	78⅝	−⅛
40	11¾	ATr sc		...	...	34	34	33¼	33½	−¼
117½	78	ATr un	5.92	5.3	...	41	112¼	112	112	+½
30	17⅞	Amern s	.96	3.9	9	75	25¼	24½	24½	−⅝
34⅝	19¼	AmesD s	.10	.3	24	857	29½	28⅛	28¾	−¾
31	19⅞	Ametek	1.00	3.8	17	848	27⅛	26½	26⅝	−¼
11⅝	9¾	AmevSc	1.08	9.5	...	119	11⅜	11	11⅜	+¼
31¾	22	Amfac		...	23	67	26¼	25⅞	26¼	−¼
8⅛	13/16	vjAmfsc		...	...	239	3¾	3¼	3¼	−½
70¼	53⅛	Amoco	3.30	6.0	8	5037	55¾	54½	54⅝	−1¼
45	27½	AMP	.72	2.0	35	5092	37	35⅜	35⅞	−1¼
16½	11¾	Ampco	.30	2.0	31	163	14¾	14½	14¾	+¼

Take a look at the fifth entry on this list.

"AmExp" is a shortened version of the name of the company whose common stock is being quoted, in this case, American Express. The numbers to the left of the name indicate the highest and

Dollars and Sense

lowest price paid for a share of American Express common stock during the previous year (last 52 weeks). In this case the highest price paid was $70.125 (70-1/8) while the lowest price paid during the last year was $40.375 (40-3/8) per share. The number immediately to the right of the company name is the per-share cash dividend paid during the last 12 months. Barring unforeseen events, this is also the per-share cash payment that can be expected over the next 12 months. (Note that as corporations earn more income, they tend to increase the cash dividend payments to investors. Extreme earnings declines are usually accompanied by cuts in the cash payout.) American Express is currently paying shareholders $1.36 for every share held. The next number, "2.3," represents the current percentage dividend yield. It is computed by dividing the current annual dividend by the current share price and multiplying the result by 100. For example, $1.36 divided by $58 is 0.023. And 0.023 multiplied by 100 gives the current dividend yield of 2.3%.

The next number is the stock's price/earnings (or P/E) ratio. It shows the relationship between a company's *earnings* and the *price* of its stock. The P/E ratio is often used to determine the value of common stock. For example, if a company is earning a great deal, but its stock is selling relatively cheap, the stock is undervalued—and the price of the stock should rise. The opposite, of course, could also be true. Generally speaking, the price of a stock should reflect how "well" the issuing company is doing in terms of earnings.

The next number, "13342," is the number of round lots of American Express common stock which changed hands on the New York Stock Exchange during the day. Remember that one round lot equals 100 shares. Thus, on this particular day, 1,334,200 shares of this company's common stock moved from the hands of sellers to buyers. The next three listings are the prices received by sellers and paid by buyers. The first, 58-3/4 ($58.75), is the *highest* price paid for a share of the company's stock that day. The *lowest* price paid was $57.50 (57-1/2) per share, while the price of the last trade of the day (called the closing price) was 57-7/8. The last number, -1-1/8, is the minus difference between that day's closing price per share and that of the previous day. Here, the day's last trade (57-7/8) was $1.125 *lower* than the previous day's last or closing trade.

To review, consider another entry:

26   19-7/8   AT&T   1.20   4.9   16   23691   24-3/8   24   24-1/4   −1/8

Here's a verbal description:

Highest per share price paid during the last year	$26.00
Lowest per share price paid during the last year	$19.875
The company is American Telephone and Telegraph	AT&T
Its current annual dividend per share is	$ 1.20
Its current yield is	4.9%

Reading Stock Market Quotations

The price/earnings ratio is	16
Total shares changing hands during the day	2,369,100
Highest price paid during the day	$24.375
Lowest price paid during the day	$24.00
The price of the last (closing) trade	$24.25
The change in closing price	−0.125

Like most things in life, reading a stock quotation is easy—once you know how!

The Dow Jones Industrial Average

The Dow Jones Industrial Average (DJIA) is the most widely quoted and used measure of stock market performance. While it is avidly followed by most stock market players, many of them don't realize that it isn't an "average" at all. The DJIA or "Dow" actually is an adjusted mean of the prices of 30 industrial stocks. The Dow Jones Industrial Average has been published since 1896 when closing share prices of 12 large industrial companies were added up and divided by 12.

The composition of the DOW hasn't been changed very often, but some substitutions have significantly affected the performance of this market indicator. (A brief history of the DJIA is given in Figure 62-1.)

The "Dow Jones Industrial Average" was born on July 3, 1894. It was the brainchild of Charles H. Dow, who was to later become the first editor of *The Wall Street Journal*. His intent was to provide a gauge of how stock market prices were moving. The first average contained nine railroad stocks and only two industrials. Various additions and deletions finally produced, in 1896, an average of 12 industrial stocks. In 1916 the list was expanded to 20 stocks, and finally to 30 in 1928. Since then the average has been revised several times. Figure 62-2 shows the stocks currently included.

When Is an Average Not an Average?

There's a good reason the DJIA isn't calculated as a straight average. (That would involve adding the price of the stocks and dividing by 30—the total number of companies included.) Since firms can and do split their shares (or distribute stock dividends), the average must be adjusted to account for these actions. For example, suppose that each of the 30 stocks is selling for $10. The value of the average would be $300 divided by 30 or $10. If one of the stocks split two for one (which would cause its price to fall from $10 to

Figure 62-1
A Chronological History of the Dow Jones Industrial Average

1896 May	The list of 12 stocks used to compute the average consisted entirely of industrial stocks

        American Cotton Oil   Laclede Gas
        American Sugar   National Lead
        American Tobacco   North American
        Chicago Gas   Tennessee Coal & Iron
        Distilling & Cattle Feeding   U.S. Leather pfd
        General Electric   U.S. Rubber

1916 Oct   List expanded from 12 to 20 industrials
1928 Oct   DJIA expanded to 30 industrials.
The list included:

Allied Chemical	Nash Motors
American Can	North American
American Smelting	Paramount Publix
American Sugar	Postum Inc
American Tobacco B	Radio Corp
Atlantic Refining	Sears, Roebuck
Bethlehem Steel	Standard Oil (NJ)
Chrysler	Texas Corp.
General Electric	Texas Gulf Sulphur
General Motors	Union Carbide
General Railway Signal	U.S. Steel
Goodrich	Victor Talking Machine
International Harvester	Westinghouse Electric
International Nickel	Woolworth
Mack Trucks	Wright Aeronautical

1929 Jan   National Cash Register replaced Victor Talking Machine
     July   Postum name changed to General Foods
     Sept   Curtiss-Wright replaced Wright Aeronautical
1930 Jan   Johns-Manville replaced North American
     July   Borden replaced American Sugar
             Eastman Kodak replaced American Tobacco B
             Goodyear replaced Atlantic Refining
             Liggett & Myers replaced General Railway Signal
             Standard Oil (Cal) replaced Goodrich
             United Air Transport replaced Nash Motors
             Hudson Motor replaced Curtiss-Wright
1932 May   American Tobacco B replaced Ligget & Myers
             Drug Inc. replaced Mack Trucks
             Procter & Gamble replaced United Air Transport
             Loew's replaced Paramount Publix
             Nash Motors replaced Radio Corp.
             International Shoe replaced Texas Gulf Sulphur
             IBM replaced National Cash Register
             Coca-Cola replaced Hudson Motor

Continued

Figure 62-1, *Continued*
A Chronological History of the Dow Jones Industrial Average

1933 Aug	Corn Products replaced Drug Inc.
	United Aircraft replaced International Shoe
1934 Aug	National Distillers replaced United Aircraft
1935 Nov	DuPont replaced Borden
	National Steel replaced Coca-Cola
1937 Jan	Nash Motors name changed to Nash Kelvinator
1939 Mar	United Aircraft replaced Nash Kelvinator
	AT&T replaced IBM
1956 July	International Paper replaced Loew's Inc.
1959 May	Texas Corp. name changed to Texaco
June	Anaconda replaced American Smelting
	Swift & Co. replaced Corn Products
	Alcoa replaced National Steel
	Owens-Illinois Glass replaced National Distillers
1965 Apr	Owens-Illinois Glass name changed to Owens-Illinois
1969 July	American Tobacco B name changed to American Brands
1972 Nov	Standard Oil (N.J.) name changed to Exxon
1973 May	Swift name changed to Esmark
1975 May	United Aircraft name changed to United Technologies
1976 Apr	International Nickel name changed to INCO
Aug	3M replaced Anaconda
1979 June	IBM replaced Chrysler
	Merck replaced Esmark
1981 Apr	Allied Chemical name changed to Allied Corp.
Oct	Johns-Manville name changed to Manville
1982 Aug	American Express replaced Manville Corp.
1984 Jan	AT&T "new" replaced AT&T "old"
July	Standard Oil (Cal.) name changed to Chevron
1985 Sept	Allied Corp. name changed to Allied-Signal
Oct	Philip Morris Cos. replaced General Foods
	McDonald's replaced American Brands
1986 Feb	International Harvester name changed to Navistar International
July	U.S. Steel name changed to USX
1987 Mar	Coca-Cola replaced Owens-Illinois
	Boeing replaced INCO
Apr	American Can name changed to Primerica

$5), an unadjusted average falls to $295 divided by 30, or $9.83 per share. However, the average isn't accurate because, in actual fact, there was only a change in the price of one stock. To compensate for this, the divisor is adjusted. In our example, if the divisor were adjusted downward from 30 to 29.5, the average would remain at

Figure 62-2
Dow Jones Industrials: (November 1987)

Company Name	Year Added
Allied-Signal	1925
Alcoa	1959
American Express	1982
American Telephone & Telegraph	1984
Bethlehem Steel	1928
Boeing	1987
Chevron	1930
Coca-Cola	1987
DuPont	1935
Eastman Kodak	1930
Exxon	1928
General Electric	1907
General Motors	1915
Goodyear	1930
IBM	1979
International Paper	1956
McDonald's	1985
Merck	1979
3M	1976
Navistar International	1925
Philip Morris	1985
Primerica	1916
Procter & Gamble	1932
Sears, Roebuck	1924
Texaco	1916
USX	1901
Union Carbide	1928
United Technologies	1939
Westinghouse	1928
Woolworth	1924

$10. With the actual DJIA an adjustment is made both in the divisor and for differences in prices. (It is *price weighted*.)

The following simplified example illustrates the method used to calculate the Dow Jones Average. Assume that three stocks are used to compute the average and the respective share prices are $5, $10, and $15. The value of the average is computed by summing the three prices and dividing by 3.

Dollars and Sense

$$A = \frac{\$5 + \$10 + \$15}{3}$$

$$= \$10.00$$

If at the close of the next trading day, the three stocks closed at $4, $12 and $17, the value of the average would be: 4 plus 12 plus 17 divided by 3 or 11.00 which is up "one point" from the previous day's close.

Suppose, however, that effective the next day, the $12 stock splits two-for-one and the stocks close at prices of $4, $6, and $17. If the three closing prices are added together and divided by 3, the result is $9 and the result gives the impression that stock prices have fallen. This is not the case since owners of the $6 stock now have two shares for every one they had before—their shares are *still* worth the same total value, they just hold more of them. To accommodate such stock splits, the divisor is adjusted downward. The computation is

$$\frac{\$4 + \$6 + \$17}{\text{New Divisor}} = 11 \text{ previous day's closing average}$$

$$\text{New Divisor} = 27/11$$
$$= 2.45$$

Note that when the three prices ($4, $6, and $17) are added and divided by 3, the average share price ($9) is different from the divisor-adjusted "average."

Over time, stock splits, stock dividends, and replacements have reduced the original divisor to its current value of less than 1.00. That is, to obtain the value of the Dow today, you must add up the share prices of the 30 firms in the average and divide by 0.754 (as of November 1987). Since this divisor is close to 1.00, a $1.00 change in the price of any stock causes the Dow to change by approximately one point. Note that the average is biased by changes in higher-priced stocks. For example, a 10% rise in the price of IBM (when trading near $133) would cause the average to rise by 13 points while a 10% rise in Bethlehem Steel (a $12 stock) only brings about a 1-point rise in the Dow. Further, because the current divisor is slightly less than one, a $1 price change in any stock would cause the average to change by more than one point.

Is the Dow Worth Watching?

The point of all this explanation is that although widely watched and quoted, the DJIA is a highly misleading gauge of overall stock market performance. First, the 30 stocks are all traded on the New York Stock Exchange (NYSE). Although the NYSE is the largest, there are several other exchanges throughout the country which trade different stocks. And a goodly number of securities are traded over the counter, not on an exchange. So, the Dow doesn't reflect the actions of other markets whose trading volume often exceeds that of the NYSE. In fact, the 30 companies included account for less than 17% of the total market value of nationally traded stock issues. Second, all of the companies included are or were billion-dollar giants. Small and medium sized firms are ignored. So, the Dow presents a somewhat lopsided view of the market. Third, price weighting greatly distorts true stock market trends. Fourth, the Dow includes a large number of industrial manufacturers like Navistar International and USX, many of which are financially troubled. This does not paint an accurate picture of U.S. corporate functioning. Finally, changes in the stocks listed have destroyed any continuity in the Dow as a measurement of stock market performance. For example, IBM was first added to the average in 1932, dropped in 1939, and re-instated in 1979. Thus, the firm's greatest growth years were never taken into account. Chrysler shares were allowed to fall from $60 in the late 1970s to slightly more than $9 before the company was replaced on the Dow in 1979. (Of course, Chrysler's rebound was also never recaptured by the average.) The addition of a fast-food concern occurred a quarter century after the industry began to bloom.

The point is this: Do not place much credence in day-to-day values of the Dow. Discussed in Dose 63 are some other measures that may be more useful for individual investors in assessing where the market (and their investments) are going.

Other Measures of Stock Market Prices

The Dow Jones Industrial Average may be the most widely quoted measure of stock prices, but its limitations, discussed in Dose 62, make it an inappropriate benchmark for judging the performance of most personally (or professionally) managed portfolios. Many investors instead use more broadly based market indicators like the New York Stock Exchange Index, the Standard & Poor's Composite Index, the Wilshire 5000 Equity Index, and the NASDAQ Composite Index.

Standard & Poor's Composite The "S&P Composite" or "S&P 500" is an index of the prices of 400 industrial stocks, 40 financial stocks, 20 transportation stocks, and 40 utility stocks. The S&P is calculated on the basis of both number of shares outstanding and price. The composite is measured against shares and prices for a base period (1941-43) with an index value of 10. The S&P Composite is a *value-weighted* index. This means greater emphasis is given to higher-value stocks. As a result, the index is affected more by price changes in the common shares of firms with greater total equity values (share price multiplied by number of shares outstanding). What this means is that the S&P may not be an appropriate basis of comparison for all investment portfolios. This would be the case, for example, if most of your investments were roughly equal in value.

New York Stock Exchange (NYSE) Composite Index This index has been published by the NYSE since 1966. Like the S&P Composite, it is a value-weighted index. The only differences between the two are that the NYSE Composite contains all stocks listed on the NYSE "big board" and a 1966 base year index value of 50 is used.

The market measure suffers the same biases as all value-weighted measures. While it is a broad measure, since all stocks listed on the NYSE are used, nonetheless, newer and smaller companies are excluded.

Wilshire 5000 Equity This market measure is the aggregate market value of all stocks listed on the two largest exchanges—the American Stock Exchange (Amex) as well as the NYSE—and those which are actively traded *over the counter* (*not* on an organized exchange). The Wilshire 5000 is also a value-weighted measure and so is most affected by price changes in the issues of the largest publicly traded firms. The measure is given in billions of dollars. Thus, a value of 1690.08 is one trillion, six-hundred ninety billion, eighty million dollars.

The NASDAQ Composite This price indicator series was first published on May 17, 1971. The index is value weighted and the method of construction is similar to that of the S&P 500 and the NYSE Index. However, only domestic common stocks traded over the counter (OTC) are used. This includes over 2,000 listed on the National Association of Securities Dealers Automatic Quotations (NASDAQ) system—a computer linkup used for OTC trading. New stocks are included when they are added to the system. The index value was 100 as of February 5, 1971. Because the index is value weighted, it is heavily influenced by the largest stocks on the NASDAQ system. However, the index does include a preponderance of stocks of smaller firms which are generally traded OTC.

Using any of these indexes to evaluate either your own investments (are they doing "better," "worse," or "the same as" the "market") or to gauge where prices are "going" can provide a general benchmark for where specific aspects of the market are headed. And because they, and the Dow, are so widely followed, they may carry a wide variety of investments with them.

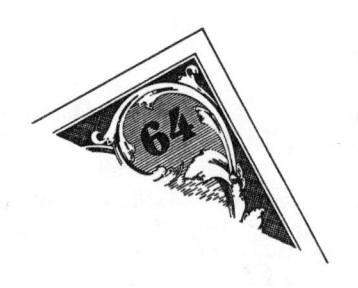

Measuring Portfolio Performance

The years 1982-87 were something else for stock market investors. A bull market to end all bull markets charged its way into stock market history, leaving a trail of broken records and swollen portfolios.

Whether you were in the stock market reveling in those rare, heady days or playing it safe on the sidelines in a money market fund, you heard the same question all over town. "How are you doing?" Everyone seemed to be buzzing with stories about their best stock or mutual fund gaining 20%, 30%, 40%, or more in just a few short months. Everyone, it seemed, was doing just fine.

But were they really? It's important to remember that one investment does not make or break your fortune. At least, not necessarily. Which brings us to the point. Investors need to know, when the year (month or quarter) is over, how all their investments—their entire portfolio—have performed. And this means everything: stocks, bonds, mutual funds, money market accounts, bank certificates of deposit, and whatever other financial assets you hold.

Why?

You, as an investor, need to know what the overall performance of your portfolio has been for two important reasons. First, you need to know whether you are earning a sufficient rate of return for the investment risks you have been taking. If you are not, you need to reduce the risks or increase the returns.

Second, you need to decide, based on your portfolio's performance, whether you should continue with your current investment strategy or make a change. This is especially important if you are planning on supplementing your retirement funds from your investments. If you find that your portfolio is not earning the minimum return you will need to meet your retirement goal, then you must modify your portfolio and investment strategy accordingly.

Although these questions are an important aspect of sound portfolio management, you would be surprised at how few investors regularly take the time to assess their investments' performance. In fact, not many even ask the question in the first place. Instead, investors generally focus their attention on those stocks in their portfolio that have advanced to new highs or have declined by significant amounts. If you asked them, most individual investors would not know what the overall return was on their investments over the past year.

Why Not?

The excuses for not regularly computing overall portfolio return are many and varied. The first excuse is time. Investors using this excuse claim that they simply do not have time to monitor their portfolios on a regular basis. The second excuse is "What's the use?" This group points out that "you can't spend a rate of return," and all that really counts is what's left at the end, anyway. The last excuse is, "I just don't know how. It's too complicated."

To all three excuses, we say consider this. First, regular portfolio review should only take a few hours each year if adequate records are available. This is a small percentage of your time when it's looked at in those terms. Second, measurement of the historical rate of return on your investment (and comparison with equivalent portfolios) provides a valuable guide to future portfolio management. The better the management, the bigger the portfolio and, therefore, the more you have to spend or save. And finally, as will be demonstrated in the following pages, measurement of portfolio return is really quite straightforward.

A True-Life Adventure

Why should you measure portfolio return? Well, consider the following true story.

Not so many years ago, I was called on as an expert witness in a lawsuit filed by an individual investor against a stockbroker. The investor was an elderly widow. She alleged that over the previous three years, the value of her investment portfolio had fallen over 80% because of her broker. The broker, she contended, made poor investment decisions, and on top of that, was churning her account. ("Churning an account" refers to excessive trading by a stockbroker to generate high brokerage commissions.)

After examining the records of the trading which had been done in her account, I reached a conclusion which startled the widow, her attorney, and even the stockbroker himself. Most of the decline in the widow's portfolio value was due to her frequent withdrawals of money from the portfolio. It was not due to the stockbroker's activities.

While the lawsuit was subsequently settled out of court, something from that episode is still amazing: The case got as far as it did without either party analyzing the portfolio's return. All that was known was that the portfolio's current dollar value was far less than its beginning value. While this case may be somewhat unusual, it points out the general reluctance of investors to assess portfolio performance.

Knowing Where You're Going

One of the marks of a successful business organization is timely management action. A plan is specified that provides a benchmark against which actual results can be compared. If results are not consistent with the initial plan, management action is required. If a change is necessary, plans must be modified or actions must be taken to improve the efficiency of operations. In either case, a comparison of results with a benchmark indicates whether or not management action is needed.

In other words, before you can know where you are going, you must find out where you've been. This is true in business and it is also true in any other pursuit where goals are set. This, of course, includes your personal finances.

Effective portfolio management requires that investment results be periodically measured and compared with the initial plan. The initial plan should specify the level of risk assumed and the rate of return expected.

A general benchmark for measuring common stock returns is the performance of the stock market itself. This is measured using an index of overall market performance like the Standard & Poor's Index of 500 Common Stocks or the Dow Jones Industrial Average. Remember, however, that these averages or indexes measure the return of the average common stock. If your portfolio contains assets that are markedly different from most common stocks, you may also wish to obtain the returns for long-term bonds, Treasury bills, gold and silver, small stocks, etc.—depending on the kinds of vehicles you're investing in.

If your portfolio underperforms similar financial instruments over prolonged periods (which we certainly hope it hasn't), this is a signal for management action—your action. Thus, the measure of past portfolio returns provides the essential input necessary to obtain optimal portfolio returns in the future.

On the surface, measuring past returns appears to be a monumental task. During the year, for example, you may have bought and sold several stocks, bonds, or mutual fund shares, added new dollars to your overall portfolio, paid brokerage commissions and taxes, and withdrawn funds. However, thanks to the dubious honor of being a taxpayer, you must keep records of all of these transactions. And using those very records, you can easily measure your portfolio's performance.

The only additional ingredients you need for this task are access to periodic quotes of your assets' price, a systematic method for summarizing transactions and cataloging the value of the portfolio, and a model for computing investment return.

Measuring Where You've Been

Before getting started, you need to decide how often you need to measure portfolio returns. The only rule that applies here is that frequency should be consistent with your ability to take appropriate action. While we will go into more detail about this subject later, let us assume at this point that annual measurement generally provides sufficient data for timely action. Thus, in the examples which follow, assume that performance measurement takes place annually, at year-end. (You will see that the prescriptions given here can be easily modified to incorporate any frequency.)

Figure 64-1 shows an example of the calculations of annual rates of return for a portfolio containing common stocks (and equity mutual funds), bonds (and other liquid assets), and "miscellaneous" investments (gold coins, in this case).

For each investment class, we have determined the market value at the beginning and end of the year, and the additions and withdrawals of capital during the year. The market values of the common stock, bond, and gold portions of the overall portfolio were obtained from data published in *The Wall Street Journal*, although a number of other data sources could have been used. The value of the money market fund was obtained from the fund's latest statement.

The values in each column were then added up and the sums entered on the "Totals" line. These sums were then moved to the corresponding lines on the "Portfolio Summary." The exceptions were "Additions" and "Withdrawals," which were combined (additions minus withdrawals) to arrive at "Net Capital Additions."

Figure 64-1
Portfolio Return Example

Year Beginning 1/1/xx			Ending 12/31/xx	
Asset Class	Beginning Value	Additions	Withdrawals	Ending Value
Equities	$12,500	$1,500	$ 0	$18,000
Bonds	6,600	0	0	7,500
Money funds	9,750	5,000	2,000	13,000
Other—Gold coins	3,200	1,600	0	4,650
Totals	$32,050	$8,100	$2,000	$43,150

Summary: Beginning portfolio value: $P(O)$ $32,050
          Net capital additions: (C) 6,100
          Ending portfolio value: $P(1)$ 43,150

$$\text{Return} = \frac{43,150 - \frac{1}{2}(6,100)}{32,050 + \frac{1}{2}(6,100)} - 1 = \frac{40,100}{35,100} - 1$$

Dollars and Sense

For simplicity's sake, we abbreviated "Beginning Portfolio Value" as P(O), "Ending Portfolio Value" as P(1), and "Net Capital Additions" as (C). In the example, P(O) is $32,050, P(1) is $43,150, and C is $6,100 (additions, $8,100, minus withdrawals, $2,000).

Now we are ready to calculate the portfolio's annual return. Simply plug the numbers into the following equation:

$$\text{Return} = \frac{\text{Ending Portfolio Value less one-half Net Capital Additions}}{\text{Beginning Portfolio Value plus one-half Net Capital Additions}}\text{ or}$$

$$\text{Return} = \frac{P(1) - \tfrac{1}{2}C}{P(0) + \tfrac{1}{2}C} - 1$$

$$= \frac{\$43{,}150 - \tfrac{1}{2}(\$6{,}100)}{\$32{,}050 + \tfrac{1}{2}(\$6{,}100)} - 1$$

$$= \frac{\$43{,}150 - \$3050}{\$32{,}050 + \$3050} - 1$$

$$= \frac{\$40{,}100}{\$35{,}100} - 1$$

$$= 1.1425 - 1$$

$$= .1425$$

$$.1425 \times 100 = 14.25\%$$

Therefore, the portfolio provided an annual return of 14.25%.

The model just used to calculate annual returns has an impressive name but, as demonstrated, is quite simple to use. It is called the "Dietz Algorithm," and it solves the measurement problem more easily than do more complicated models. Other models involve the problem of what to do about the cash that is added to, or withdrawn from, the portfolio during the year. These models treat additions and withdrawals in a more complicated manner, calling for many, more complex calculations. But the Dietz Algorithm simply assumes that exactly one-half of such additions and withdrawals are made at the beginning of the year and the other half at the end. Since this assumption may not accurately describe the annual cash flow of your portfolio (e.g., all additions may have been made at the beginning or at the end of the period), the resulting rate of return is only an approximation of the "true" portfolio rate of return. However, if you do not make cash contributions and withdrawals frequently, the return calculation provides quite accurate results.

Figure 64-2
Calculating Quarterly Portfolio Return Worksheet

Year Beginning _____   Ending _____

Asset Class	Beginning Value	Additions	With-drawals	Ending Value
Equities	_____	_____	_____	_____
Bonds	_____	_____	_____	_____
Money funds	_____	_____	_____	_____
Other—	_____	_____	_____	_____
Totals	_____	_____	_____	_____

Summary: Beginning portfolio value: $P(0)$ _____
Net capital additions: (C) _____
Ending portfolio value: $P(1)$ _____

$$R = \frac{P(1) - \tfrac{1}{2}C}{P(0) + \tfrac{1}{2}C} - 1 \quad _____$$

If you want to improve the precision of your return calculations, quarterly rates of returns should be calculated. Simply convert the annual worksheet to four one-quarter worksheets. Your worksheet for the first quarter contains values at the beginning of the quarter (January 1), the end of the quarter (at March 31), and any contributions or withdrawals made in January, February, or March. Using the Dietz Algorithm in exactly the same way as for the annual return, calculate the portfolio's return for the quarter. Figure 64-2 gives the format.

Proceed in a similar fashion for the second, third, and fourth quarters. The first quarter's return is R1, the second quarter's return is R2, the third quarter's is R3, and the fourth quarter's return is R4.

Now you need to convert these four quarterly returns into one annual rate of return. Simply plug your values for R1, R2, R3, and R4 into the following equation.

Annual Return = $[(1 + R1)(1 + R2)(1 + R3)(1 + R4)] - 1$

For example, suppose that during the previous year, a hypothetical investor earned quarterly returns of 4%, 10%, -5%, and 3%. These percentage rates of return must first be converted to decimals: 0.04, 0.10, -0.05, and 0.03. Next, the number "1" is added to each quarterly rate of return and the results are multiplied.

$$= (1.04 \times 1.10 \times 0.95 \times 1.03) = 1.1194$$

Finally, the number "1" is subtracted from the result.

$$= 1.1194 - 1$$
Annual return $= .1194$

To convert this to a percentage, multiply by 100.

$.1194 \times 100 = 11.94\%$

Use Figure 64-2 as a worksheet to calculate annual rates of return for your portfolio. A personal computer with a spreadsheet program makes the calculation easier. Note that separate worksheets can be prepared and used to monitor the return performance of segments of the overall portfolio (e.g., IRA portfolios, Keogh portfolios, etc.).

Once the quarterly and annual rates of return have been determined, compare them with the results which could have been obtained over the investment period. This is commonly done by comparing portfolio returns with the returns from an index of stock market prices such as the S&P 500. However, in this case, performance was determined on a total return basis, so cash dividend payments must also be taken into account. Further, when making comparisons, risk must also be accounted for. This means you should compare your portfolio's performance with an index of similar investments. For example, if you have invested in relatively liquid assets that can easily be converted into cash with relatively little risk of loss of principal—like bank CDs or money market funds, etc.—compare your portfolio's performance with the yields on Treasury bills, which are almost completely liquid. If you have been in common stocks, compare returns with those of the S&P 500 or another stock index. If you have invested in a combination of liquid assets and common stocks, compare returns with a weighted average return from Treasury bills and S&P 500 stocks.

Now is a perfect time to spend a few moments assessing the performance of your investment portfolio. The records of investment transactions required for such assessment are the same ones required for income tax purposes. Thus, while you are paying Uncle Sam, you have the opportunity to "pay" yourself. Such payment will give you a new awareness of your portfolio management skills and a set of data which can lead to better portfolio performance in the future.

Speculation Is In The Eye of the Beholder

Our ancient ancestors were smarter than we are. When they were worried about the future, they turned to their tarot cards or consulted a palm reader. They peered at crystal balls and tea leaves. It didn't work, of course, but at least they understood that it would take magic to be able to inspect the future in the present. Short of sorcery, nobody can tell you tomorrow's news today.

Investment vs. Speculation

This dash of philosophy was prompted by something we heard on television the other day—a bit of bad advice from a generally good financial program. The host got to talking about the difference between investment and speculation. One of the things that "everybody knows" is that to be an investor is a Good Thing, and to be a speculator is a Bad Thing. But apparently, even some well-informed people (like the host) aren't clear which is which. To follow the program's rules for sticking to the first and avoiding the second, you need to be able to foretell the future.

Most people believe that the distinction has something to do with risk. "Speculating" is risky; "investing" has a safe, solid, virtuous sound to it. In recent years, people in the investment business have liked to define risk as the possibility that, in the future, your investments won't earn exactly the return you expect them to. By that definition, "speculating" means buying securities whose returns are unpredictable; on the other hand the results of "investing" are supposed to be predictable.

The TV show's host agreed. He offered his viewers these definitions:

- Investment means putting your capital in any vehicle whose future returns are set in advance.
- Speculation means putting your capital in any vehicle whose returns can vary.

He also offered these examples of investing:
- Putting your money in a bank account or certificate of deposit.
- Buying a government or corporate bond and holding it until your principal is repaid when it matures.
- Placing your savings in a guaranteed income contract with an insurance firm.

The reasoning is plausible, but it just ain't right. There are no sure things, and every one of these "investment" examples actually yields a return that is at least somewhat uncertain. This is because any return that's predictable in *dollars* is unpredictable in *purchasing power*. Inflation will reduce the value of the returns on all of the "investments" listed, and reduce them by an unpredictable amount. (People who have had to live on fixed incomes over the last 10 years can testify to that.) Deflation—a falling price level—would increase purchasing power unpredictably, but that hasn't been a problem for several decades.

According to the definition above, these are all "speculations":
- Holding common stocks directly,
- Owning stocks indirectly through a mutual fund or variable annuity,
- Owning real estate,
- Buying variable-interest-rate bonds.

But if a steady *real* return, in terms of purchasing power, is what you want, some items on this "speculation" list offer you a better shot at your goal. Variable-rate bonds, for instance, were invented to shield returns from the corrosive effects of inflation. Their interest rates move up and down with the rates on newly issued bonds. Clearly, this is speculation. But since interest rates tend to rise as inflation speeds up, and fall as it slows, a variable-rate instrument may be the best way to fix a bond's return in terms of real purchasing power.

The same applies to common stocks. Their returns are notoriously unpredictable over short periods, and none too stable even over several years. On the other hand, company managements are always working hard to keep the long-term value of their firms growing. And history shows that most firms cut the dividends they pay to shareholders only as a last resort. In recent years, many companies have publicly adopted the goal of maintaining and increasing the purchasing power of their dividends, not just the dollar amounts. Over the past 20 years, the purchasing power of the total dividends paid by U.S. corporate business has seldom even dipped.

So if both categories of holdings yield uncertain returns, how can you tell an investment from a speculation? The answer is suggested by one characteristic that all the "investments" share: none of them exposes the individual investor to the day-to-day fluctu-

Speculation is in the Eye of the Beholder

ations of the securities markets. Bank certificates and insurance contracts can't be traded by individuals. Bonds can be traded, but according to the TV show host, his "investors" could hold their bonds to maturity, when the issuer of the bond pays back the principal. Thus, the bond's yield is fixed.

In the stock market, of course, the only way to get your money out is to offer your shares for whatever price they'll bring on the open market on the day you sell. We'd bet it's that kind of exposure to the markets that some people think investors should avoid. Well, it's impossible to avoid it forever. But in fact, you can invest in common stocks or stock mutual funds without being vulnerable to every shifting wind of the market. The difference between investment and speculation depends not on what you buy, but on why you buy it.

Consider the definitions offered by one of our all-time favorite investment philosophers, Robert G. Kirby of Capital Guardian, at a seminar sponsored by the Financial Analysts Research Federation:

> *Speculation* is the purchase of an asset solely or principally on the expectation that it can be sold to someone else at a higher price sometime in the future.
>
> *Investment* is the purchase of a claim on a present and/or future stream of income—for instance, a share of stock (which is a claim on a corporation's earnings) or a rentable building. An investment does not have to be sold to someone else at a higher price in the future to be successful.

When you buy a stock, or shares in a stock mutual fund, you can look for companies that earn a good profit on their operations and can make their earnings and dividends grow over the years. You won't know in advance exactly how much those earnings will be. But over the long run, a group of well-selected companies will produce dividends as surely as a cow produces milk.

That stream of income is your investment return—it will come through no matter what the stock's prices do from day to day. And when your financial needs change, and you finally do sell some of your holdings, you'll probably find that their market prices reflect their dividend record and prospects. Over a full investment lifetime, stocks do tend to appreciate roughly in line with their earnings and dividend progress—although they can easily run ahead or lag behind for periods of several years at a time.

Exactly the same kind of earning power supports fixed-income investments, such as bank certificates of deposits or bonds. The amount of interest they pay is set in advance, but the money to pay it is generated by the business operations of the issuer. These operations also earn a profit for the company's stockholders in the sense that profitable operations mean the company—and thus the inves-

Dollars and Sense

tor's share in it—are worth more. Stockholders probably regard their holdings as "investments" even though the earnings remaining after the issuer pays interest fluctuate from year to year.

Speculation á la Kirby, on the other hand, depends on short-term trading. Any "investment" offered to you on the argument that its price will soon go up and you can sell out at a gain, is actually a speculation. Its success depends on your ability to outguess the other traders in the market. The speculator's reputation as a wild-eyed gambler stems from the fact that so few of us are good at outguessing. (It should be noted that Mr. Kirby himself strongly advocates investment, not speculation, and he practices what he preaches. When he was asked on a popular TV show whether the stock market would be higher a year from now, he replied, "If I had the slightest idea where the market is going next, I wouldn't have to eke out a meager living managing other people's money.") By definition, speculation can't work for everybody. If you buy a stock whose price then shoots up, the guy who sold you his shares will be kicking himself. If the price drops, you'll be kicking yourself. What one party wins, the other loses.

Investors on the other hand, can all win at once. Some companies will always earn a better return than others, but as long as a corporation is operating at a profit, its shareholder owners will be accumulating some investment returns. As long as the private sector of the economy is growing, investors as a group will be increasing their wealth.

There's no law against speculating; some people make a profession of it and are highly successful. But speculation is a tough dollar. The individual who speculates has chosen to go head-to-head in the market against savvy, full-time professionals who have much better information and, taken together, centuries more experience at the job than he has.

The investment process is much more forgiving. You may make mistakes—in fact, you often will; you may not make a killing—you usually won't; but you will, almost certainly, make progress.

And finally, remember that a speculation doesn't turn into an investment just because the investor (or the salesperson) believes very strongly that its price will rise. Believing hasn't saved anybody since Tinkerbell.

Finding the Next Superstock

How do you earn abnormally large rates of return on your investment portfolio? One answer, of course, is to assume abnormally large risks. Another is to find significantly undervalued assets. That is, find the IBMs, the Haloid Xeroxes, and the Walt Disneys in their infant stages and position your portfolio for significant return. In a recent book, *Finding the Next Super Stock* (Liberty Publishing Company), Frank Cappiello, an investment adviser and regular panelist on "Wall Street Week," identified nine characteristics common to most superstocks of the past. But even if a stock fits all nine categories, according to Cappiello, this does not ensure that it will be a superstock. However, the screen "tells us that the company is well positioned ... to return a good profit to the stockholders."

The following are Cappiello's nine "superstock" screens:

Size: Company sales should be between $25 million and $500 million. That is, the companies should be relatively small.

Sales Volume: Company sales must have increased by more than the rate of inflation (measured by changes in the Consumer Price Index) over the past three years. (See "What is the CPI, Dose 99.)

Profit Margin: Company pretax profit margin (earnings before taxes divided by net sales) should be currently above 10% and show a rising trend over the past five years.

Return On Equity: Current company return on its stock ("equity") should be at least 15% with a rising trend over the last five years. (Exceptions can be made to account for the possibility that recent figures may have been unduly depressed by an economic recession.)

Earnings Per Share Growth: Growth in earnings per share should be greater than that reported for the Dow Jones Industrials over the past three years.

Dividends: Companies that pay some cash dividends are preferred. The payout ratio (dividends divided by company earnings) must also be below 40% and dividends per share must show a rising trend over the past five years.

Debt: Company long-term debt must be less than 35% of stockholders' equity.

Institutional Holdings: No more than 15% of the company's outstanding stock should be held by large institutional investors like pension funds and insurance companies.

Price/Earnings Multiple: This is the relationship between the earnings of a company and the price of the stock it issues. The multiple for super stocks will be better than the multiple for the overall market over the long-term, and equal the Dow Jones Industrial Average in a favorable market.

Cappiello's book contains a detailed scoring method based on the nine screening characteristics. Thus with a little time and access to corporate financial data, investors should be able to narrow a long list of stocks down to a manageable number of potential super-stocks. However, Cappiello warns that the actual selection process is not a simple process and requires that the analyst confirm initial suspicions with more detailed financial research.

The Original "Value Approach to Investing"

Benjamin Graham published the first comprehensive guide to the fundamental analysis of common stock in 1934. His book, entitled *Security Analysis*, was so enthusiastically received by the investment community that Graham became known as the "Father of Security Analysis." For over 50 years, his valuation approach has been extensively employed by both professional investors and individuals alike.

In addition to *Security Analysis*, Graham authored another book entitled *The Intelligent Investor* which was written for the novice investor. In that book, Graham outlines his approach to the valuation of common stock. He writes, "The ideal form of common stock analysis leads to a valuation of the issue which can be compared with the current price to determine whether or not the security is an attractive purchase. This valuation, in turn, would ordinarily be found by estimating the average earnings over a period of years in the future and then multiplying that estimate by an appropriate 'capitalization factor.'" In other words, a stock's value depends on what the company is anticipated to earn in the future and a special "capitalization factor."

The "capitalization factor" was intended to take into account a number of considerations which are not accounted for in the earnings estimate. Factors such as the firm's long-term prospects, its management, financial strength and capital structure, its dividend record, and its current dividend rate all must be considered when valuing its common stock.

One can imagine the difficulties that would be encountered in attempting to quantify these factors and then relate them to the firm's future earnings to arrive at an appropriate valuation for the firm's stock. Ben Graham recognized this problem and solved it by dividing the process into two parts. First, he applied a certain set of screens to the stocks to be analyzed. Those that passed the screens could then be valued using the simple calculation that is explained below. This formula yielded figures fairly close to those resulting from more refined, and more complex, mathematical models. His original model follows:

$$V = E(8.5 + 2G)$$

The term, 8.5 + 2G, represents a multiple against which a company's expected earnings, E, can be multiplied to arrive at a value, V, for the stock. Let us now examine that odd term, 8.5 + 2G, to determine where it comes from.

The "G" is simply growth, that is, the expected annual average growth rate in earnings for the firm over the next 7 to 10 years. If a firm was not expected to grow, then its value could be calculated as follows:

$$V = E(8.5 + 2G) \quad \text{But } G = 0, \text{ so}$$
$$V = E(8.5 + 2(0))$$
$$= E(8.5 + 0)$$
$$= E(8.5)$$

In other words, it was thought that a firm with a zero growth rate should sell for 8.5 times its earnings projected for next year.

This model was subsequently modified to account for the changes in bond yields over time. At the time the model was originally formulated, AAA rated bonds (AAA is the highest rating a bond can receive) possessed an historical average yield of 4.4% Thus, it was reasonable to assume that zero growth stocks would yield about 1/8.5 (the reciprocal of the multiplier), or about 12%. However, yields on high-grade corporate bonds have been far higher over the past decade than the old 4.4% level. Thus, the yields on zero-growth common stocks would also be expected to increase beyond the original estimated yield of 12%. In 1974, Graham added an adjustment factor to his model to account for interest rate changes which have occurred over the years. The revised model is shown below.

$$V = E(8.5 + 2G)(4.4/AAA)$$

The new adjustment factor is the ratio of the original historical bond yield (4.4%) to the current AAA bond yield. An increase in bond yields serves to reduce the earnings multiplier, while a decrease in AAA bond yields increases the earnings multiplier. For example, if AAA corporate bonds currently yield 10%, the appropriate earnings multiplier for a zero growth company is 3.74.

$$V = E(8.5 + 0)(4.4/10)$$
$$= E(8.5)(.44)$$
$$= E(3.74)$$

The appropriate multiplier for a company for which a 5% annual growth rate is expected is 8.14 and is computed as follows:

$$V = E\,(8.5 + 2(5))\,(4.4/10)$$
$$= E\,(18.5)\,(.44)$$
$$= E\,(8.14)$$

But Here's the Catch

Ben Graham's formula method of stock valuation is quite simple to follow but it had one serious flaw. If you recall, earlier I explained that Graham developed a series of screens to weed out those firms which could not be valued using his model. The reason was that his model had no way to adjust for much of the risk that is inherent in common stock investment. Therefore, instead of trying to modify his model to account for risk, he modified his universe of stocks so that all those which were used had low levels of risk. He used four screens which were designed to weed out all high-risk firms.

1. Eliminate all firms with negative earnings (losses).
2. Eliminate all firms with debt/total assets ratios greater than 0.60. (Those which have debt greater than 60% of their assets.)
3. Eliminate all firms with share prices greater than net current assets per share. ("Net" current assets equal current assets minus all debt, divided by the number of shares outstanding.)
4. Eliminate all firms with earnings/price ratios less than twice the existing AAA bond yield.

At one time, many firms were able to pass these four screens and thus could be valued using Graham's formula. Today, however, the same four screens are simply not an appropriate way to weed out high-risk firms while letting through firms with average levels of risk. Here's why.

While there is no problem with the application of the first two screens, the third screen fails to account for differences among industries. Low-risk firms can employ more debt to finance their operations than can high-risk firms. Furthermore, firms with larger amounts of fixed assets are usually large borrowers, since such assets serve as collateral. The result of the application of this screen would be to eliminate all firms with a large dollar amount of fixed assets and a large borrowing capacity. For example, let us take a look at Commonwealth Edison, a $5 billion (revenues) electric utility which has long been considered a high-quality stock by the investment community. At year-end 1984, the firm had $958 million in current assets, $8 billion in total debt, and 176 million common shares outstanding. At year-end 1984, the stock was selling at $28 per share.

Dollars and Sense

To apply the third screen, we subtracted total debt from current assets and divided the result by the number of shares outstanding.

$$\$958{,}000{,}000 - \$8{,}000{,}000{,}000/176{,}000{,}000 \text{ Shares}$$
$$= -\$40 \text{ Per Share}$$

According to the third screen, if the stock is selling at a price greater than the value calculated above, it is too risky to be considered. Commonwealth Edison's selling price of $28 was greater than the nonsensical -$40 calculated in the application of the third screen. Therefore, according to the screen, investment in Commonwealth Edison is too risky to consider. In fact. there is not a single utility stock in this country that could pass this third screen.

The fourth screen presents a problem as well. It fails to account for future firm growth since both high-growth and low-growth firms are subjected to the same earnings capitalization screen. Rapidly growing firms will possess high P/E ratios and much lower earnings/price ratios than slower growing firms. Therefore, this screen eliminates most new, rapidly growing firms and, instead, lets in firms which tend to produce returns from income dividends rather than long-term capital gains.

To surmount these shortcomings, I suggest that investor's apply the first two screens and then utilize the following model:

$$V = E\,(8.5 + 26)\,(6.2/AAA)\,(1/beta)$$

The factor beta accounts for the risk level of the stock, and the substitution of the 6.2 figure for the 4.4 figure gives an up-to-date estimation of average bond returns over the last 40 years. While much of Ben Graham's philosophy is still valid in today's marketplace, changing conditions require that any stock market valuation model be continually updated.

Paying Your Broker, Your Banker, The Candlestick Maker

It's difficult to make a financial move without a middleman. Still, there are some things you can do yourself and ways to stop spending for services you don't need. More help is now available with organizing and conducting your finances than anyone would have dreamed of just a few years ago. But if it seems that transaction costs and other fees eat up your profits, take heart: Wisely choosing which services are worth the price tag will keep you ahead of the game.

Granted, it's hard just keeping up with the players. In the hotly competitive new world of deregulation, bankers are trading stocks, brokers are offering checking accounts, and insurance companies are marrying up with credit card issuers and mutual funds. Nearly every major institution is aiming to eventually bring all kinds of financial services together under one roof. Fees for those services add up. And any commissions, sales charges, or other transaction costs connected with your investments reduce your "real" return. How do you avoid spending more for financial services than you have to? The answer calls for a good look at what you are paying for them now, then considering some possible alternatives for accomplishing the same goals.

Are One-Stop Accounts for You?

Perhaps the most striking example of the "supermarket" trend so far is the *asset management account*. Developed by Merrill Lynch in 1977 and widely copied since then by other brokerage houses as well as banks, these accounts give you free checking and often a Visa, MasterCard, or American Express card, and let you borrow on your investments and earn money market rates on idle cash. The admission ticket to all this convenience is high. You usually need to deposit cash or securities worth at least $10,000. And then there are annual fees, which can run anywhere from $25 to $120. Still, if you are an active investor, an asset management account might be a bargain. The yearly fees could total less than the separate charges you pay now for a checking account, credit cards, travelers' checks, and other incidentals.

Asset accounts at banks and brokerages are probably equally safe. Although only banks can offer federal deposit insurance, most large brokerages pay to insure their customers privately through the Securities Investor Protection Corp. Whether to choose a bank or brokerage for an asset account depends on your needs. For instance, check on borrowing policies. With your securities as collateral, a brokerage firm will usually loan you money for only half a percentage point more than the prime rate. Some banks charge a full 1% over prime. If you are looking for stock recommendations and information about companies, a full-service broker is the ticket. The quality of information you get elsewhere typically can't compete with the tonnage churned out by analysts at the big Wall Street securities firms.

But you have to look closely to compare other differences between bank and brokerage asset accounts. Some questions to ask:

- *How often are reinvestments made?* One of the biggest advantages of an asset management account is the so-called "sweep" which *automatically* reinvests dividends and bond income for you, typically in a money market fund yielding much more than an ordinary checking account. Sweeps are sometimes done daily, but may be done weekly, and may include all your current cash or only an amount above a certain minimum. Obviously, frequency and amount will affect your overall return. You may also have a choice of directing the money into a tax-exempt or government securities fund rather than a regular money market fund, which may be an advantage for some investors.
- *Do you want your canceled checks?* Then go with a bank asset account. Brokerage firms typically don't return the actual checks. Instead, their monthly statements usually just list the payee, the amounts, and the dates.
- *Does the account offer a debit card or a credit card?* With a credit card, which is what most of us mean by a "charge card," purchases you make using it are totaled each month and you receive a bill for the amount. With a debit card, charge purchases are immediately *deducted* from your account. Whether you choose a bank or brokerage firm, odds are you will get a debit card. Which brings us to . . .
- *What sort of overdraft protection does the account offer?* Accidentally overspending on any asset account typically activates a line of credit which covers the amount of the overdraft. The catch, of course, is the interest rate you are charged on the "loan."

Sizing Up Regular Bank Fees

Most of us don't have $10,000-plus of liquid assets to put in an asset management account. But banks and other financial institutions are offering a variety of products aimed at the average investor. As a result, even "simple" checking and savings accounts aren't simple anymore. Most banks now offer NOW and SuperNOW accounts that pay interest on checking balances.

Who's covering the cost of these new services? The consumer, of course. So shopping for the best deal on straight bank accounts can definitely save you money. A 1984 Consumer Federation of America survey of banks around the country found that fees vary widely for most services, including bounced checks and deposits drawn against insufficient funds. There was also a wide range in the service charges assessed customers who let regular checking account balances fall below specified minimums. Moreover, the survey revealed that bank policies also differ greatly on *check-holds*, or how long you have to wait before deposited checks are cleared and you can draw money against them. Another consumer federation found that the hold on out-of-state non-payroll checks, for instance, was anywhere from 2 to 20 days. In effect, this is a "hidden fee" that may penalize you in two ways: You can either use that money during the waiting period or, in a NOW or SuperNOW account, it is earning interest.

Banks tend to hold checks for less time than do savings and loans. This is because S&Ls sometimes turn their checks over to banks for processing. If you maintain a reasonable balance and do other business with your bank or S&L, you might be able to haggle over check-holds, particularly on payroll checks. Ask your financial institution what its policy is, then see how it and the service charges you are currently paying compare with the range discovered by the Consumer Federation listed in Figure 68-1.

Figure 68-1
Range of Service Charges

Type of Account	Fees/Requirements	Fee Range Low	Fee Range High
Savings	Minimum balance for interest	$0.00	$ 200.00
	Monthly fee if below minimum	0.00	3.00
Regular checking	Bounced check	7.00	20.00
	Returned deposit	0.00	12.00
NOW accounts	Minimum balance for no monthly service charge	50.00	2,500.00
	Monthly fee if below minimum	2.00	8.00
	Per check charge if below minimum	0.20	0.50

Using a Discount Broker

You can also comparison shop when it comes to broker's fees. It used to be that discount brokerage firms were "transaction-only specialists" who bought and sold stocks for a fee—period. They provided no auxiliary services like research or investment advice, which meant that the cost of trading through a discount broker was lower. In some cases, this is still true. With charges on a straight transaction (buy or sell), for example, specialty brokerage houses typically charge 25% less than full-service firms. But now the line between discounters and regular brokers—and the difference in fees they charge—is blurring. For instance, some discounters now assign you to an account executive who may try just as hard to sell you something you aren't interested in as a sale representative at any Wall Street firm. And the investment "advice" isn't free. Compare rates for the extra service with transaction-only fees and you will find the former are anywhere from 10% to 20% higher.

Some of the big discounters offer you a choice of both kinds of service. For instance, say you want to purchase 200 shares of $20 stock. If such a "straight" transaction is handled by any salesperson who happens to answer the phone, the commission might range from about $45 to $60 on this $4,000 purchase. (Typically, the percentage discount you get from any of these firms increases with the number of trades you do in a given year.) On the other hand, if you want a discount house broker to monitor your portfolio and make buy-and-sell recommendations, it might cost $62 if your account executive makes the same purchase. At a full-service firm, that $4,000 transaction would theoretically cost about $95, according to the rate schedules that most brokers use. But in practice, all the full-service firms discount, too. Depending on how much business you do with one of them, you could pay as little as $50 at one of the giants for buying the same 200 shares.

Sound confusing? It is, but there are some guidelines for deciding whether to use a discounter:

If you typically buy stock, for instance, in odd lots (fewer than 100 shares) and tend to favor low-priced shares, you will almost always pay less at a full-commission firm. Discounters usually have minimum fees. Generally, their rates only become bargains on transactions of more than $1,500.

Say you're seeing an increase in your shares of XYZ, Inc. and figure now is a good time to take your profits. A discounter probably won't tell you that "the Street" is betting on a merger you didn't know about, whereas a full-service broker who wants to keep customers will. Even if you consider yourself a well-informed investor, such advice can be well worth the price.

Are your investment needs complicated? Many discounters are expanding rapidly beyond stocks and bonds to handling other types of trades, including commodity-future contracts and switching your

Figure 68-2
Brokerage Fees: Discount versus Full Service

Discounter's Basis for Fees	Minimum Fee Per Trade	Cost to Buy/Sell 100 Shares @ $20 Share	200 Shares @ $40 Share	Municipal Bonds @ $1,000 each
Number of shares traded	$20–50	$30–50	$50–80	$5
Dollar value of shares traded	$18–20	30–40	65–80	5
Combination of number/dollar value of shares traded	$20 plus 5 cents a share/$30 flat	25–40	40–85	5
Typical Full Service Broker	None-Nominal	54	150	10

mutual fund shares. Several also offer Individual Retirement Accounts, Keogh plans, and asset management accounts. But there are other types of investments they don't handle, like new issues or tax shelters. So for one-stop shopping, the full-service firms are still the better choice.

Full-service brokers usually base their commission rates on the dollar value of trades. Discounters' fee policies vary. Some set charges according to the number of shares traded; others peg them to the dollar value of the transaction. Still others take both variables into account. Figure 68-2 provides some examples of how much discounters' fees can vary depending on the rate basis they use and how the range of their fees compares with charges for the same transactions at a typical full-service broker.

Should You Buy Treasury Securities Direct from Uncle Sam?

Whether or not to pay brokerage fees also depends on what you're investing in. For example, securities issued by the U.S. government are one of the safest investments you can make. Most banks and brokerage firms charge anywhere from $25 to $50 to buy these Treasury securities for you. But there are two types of Treasury issues—short-term bills and long-term notes and bonds. If you invest in Treasury bills and expect to sell them before they mature (anywhere from 3 months to 1 year), it's probably worth it to pay the broker's fee. That's because instead of issuing actual bills, the government uses a computerized "book entry" system that can make it difficult to get your cash early. Going through a broker can

Dollars and Sense

facilitate the process. In the case of notes and bonds, you're better off buying direct through a Federal Reserve bank or branch and saving the fees.

As is obvious by now, the question of fees very much depends on how you invest and in what. Before you do any comparison shopping, take a serious look at the kind of services you really need, then find the best price.

Time is Money

Help Wanted: Desk job in pleasant surroundings. Interesting work, almost unlimited potential for advancement. Starting pay: $50 per hour and up. Sound good? The job is really available. We're talking, of course, about the job of managing your own savings and investments.

The rate of pay isn't guaranteed. In the riskier types of investment, some of your decisions, no matter how well reasoned, may end up losing money. But the time you spend gathering information and using it to manage your assets can be very well compensated. In general, the more complex and demanding the investment, the higher its potential returns over time—if you do your homework.

The other side of the coin is the potential for loss if you don't spend enough time selecting and following your investments. A snap decision or not bothering to keep track of your program can save you a few minutes or hours—and cost you a few thousand dollars. So before you decide to buy stocks, or mutual funds, or annuities, or bank certificates of deposit, you should count the cost, in minutes as well as in dollars.

Bank Vehicles—Starting Simple

The most straightforward example of the benefit of time investment comes in bank accounts and certificates of deposit. There aren't too many variables to consider. The so-called term accounts and certificates guarantee you a specific rate of interest for a given period, and also tie your money up for that period. Federal deposit insurance (which nearly all banks have) ensures that you won't lose any principal or accumulated interest, so you don't have to worry about risk. For this type of investment, your job is to find the bank that offers the best return over the period you prefer to invest for, along with sufficient convenience in opening and handling your account. Since there are more than 14,000 banks in the country, you can't check them all. But within the category you want to deal with—banks where you already do business, for example, or banks in your own city—you can compare quite a few in a short time by phone. At an easy pace of 10 minutes a call (to allow for finding phone numbers, reaching the right bank officer, and taking notes), you can get the available rates and terms at six banks in an hour, a dozen in two hours.

What do you get for your two hours' work? A recent survey of 225 commercial banks, savings and loans, and mutual banks found differences of nearly a full percentage point in the effective annual yields they offer on some accounts and certificates of deposit, even among the dozen or so institutions with the highest rates. If you put $4,000 of your IRA money in, say, a 30-month certificate, you could easily end up with an extra $100-plus for your two hours' trouble. Not a bad rate of pay.

The work isn't quite over when you've found the right account. You'll need to maintain records, including your statements, and keep track of the maturity dates of your certificates. (If you leave your money sitting there past maturity, it will stop earning the high term rate and drop to the passbook level.) But this is a tiny chore. In essence, a few hours' work at the outset will let you do a professional job of investing in most bank offerings.

Insurance and Annuities

Insurance and *annuities* (also an insurance vehicle, but one that provides a series of payments rather than a lump sum) have definite terms and rates that can be directly compared. (This is the case for fixed-rate annuities which pay a specified periodic sum; variable-rate annuities are more like mutual funds in that payment varies depending on market conditions.) But aside from that, buying life insurance and buying annuities are two very different jobs. Buying insurance with an investment component—that is, a policy that builds up cash value for you—involves working through a number of alternatives with your insurance agent, and matching the policies available against your needs for protection plus a conservative investment vehicle. It can be a complex job. Buying a fixed rate annuity is simpler, since there are fewer options.

If you want to understand what you're getting when you buy life insurance, be prepared to spend at least two multi-hour sessions with your agent. (We're assuming that you've already done the job of tracking down a top-notch professional agent.) The first meeting will be spent mostly on fact-finding, with you filling the agent in on your situation, and the agent explaining briefly several of the possible ways of meeting your needs. He or she will then go off to work up a proposal for you, probably leaving some literature on policies for you to study. At a minimum, you should spend the time—say an hour or so—reading what the agent has provided and jotting down any questions you have. Better still, add several more hours to your time budget, and spend them at your library reading up on how insurance works and what current products are like. This is a once-only time cost, and it can pay back richly. (Also see Doses 25 and 26.)

At your second meeting with your agent, a week or so later perhaps, he or she will suggest a specific policy and answer your questions about it. If you've done some homework, you stand a much better chance of evaluating the proposal and getting insurance that's tailor-made for you, rather than force fit. Their terms and interest rates for different fixed-rate annuities can be compared relatively easily. Points of difference might include the rate of interest guaranteed at the time of purchase, how long the guarantee lasts, sales charges or loads, and withdrawal terms. Your agent may be able to provide you with a summary of these items for several annuities, which you can read through quite quickly.

However, it also makes sense to read carefully through the prospectuses of several annuities that seem to meet your requirements, to get a firm understanding of how the product works and an idea of how details differ from one annuity to another. Most of these prospectuses, like many financial documents these days, are 100% more intelligible than they were in the past. Still, if you haven't bought an annuity before, you might well spend an hour or two plowing through the first one. The next few will go much quicker. It makes sense to look at products from more than one company.

There's still one more job to do before settling on an annuity. As investors in Baldwin-United annuities learned to their cost, all insurance companies are not created equal. You can't just pick the highest interest rate and walk away. You want assurance that the company you invest with is unshakably solid. The first cut (and most of the work) on this point should be done by your agent. If you've picked one who's really on the ball, you'll never be offered an annuity from an obviously weak or unreliable company.

But it doesn't hurt to wear a belt and suspenders. A.M. Best Company rates insurance companies for financial soundness. Be sure that the information you get from your agent includes their rankings, and stick with high-rated, established firms. In addition, you'd do well to make one phone call to the insurance commission of the state in which the company is based, before you actually invest. The commission can tell you whether the company has had any financial or consumer problems.

Mutual Funds

As with bank and insurance investments, the work of investing in mutual funds is concentrated at the beginning. The big job is

Dollars and Sense

selecting the fund. Record-keeping and monitoring are somewhat more complex than for a bank certificate or an annuity, but still not burdensome.

To sum up, you'll want to go through these steps when selecting a fund.
1. Set your goals. Decide how much risk you can take on, how long you can leave your money at work, and what your income needs are.
2. Screen a large number of funds—at least a dozen— preferably using an independent source of information, such as Wiesenberger's Investment Companies Service. (It's available at public libraries.) Narrow down the possibilities to a few funds. (See Dose 44—Mutual Fund Evaluation.)
3. Send away for the fund prospectuses, current annual and quarterly reports, and statement of Additional Information. Go through each set, comparing the information on investment objectives, philosophy, and performance with your initial impression of the funds from Wiesenberger.

Even if you already have your overall investment plan in good order and know pretty well what kind of fund you need, each of these steps is at least a multi-hour job. If you do it right, you'll probably put in the equivalent of several full days' work, interrupted by the wait for the prospectuses to arrive. Once you buy a fund, the record-keeping is perfectly simple. With the advent of computers, mutual fund account statements have become so complete, frequent, and prompt that all you have to do is read and file them or use the "Mutual Fund Recordsheet" provided in Dose 50.

But in addition to the bookkeeping, it's your job to ride herd on your fund manager. Short-term investment results seldom mean much, but as the quarters and the years go by, you should know how your fund has done, compared both to your expectations and to other funds with similar objectives. This means periodic study of a mutual fund information service, such as Wiesenberger, and preferably keeping your own running record of the fund's results. Also, you should carefully read the fund manager's regular reports, especially concerning the changes in the portfolio and the reasons for them. Funds can change over time—sometimes as a result of announced management policy, but also through sheer drift, as when a fund manager wanders from the fund's stated goals and methods in search of greener pastures (or more fashionable holdings). If your fund changes, but your goals haven't, you need a new fund.

This job of monitoring your fund isn't burdensome: a couple of hours a quarter and an occasional trip to the library should do it. But if you just sock your shares away and ignore them instead, you may end up with worse results than you bargained for, from a kind of fund you didn't know you owned.

Your Own Portfolio

Learning enough to make sensible stock and bond selections is the big time in investment. If you want to pick your own portfolio of stocks and bonds, you'll not only have to get a good deal of education before starting, but you'll also be taking on a permanent assignment of research and monitoring. Learning the basics of the market on your own time is a multi-month job, at the very least. There's no shortage of books on the subject, or of adult education courses and seminars. And absorbing this education is definitely work. Avoid any book or course with the theme "It's Perfectly Simple" or "Anyone Can Make a Million in Ten Minutes a Day."

Once you feel you know the ropes, you still won't be ready to plunge into the markets with real money. Invest on paper for a while. If you're a long-term investor (as all nonprofessional investors should be) you won't be able to duplicate the full course of an investment plan on paper, since that would delay your actual start-up for one or two business cycles (which could be a matter of a few years)! But you can experiment on paper with the job of selecting a small, but balanced and diversified, group of stocks, doing the calculations, and keeping your records. Hardest of all, you'll have to face your own mistakes, including the job of trying to figure out whether they are mistakes.

Once started in the real market, you'll have to monitor your holdings. No matter what your investment philosophy, each day brings new information on the economy and the market which changes the prospects for, and the values of, your securities. You'll need to keep up with these developments, make the calculations that let you draw your own conclusions, and then make any needed changes in your portfolio.

How long will that take? There's no hard and fast rule, but here are a few indicators:

The average subscriber to *The Wall Street Journal* spends 51 minutes a day reading it. An individual investor might spend less, but probably not much less. (My own opinion—prejudice, if you like—is that a willingness to spend some time with *The Journal* every day is the single best indicator that you're ready to choose your own stocks.) You should also scan the weekly and monthly business press, such as *Business Week* and *Dun's Business Month*.

Each company whose stock you own will send you one annual and four quarterly reports. You should study them all carefully. Most stockbrokers can provide regular reports on the companies whose stocks you own as well as on their competitors and their industries. These reports are prepared by the research departments in most brokerage houses. So-called "discount brokers" do not provide such services, which is one reason that their fees are lower. You should read all the research reports as they come out. You'll need to keep some perspective on the current market for your securities and

Dollars and Sense

also for stocks in companies and industries you haven't invested in. Only if you do this will you have a good sense of the relative values of the securities you own. Information provided by a factual market service (not "market opinion" newsletters that describe over 1,700 listed and unlisted stocks and tend to reflect only the views of the "experts" who write them) is a must. I always found the Value Line Investment Survey useful.

The exact amount of time invested depends on you, but it won't be small. For comparison, we telephoned a friend who's a talented amateur golfer. It seems that her row of trophies was achieved at a time price of about 15 hours a week during the golfing season. For most of us, running home, holding down jobs, and raising families, 15 hours pushes the absolute limit of time that could be spent on any extra activity. You can regard your stock portfolio as a competitor for the time you might otherwise spend on a totally absorbing hobby.

The comparison to a hobby isn't frivolous. Investing is a fascinating pastime to some people, one that pays them well for doing work they enjoy. But if you don't enjoy the work, you're going to regret the commitment and the time lost because of it. Worse still, you may stop keeping up with your holdings in favor of an extra round on the course (or an afternoon in the garden or an episode of "Dallas"). In that case, you can count on losing your money instead of your time.

There's no "right" amount of time to spend managing your money. But there is a connection between the time you can spend and complexity of the investments you can handle. If you match these correctly, any sensible program can give you highly satisfactory results.

How Risky Are Your Investments?

Risk—the possibility that you will lose money on an investment—is an important consideration when you're choosing investments. Of course, there's a trade-off. The greater the risk, the greater the potential return from an investment—but the greater, too, the potential for loss. Low-risk investments also offer relatively low returns—but the returns are almost assured. To create an optimal portfolio—according to theory, at least—an investor has to decide how much risk he or she is comfortable with and invest for the highest possible returns at that risk level. This is sound financial management practice, but often risk considerations are applied only to an investor's stock and bond portfolio without considering the overall investment portfolio. In addition to financial assets (stocks and bonds), your portfolio includes human capital, real estate, and other economic assets. The risk/return characteristics of these assets should dictate the level of risk you can and should assume in the financial asset portion of your overall portfolio.

Personal Wealth

Most investors are familiar with the financial statements prepared by public corporations. The annual income statement shows the financial activities of the firm over the last 12 months. The "bottom line" of such statements is net income which shows the increase in value of the firm over the previous year. Firm value (or wealth) is shown on another financial statement, the balance sheet. This document lists the value of assets controlled by the firm and how these assets were financed. The total value of the firm's assets minus financing/supplied by creditors (total debt) equals the firm's net worth.

To determine personal net worth, you must prepare your own personal balance sheet. Figure 70-1 (Part I) shows the asset side of the personal balance sheet. (Note that, to determine personal net worth, the current market value of assets, not historical cost, is

Dollars and Sense

Figure 70-1
Personal Investment Balance Sheet

I. Value of Overall Portfolio

	Dollar Value	Risk Level Low, Moderate, or High
Human capital	_____	_____
Residence (net)	_____	_____
Other real estate (net)	_____	_____
Liquid assets	_____	_____
Pensions	_____	_____
Financial asset portfolio	_____	_____
Collectibles and other "hard assets"	_____	_____
Value of business interest	_____	_____
Other investments	_____	_____
Total	_____	_____

II. Portfolio Composition

	Dollar Value	Percent of Total Portfolio
Human capital	_____	_____
Real estate (net)	_____	_____
Liquid assets	_____	_____
Stocks (including mutual funds)	_____	_____
Bonds (including mutual funds)	_____	_____
Business equity	_____	_____
Hard assets	_____	_____
Other	_____	_____
Total	_____	_____

III. Summary of Portfolio Risk

	Dollar Value of Assets With that Risk	Percentage of Total Assets at that Risk Level
High risk	_____	_____
Moderate risk	_____	_____
Low risk	_____	_____
Total	_____	_____

used.) Assets listed include the major subclassifications of overall personal wealth: the value of human capital (the present value of your future earnings), the market value of your home (net of any existing mortgages), other real estate holdings (net), liquid assets (bank accounts, money market mutual funds, Treasury bills, etc.), the current value of any pension assets (if you are vested), the value of your stock and bond portfolio, collectibles (including gold and silver), the market value of any business interests you hold, and other investments. The total is personal wealth.

We have excluded the value of automobiles and other personal assets like furniture since these items are generally not investments in the sense that they are not purchased with the intention of making a profit. Also, we have not included liabilities like an auto loan, credit card debt, or other consumer installment debt for the same reason. These debts represent payment for noninvestment assets.

Remember, our ultimate goal is to decide the composition of your financial asset (stock and bond) portfolio. We begin by filling out Part I in Figure 70-1. "Human capital" is the present value of your expected future earnings. This item is generally the largest component of personal wealth. A young college graduate with few tangible assets, for example, may find that future earning power represents nearly 100% of personal wealth. A retiree, on the other hand, may find that future earning power is a negligible component of total net worth. To determine the value of your "human capital," you must forecast future aftertax earnings for each year you plan to keep working and then "discount" those earnings back to the present. This somewhat complex procedure involves expressing future earnings in terms of what they are worth today. To do this, an appropriate discount rate is used. See "What Is Your Future Worth", Dose 5.

The value of your personal "residence" is an estimate of the net proceeds if you sold your home. The estimate is reduced by any sales fees, repayment of any mortgages, and capital gains taxes if applicable. The value of other real estate holdings (rental property, a vacation home, or other investment property) is determined in a similar manner.

"Pension" assets include the value of vested rights in any company-sponsored plans plus the assets held in an IRA, Keogh, or any other plans that you invest in personally. If you are unsure of the value of any vested corporate pension rights, your employer or pension trustee can supply the data.

The dollar value of these various components is your net worth. The next step is an analysis of the risk of each component. We've simplified this somewhat by assigning each to a category—low, moderate, or high—but a certain amount of subjective judgment will be needed to classify the components.

The risk of an asset is affected by several factors, including how it is financed. For example, consider two individuals living side by side in identical condominium apartments in downtown Chicago. Both have assessed the resale value of their residence at $200,000 (the price recently obtained by a seller down the hall). But, one purchased the condo for cash while the other has a $175,000 variable-rate mortgage, which means that monthly payments could rise substantially, which would also lower the value of the condo as an asset. Even though both residences are identical in all other respects, the method of financing has made the $25,000 net value of one residence very risky while ownership of the other involves only moderate risk.

Further, the riskiness of one component is frequently affected by its relationship to other components. Consider a second example. Suppose that both residences have been financed with a $150,000, 30-year, fixed-interest mortgage. However, one owner is a physician who has been practicing in the Chicago area for 20 years. The other residence is owned by a highly paid linebacker for the Chicago Bears football team. An injury could prematurely end the career of the pro athlete and abruptly terminate his high level of anticipated future income. This could also lead to a forced sale of his residence at a distress price. Thus, the high level of risk associated with the value of the athlete's human capital has caused the risk of his real estate holding to increase substantially beyond the risk level of the residence of the physician next door.

As you can see from these examples, it is important to consider the riskiness of a single component of your wealth in the context of the total package of assets you hold.

Portfolio Composition and Overall Risk Position

Part II in Figure 70-1 restates the value of the assets listed in Part I in terms of the *type* of asset held (real estate, stocks, bonds, etc.). Both the dollar value of the assets and the percentage they represent in your overall portfolio are specified. To complete this section of the table, enter the value of human capital, the total net value of real estate holdings, and the value of all assets (regardless of whether these are held in pension plans, personal bank accounts, etc.). The same determination should be made for stock and bond holdings. Note that these two categories include assets held directly and indirectly (actual shares, pensions, and assets held in trust). The total dollar value of Part II should agree with the total value in Part I. To determine the percentages, merely divide the total value of your overall portfolio by the value assigned each component and multiply by 100%.

Part III of Figure 70-1 allows you to summarize the composition of your total portfolio in terms of our three risk categories—both as a dollar amount and as a percentage of your portfolio. The figures are simply the sums of the values you assigned to each risk level in the first two parts of the figure. Parts II and III give you a quick assessment of the composition of your overall portfolio and your overall level of risk.

This assessment is very important. The composition of your investment portfolio is a discretionary decision, as is not true of many other aspects of your total net worth. By varying the composition of your investment portfolio, you can change the overall riskiness of your entire wealth portfolio. Reviewing the risk levels of the nondiscretionary portions of your overall wealth portfolio will dictate the composition and risk level which *should* be assumed in your investment portfolio. For example, if your nondiscretionary assets involve very low levels of risk, you can and should assume large risks in the discretionary portions of your investment portfolio. Once the level of risk of the investment portfolio has been specified, investors can narrow their search to specific assets with the desired risk characteristics.

Portfolio Composition: An Example

The following example shows how the various items in Figure 70-1 are calculated and how an assessment of worth can be used to guide the composition and maintenance of the discretionary investment portfolio.

John Robinson, a 40-year-old engineering professor, has been teaching at a Midwestern university for the past 12 years. He is a valued faculty member and has tenure with the university which means his job is pretty secure. John's wife recently resigned from an administrative position when their son was born. John's annual salary is $50,000 and he nets $44,000 after taxes. He expects his salary to grow at the average rate of 5% per year over the 25 years before he retires at age 65. The Robinsons own a home with a current market value of $120,000 and owe $80,000 on a first mortgage. They also own a vacation cottage valued at $60,000 on which they have a $30,000 mortgage. A few years ago, John and a colleague founded a small metal stamping company and John was recently offered $100,000 for his 50% ownership in the firm. The university participates in a private teachers' pension plan, and John has vested rights which amount to $52,000. Approximately 75% of the plan's assets are invested in S&P 500 stocks and 25% are invested in long-term bonds. In addition to $25,000 held in bank accounts and money market mutual funds, John has also invested $10,000 in gold coins, $25,000 in growth-oriented common stock mutual funds, and $10,000 in municipal bonds.

Figure 70-2 shows the Robinson family's wealth profile. Their net wealth is $700,000 and largely consists of the current value of John's expected future income from his teaching career (62% of total wealth). John's ability to continue teaching is the family's most valuable asset. Due to university tenure, John has rated the risk of this asset as low. Stability of current employment also means that the family's real estate holdings have a moderate risk rating. In terms of the overall portfolio, 11% of the family's total wealth has been classified as high risk, 24% as moderate risk, and 65% as low risk. As a result, the overall portfolio contains very little risk.

The discretionary portion of John's portfolio (liquid assets, financial asset portfolio, and gold coins) represents approximately 9% of the family's total wealth and involves moderate to low risk.

Dollars and Sense

Figure 70-2

I. Value of Overall Portfolio

	Dollar Value	Risk Level
Human capital	$435,000	Low
Residence (net)	40,000	Moderate
Other real estate (net)	30,000	Moderate
Liquid assets	25,000	Low
Pensions	50,000	Moderate
Financial asset portfolio	35,000	Moderate
Collectibles and other "hard assets"	10,000	Moderate
Value of business interest	75,000	High
Other investments	0	
Total	**$700,000**	

II. Portfolio Composition

	Dollar Value	Percent of Total Portfolio
Human capital	$435,000	62%
Real estate (net)	70,000	10
Liquid assets	25,000	4
Stocks (including mutual funds)	62,000	9
Bonds (including mutual funds)	23,000	3
Business equity	75,000	11
Hard assets	10,000	1
Other	0	0
Total	**$700,000**	**100%**

III. Summary of Portfolio Risk

	Dollar Value of Assets With that Risk	Percentage of Total Assets at that Risk Level
High risk	$ 75,000	11%
Moderate risk	165,000	24
Low risk	460,000	65
Total	**$700,000**	**100%**

Given the low level of risk in the overall portfolio and the fact that John has a long time to accumulate additional wealth before he retires, he can and probably should increase his level of risk. Aggressive growth mutual funds and high-risk common stocks should be substituted for the more conservative mutual funds and municipal bonds which he currently holds. Finally, additional investment funds obtained in the future should be committed to higher risk, growth-oriented equity investments. In this way, the risk level of the overall portfolio can be gradually increased. Increasing the overall risk level will ultimately lead to greater long-term returns.

The Price You Pay For the Best Investment Returns

Over the long run, the best way to consistently "beat" inflation and thereby increase the real value of your investment portfolio is by holding a well-diversified portfolio of common stocks. Other types of financial assets have historically offered little or no "real" (after-inflation) returns. However, the "extra" return that you can earn by investing in common stocks is only half the story. Greater potential returns in the financial markets are almost always accompanied by greater amounts of risk.

To illustrate the additional risk you assume when you invest in common stocks, consider the following scenario. During the 20-year period 1965-84, common stocks (as measured by the Standard & Poor's 500 Index) provided investors an average compound annual return of 7.8%. Treasury bills which, because they are issued by the Federal government, involve almost no risk, returned an average of only 7.0% per year. But consumer prices over the same period rose at the average rate of 6.3% annually. Common stocks, therefore, would have been the best way to achieve a real increase in wealth during that period.

Here is where risk comes into play. The 1965-84 period was marked by two subperiods during which common stock prices declined sharply. From June 1968 through June 1970, the S&P 500 Index of common stocks dropped by nearly 26%. Thus, while common stock returns "beat" inflation over the entire period, during shorter periods, stock market investors were subject to a roller coaster ride. For example, if you had invested $1,000 in common stocks in June 1968, your portfolio would have declined by $262 over the next two years, as Figure 71-1 shows. On the other hand, if you had invested that $1,000 in "risk-free" Treasury bills over the same period, the value of your portfolio would have increased by $103.

Figure 71-1
Portfolio Strategies

	100% Stocks, 0% T-Bills	75% Stocks, 25% T-Bills	50% Stocks, 50% T-Bills	25% Stocks, 75% T-Bills	0% Stocks, 100% T-Bills
June 30, 1968—June 30, 1970					
Beginning portfolio value	$1,000	$1,000	$1,000	$1,000	$1,000
Return (loss)	(26.2)%	(17.1)%	(8.0)%	+1.2%	+10.3%
Ending portfolio value	$ 738	$ 829	$ 920	$1,012	$1,103
December 31, 1973—September 30, 1974					
Beginning portfolio value	$1,000	$1,000	$1,000	$1,000	$1,000
Return (loss)	(37.3)%	(24.1)%	(10.9)%	+2.3%	+15.5%
Ending portfolio value	$ 627	$ 759	$ 891	$1,023	$1,155
1965-85 Compound Annual Rate	8.8%	8.4%	8.0%	7.5%	7.1%

Dollars and Sense

How, then, can a conservative investor achieve real growth of wealth without assuming a great degree of risk? The answer is to build a portfolio consisting of a combination of common stocks and risk-free securities. Such a portfolio can easily be tailored to "fit" the amount of risk an investor is willing to accept. Figure 71-1 illustrates several possible portfolio combinations, their returns during the two market downturns mentioned above, and their compound annual return over the period 1965-85. A moderately "aggressive" investor (in terms of risk) may choose a combination of 75% common stocks and 25% Treasury bills. While such an investor's losses during the market downturns would have been sizable, the superior long-run performance of his portfolio (7.5% compound annual return) may be high enough for him to justify the added risk. A more conservative investor, however, may prefer an even split between common stocks and Treasury bills. Of course, the actual combination of common stocks and risk-free assets that would be best for your portfolio depends upon your own attitudes toward risk and your need for investment return.

Portfolio Diversification: A Matter of Time and Assets

It goes without saying that investors in common stock assume risk in their quest for investment returns. However, investors who hold a *diversified* portfolio—who invest in a variety of assets—better their odds because they spread their risk over a number of investments. Chances are, when some go down, others will go up. As a result, investors who have a diversified portfolio are really only affected by major changes in the overall market—what is referred to as *market risk*. Current research suggests that common stock portfolios should contain *at least* 12 different issues and a maximum of about 30 for proper diversification.

But diversification is more than just how many assets you hold. It also involves when you buy and sell different assets—*time diversification*. By spreading their purchases or sales over time, investors are protected against making large investments at market peaks—and thereby paying premium prices—or selling at a market bottom and "taking a bath." Investors who hold several assets and gradually spoon in and out of the market—who don't commit a large amount of capital at any one time—avoid taking unnecessary investment risk.

While this is easy in theory, diversification can be quite complex for most of us in practice. For example, if you have a limited amount of capital to invest, you may not be able to diversify your assets. Investors who, for various reasons, find themselves completely "out" of the stock market but want to invest in stocks face the problem of time diversification. Finally, if you're in the fortunate position of having large amounts of new capital to invest each year, you also face the problem of time diversification. If these descriptions fit, help is on the way! Here are three examples that may help with your diversification problems.

Example I John Little currently has $10,000 to invest. He intends to add about $5,000 each year to his portfolio. Although John does not own any stocks, he's convinced that he should be investing in the "market." His investment goal is appreciation of the capital he invests, and he is willing to assume the necessary investment risks (in fact, John classifies himself as an aggressive investor). He does not need income from his investments to meet current living expenses.

Our recommendation for aggressive investors such as John is to commit 70% of his investment capital to equities and 30% to liquid assets. (Liquid assets are investments that can be called in almost immediately with no loss. A bank savings account is an example, so is a U.S. government Treasury bill. A house or a stock isn't liquid because it can't be sold immediately—at least not at the price the seller wants. Any investment portfolio should contain some liquid assets, just in case.) John should now hold $7,000 in common stocks and $3,000 in liquid assets. However, since John does not currently have enough capital to build a diversified portfolio of common stocks, and since he currently holds no stocks, he is faced with both asset and time diversification in building a portfolio.

The problem of asset diversification can be solved if John initially invests in common stock mutual funds rather than directly in common stocks. Mutual funds are discussed in greater detail in Doses 42 through 53. At this point, suffice it to say that a mutual fund is a portfolio of various stocks (or other investments) managed by a professional analyst. A share in a mutual fund gives you an investment in all the assets in the fund's portfolio. Once John has accumulated enough to let him invest directly in common stocks, he can begin shifting his mutual fund investments. Until that time, he should invest in two to four different common stock mutual funds.

The second problem—time diversification—can be solved through using *dollar cost averaging* (discussed in Dose 73). This involves investing a fixed amount at preset intervals. In our example, John would invest no more than 10% of his available capital in the stock market at any one point in time. First, John would invest $1,000 in common stock mutual funds every six months or whenever stock prices fall by 10% (whichever occurs first). Thus, John would invest $1,000 in a common stock mutual fund now. If stock prices do not fall by 10% over the next six months, he would make his next purchase at the end of the period. If stocks fall during the specified time (six months), John would buy earlier, taking advantage of lower prices. John should also consider adding a second common stock mutual fund at the time of the second purchase.

Since an additional investment of $5,000 is planned each year, the same technique can be used to invest this additional capital (i.e., invest half every six months or when stock prices fall by at least 10%). As total investment capital grows (due to new cash injections, rising stock prices, and dividends and interest from investments), John may wish to begin building his own portfolio of common stocks rather than continue adding to his mutual fund investments. This might be accomplished as follows. Suppose that John's portfolio consists of $40,000 in common stock mutual funds, and $17,000 in liquid assets. At this point, instead of continuing to purchase additional mutual fund shares with new investment capital, he might acquire the common stocks of two or three companies (approximately $2,000 invested in each). While a portfolio consisting entirely of two stocks does not provide adequate asset diversification, when these stocks are coupled with mutual fund investments, the overall portfolio risk is greatly reduced. When at least eight different stocks have been acquired, mutual fund shares can be periodically sold and the proceeds invested in additional common stock issues until the minimum number for adequate diversification has been reached. At that time, common stock mutual fund investments can be abandoned.

Example II Sally Wilson, an attorney in her mid-40s, has $60,000 to invest. Currently, her only financial asset is a bank certificate of deposit which will mature this month. She classifies herself as an aggressive investor and believes that she should be investing in the stock market. She plans to add about $10,000 each year to her investment portfolio.

As in the previous example, our recommendation would be to hold a portfolio consisting of 30% ($18,000) in liquid assets and 70% ($42,000) in common stocks. While Sally has sufficient assets to invest directly in common stocks while holding the required minimum number for proper asset diversification, the fact that she is not in the stock market at this time presents the problem of time diversification.

To solve this problem, she should follow the plan outlined for John (i.e., invest approximately 10% of her existing capital in common stock mutual funds every six months or when stock prices fall by 10%, whichever occurs first). In addition she can invest the $10,000 she plans to add each year as follows: $3,500 in common stock mutual funds every six months or on market declines. Once the common stock portion of the overall portfolio grows to approximately $20,000, she can begin adding individual common stocks to the portfolio and begin to gradually shift mutual fund assets to common stock investments. In this way her portfolio is being built without violating the principles of both asset and time diversification.

Example III Bob Carpenter, 50, has $200,000 to invest and considers himself a conservative investor. He owns no common stocks at this time, will only be able to add modest amounts of additional capital to the portfolio each year, and does not need investment income to meet present needs.

Conservative investors like Bob (who do not need current income), should put 60% ($120,000) in common stocks and 40% ($80,000) in liquid assets. Although Bob has no common stock investments at this time, he has enough capital to buy common stocks right from the start and still obtain asset and time diversification. The accumulation process would be as follows. First, he should invest equal amounts in each of 12 different common stocks (approximate value $20,000). In six months or when stock prices fall by 10% (whichever occurs first), he should invest an additional $20,000 in an *additional* 12 common stocks. In another six months (or after stock prices decline by 10%) he should invest approximately $20,000 in the common stock issues that he *now holds*.

Note that with a larger amount of capital, Bob has the advantage over the previous investors in that he can begin building a common stock portfolio directly from the start without sacrificing either time or asset diversification.

These examples were not meant to be all-inclusive. Investment portfolios must be built around the unique needs and objectives of each individual investor. However, while many investors know where they want to invest their capital, they become confused about the best road to take when building the desired portfolio. Especially in periods of rapidly rising stock prices, investors who do not currently hold common stocks are afraid of being left behind if the stock market continues to surge to new highs. At the same time, they are also aware that buying anything when it is selling at an all-time high price could be dangerous to their financial well-being.

Through these simplified examples, we showed how an investor can enter the stock market without taking undue risks. Further, if you held a mirror to these examples, the reverse image would indicate how you should get out of the stock market while preserving asset and time diversification (i.e., reducing investment risk) along the way.

Dollar Cost Averaging: The Ins and Outs of Playing the Market by Numbers

More than 50 years ago, a successful investor was asked how he amassed his fortune in the stock market. Supposedly, he answered, "It's rather simple. I buy low and sell high." Sounds simple. But many modern-day market players have found that turning this into action is a difficult task indeed. In fact, a great many investors end up playing the game in reverse. They buy high (when the financial world is full of optimism) and sell low (when the doomsayers are ringing the death knell for equities). Even the pros get caught up in stock market emotionalism and find it difficult to buy at market bottoms and sell at market tops.

In an effort to reduce the emotional aspects of investing, many have turned to playing the market by numbers. The most widely publicized and most practiced numerological games played by investors are dollar cost averaging and formula planning.

In reviewing what securities salespeople and the financial press have said about these number games, we found a great deal of misinformation. Some tout these strategies as panaceas while others summarily dismiss them as a gimmick used to sell stocks and as a waste of investors' time and money.

In an effort to straighten out a few misconceptions, we decided to explore the nature of these investment strategies: how they work and their advantages and disadvantages. Here we will focus on dollar cost averaging. Formulas are discussed in "Investing by Formula," Dose 74.

Take a Taste First

The principle behind dollar cost averaging applies to all of life, as well as investing: Just because you have a good idea doesn't mean you should instantly jump in with both feet. When you're buying common stocks, this translates into "spooning in." If a stock looks attractive, you buy a little now, keep an eye on the company, buy a little more later, keep watching ... and so on, until you've built up a complete holding.

This gives you time to check your first impression of the company. It has another advantage as well: It averages your purchase cost over a fairly long period. You're protected from the market enthusiasms that lure investors into buying stocks just when everyone loves them—when they're most likely to be overpriced. Further, regular stock purchases of equal (or nearly equal) dollar amounts allow you to accumulate more shares at lower prices—at the time when it seems as though the love affair with stocks has terminated and everyone is selling out—when stocks are most likely to be underpriced.

Dollar cost averaging your way into the stock market works best when you expect to be able to constantly inject new capital into your investment portfolio over a long period of time. Thus, dollar cost averaging appears to be especially attractive for IRA, Keogh, or pension plan investors.

How It Works

To understand how dollar cost averaging works, let's consider the story of our favorite hypothetical investor, D.C. Anderson. Back in January 1980, D.C. decided to take a flyer in the stock market. He singled out Eastern Airlines as his intended purchase and committed his entire nest egg of $9,600 to this one stock. With the stock selling for $8 per share, he obtained 1,200 shares. Since January 1980, the share price of this stock has wandered between $13 and $3.50 and is currently trading at $9. Since this company did not pay any dividends over this period, the current value of D.C.'s portfolio is $10,800 (1,200 times $9.00) which represents an increase of 12.5%. D.C. could have improved his return by selecting a better investment—easy to say now! He also could have improved the return on *this* investment by "spooning in" rather than jumping in all at once.

Equal Share Purchases Suppose that D.C. purchased 100 shares of Eastern Airlines common stock twice each year (in January and July). By buying 100 shares twice a year, D.C. would have acquired 1,200 shares by July 1985. But, the total cost of his investment would have been $8,800, and the average price paid per share would have been $7.33 (instead of the $8 he paid at the beginning of 1980). With a current value of $10,800, systematic purchase of *equal share* amounts would have resulted in a gain of 22.7%. The results of these systematic purchases are illustrated in Figure 73-1.

Dollar Cost Averaging The right-hand side of Figure 73-1 illustrates systematic investing using dollar cost averaging. Rather than the regular purchase of equal numbers of shares, dollar cost

Figure 73-1
Equal Share Purchases vs. Dollar Cost Averaging—Eastern Airlines

Date	Share Price	Purchase Equal Share Amounts Amount Invested	Shares Acquired	Dollar Cost Average (DCA) Amount Invested	Shares Acquired
1/80	$8	$800	100	800	100
7/80	10	1,000	100	800	80
1/81	7	700	100	770	110
7/81	9	900	100	810	90
1/82	5	500	100	800	160
7/82	5	500	100	800	160
1/83	9	900	100	810	90
7/83	10	1,000	100	800	80
1/84	7	700	100	770	110
7/84	4	400	100	800	200
1/85	4	400	100	800	200
7/85	10	1,000	100	800	80
Recent	9				
Totals		$8,800	1,200	$9,560	1,460

	Purchase All 1,200 Shares on 1/80	Purchase Equal Share Amounts	Dollar Cost Average
Current portfolio value	$10,800	$10,800	$10,800
Average cost	$8.00	$7.33	$6.55
Increase in portfolio value	$1,200	$2,000	$3,580
Percent increase	12.5%	22.7%	34.7%

275

averaging involves periodic purchase of equal dollar amounts of stock. As an example, perhaps $1,000 worth of stock is purchased every four months. With this strategy, fewer shares are purchased when the stock price rises, and more shares are bought when the price falls because a *fixed amount* of money is invested. Using this strategy, had D.C. purchased (nearly) equal *dollar* amounts of Eastern Airlines stock, he would have accumulated 1,460 shares at a total cost of $9,560. His average price per share ($9,560 divided by 1,460) would have been $6.55. With his current portfolio valued at $13,140, he would have gained 37.4% on his investment. Notice that if he purchased *equal dollar amounts* of stock rather than *equal number of shares*, the average price per share decreased from $7.33 to $6.55. The lower average price per share results from the acquisition of more shares when the stock price falls and the purchase of fewer shares at higher prices. Notice also that in January 1980, with the share price at $8, $800 purchased 100 shares, while $800 purchased 200 shares during July 1984, when the share price had fallen to $4.

While dollar cost averaging does not automatically result in buying low and selling high, at least you are buying more at lower prices and tempering your purchases when prices are relatively high. Furthermore, systematic investing allowed D.C. to spoon in and thus avoid the possibility that the stock price on the day of a single purchase is at an all-time high.

Before You Get Carried Away

Some alleged market experts have touted dollar cost averaging as a foolproof way to make money trading stocks. If you use this technique, they say, your cost per share is mathematically guaranteed to be lower than the average of the prices on the days you bought, since you bought larger numbers of shares on days when the price was low. Assuming that the average price of the stock continues to be the same over the period when you're selling out, you automatically have a gain.

Anyone not unconscious or hypnotized can see the fallacy in this logic: There's no reason for that assumption to hold. Your stock's price may dip temporarily during the buying period and then recover completely. But it may just as likely continue to spiral downward, belching black smoke, and finally crash in flames. In that case, dollar cost averaging will merely reduce the amount you lose per share, while increasing your total losses. Consider, for example, a dollar cost averaging investment program applied to Continental Illinois Holding Corporation common stock over the same period. (See Figure 73-2.) In this case, our hypothetical dollar cost averager began buying Continental Bank Holdings at $24, paid as much as $34 per share and as little as $2 per share. Alas, however, the 848 shares accumulated over the course of the dollar cost aver-

Figure 73-2
Dollar Cost Averaging
Continental Illinois Holding Corp.

Date	Share Price	Amount Invested	Shares Acquired
1/80	$24	$1,200	50
1/81	33	1,188	36
1/82	34	1,190	35
1/83	20	1,200	60
1/84	18	1,206	67
1/85	2	1,200	600
Current	0.75	—	—
Total		$7,184	848

Average cost	$8.47
Current portfolio value	$636
Loss on investment	91.1%

aging program commanded a per share market value of $0.75. The current portfolio value of $636 represents a loss of 91%.

Don't let anyone tell you that dollar cost averaging will guarantee investment profits. The results of any long-term investment depend far more on the fortunes of the underlying company than on any other factor.

Although easing in and out of investments is a good idea, as was illustrated in the previous examples, systematic purchases and sale of securities through dollar cost averaging does not provide a guarantee of investment success. Remember, dollar cost averaging works best when investing in an asset whose price varies considerably over the economic cycle yet always ends on a higher note. Such is the case with the stock market as a whole.

Averaging and Mutual Funds

Given the above, dollar cost averaging appears to be ideally suited for mutual fund investors. First, since you can purchase fractional shares of most funds, it is possible to invest equal dollar amounts. Second, with no-load mutual funds, investors do not pay a sales commission and thus can regularly make small purchases without having to bear excessive transactions costs. (The transaction costs in equity trading may offset any gain from dollar cost averaging.) Third, and most important, is the fact that most common stock mutual funds are *widely diversified* and thus to some degree track the stock market averages over time. That is, like the stock market, they are subject to highly variable swings in value but over the long term generally head to higher ground.

Figure 73-3 illustrates a dollar cost averaging program applied to the Vanguard Index Trust over the period 1977-84. This particu-

Figure 73-3
**Dollar Cost Averaging
Vanguard Index Trust**

Quarter	Amount Invested	Number of Shares Acquired	Number of Cumulative Shares	Per Share Dividend	Number of Shares from Reinvestment of Dividend	Total Shares	Portfolio Value
1977 1Q	$500	33.944	33.944	$.13	.327	34.271	$462.32
2Q	500	37.065	71.336	.13	.674	72.010	990.86
3Q	500	36.337	108.347	.13	1.065	109.412	1447.52
4Q	500	37.793	147.205	.18	2.037	149.242	1941.64
1978 1Q	500	38.432	187.674	.14	2.155	189.829	2314.02
2Q	500	41.017	230.846	.14	2.477	233.323	3044.86
3Q	500	38.314	271.637	.14	2.709	274.346	3851.82
4Q	500	35.613	309.959	.23	5.434	315.393	4137.95
1Q	500	38.110	353.503	.15	3.823	357.326	4956.11
2Q	500	36.049	393.375	.15	4.188	397.563	5601.66
...	...	...	...	...	...	...	...
1984 1Q	500	25.381	1,268.767	.18	11.969	1,280.736	24,436.45
2Q	500	26.205	1,306.941	.18	12.785	1,319.726	24,282.96
3Q	500	27.174	1,346.890	.18	12.134	1,359.024	27,153.30
4Q	500	25.025	1,384.049	.82	58.141	1,442.190	28,151.55

lar no-load mutual fund was selected for the example because it seeks to duplicate the movement of the Standard & Poor's Composite Stock Index by investing in the 500 companies that make up the index. We could have selected a more aggressive fund, which would have given even better results. However, we did not want to bias our results by selecting a more variable but more rapidly growing fund.

We began the dollar cost averaging program in 1977 and made the first of four annual purchases of $500 at the end of March. Thus, $2,000 (in addition to automatic reinvestment of dividends paid on the shares) was invested in the fund each year. Note that after eight years of investing (a total of $16,000), the value of the portfolio at the end of 1984 was $28,152. Of the total 1,442 shares obtained at the end of the program, 1,061 were purchased through dollar cost averaging and 381 were accumulated through automatic reinvestment of dividends. The average price paid for the shares accumulated through dollar cost averaging was $15.08 ($16,000 divided by 1,061). This is $0.78 lower than the average price per share of $15.86 over the period.

This example also illustrates the limits of dollar cost averaging. Remember that the goal of investing this way is to lower the average cost of investments. This is done by purchasing more shares when prices sag and purchasing fewer when prices rise. However, note that just before the last purchase, the portfolio was valued at $27,153. The last purchase of $500 would only increase the value of the portfolio by 1.8%. On the other hand, when the second purchase was made back in June 1977, it represented an increase in portfolio value of approximately 50%. Thus, the largest benefits of dollar cost averaging are obtained in the early stages of the investment program. A sharp fall in security prices followed by a subsequent rise will lower average investment cost by a considerable degree in the early years of the program, but only by a slight amount during later years when portfolio value dwarfs the size of the regular investments being made.

This example also illustrates the residual benefit of a systematic investment program. Regular injections of small amounts of capital over a lengthy period of time can build significant wealth. A dollar cost averaging program may only lower average purchase price by a small amount. The real benefits come from regular injections of new capital.

First the Bad News

While we believe that dollar cost averaging is a good idea for individuals trying to accumulate wealth, there are a few drawbacks. First, as was seen, the impact of dollar cost averaging diminishes as the value of the portfolio grows relative to the amount being invested. Second, the program works only when share price is highly variable but is generally increasing. Third, dollar cost averaging will not result in *automatic* investment gains and is not a substitute for proper asset selection. Finally, since the program requires regular purchases, it may not be suitable for individuals with a fixed pot of investment dollars (although it can be used to switch investment from one asset to another).

And Now the Good News

There are distinct advantages to dollar cost averaging. First, the program allows you to spoon in and, therefore, results are not dependent on when you made the investment. (How many times, when you made an investment, does it seem that you bought at the top?) Second, it allows for purchase of more shares at lower prices and thus automatically lowers average investment cost of a series of purchases. Third, it eliminates the emotional element of investing. Regular injections of new capital are made regardless of the extreme swings in the "mood" of the market—the times when the biggest investment mistakes are usually made. Finally, dollar cost averaging is highly compatible with a wealth-building program since individuals make regular "installment" payments toward their financial independence.

Dollar cost averaging won't make a silk purse out of a sow's ear, and don't let anybody tell you otherwise. But a program of regular investment—applied as rigorously as possible—will let your portfolio grow with the growth of the companies or mutual funds in it, without exposing you to the risks of trying to time movements in markets or stock prices.

And more importantly, dollar cost averaging will get you into the habit of saving and investing regularly, almost automatically. Even moderate investment success will do more for you than the shares you never got around to buying.

Investing By Formula

Like gamblers, many investors want a method—a system that will allow them to "win" on a regular basis. Investors try to do this by timing the market to take advantage of anticipated price changes. Unfortunately, most of these timing methods simply don't work—you'd do just as well merely buying stocks and holding on to them.

Formula planning is an alternative strategy. Although it involves timing ups and downs in the market, it does not rely on forecasts of future stock prices per se. Rather than attempting to "buy low - sell high," these plans require that investors sell some stock when prices rise and buy more when prices decline. Formula planners seek to protect their overall investment portfolios against some of the losses during a market decline and to preserve some of the gains obtained during a market rise.

How the Formula Plans Work

While specific formula plans may differ, all are characterized by the following elements. First, they incorporate certain assumptions about the future. Second, the portfolio is divided into aggressive (risky) and defensive (risk-free) portions. Finally, a set of rules is employed that allows for the systematic purchase and sale of securities.

The aggressive portion of the portfolio generally consists of common stocks and convertible securities, while the defensive portion consists of investment in short-term maturity bonds or money market mutual funds. (In the examples that follow, the defensive portion of the portfolio is short-term Treasury bills. Such government assets are considered risk-free because the possibility of default is virtually nonexistent.)

To initially establish a plan, the investor determines the proportions of aggressive and defensive assets in the overall portfolio.

The defensive portion serves as liquid assets which are used to purchase common stocks or other aggressive assets when prices fall. The investor also determines specific changes in price levels at which he will buy or sell an aggressive asset like common stock.

There are two broad classes of formula plans: constant ratio and variable ratio. A *constant ratio* plan maintains a pre-established ratio between the amounts invested in aggressive and liquid assets *irrespective* of changes in the level of asset prices. A *variable ratio* plan varies the aggressive portion of the portfolio as prices change. In both cases, the investor makes an *arbitrary* decision in terms of proportions and the prices at which he or she will buy or sell.

Constant Ratio Plan An investor employing a constant ratio plan must first decide what proportions of the portfolio will be placed in equities and money funds. For example, an investor might decide to initially split the portfolio 50/50 between stocks and liquid assets. If the value of the equity portion is reduced to, say, 40% of the total portfolio as a result of a market decline, money fund assets are used to purchase stocks until the two portions are brought back to 50/50. Conversely, when a stock market rise increases the value of the aggressive portion to, say, 60% of the total portfolio, stocks are sold and the proceeds are reinvested in money funds until the 50/50 ratio is again restored. Note that whether stock prices rise or fall, the constant ratio plan always restores the initial stock/money fund proportions.

Variable Ratio Plan Investors who employ a variable ratio plan also begin by splitting the total portfolio into common stocks and liquid assets. But in this case, the intention is to take advantage of market swings. If equity prices rise to a predetermined level, stocks are sold, which shifts the ratio. If prices fall to a certain level, stocks are purchased, again changing the ratio. A variable ratio plan might operate as follows. Suppose that initially the stock/money fund ratio is set at 50/50. If stock prices fall by 20%, money fund assets are used to bring the stock/liquid asset ratio to, say, 70/30. On the other hand, if stock prices were to rise by, say, 25%, stocks would be sold to reduce the stock/liquid asset ratio to, say, 30/70. Thus, the overall portfolio is weighted heavily in favor of liquid assets when stock prices rise, and tilts in favor of equities following periods of severe declines in stock prices.

Ratio Choice

Formula plans are timing devices meant to tell investors *when* to buy or sell stocks. *How much* stock should be bought or sold must be determined by each investor. The particular ratio used in either case must be tailored to meet an individual's specific investment risk and yield requirements. (Note that current yield can be increased by reducing the stock portion and increasing the liquid asset portion.) Most often an initial 50/50 split is used. However, aggressive investors who have very little need for current income and those who plan to invest over a long period of time might tilt this initial ratio toward equities. Our suggestion is that the equity portion of a constant ratio plan should not be more than 70% of the overall portfolio. Conservative investors, or those interested in current yield, might want to tilt the ratio toward liquid assets. Variable ratio plan investors should most likely stick with a 50/50 split to allow room for the ratio to be tilted in either direction as stock prices rise and fall.

In setting up a constant ratio plan, determining whether the stock market is high or low is significant. Thereafter, the action of the market and the relative amounts invested in stocks or liquid assets dictate portfolio adjustments, so it won't be necessary to make periodic assessments of whether the market is high or low. Users of variable ratio plans, however, must continually evaluate stock market conditions, since a larger percentage of the portfolio is placed in stocks when the market is "low" and a smaller percentage of common stocks is held when the market is "high."

Once the initial ratio has been set, the investor must decide when to buy and sell. Care must be taken in setting the points at which to trade. If the percentage change is too low, too many transactions would be made and the concomitant brokerage fees and income tax liabilities would erode profit potential by a significant amount. On the other hand, if the percentage is too high, the investor wouldn't trade very often and wouldn't take advantage of market swings. In effect, the yield from these investments would be the same as merely buying and holding the asset. The level must be set so that trades are not made too frequently, but occur often enough to allow investors to periodically preserve profits and buy in at lower prices. How to establish this level is obviously a problem.

Trading Based on a Market Index

Purchase and sale under a formula plan may be governed by changes in the value of the stocks in the portfolio. However, a simpler method is to base trades on changes in the general level of the market. There are several indicators that are calculated to reflect overall changes in the market, such as the Dow Jones Industrial Average (DJIA), the Standard & Poor's 500 Index, or the Value Line Composite Index. Any of these may be used to trigger trading action. Using these indexes as an indicator of change means that the investor does not have to value his or her portfolio in determining when to trade. Furthermore, since most diversified common stock portfolios tend to track the action of these market measures, the use of an index provides a broad gauge of fluctuations in the market value of the equity portion of the overall portfolio.

The portfolio may also be changed at established time intervals rather than on the basis of stock price fluctuations. The portfolio is valued and stock/liquid assets transfers are made quarterly, semiannually, or at some other regular time interval. To avoid the expense and bother of inordinately small transfers, the stock/liquid asset ratio may be required to be out of balance by a minimum number of percentage points before a transfer is made. (Our preference is the use of a market indicator to make a change in assets.)

Easing into the Program

Investors who do not already have a portfolio of common stocks run the risk that the market will be at an unusually high level when they construct a formula investment plan. In this case, if stock prices fall by a significant amount shortly after the plan is established, the value of the new portfolio would tumble. And even though additional stock purchases would be made as prices fell, the overall value of the portfolio could remain in a loss position for a considerable time. Over the longer run, stock price appreciation would ultimately enhance portfolio value, but a considerable amount of time could elapse before the plan began to work as it was intended.

To remedy this problem, many formula planners suggest that the pre-established target proportion of stocks be built up gradually over time using a modified dollar cost averaging approach (discussed in the "Dollar Cost Averaging" Dose 73). For example, suppose you are not currently "in" the stock market but want to start a constant ratio formula plan with an initial 50/50 equity/liquid asset ratio. You might begin with a 10/90 split between stocks and liquid assets. If the market does not decline over, say, the next six months, the ratio might be brought up to 20/80. Without major fluctuations in stock prices, the ratio could be expanded to 30/70 in another six months, to 40/60 in another six months, etc.

However, if stock prices wander downward during the accumulation stage, purchases could be speeded up each time the established trigger is reached. In other words, a purchase would be made every time the trigger is reached on the downside or after six months, whichever occurred first. Thus, you would obtain the benefits of spreading your investment over time while bringing the stock portion of your overall portfolio up to the desired ratio.

Adding New Dollars to the Program

Investors who anticipate making significant and regular injections of new capital into the overall portfolio are also faced with some complications, namely, when and where to invest these new dollars. Our advice is that these investors also use a modified dollar cost averaging approach. For example, suppose that a portfolio contains $10,000 in equities and $10,000 in liquid assets (and that a constant ratio plan with a 50/50 ratio is being employed). Also suppose that another $10,000 is added to the portfolio. Investing the $10,000 in liquid assets would change the ratio to 33/66, which is undesirable. On the other hand, if $5,000 is placed in each portion, the constant 50/50 ratio would be maintained. However, this investor would have increased the equity portion of the portfolio by 50%, which is a significant amount, and would have lost the benefit of diversification over time. Thus, our suggestion is to place small portions of the new capital in equities at regular intervals or whenever the stock market declines to levels that would "trigger" investment, whichever comes first. Thus, this investor again doesn't have to commit large amounts of capital at a single point in time.

The problems of market timing and capital management are greatly compounded by variable ratio formula plans. In fact, we believe that forecasting problems are insurmountable, and that most investors can't use variable ratio plans. Thus, our suggestion for investors who are intrigued by the prospect of using a formula plan is to concentrate their attention on the constant ratio plan.

Real Life

The following two examples illustrate how various formula plans work in actual practice.

Constant Ratio Plan We began with an initial portfolio of $10,000 divided equally between investment in one-month Treasury bills and the Vanguard Index Trust. This trust is a no-load mutual fund which seeks to duplicate the actions of the stock market by investing in the 500 stocks in the Standard & Poor's Composite Index. Thus, the aggressive portion of the overall portfolio consisted of a widely diversified portfolio of common stocks of average risk. (Of course, we could have chosen a stock-oriented mutual fund or an individually tailored portfolio of stocks.) The defensive portion of the portfolio consisted of investment in a "riskless" asset—Treasury bills—although as mentioned earlier, a money market mutual fund or bank money market account could have been substituted. These two investments were used here because return data were readily available.

The rule used to trigger switches back and forth between aggressive and defensive portions was as follows. When the stock market (as measured by the Dow Jones Industrial Average) rose by 25%, a sufficient number of shares of the Vanguard Index Trust were sold to rebalance the portfolio back to the original 50/50 ratio. (Note that since fractional shares of a mutual fund

Dollars and Sense

may be bought and sold, we were able to shift exact dollar amounts between the two portions to rebalance the overall portfolio.) When the Dow Jones Industrial Average fell by 20%, a sufficient amount of Treasury bills were sold and the proceeds reinvested in the Vanguard Index Trust to bring the common stock/liquid asset ratio back to 50/50. The reason we chose the 20% downmarket and 25% upmarket triggers was to insure that while some trades would be made over the eight-year period, trading would not be excessive. Note also that a 20% decline followed by a 25% rise brings the index back to its original position.

Initial investment took place at the beginning of January 1977 with the DJIA at 945. At the end of February 1978, the Dow Industrials had fallen by 20% (to 756), triggering a rebalancing of the overall portfolio. At that time, the equity investment was worth $4,260 and the liquid assets were valued at $5,306 for a total portfolio value of $9,566. We then sold $523 Treasury bills and purchased an equivalent dollar amount of Vanguard Index Trust shares. This action restored the 50/50 balance between stocks and Treasury bills. In late August 1980, the Dow Industrials reached 945 (up 25% from its interim low), and the portfolio was again rebalanced. Since the total value of the portfolio was then $14,688, we sold shares of the Trust worth $232 and reinvested in liquid assets. This rebalancing process was continued until year-end 1984. The purchase and sale points are illustrated in Figure 74-1 and the entire trading process is summarized in Figure 74-2. By year-end 1984, the portfolio was valued at $24,302 consisting of $11,761 in common stocks and $12,541 of liquid assets.

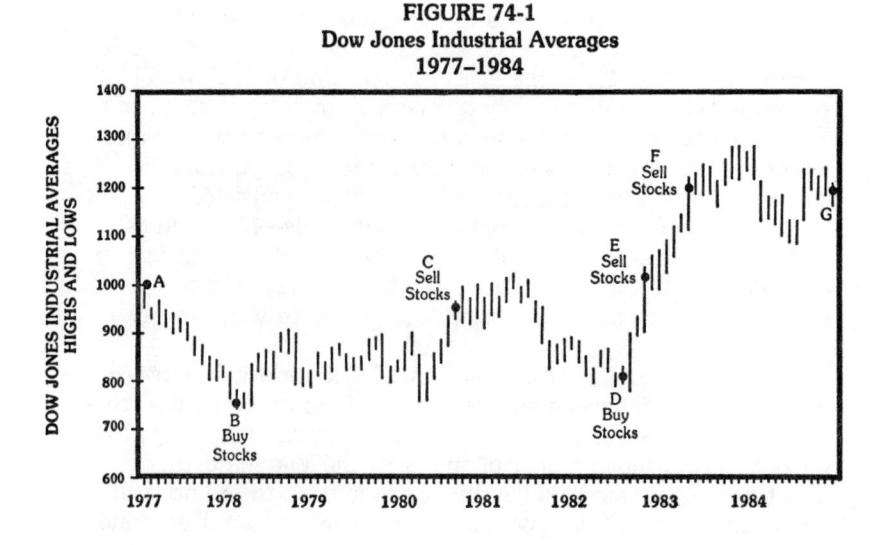

FIGURE 74-1
Dow Jones Industrial Averages
1977–1984

Figure 74-2
Constant Ratio Plan

Event	Date	DJIA	Equity Portion	T-bill Portion	Action
A	1/77	945	$ 5,000	$ 5,000	Initial investment
B	2/78	756	4,260	5,306	Sell $523 T-bills and reinvest in equities
C	8/80	945	7,576	7,112	Sell $232 equities and reinvest in T-bills
D	7/82	756	7,079	9,385	Sell $1,135 T-bills and reinvest in equities
E	10/82	945	10,387	8,407	Sell $990 equities and reinvest in T-bills
F	4/83	1181	11,766	9,784	Sell $991 equities and reinvest in T-bills
G	12/84	1211	11,761	12,541	End of period— Total Portfolio Value $24,302

Variable Ratio Plan As with the constant ratio plan, we began in early January 1977 with a $10,000 initial investment split evenly between the Vanguard Index Trust and one-month Treasury bills. This plan calls for an increase in the proportion committed to common stocks when market prices fall by 20%, and a decrease in the common stocks proportion when the stock market prices increase by 25%. In this way, a higher commitment to stocks is made when prices fall and "lighten up" when prices rise. Specifically, we planned to decrease the equity proportion of the overall portfolio from 50% to 25% on the first 25% rise in stock prices. If the stock market continued to rise by another 25%, we planned to abandon common stock investment in favor of 100% investment in liquid assets. On the other hand, if stock prices fell by 20% the 50/50 ratio would be changed to 75/25 in favor of common stocks. That split would become 100% common stocks if the market continued to fall by another 20%.

Figure 74-3 contains a summary of the transactions which occurred over the eight-year period of 1977-84. Note that after making a stock purchase in July 1982, which resulted in a 75/25

Figure 74-3
Variable Ratio Plan

Event	Date	DJIA	Equity Portion	T-bill Portion	Action	Split Between Stock and T-bills
A	1/77	945	$ 5,000	$ 5,000	Initial investment	50/50
B	2/78	756	4,260	5,306	Sell $2,915 T-bills and reinvest in equities	75/25
C	8/80	945	11,365	2,983	Sell $4,191 equities and reinvest in T-bills	50/50
D	7/82	756	6,916	9,169	Sell $5,148 T-bills and reinvest in equities	75/25
E	10/82	945	15,222	4,108	Sell $5,557 equities and reinvest in T-bills	50/50
F	4/83	1181	12,103	10,063	Sell $6,561 equities and reinvest in T-bills	25/75
G	12/84	1211	6,049	19,349	End of period—Total Portfolio Value $25,398	

stock/Treasury bill ratio, two successive stock sales and portfolio realignments were made in October 1982 and April 1983 which resulted in a 25/75 stock/Treasury bill ratio. When terminated, this plan had increased the initial $10,000 investment to $25,398. When compared to a buy-and-hold posture (i.e., invest the $10,000 in the Vanguard Index Trust in January 1977 and hold on until December 1984 with all dividends being reinvested when earned) both the constant ratio and variable ratio plans produced superior results before taxes. (See Figure 74-4.)

The constant ratio plan produced an additional $1,862 return while the variable ratio plan generated an additional $2,958 over the buy-and-hold approach before taxes.

Diversification is the Key

As I have illustrated, formula plans can improve investment results. While they come nowhere near the results that could be achieved if an investor were able to take full advantage of each rise and fall in the market, they avoid the disasters which can, and frequently do, result from the implementation of poorly thought out market timing schemes. However, the improvement in returns over a buy-and-hold investment strategy is only marginal. Thus, the slight improvement may not be worth the extra time and effort that it takes to implement them. Further, since the examples above did not include the impact of income taxes on investment results, the gains of formula planning are overstated for tax-paying investors.

When implementing any investment strategy, we cannot overemphasize the need for proper diversification. Formula plans are

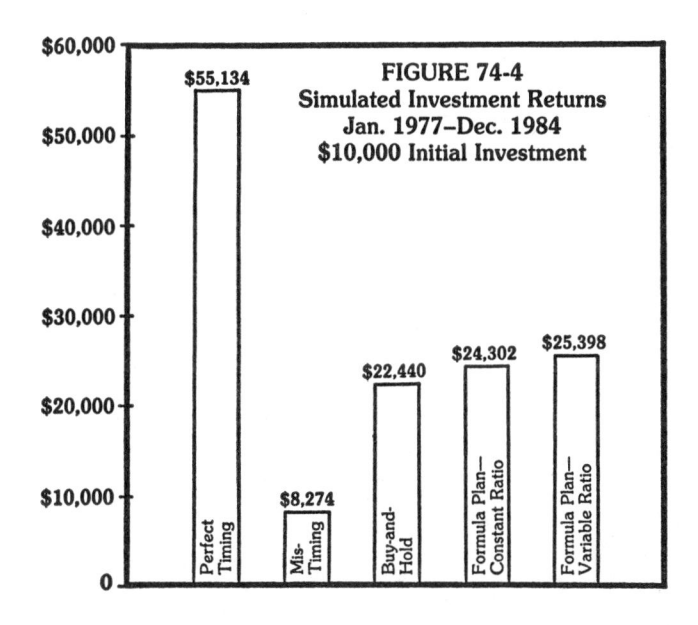

FIGURE 74-4
Simulated Investment Returns
Jan. 1977–Dec. 1984
$10,000 Initial Investment

Perfect Timing	$55,134
Mis-Timing	$8,274
Buy-and-Hold	$22,440
Formula Plan—Constant Ratio	$24,302
Formula Plan—Variable Ratio	$25,398

built on the assumption that the assets being managed will fall in value periodically, then track back upward and, at the very least, return to values reached at previous points in time. That is, formula plans will not produce a positive investment return if a portfolio, once assumed, only falls in value. While some stocks sink in value, never to rise again, a widely diversified portfolio of common stocks will always rise in value over time. Thus, it appears that formula plans are best suited for investment in mutual funds.

Finally, variable ratio formula plans require that the stock/liquid asset proportion be periodically changed over a stock market cycle. An investor using such a plan must be able to make accurate forecasts about future stock prices. Since this is the very element that the investor who is using formula plans is trying to avoid, we suggest that risk-averse investors avoid such plans entirely. Given the marginal returns over the buy-and-hold and constant ratio plans, we suspect that the incremental returns provided by the variable ratio plan are not worth the additional risk assumed.

The "Dividends" From Common Stock Investments

Bonds, unlike stocks, are typically regarded as income-producing assets. This is because, when you purchase a bond, you are entitled to regular payments of interest at a specified rate. Since the interest rate is specified and doesn't vary over the life of the bond, the *income* from bonds is *fixed*. With interest rates on high quality corporate bonds exceeding the rate of inflation by over 6% per year, investors of all types have stampeded into the bond market. Income-oriented investors have been rushing to buy bonds in an effort to lock in prevailing high interest yields on long-term government, corporate, and municipal bonds. To these investors, I say *caveat emptor* (buyer beware).

For years now I have been cautioning investors against committing their hard earned dollars to long-term "fixed income" assets. I am not alone. David Sergent, president of United Business Services, and an investment adviser for over 40 years says, "Never buy bonds." Venita VanCaspel, author of the best-selling book *The Power of Money Dynamics* agrees, and so do most knowledgeable investment advisers.

A peek at the historical record of bond returns (versus the returns from nearly everything else) should discourage those who are considering the purchase of these fixed-income assets. For example, over the period 1940-84, long-term U.S. government bonds provided investors with an average total return of 3.3% annually. Investors in corporate bonds earned only marginally more (3.8% total annual return). But over this period the rate of increase in consumer prices averaged 4.6%. As a result, long-term bond investors "lost" nearly 1.5% per year in purchasing power *before* accounting for tax payments on interest income.

The recent historical experience of bond buyers has been little better. Over the 16 year period 1970-85, long-term government bonds returned 8.2%, while long-term corporates returned 9% annually. When these returns are reduced by the 6.8% annual rate of inflation over this period, tax-paying investors would have again suffered a decline in the purchasing power of their bond portfolios—even if they had reinvested the interest received.

An Alternative for the Income-Oriented Investor

Of course, today's economic climate and the prevailing level of long-term interest rates may provide bond investors with much greater returns. While this *may* be true, we would not want to bet our hard-earned dollars on the prospects.

What then is an income-oriented investor to do? I suggest investment in a diversified portfolio of *dividend-paying* common stocks. While some investors may scoff at this recommendation (the risks are too high and the yields too low), it makes good economic sense when you consider the nature of bonds and common stocks.

When you invest in a long-term bond with a coupon rate of 10%, you get a promise of $100 each year for the next 20 years if you buy a $1,000 bond paying 10%, along with a *promise* of a return of capital 20 years hence. On the other hand, if you buy common stock you are promised nothing. However, consider the fact that at a 4% annual rate of inflation, each year's interest payment will buy (and hence is worth) 4% less than the payment made the year before. For example, $100 paid next year will be worth $96, and a payment two years from now will be worth $92.30. At this rate of inflation, the last interest payment made by a 20-year bond would be worth $45.64 in today's dollars and the $1,000 principal repayment would have a current worth of only $465.

The solution to the problem of the shrinking purchasing power of income-producing investments is to acquire assets with income that grows along with the rate of increase in consumer prices. Such is the case with common stocks. Figure 75-1 shows the growth in dividends of the S&P 500 stock index relative to the rate of inflation over the period 1970-85. In 1970, per-share dividends (stated in index terms) were $3.69. By the end of 1985, these annual cash payments had grown to $7.90. Although the payments have not grown as fast as the rate of inflation, when compared to a bond's interest payments, which remain constant, common stocks win hands down. Further, the S&P 500 index had grown from 93, in 1970, to nearly 211 by year-end 1985. Thus, the value of common stock has increased by over 100% while the maturity value of a bond held over this period remained the same. Given these figures, common stock investors would have won in the battle for income while bond investors would have lost.

Figure 75-2 shows the results over the period 1975-85 for an income portfolio of either common stocks (the S&P 500) or bonds. In 1975 high-quality, 20-year corporate bonds were yielding ap-

The "Dividends" From Common Stock Investments

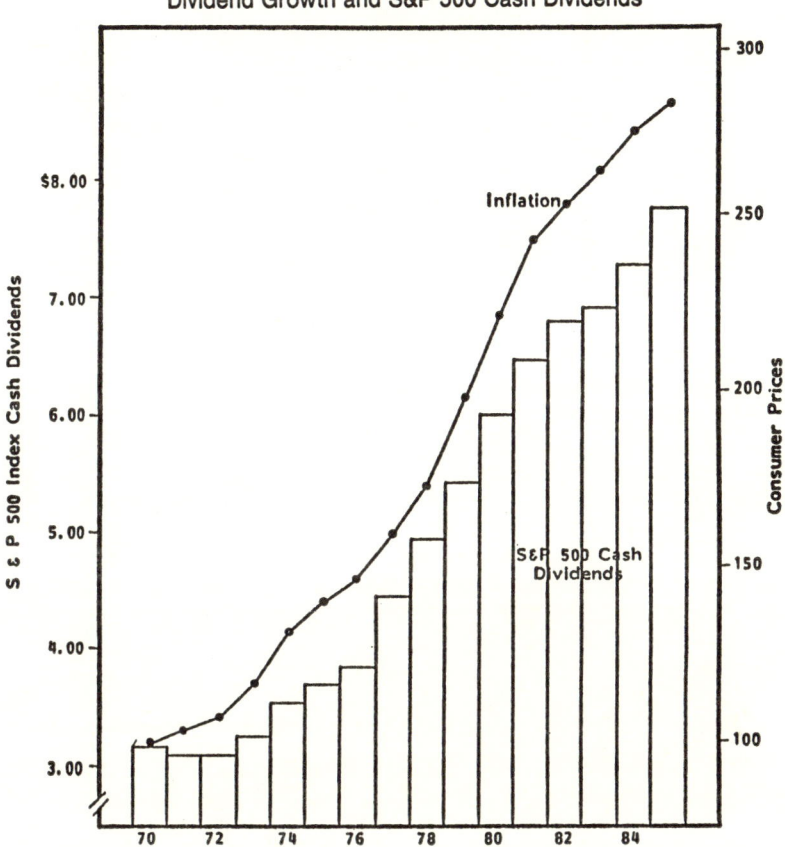

Figure 75-1
Dividend Growth and S&P 500 Cash Dividends

proximately 8.5%. Thus, a $1,000 par value bond would have provided its holder with $85 in interest each year. On the other hand, if the investor put $1,000 in the S&P 500 index at the same time, he would have received 14.29 shares which would have paid $52.73 in dividends during 1975. Since this is $32.27 less than the income received by the bond investor, the common stock investor would have had to sell 0.36 shares of the index to match the bond investor's income. Thus, at the beginning of 1976, the common stock investor would have held 13.93 shares of the index. However, since per-share dividend payments increased from $3.69 to $3.84, total dividend income would have increased to $53.49 and thus reduced the income differential to $31.51.

Note that by 1982, the dividend income from common stock would have exceeded bond income even though a total of 1.28 stock shares had been sold over the previous five years. By year-end 1985, the investor in common stock would have held 13.13 index shares

Figure 75-2
An Income Portfolio: Bonds Versus Common Stocks

Year	S&P Dividends Per Share	Number of Shares Owned	Total Income	Fixed Bond Interest	Difference In Income	Action Buy or Sell
1975	$3.69	14.29	$ 52.73	$85	$ (32.27)	Sell 0.36 shares
1976	3.84	13.93	53.49	85	(31.51)	Sell 0.29 shares
1977	4.43	13.64	60.43	85	(24.57)	Sell 0.26 shares
1978	4.95	13.38	66.23	85	(18.77)	Sell 0.19 shares
1979	5.42	13.19	71.49	85	(13.51)	Sell 0.13 shares
1980	6.00	13.06	78.36	85	(6.64)	Sell 0.05 shares
1981	6.46	13.01	84.04	85	(0.96)	Sell 0.01 shares
1982	6.81	13.00	88.53	85	3.53	Buy 0.03 shares
1983	6.98	13.03	90.95	85	5.95	Buy 0.04 shares
1984	7.35	13.07	96.06	85	11.06	Buy 0.06 shares
1985	7.90	13.13	103.73	85	18.73	—

The "Dividends" From Common Stock Investments

which produce $103.73 in annual income. The bondholder, on the other hand, would still be receiving an annual income of $85. Further, given the conditions currently existing in the stock and bond markets, the common stock investor's holdings would be worth $2,200 while the value of the $1,000 20-year bond would have fallen to approximately $750.

This illustration amply points out the advantage of using a common stock over a "fixed income" strategy. The strategy can and will work well for the common stock investor who holds a diversified portfolio of common stocks and holds onto the portfolio over the long run.

Small Investors, Small Stocks, Big Profits

If you feel you've got all the rest of your financial house in order, and have decided it's time to consider building your own portfolio of stocks, you may be casting about for a really reliable investment approach. Unfortunately, no one method has ever proved infallible at choosing stocks that outperform the market averages (such as the Dow Jones Industrial Average, the Standard & Poor's 500, and the New York Stock Exchange Index). Yet "beating the market" is the goal of most investors. It seems only logical that if the stock market as a whole returns 10% a year, smart investors should be able to rack up a higher return by zeroing in on just a few stocks with above-average prospects.

Of course, some investors are successful some of the time. However, not even professional money managers are able to choose stocks that outperform the market averages all the time. Compare their investment returns with the amateurs' for any one year and you get about the same picture: a few investors suffered monumental losses, a few enjoyed terrific gains—the majority were in the middle and did about as well as the market averages.

Small is Mighty

If you own a diversified portfolio of stocks and hold them long enough, you are bound to do better than the averages in some years. But it works both ways. In other years, you won't do as well as the averages.

With the goal of rising above mediocrity, academic types and other serious market watchers over the past 50 years have attempted to isolate the characteristics of superior-performing stocks. Most recently, they have focused on the size of companies and found that small is mighty. The so-called "small-firm effect" has some big advantages for individual investors. Why this is so is a reflection of how the market works as well as of recent changes in investment patterns.

The Efficient Market

The stock market, so the theory goes, is "efficient." Basically, this means that the price of a stock is a pretty fair reflection of what the stock is worth. Stocks of companies with bright futures are priced relatively high (expressed as a ratio of current stock price to recent company earnings, the "price/earnings"—P/E—ratio) to reflect those happy expectations. On the other hand, stocks of companies with poor or uncertain prospects are priced relatively low because their futures look dim.

No wonder it's tough to beat the averages, even for professionals. According to the efficient market theory, the stock market stays efficient by constantly absorbing news that makes investors willing to pay more—or less—for a company's stock. The "news" may be earnings reports, the company's announcement of a new strike, a takeover bid, or a whispered scandal in the executive suite. Every scrap of information, fact or hearsay, is quickly digested by the market and reflected in the next move up or down in the price of the stock.

Enter the Institution

OK—if the market really is efficient, you already have one strike against you when you try to beat it. And you're also up against the pros—professional money managers who oversee huge portfolios for pension funds, insurance companies, and mutual funds. These "institutional investors" account for nearly 70% of the trading on organized stock exchanges. With that kind of percentage they exert substantial influence over the market. And professional portfolio managers are likely to react with lightning speed to any new market information. In contrast, the individual investor often hasn't a prayer of moving fast enough, especially when the news is bad. By the time he reads the next morning's newspaper and learns of a sell-off of his favorite stock, he may already have lost a big chunk of his investment. In fact, since the late 1970s, a spate of investment books has appeared offering tips on how to survive in the "new stock market" that is dominated by institutional investors. The implication, not so subtle, is that jittery big investors have made the stock market absolutely unsafe for the common man. Not so! There is a heaven of sorts for the individual investor who concentrates on stocks of small companies instead of competing with the pros. Those folks are getting paid to spend all their time trying to beat the market averages and for the most part, they stick with the big companies. While this is partly due to government regulation, it still means that virtual armies of stock analysts follow the securities of large "safe" companies, providing the information that our efficient stock market absorbs and immediately reflects in stock prices. Therefore, no individual investor (except one with inside information) could hope to consistently discover securities of large companies that are undervalued. But if the market is indeed efficient, it should follow that there aren't many bargains among small-company stocks either. Not so; an interesting exception to the efficient market theory is the so-called "small-firm effect."

Small May be Better

The bright fellow credited with discovering it in 1978 is Rolf Banz, then a University of Chicago Ph.D. candidate. Looking through data that went back almost 50 years, Banz was surprised to find that the common stocks of some of the smallest firms rewarded investors with relatively high rates of return. Banz found that over the 43-year period he studied (1931-74), the small firms provided an excess return of 5% a year. An extra 5% annual rate of return, over 50 years, is no small amount. For comparison's sake, let's use just one yardstick of the overall market's performance, the S&P 500 Index. Over the period 1932-81, the market average had a compound annual rate of return of 10.7%. Banz's mighty midgets, by contrast, returned 16.8% annually over the same period. How much is that in dollars? Well, if you had been able to invest $1,000 in the S&P stocks at the end of 1931 and reinvest all cash dividends, your initial investment at the end of 1981 would have been worth $157,700. The same amount invested in the small-company portfolio developed by Banz from companies listed on the New York Stock Exchange would have grown with dividend reinvestment to $2,336,300 over the same period!

"Are You Sure About That?"

All this was understandably unsettling to Banz's colleagues at the University of Chicago, the university most readily identified with the development of the efficient market theory in the first place. After all, according to the theory, there isn't supposed to be any free lunch. But the doctoral student found one. What's more, his original work on small-company stocks has since been backed up by more evidence that the free lunch is still there for the taking.

A study done by University of Chicago professor Roger Ibbotson found that the smallest companies listed on the New York Stock Exchange returned 17.6% a year, compounded annually, between 1964 and 1983. That rate beat the S&P 500 stock index by 9.3%. Moreover, adjusting for inflation, these small companies served up a real rate of return of 11.5% a year, compared with an inflation-adjusted rate of only 2.2% for the market as a whole.

The Small Stock Edge

Investment Return by Investment Class: 1965-1986

Investment Category	Total Annual* Return %
Small Company Stocks	16.4%
Common Stocks	8.8%
Long-Term Corporate Bonds	6.3%
Long-Term Government Bonds	5.7%
Treasury Bills	7.1%
Consumer Price Increase	6.1%

*Includes reinvestment of dividend or interest income.
Source: "Stocks, Bonds, Bills and Inflation: 1986 Yearbook," Chicago: R.G. Ibbotson Associates, Inc.; 1986

While the stocks of small firms provide investors with higher rates of return than do large firms over the longer run, the stocks in both groups tend to move together over shorter time periods. But the small firm stocks are considerably more volatile. That volatility versus the extra return they offer is a trade-off the investor must consider.

Weigh the evidence and you may become a small-stock believer. Or, you may say, there's a hitch in here somewhere. And, you'd be partially right. In fact, the "small-firm effect" doesn't hold true for all small-company stocks. But Banz's work and the research of several other respected market theorists has clearly defined stocks of many small companies that do fit the pattern. The key to this particular "beat the market" system is company size in terms of the market value of its stock (number of shares multiplied by share price). The rule of thumb is to stick to companies with market values of less than $100 million that are listed on the New York Stock Exchange, the American Stock Exchange, or on the National Association of Security Dealers Automated Quotation service (NASDAQ). The first two are the largest organized securities exchanges in the country; the third is the national listing for stocks traded over the counter, not on an exchange. At present, shares of more than 1,000 companies meet those criteria. And individual investors have a clear field. Small firms in general have so few shares outstanding that it isn't practical, or sometimes even legal, for financial institutions to buy them.

Why the Big Boys Stay Out

One problem for institutional money managers is liquidity. To an institution, illiquidity is being unable to sell—on a moment's notice and at any price—the 100,000 shares of little Up-and-Comer, Inc. it gradually acquired over several months. Shares of smaller firms may take longer to sell, but this is often less important to the average investor.

The constraints on financial institutions interested in small stocks are further complicated by the financial industry's regulators. For instance, suppose Up-and-Comer, Inc. has 700,000 shares of common stock outstanding that are currently trading at $30 a share. That gives the company a market value, or *equity capitalization* as it's also called, of $21 million. A mutual fund, by law, can't invest in more than 10% of a single firm's securities. So a fund could buy up to 70,000 shares of Up-and-Comer, or invest $2.1 million in the company. But to stay on the safe side, many mutual funds would limit their purchases to about 5% of Up-and-Comer's shares, or a $1 million investment.

But a medium-sized mutual fund with net assets of, say, $200 million probably wouldn't consider a $1 million investment worthwhile. It would amount to only 0.5% of the fund's assets which, at that rate of investment, would mean that the fund must hold the stocks of 200 or more different companies. Moreover, trying to buy up 30,000 or 40,000 shares of Up-and-Comer within a reasonable time frame without driving up the share price would pose considerable trading problems.

Why—and How—Should You Get In?

Exactly how do you make the most of the "small-firm effect?" If your last name is Rockefeller, you could buy all of the small stocks listed. That, of course, isn't practical. Besides, a diversified portfolio should include the stocks of both small and large firms. Nonetheless, there's a case to be made for weighting a portfolio with more little stocks than big ones. Obviously, it's a cheaper way to diversify your investment risk. For what you might pay to own the stocks of 10 large firms (about the minimum for proper diversification), you could probably buy shares of 20 to 30 companies (the minimum number to ensure diversification in this market segment).

A few caveats: returns tend to do better on stocks issued by small firms that regularly pay some cash dividends. Stocks with lower price/earnings ratios also tend to return more than stocks with higher ratios. Institutional ownership plays a big role in the small-firm effect. Stocks that aren't actively owned by institutional investors tend to provide superior returns. The cutoff is stocks for which institutional investors hold 15 percent or more. Small companies with demonstrated growth—both in sales and earnings per share—have an added investment dimension. After all, the growing small firm may well become a large firm, and large firms draw the big institutional investors. The thundering herd rushes in, the stock's price soars, and now the pros are playing your game.

Where to Look

Roughly the stocks of 6,000 public companies are traded nationally. How do you identify which ones are small? You don't need a computer or the high-priced stock selection services the pros use. All you need to screen the small firms is share price and the number of shares outstanding (multiply these two items together to obtain the market value of the firm).

A few references contain the needed data; the number of companies they list is given in parentheses:
1. Standard & Poor's Stock Guide (5,200)
2. Media General Financial Weekly (4,800)
3. The Value Line Investment Survey (1,700)

These publications should be available in the business section of your local public library or at any brokerage firm.

Investment Strategies and Bear Markets

Unfortunately, overall declines in stock prices—so-called "bear markets" seem to trigger a panic response in many investors. In their haste to cut their losses as prices decline, investors sell. The net effect is not only a loss for sellers, but also a continued decline in prices as more issues flood the market. What should the smart investor do in bear markets? Quite simply, buy. Following is a relatively straightforward strategy that lets the investor take advantage of a bear market.

Strategy

The first buying opportunity presents itself when the market moves down by 10%. The second opportunity occurs (during steep bear markets) when stock prices drop by another 10%. The final purchase opportunity occurs during the sixth to eighth month of an economic recession. To take full advantage of the decline, you should invest one-third of your cash reserve at the first purchase opportunity; one-half of your remaining cash reserves should be used for additional purchases at the second buy point, and all remaining cash reserves should be committed during the sixth to eighth month of a recession. As a result of this strategy, when prices begin their rise—in a "bull market" you'll be able to take full advantage. While this strategy does mean that the *value* of your stock portfolio will be lower during bear markets, the net *cost* of your investment is averaged downward as you buy at "sale" prices. Admittedly, the strategy is aggressive. However, many investors receive a less-than-adequate return not because they stayed with a bear market too long, but because they sold too early in a bull market! Therefore, *hold* your stocks during bull markets and reserve *buying* for bear markets.

Figure 77-1 lists the buying opportunities signaled by this strategy since January 1950. If an investor had followed this strat-

Figure 77-1
Subsequent Purchase Opportunities*

Date	Action Required
September 1, 1953	Invest ⅓ of available cash in S&P 500
March 1, 1957	Invest ⅓ of available cash in S&P 500
October 1, 1957	Invest ⅓ of available cash in S&P 500
October 1, 1960	Invest ⅓ of available cash in S&P 500
June 1, 1962	Invest ⅓ of available cash in S&P 500
August 1, 1966	Invest ⅓ of available cash in S&P 500
August 1, 1969	Invest ⅓ of available cash in S&P 500
February 1, 1970	Invest ⅓ of available cash in S&P 500
June 1, 1970	Invest ½ of available cash in S&P 500
December 1, 1971	Invest ⅓ of available cash in S&P 500
December 1, 1973	Invest ⅓ of available cash in S&P 500
June 1, 1974	Invest ½ of available cash in S&P 500
September 1, 1974	Invest balance of cash in S&P 500
October 1, 1975	Invest ⅓ of available cash in S&P 500
June 1, 1977	Invest ⅓ of available cash in S&P 500
February 1, 1978	Invest ⅓ of available cash in S&P 500
April 1, 1980	Invest ⅓ of available cash in S&P 500
September 1, 1981	Invest ⅓ of available cash in S&P 500
July 1, 1982	Invest ⅓ of available cash in S&P 500
June 1, 1984	Invest ⅓ of available cash in S&P 500

*Initial portfolio as of January 1, 1950 $7,000 in S&P 500 Stock Index; $3,000 in Treasury bill.

egy since January 1, 1950, he would have had 20 buying opportunities. The bear market of 1969-70 signaled two successive buying opportunities (February 1970 and June 1970) and the great bear of 1973-74 flashed three buying opportunities (December 1973, June 1974, and September 1974). In all other instances, stock price declines fell short of the 20% required to signal a second buying opportunity. The first buy signal since that market decline began on June 22, 1983, was flashed some 11 months later, in late May of 1984.

Using this strategy requires both patience and discipline. Patience is needed since there were only 20 buying opportunities during the period from January 1, 1950 to June 1, 1984. This represents an average of one buy signal every 15.5 months. The strategy requires great discipline since investors must accumulate cash (and invest in cash instruments like money market mutual funds and Treasury bills) during roaring bull markets even though everyone else is converting their liquid assets to stocks. But they are thus merely trying to scramble aboard lest they be left at the station. You were already aboard before the parade began. Also, the strategy requires that you convert liquid assets to equities during bear markets when (it sometimes seems) everyone else is selling out. With each move you are required to go against the prevailing investment activity of a majority of individual investors. However, *you* must remember that you are buying low and holding while everyone else is *buying high* and *selling low*.

Cash Management Provides the Key

The key to implementing the investment strategy outlined above is proper cash management and not market timing because investors must have sufficient cash balances to be able to buy during bear markets. In contrast, the average investor is often fully invested at market tops and thus is unable to invest more as prices fall. In fact, it is usually this fully invested position that leads the investor to sell during market breaks.

To follow this strategy, you must first establish the relative proportions of wealth targeted for "safe" money market securities and "risky" equity securities. The proportions should be set on the basis of your personal income needs and your desire and ability to assume investment risks. (For example, conservative investors may want to apportion 40% of their investment in money market securities and 60% in common stocks, while aggressive investors may opt for an 80/20% split in favor of common stocks.) However, you will find that over time, the ratios will vary as a result of new cash injected into the investment program, the receipt of cash dividends and interest income, the rises and falls in the value of the common stock portion of your portfolio, and cash withdrawals made to pay taxes on investment income.

Here is a simplified example of how the strategy works. Suppose that an aggressive investor decides to put 80% ($8,000) in the stock market and 20% ($2,000) in a money market mutual fund. Also, suppose that over the next year, stock prices (and the value of the stock portfolio) rise by 20%. The stock portfolio earns a dividend yield of 4% and the money market fund provides an interest yield of 10%. At the end of the year, the overall portfolio is as follows:

Common stocks now represent $9,600/$12,165 (the new portfolio total) or 78% of the total portfolio, and the money fund represents 22%. If stock prices fall by 12%, a buying opportunity is

Common Stocks		Money Market Fund and Dividend Income	
Initial investment	$8,000	Initial investment	$2,000
20% Capital appreciation	1,600	Dividend income	350
Current value	$9,600	Interest income	215
		Current value	$2,565

signaled and one-third of the money fund balance ($820) is shifted to common stocks:

Common Stocks		Money Market Fund	
Initial value	$9,600	Initial value	$2,565
12% Capital loss	1,152	Less stock investments	(820)
Adjusted value	$8,448	Current value	$1,745
Plus new investment	820		
Current value	$9,268		

The total portfolio has a value of $9,268 plus $1,745, or $11,013. Common stocks represent $9,268/$11,013 or 84% of total investment, and money funds represent 16%. As additional cash dividends are received and interest is earned on the money fund investment, the absolute amount of cash held will increase and the relative proportion of cash in the overall portfolio will begin to move back toward the desired 20%. The result will be maintenance of the desired split between aggressive assets (common stocks) and defensive assets (money market funds) and the acquisition of additional shares of common stocks at lower prices.

An Investment Simulation

While this investment strategy is theoretically appealing, I decided to put it to the test using investment returns over the period January 1, 1950 to June 1, 1982. January 1950 was chosen as a starting point since this was in the middle of a bull market that began on June 15, 1948. Thus, results are not biased either upward or downward by setting the beginning or ending of a bull market as the point of initial investment. Also, investments were apportioned between the Standard & Poor's 500 Index and one-month maturity Treasury bills. Since the S&P 500 Index was used, our simulated results reflect the returns from a common stock portfolio of average risk.

A moderately aggressive posture was assumed initially. The initial "investment" of $10,000 was split 70/30% in favor of common stocks. It was assumed that cash dividends paid by S&P 500 firms were placed in one-month Treasury bills on the first of each month and that interest on the Treasury bill investments was compounded monthly. Transaction costs or income tax in determining the end value of the investment portfolio were not included. The decision rule used to make stock purchases was: Buy on the first trading day of the month following each 10% decline in the value of the S&P 500 stock index. During these bear markets, one-third of available cash was invested after the first 10% decline in stock prices. One-half of the remaining cash balance was invested following the second successive decline in stock prices by at least 10%. All remaining cash was committed to the common stock portion of the portfolio when stock prices fell by another 10%. Stock purchases were made the first trading day of the appropriate month because this made calculation of dividends and interest income easier. In actual practice, such purchases should be made on the day following the signal of a buying opportunity.

The buy signals and the investment actions taken are listed in Figure 77-1. As a result of these transactions, the initial $7,000 investment in the Standard & Poor's Stock Index would have grown to $127,088 by July 1, 1982. In addition, the T-bill account would have contained $16,406. Since a buying opportunity signal was flashed on July 1, 1982, implementation of the strategy would have resulted in $5,370 being invested in common stocks one month before to the start of the most recent bull market. Thus, the equity portion of the overall portfolio would have grown to $196,034 by January 1, 1984.

I always advocate long-term holding of common stock and express this view at every opportunity. However, some investors are confused about how to do this in actual practice. The strategy outlined above is a method of doing just that while accounting for the injection of new investment funds and for cash accumulated from dividend and interest payments. While the word "sell" was never mentioned, we do not advocate that common stocks, once purchased, be held forever. The common stock portfolio must be continually upgraded as companies fail to deliver on their promises of future growth. However, security sales should only be made to affect switches between stocks of varying quality. While the simulated results are not a guarantee of future results, we believe very strongly in buying common stocks at reduced prices and holding them for long-term appreciation. As one wag put it, the phrase "buy low and sell high" may, in fact, be only half correct.

Games Money Plays

First, a short and completely unscientific quiz:
1) If you had to choose, would you say you were most like:
   a) Ben Franklin's "Poor Richard"
   b) One of "The Waltons"
   c) Rhett Butler
   d) Art magnate Joseph Duveen
2) Would you rather:
   a) Plan an addition to your house
   b) Make your own raspberry preserves
   c) Bargain in an Arab bazaar
   d) Attend a "Dare To Be Great" meeting

We were inspired to create the quiz when we saw a recent survey of investment returns. This survey listed gains and losses for 14 kinds of investments, ranking them for 1-, 5-, 10- and 15-year periods. It occurred to us that the survey really summed up the fates of four kinds of investors over those periods. How well you did depended on what kind of investor you are.

Given that the survey was begun in 1977, it isn't surprising to find that the focus is on the choice between tangible assets—from farm land to stamp collections—and financial assets, represented by stocks, bonds, and Treasury bills. It was during the mid-'70s that investors began to wonder whether they would ever again make a decent return on securities, and to look for things to own that would at least keep them whole in terms of purchasing power.

But in 1982, returns on stocks and bonds finally made it to the top of the list (bettered only by the rise in the price of silver, which was bouncing back from a disastrous slump). In fact, returns on securities were so good for that single year that financial assets came out fairly well on the five-year comparison, too.

There is an explanation for this situation—a sustainable change for the better in inflation, government intervention in the economy, and the outlook for growth, at least in the eyes of the firm that made the initial studies. Inflation-hedged investments are therefore losing their attraction; productive investments are gaining. The bull market in stocks has been fueled in part by a shift of funds, as investors sold out their gold and art, replacing them with stocks and bonds.

If this analysis is right, there may be still more funds to be shifted, and more particularly into the securities market (although the rise so far has surely used up the proceeds of an awful lot of stamp collections). If these assumptions are wrong, a countershift would send tangibles up again at the expense of conventional investments.

Four Options

This analysis of the competition between tangible and financial assets seems reasonable, as far as it goes. But all tangibles are not alike. Depending on the business climate and public economic policies, some can be reasonable investments when others are wild speculations. Which brings us back to our four categories of investors—and, by implication, investments.

The first, financial assets, are what most of us think of as "investments." These would include bank accounts, some insurance products, mutual funds and so forth, as well as the securities listed. The second, productive tangibles, are "hard" assets—real physical objects—but they are usually valued for the goods and services they produce: tons of wheat, say, or a rain-free place to sleep. The third, commodities, are also used in the process of production. But those who deal in them do not hold them as productive assets. Instead, they buy and sell for trading profits. (Gold and foreign currencies are different, of course, since they are themselves money. But we've included them here because they are traded on markets that operate like those for more conventional industrial commodities.) The fourth group we've named "tulip bulbs," with reference to the 17th-century craze for investing in those flowers. Although "tulip bulbs" are alleged to be investments, their value has nothing to do with economic production. They are just tradable, high-unit-value items whose price is determined by their scarcity. (In the 17th century, tulips were new to cultivation and very scarce.)

Games Investors Play

Each type of asset generates its own type of investing—its own game. All four games are going on in the markets all the time. There is nothing more important to the investor than knowing which one he or she intends to play, and how to play it. But over the past 15 years, economic and political conditions have favored some games over others.

Figure 78-1
Investment Categories Compounded Annual Rates of Return

	1967–72	1972–77	1977–82	1982
Financial Assets				
Treasury Bills	6%	8%	13%	11%
Bonds	6	6	7	39
Stocks	2	1	15	52
Avg.	5%	5%	12%	34%
Productive Tangibles				
Farmland	7%	17%	7%	−6%
Housing	7	11	7	2
Avg.	7%	14%	7%	−2%
Commodities				
Oil	11%	35%	16%	−15%
Gold	19	14	18	29
Silver	4	15	20	110
Foreign Exchange	7	6	−3	−4
Avg.	10%	18%	13%	30%
"Tulip Bulbs"				
Coins	4%	40%	13%	17%
Stamps	12	18	22	−6
Chinese Ceramics	38	−4	13	nil
Diamonds	10	15	5	nil
Old Masters	7	13	4	2
Avg.	14%	16%	11%	3%
Consumer Price Index	5%	8%	9%	4%

Source: Solomon Brothers, Inc. (some figures recalculated)

Poor Richard The basic game played with financial assets can be called "Poor Richard"—hence the first choice in our quiz. In this game, investors buy securities to get a claim on the income produced by the businesses that issue them (or, in the case of Treasury bills, on the taxes paid by the whole economy). The object of the game is to get the best trade-off between the price you pay for the asset and the income it produces. Returns depend on the long-term productivity and business success of real companies. They aren't often huge, but they're seldom negative. Even the investor who aims to rack up the top score with a "Poor Richard" strategy can accumulate a comfortable number of points.

Unfortunately, business rates of return have been undergoing a downward trend since 1967. At their worst a few years ago, corporate assets were generating profits of about 3% per year after adjustment for inflation. The values of the securities issued by these businesses followed suit, and all Poor Richard's savings left him barely even. Common stocks did worst of all, lagging behind inflation from 1967-77, and in the first four years of the 1977-82 period as well.

The Waltons Productive tangibles are the game pieces in "The Waltons" because the typical investor in this group plays it by owning a home. In this game, you buy the asset itself, rather than a general claim on a collection of assets organized into a business. When inflation is on the rise, owning the assets that produce what you consume can be a winning strategy. No matter how slowly the price of a home goes up, once you own your house you can't fall behind on the cost of housing. Note that the object of the Walton strategy, properly played, is simply to nail down your supply of housing—i.e., put a roof over your head, regardless of the ups and downs of home prices or rents.

Beat the Market Like Rhett Butler making a killing during the Civil War, investors in commodities try to beat the market. Professional commodities dealers play constantly, whether inflation is epidemic or hardly there at all. Armed with detailed knowledge of the markets for copper, pork bellies, or heating oil, they stake their capital on their ability to foresee price moves earlier than their competitors do. Every winning trade is made with some other dealer who, by definition, had a losing trade. The object of the game is to "win" your opponent's stake. Amateurs in the commodities markets attempt the same feat. We've seen quite a few ads for commodities brokers, appealing to the Rhett Butlers among us—those rare individual investors who have the brains, talent, and guts to go head-to-head with the pros—and win! The old David and Goliath match. Daffy Duck versus Albert Einstein is more like it. The odds that an unassisted individual will consistently beat the professional traders are astonishingly small. But when inflation shot up during the 1970s, and the media got excited about tangible assets, quite a few individual investors tried to beat the market. Mostly, they didn't.

Tulip Bulbs Tulip-bulb enthusiasts are closet Joseph Duveens. Having observed that the price of so-called collectibles can move up much more rapidly than the rate of inflation, they buy in eagerly, sure there will always be someone else who'll pay them an even higher price. In ordinary times, rising prices for these investments are the result of little more than fashions in the markets for art, antiques, and, generically, "collectibles," with perhaps some help from a good economy. Fashion can push prices down, too; some schools of painting, for instance, have been acclaimed as great art by one generation of collectors, only to be discarded by the next.

But when inflation is a serious problem, there are two added forces behind the rise in the price of collectibles. First, some of them really are suitable stores of purchasing power: small, high-unit-value items with well-established markets are in great demand when the value of currency is falling. Under those conditions, expert collectors, who know so much about their specialties that they are almost in the business of collecting, can make good use of "tulip bulb" investments.

The second source of upward pressure on collectibles prices is nonexpert interest in the field. When inflation was at its worst, individual investors came into the art markets at the small-ticket end. Unable to buy Rembrandts, they bought whatever they could afford. This helped bid up prices across the whole price spectrum. Unfortunately, the free market system responded in its usual way: there was a demand for collectibles and the market set about supplying them. Commemorative plates, special editions, and medallions poured forth from the factories. Franklin Mint, one of the biggest producers of these "scarce" items, was a real winner for a while. Naturally, it all collapsed. Inflation eased and the supply of collectibles seemed endless. At that point, whoever still owned the Millard Fillmore commemorative wall plaque won the title of Greatest Fool.

The Scoreboard

In our example, Poor Richard was clearly the game for individual investors if the business climate improved, and if returns on corporate assets recovered and stayed strong. The Waltons were insulated from the rise in home prices, whether 2% or 20%, and their return in the form of shelter for their household came through right on schedule.

Rhett Butlers had their ups and downs. Commodity prices in general were weak, but trading profits can be made on the sell side as well as the buy side. What had changed by the end of the three-year recession was the public impression that prices could go nowhere but up. The bust in the Joseph Duveen markets was inevitable, and in some ways the result of Poor Richard's rise. As long as inflation seems to be under control, it isn't likely to have another strong run on collectibles. But for those who like it, there's always a hand being played somewhere.

The Warning Signs

Is it possible to know in advance when and if Poor Richard is going to become a losing game again? Not for sure. The individual investor can keep track of economic and political developments. A habit of closely monitoring the inflation statistics may be your most useful weapon. But as we put this chapter together, another sign occured to us—one that shows up in the markets themselves. When inflation heats up, and returns on productive investments head down, investors begin to play the wrong games with the right pieces.

In the mid-'70s, securities analysts began to appraise common stocks in terms of the productive assets held by the issuing businesses. Replacement-cost valuation of plant and equipment became a topic of interest. Later in the decade, business ownership of commodity resources became a selling point. Just before the oil stocks peaked out, analysts were frantically calculating the per-share market value of their crude reserves to justify sky-high stock prices. At the same time, Waltons became Rhett Butlers. Back in the late '70s, the chief economist at the investment firm of Donaldson, Lufkin & Jenerett told us he knew the California housing market was in trouble, because a friend of his had taken out a second mortgage on his home there to buy another single-family house as a speculation.

Finally, individuals began to treat commodities like tulip bulbs. Franklin Mint brought out a series of gold and silver medallions and sold them at a price wildly in excess of the market value of the metals in them. But they sold—because how could you go wrong owning gold? As this trickle through of change occurs, it may be time to batten down the hatches. However, we have no information on how long the shift will continue or how far it will go. In 1929, from all we've heard, the corner grocer was trading shares of General Electric for all the world as if they were tulip bulbs.

The Rule of 72: Cheaper Than a Calculator

While speaking to a group in Cleveland, I casually mentioned that financial calculators are preprogrammed to figure compound interest and run various other calculations useful to the individual investor. I suggested that everyone should have such a gadget. At the end of the meeting one participant stated that he thought I was all wet, and he made a good case. He pointed out that a shorthand method, known as the rule of 72, will give you approximate answers to compound interest problems almost instantly, and you can do them in your head. Here's how it works:

If you know the interest rate or rate of return on an investment, you can divide that number into 72 and get, approximately, the number of years it will take that investment to double the money you originally put into it. Alternately, if you know that your money has doubled in a certain number of years, dividing the number into 72 will tell you roughly the rate of return you earned. The method works for returns other than exact doublings, too: if, for instance, your investment's value rose 76% in 7 years, dividing the 7 into 55 (76% of 72) reveals a rate of return just under 8% per year. Our trusty financial calculator makes the correct answer just over 8%.

Well, it's the late 80s and financial calculators are relatively inexpensive. Why settle for "approximately?" Why not just get the calculator and work with precise answers? On that point, the participant's reasoning is so close to one of my own favorite investment rules, I wouldn't even talk back. He suggests that individuals work calculations out themselves, so, he says, they'll know almost without having to think about it whether their answer to a problem is reasonable or not. It matters less that your seven-year, 76% gain amounts to 8.4% per year, not 7.8%, than that you know instantly that a return of 20% or 30%, compounded over several years, is fantastically good—and fantastically unlikely. I had to agree. I must stand

Dollars and Sense

by my suggestion that every individual investor should own a financial calculator. However, the rule of 72, as well as several other shortcut rules, should be applied to check the "reasonability" of the solutions given by machine. That way you avoid the danger that the answers you calculate will travel directly from the display panel to your paper, bypassing the brain.

Investment Games You'd Be Better Off Not Playing

Investing can be fun. It can also be quite profitable. While the primary object of investing is profit, many investors sometimes get caught up in the fun and forget the real reason they were investing in the first place. These investors do have fun playing "the money game"—at least for a while. However, eventually some of the games they are lured into playing erode investment capital so much that pleasure gives way to extreme pain.

Bull markets can indeed be dangerous. The prospect of easy money frequently leads some investors into playing investment games they otherwise would avoid. As stock prices rise and tales of instant riches dot social gatherings, long-term risk averse investors unwittingly begin to change their investment strategies. As a result, investment portfolios become more risky and the probability of meeting the initial objective (to earn investment return) decreases.

As more and more individuals begin to invest, the danger of being led into playing investment games "for the fun of it" has never been larger. Thus, I decided to outline a few games which can be upsetting to your financial health. These are games that can pay off for some investors but, unfortunately, usually only pay off for investors' brokers.

Game #1: Retire Today With a GNMA

Equipment:
Available cash. About $25,000 if you invest directly, much less if you invest indirectly through a mutual fund.

Object of the Game:
To earn a high rate of return on a low risk federally "guaranteed" investment.

Start of Play:

Play usually begins when your broker calls and pitches you the opportunity to invest in a pool of federally backed mortgages which currently provide a higher current yield than the existing rate on long-term government bonds.

Strategy:

Since many people who invest in GNMAs don't fully understand what they have gotten themselves into, they don't know what type of strategy to employ. For example, distribution checks received monthly from an investment in a GNMA include both interest and a return of principal. Individuals who do not realize that they are receiving some of their principal back and who do not reinvest the principal portion of the distribution are often shocked to find that at maturity their initial investment has completely "disappeared." On the other hand, those who realize that such payments include a return of capital frequently delay putting the money back to work and thus earn much less than those individuals who keep their investment capital continually working for them.

Continuation of Play:

Play usually continues when your broker calls on the telephone and pitches you the merits of investing in another GNMA. This play is virtually certain of success since the broker knows that you have fallen for the pitch before.

Winning the Game:

Unfortunately, the player usually never wins this game. You see, GNMAs are mortgage backed income securities. Like all so-called fixed income securities, they fall in value when interest rates rise and rise in value when interest rates fall. However, when interest rates fall, home buyers tend to refinance their mortgages at the lower rates. Thus, when interest rates fall by a significant amount, GNMA investors find their capital being returned. In short, when interest rates rise, GNMA investors lose; when interest rates fall, they generally break even. Recently, we looked at the returns for two GNMA mutual funds over the period 1982-86. Here's what we found. One fund provided a total compound return of 97.4% over this five-year period while the other fund returned 121.7%. On the other hand, an investment in a portfolio of long-term U.S. government bonds would have returned a total of 165.4% over the same period. Last year, six GNMA funds returned an average of 11.5% while long-term government bonds returned 24.4%. Of course, if you are a successful GNMA salesman, you can win this game every time.

Game #2: Write Covered Calls Boost Current Income

Equipment:

A common stock portfolio usually consisting of blue chip stocks for which listed options exist.

Object of the Game:

To earn approximately 15% per year by employing a low risk investment strategy.

Start of Play:

Play usually begins after the stock market has moved sideways for a period of time. Investors who have obtained little more than the dividend return on their investments begin looking for a way to increase returns.

Strategy:

The strategy is quite simple: You hold onto your blue chip stocks and write options on the underlying shares. The option buyer pays you a premium for the right to purchase your stock at a fixed price for a short time interval (usually six months). All the while you continue to receive the dividends on your blue chip stocks.

Continuation of Play:

When the option you have written expires, you write another option and again pocket the premium paid by the buyer. This play is continued each time the options expire. Of course, you continue to receive dividends on your common stock holdings.

Winning the Game:

This is a very tough game to win. What players usually forget is that if stock prices rise, their blue chip stocks are called away from them at the option price. This generally limits capital appreciation. On the other hand, if stock prices fall, options expire and investors keep their stocks. However, usually the fall in stock price more than wipes out the option premiums which were received. Thus, what looks like a low risk/high return game turns out to be a high risk/low return game over the longer run.

Game #3: Leverage Your Way to Investment Succe$$

Equipment:

A margin account at a brokerage firm and a large amount of intestinal fortitude.

Object of the Game:

To earn huge investment returns in a short period of time.

Dollars and Sense

Start of Play:
Play begins when you open a margin account with your broker and place at least $2,000 in cash in the account or marginable securities with a current market value of $4,000.

Strategy:
Find a stock or two that you think is going to rise in price in the near future. Buy some shares with your investment stake and borrow an equal amount of dollars from your broker and buy more shares. Interest on the loan is debited to your account, and thus, you do not have to make installment payments.

Continuation of Play:
When your stocks rise in price, the value of your equity increases, and you may continue to borrow money from your broker using your stock holdings as collateral and increase your share holdings.

Winning the Game:
When stock prices top out, you close out your positions and return the borrowed capital to your broker. Investors who win this game win big. For example, an investor who bought 100 shares of XYZ Company stock in February at $128 per share would have invested a total of $12,800. If that investor had sold his XYZ Company shares two months later when the stock traded at $157, he would have earned $2,900, or 22.6%, on his initial investment. On the other hand, if the investor had purchased 200 shares by investing $12,800 cash and $12,800 borrowed from his broker, he would have earned $5,800 on the investment. That's a return of 45.3% in just two months! On the other hand, when the players of this game lose, they can lose big. For example, the cash buyer of XYZ Company would have lost 50% of his investment capital if the stock fell to $64 instead of rising to $157. The margin buyer would have been subject to a margin call (i.e., the broker calls and asks for more money). Investors failing to post more collateral would have been sold out at a loss. If the price of XYZ then rises back to $128, the cash buyer is back to the break-even point while the margin buyer, who was eliminated from the game earlier, continues to cry over his losses.

Game #4: Invest in New Issues and Find the Next IBM Before Nearly Anyone Else

Equipment:
A full-service broker whose firm participates in underwriting a large number of new issues, a hot stock market, some spare cash and dreams of investing in a start-up IBM.

Object of the Game:
Get in on the ground floor of a start-up company which makes an initial public offering (IPO) of its common stock. Although you get in on the ground floor, the object is to get out at the penthouse level when you cash in.

Start of Play:
Your broker calls with an offer to sell you an upcoming IPO "commission free." Before you begin this game, you must first get on the good side of your broker. Hot new issues are in great demand, and your broker must limit sales to only his best customers. To get on the good side of your broker, don't send candy, send a lot of commission business instead. (See other games for ways to generate commission business.)

Strategy:
Get in on the good deals early, hold on and watch your wealth skyrocket.

Continuation of Play:
Sometimes it's difficult to continue playing this game. (See "Winning the Game" section for specific reasons.)

Winning the Game:
This is one of the biggest games in town. During the 1975-85 period, 2,800 companies went public by offering $27.5 billion in newly issued common stock to investors. Although IPOs are pitched as being commission free, brokers earn fat underwriting fees which are paid by stock buyers. During 1975-85, such fees totaled more than $2 billion. In addition, founding shareholders often get rich by including a few of their shares in the IPO. While this game always has a winner, the odds of it being an investor are slim. To quote a recent *Forbes* article, this game is: "Great for brokers. Great for the founding shareholders. Great for American enterprise. But no so good for John Investor." Here's why. A recent study of those 2,800 companies mentioned earlier revealed that if an investor would have bought some of each issue, he would have pocketed a total return of 12%, or less than 3% per year. Of course, since a player can't buy new every issue, he must settle for just a few at a time. However, buying just a few can be unrewarding and sometimes downright dangerous. Less than one of six new issues beat the market three or four years down the road. Nearly one-half drop in price by 50%, and one in eight nearly wipe out their investors. Of course, if you hit on the right IPO you can win this game big. An $18,000 investment, in the Home Shopping Network IPO, for example, last year would have netted a profit of $264,000—if you had sold out at

its peak. Stories like that are what make this game a perennial Wall Street favorite.

Game #5: Churn Your Portfolio for Fun and Profit

Equipment:

Very little patience, access to a telephone and a stock broker that enjoys earning a large amount of commissions..

Object of the Game:

To make a quick profit by darting in and out of the stock market. Since the new tax law has eliminated the preferential treatment of long-term capital gains, this game is gaining in popularity with investors. Of course, it has always been popular with brokers.

Start of Play:

The game usually begins when the investor consults a chart of stock prices and trading volume. Investors sometimes opt instead to subscribe to an investment newsletter written by a technical analyst. Most often these newsletters offer a "hotline" telephone service in addition to their regular newsletter which provides the day's latest trading tip.

Strategy:

This game is best played by locating a few stocks expected to climb a few points in the near future. Stocks are bought and left in street name since most are expected to be sold long before certificates can be delivered. In addition, registering securities in street name saves investors frequent trips to their broker.

Continuation of Play:

Actually, this game is played continuously during the hours that the exchange is open. Investors watch the tape to locate the most favorable entry and exit points. Some lazy traders have their brokers watch the tape and request that the broker call when target prices are reached. Still other investors place limit orders which are automatically executed when the triggering price is reached.

Winning the Game:

Although I don't believe that this game can be won, every time I write an article on the dangers of "churning" your own account by dipping and darting in and out of the market, I invariably receive a letter from some investor detailing how they have made a better than average return by timing the market. The real problem with playing this game is that it is expensive. Every time a trade is made, investment return is reduced by the payment of the transactions cost. This cost consists of brokerage commissions and payment of the market makers bid-ask spread. On average, the total transactions cost for a round-trip trade (purchase and subsequent sale) amounts to approximately 4% of the value of the transaction. Thus, if an investor turns over his portfolio four times a year, he must earn a 16% return annually before the assessment of transactions costs just to break even. Since common stocks, on average, have returned 12% annually over the last sixty years before brokerage commissions and taxes, this trader must earn a gross return in excess of 28% annually to beat the return earned by a long-term buy-and-hold investor. The interesting factor of this game is that while investors are allowed to churn their own accounts, it is against the rules for their brokers to do so—not that this has necessarily stopped some brokers from trying.

Taxable Versus Tax-Exempt Returns: What's the Difference?

Most investors are all too aware that most of the returns from their investments are taxed. You may receive a 10% return from a corporate bond, but after you pay taxes on your "profit," the net return falls to 8.5%, 7.2%, or even lower. Of course, your net (aftertax) return is dependent on your personal tax bracket—the higher your bracket the lower will be net return.

But there is one investment that has escaped the federal tax bite—so-called municipal bonds. These bonds are actually issued by county and state governments as well as municipalities. Most are general-purpose revenue bonds sold to finance the day-to-day operations of the issuer. Some are special-purpose bonds that cover the cost of a specific project like sewers or a new bridge.

Compare Net Yield after Taxes

Regardless of purpose, the overall yield (interest) on municipal bonds is generally lower than the yield from other interest-bearing securities. But when you examine the net yield after taxes, the picture may change. For example, suppose that a fully taxable bond has a stated yield of 10% while a municipal bond of similar risk has a stated yield of 8%. If your marginal tax rate is 15%, you would earn a greater net yield from the corporate bond after taxes (8.5%). But if your marginal tax rate is 28%, the municipal bond would give you a higher net yield after taxes (8.0% versus 7.2%).

To compare the yield from corporate bonds (or any other type of investment, for that matter) and a tax-free investment, the following equation is used:

$$\text{Corporate bond yield} = \frac{\text{Municipal bond yield}}{1 - \text{Your marginal tax rate}}$$

This equation shows what you would have to earn on a corporate bond to provide a net (aftertax) yield comparable to the yield from a tax-free municipal bond. For example, suppose that municipal bonds currently yield 7%, and you are in the 27% marginal tax bracket. Using the equation:

$$\text{Corporate bond yield} = \frac{7.0\%}{1 - .28}$$

$$\frac{7.0}{.72}$$

$$= 9.72\%$$

In other words, you would need a yield of at least 9.72% on a taxable investment to equal the net yield on the 7% tax-exempt bond. Yields greater than 9.72% will provide higher net returns from the taxable investment.

Figure 81-1 shows equivalent taxable and tax-free yields for several tax brackets. First determine your marginal tax bracket to find the corporate bond yield which equates with a municipal bond yield. Next locate the current municipal bond yield. The number at

Figure 81-1
A Comparison of "Tax-Free" and Fully Taxable Bond Yields for Various Tax Brackets

Tax-Free Yield	Equivalent Taxable Yield/Marginal Tax Rate*		
	15%	28%	33%
3.0%	3.53%	4.17%	4.48%
3.5	4.12	4.86	5.22
4.0	4.71	5.56	5.97
4.5	5.29	6.25	6.72
5.0	5.88	6.94	7.46
5.5	6.47	7.64	8.21
6.0	7.06	8.33	8.96
6.5	7.65	9.03	9.70
7.0	8.24	9.72	10.45
7.5	8.82	10.42	11.19
8.0	9.41	11.11	11.94
8.5	10.00	11.81	12.69
9.0	10.59	12.50	13.43
9.5	11.18	13.19	14.18
10.0	11.76	13.89	14.93
10.5	12.35	14.58	15.68
11.0	12.94	15.28	16.42

*Federal income tax rate on the next dollar of taxable income.

Dollars and Sense

the intersection of this row and column is the fully taxable bond yield which will provide a net return equal to the municipal bond yield.

As the figure shows, if municipal bonds currently yield 9%, an investor in the 15% marginal tax bracket would need a fully taxable yield of 10.59% to earn an equivalent net return. An investor in the 27% marginal tax bracket would need a taxable yield of 12.50% to equal the net return on the tax-free bond.

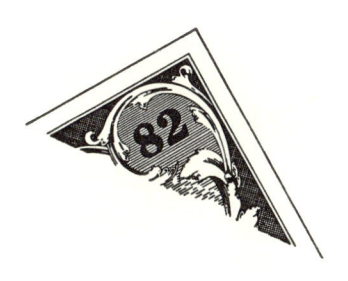

An Investment Riddle: When is a 5% Investment Return a 7.6% Investment Return?

I clipped an ad for a tax-exempt money market fund a few months back. The headline read, "Our 5.07% can be your 7.57%." I wish they wouldn't do that. I can understand that the fund's sponsors like to have a nice high number to put in their advertisement. But they've got it precisely backwards.

It's not that the tax-exempt features make the *yield higher*. Quite the contrary. Taxes make the earnings from nonexempt investments lower. So the 5.07% yield is just what it looks like: 5.07% and no federal taxes due. A taxpayer in the 33% bracket could buy a taxable bond yielding 7.57%, pay the taxman, and end up with exactly the same return: 5.07%. In that sense, the 5.07% fund is equivalent to the higher-yielding bond. But for people below the 33% bracket, 5.07% after taxes could be achieved with taxable investment yielding anywhere from 5.96% (for those in the 15% bracket) to 7.04% (in the 28% bracket). The average family can pay taxes on yields above the 7% and end up with more than 5.07% after federal taxes.

In any case, no one gets to keep 7.57% (except tax-free groups like churches, of course.) Investors who focus on that number may not stop to check out all the taxable alternatives and crank in their own marginal rates. In addition to making the tax-free/taxable comparison, the investor needs to compare both with current inflation. The tax-free money market fund in this ad, yielding 5.07%, was just skimming the current rate of inflation at that time—in other words, it was offering no real return at all.

This kind of "doubled-yield" headline in ads for tax-free securities was the norm before the 1986 tax laws reduced everybody's tax bracket. In today's environment, such ads are quite misleading: "caveat emptor."

A Close Look at Ginnie Mae Funds

One of the newest and most popular types of mutual funds is one that invests in securities guaranteed by the Government National Mortgage Association (GNMA). Dubbed "Ginnie Maes" by investors, the securities are backed by a pool of mortgages held by the association. While a few Ginnie Mae funds have been around since the first GNMA certificate was issued in 1970, most have made their debuts within the past two and a half years.

Utopia

Investors have become attracted to the funds because of their high yields and seemingly low risk. That is, they tend to provide a yield higher than that available from any other government security, with little additional risk. This has so enticed investors that they have pumped more than $3.5 billion into these mutual funds. It would certainly seem as though mutual funds that invest in Ginnie Maes provide an investment utopia for many types of investors, but it's important to understand the drawbacks (and there are a few) as well as the benefits before you buy.

GNMA Certificates

A certificate issued by the GNMA represents a share in a pool of mortgages on residential housing insured by the Veterans Administration or the Federal Housing Administration. These certificates are guaranteed by the GNMA for full principal and interest due, and that guarantee carries the same iron-clad backing of the U.S. government that is behind every Treasury security.

When an investor purchases a GNMA certificate, he is entitled to the interest and principal due each month on the mortgages backing the security. So, a GNMA certificate pays off its principal, as well as interest, throughout its life. The mix of principal and interest varies each month and depends on a number of characteristics of the mortgage pool, such as the types of mortgages held, the distribution of maturities of the mortgages, and the distribution of the rates on the various mortgages. Payments also depend on the geographic distribution of the mortgages held as well as on how many are held and how large they are.

The Nightmare As you can imagine, obtaining all the information necessary to evaluate a GNMA pool is very difficult indeed. And because the mix of principal and interest varies each month, as one bond expert put it, "The bookkeeping alone for Ginnie Mae payments can be an accounting nightmare." Additionally, as portions of the principal are returned to the investor, he faces the task of finding a suitable place to reinvest them. Another obstacle to investing in GNMA certificates is their high minimum purchase requirement—a whopping $25,000. It is very difficult for most average investors to commit a sum that large to a single investment. Because of the problems associated with direct purchase of GNMA certificates, investors have looked for other methods of participating in the home securities market.

Enter the Ginnie Mae Funds

Ginnie Mae mutual funds opened up a new market for the average investor. For as little as $100, investors can now purchase shares of a mutual fund specializing in mortgage-backed securities. This way, investors do not have to worry about obtaining hard-to-find information on the individual mortgages in each GNMA pool. The mutual fund's investment adviser handles these decisions. By investing in Ginnie Mae funds, investors can also avoid the hassle of reinvesting the monthly principal repayments because the mutual fund keeps the portion of the payment which represents the principal and passes along only the interest to the shareholders. The fund then combines all the principal repayments and uses them to purchase additional GNMAs. Interest payments from the new securities are also passed on to the shareholders, and the fund becomes a continuous operation, unlike a single GNMA certificate which, by nature, is self-liquidating. The yields investors can earn from Ginnie Mae funds are relatively high—and better than those of any other government-backed security. Sometimes these yields even rival those from long-term corporate bond funds.

Risk While Ginnie Mae funds make participating in the home securities market easier, they cannot protect investors from all the risks inherent in holding GNMA certificates. The first is *interest rate risk* and is common to all fixed-income investments. Interest rate risk works like this: When interest rates rise, the market value of the GNMA certificate (or any other fixed income security) falls because the fixed rates don't keep pace with the overall increase. When interest rates decline, the market value of the certificate rises because it offers a higher comparative yield. How much the market value of a security will rise or fall depends on a number of variables. One of the most important is the number of years remaining until the security matures. The longer the maturity, the greater the price fluctuations. This is because the effect of changes in interest rates is greater with a longer time to maturity. Home mortgage securities are medium- to long-term, so they are subject to relatively wide fluctuations in price.

The second risk associated with Ginnie Mae funds involves *purchasing power* and is also common to other fixed-income securities. This is the risk that inflation will reduce the value of an investment in *real* dollars—or purchasing power. This risk is far greater for fixed-income investors because, by definition, their returns are fixed and won't rise with inflation. Purchasing power risk is, therefore, lower for common stock or real estate investors than for GNMA or other fixed-income investors during inflationary periods. To bring this point home, consider what happened to property values and interest rates during the inflationary 1970s. Many homeowners had borrowed at mortgage rates of around 6% before double-digit inflation took hold and drove interest rates up and the purchasing power of a dollar down. The net effect was very favorable for the homeowners, of course, because they were repaying their loans in "cheaper" dollars, and at an interest rate far below what was currently charged. But it was very unfavorable for the lenders who were locked into those interest rates. Today, every GNMA investor, and every other fixed-income investor, runs the same risk of this severe loss of purchasing power should inflation take off again. But even small increases in the inflation rate will eat away at the values of these fixed-income securities.

Home mortgage securities are also subject to a risk that does not affect other fixed-income securities: *prepayment risk.* As mentioned earlier, when interest rates fall, the market price of the GNMA certificate rises which, of course, is very favorable to the certificate holder. At the same time, however, declining interest rates encourage homeowners to refinance to take advantage of lower rates. When they refinance, homeowners pay off the old mortgage. The GNMA certificate holder gets back the entire mortgage principal sooner than expected, but he or she misses out on all the interest that would have been earned if the mortgage was held to maturity. And because rates are low at that time, the certificate owner is also forced to accept a lower, less attractive rate if he wants to reinvest that principal. This process causes the value of the investment (or in the case of a mutual fund, the net asset value) to fall. So, while investment in a Ginnie Mae fund can minimize many of the problems associated with purchasing GNMAs directly, even a large Ginnie Mae mutual fund is not immune to interest rate risk, purchasing power risk, and prepayment risk.

A Dealer's Delight

Over the past several years, Ginnie Mae funds have been praised for their high yields and high degree of safety. And, even more recently, they have been proclaimed the "ideal" Individual Retirement Account (IRA) investment for almost everyone. It certainly sounds like Ginnie Mae funds are too good to be true, which led me to believe that they probably are. So, I took a closer look at where all this glowing praise was coming from. The answer was no surprise.

Of the eight primary Ginnie Mae funds available today, only two are no-load—that is, they involve no extra sales charge when you purchase your share. The Fidelity fund charges a modest 1% sales fee. The others are all sold through brokers who get anywhere from about 4% all the way to a hefty almost 7% commission of the dollars invested. So less of your money will be invested to begin with.

As mentioned earlier, because the actual mechanics of a Ginnie Mae certificate and/or fund are quite complicated, most investors are not aware of the risks associated with them. It is much easier to understand the benefits of a "high yield" and a "government backing," particularly when it is presented in persuasive sales literature. Which leads us to ask how well Ginnie Mae funds have actually done over the long term, and whether they really are suitable IRA investments. Figure 83-1 illustrates the five-year performance of several funds compared to the results with other types of invest-

Figure 83-1
**Ginnie Mae Mutual Funds vs. Alternative Investments
Five-Year Performance**

Investment	1981	1982	1983	1984	1985	Five-Year Total
Franklin U.S. Govts.	+ 6.3%	+30.4%	+ 8.7%	+11.6%	19.4%	NA
Kemper U.S. Govt.	+ 0.6	+28.5	+ 8.9	+12.3	22.3	93.3%
Lexington GNMA	+ 1.1	+24.5	+ 7.2	+11.9	17.1	76.3
Vanguard GNMA	+ 4.0	+29.0	+ 9.1	+12.8	20.7	108.0
Small-firm common stocks	+13.9	+28.0	+39.7	− 6.7	24.7	136.6
Corporate bonds (long-term)	− 1.0	+43.8	+ 4.7	+16.4	30.9	126.8
Govt. bonds (long-term)	+ 1.9	+40.3	+ 0.7	+15.4	31.0	117.4
Treasury bills	+14.7	+10.5	+ 8.8	+ 9.8	7.7	63.3
Inflation	+ 8.9	+ 3.9	+ 3.8	+ 4.0	3.8	26.4
S&P 500 Index of Common Stocks	− 4.9	+21.4	+22.5	+ 6.3	31.8	98.5

ments. As you can see, the Ginnie Mae funds lagged the average fixed-income fund by as much as 50% over the five-year period. And compared to the return provided by small-firm common stocks over the same period, the Ginnie Maes performed very poorly indeed. From this figure it appears that Ginnie Mae funds offer little to the IRA investor in long-term returns.

Many investors have asked, "Isn't a Ginnie Mae fund really just like a bond fund?" The answer is no. While Ginnie Mae funds share similar characteristics with certain bond funds, particularly intermediate- to long-term bond funds, they are different in terms of risk and long-term return. The similarities are the length of maturity (GNMAs have an average maturity of 20 to 30 years, but are often paid off after 12 years) and the size of their yields—or interest payments (GNMA funds tend to have yields slightly lower than those of intermediate- and long-term bond funds).

But in terms of risk, Ginnie Mae funds are touted as being less risky over the long run because they invest in government-backed securities. These securities are among the safest you can find. Since corporate bond funds do not carry the same insurance for their holdings, the story goes, they are riskier than the Ginnie Mae funds and should provide higher yields to compensate for this risk. However, this credit risk is actually minimized when a bond fund holds a large portfolio of many different issues. The default of one issue in a well-diversified portfolio will have little impact on the portfolio's overall performance. Therefore, many corporate bond funds actually entail little more credit risk than the Ginnie Mae funds.

On the other hand, Ginnie Mae funds carry a "prepayment risk" which bond funds are free from. Although Ginnie Mae fund managers carefully analyze the possibilities when selecting GNMA certificates, they still cannot eliminate the risk of an investor ending up with large principal prepayments which may have to be reinvested at unfavorable interest rates.

Bond Funds are a Better Bet

Bond funds and Ginnie Mae funds differ in terms of return, as well. The short-term returns from Ginnie Mae funds can be expected to be affected unfavorably by prepayment risk, while bond funds would not. And over the longer term, based on what limited historical data is available on Ginnie Mae funds, it appears that they will not perform as well as the average bond fund when held for several years. Thus, while Ginnie Mae funds do provide higher yields than any other government-backed security, an investment in a Ginnie Mae fund is not completely without risk. Changes in interest rates and mortgage prepayments both threaten the share prices and current high yields on these funds. Share prices are also adversely affected by these factors. And inflation always threatens the purchasing power of a GNMA investment (or any fixed-income investment.) Figure 83-1 tells the story clearly. Over the long run, investors have earned the best returns from common stock investments. But if investors still desire fixed-income securities, bond funds are a better choice than Ginnie Maes.

Commodity Funds—Future Speculating for the "Little Guy"

Every year, scores of amateur, part-time commodity traders jump into the rollicking futures market hoping to grab some of the big, speculative profits that can be made there. And every year, many of them slink away, poorer but wiser.

As the name implies, futures contracts give the owner the right to purchase something at a specified price at some date in the future. If the price of that "something" increases before the contract matures, the owner will make a profit. Sounds simple, but trading futures contracts is risky at best. That goes for the traditional contracts—agreements for the future delivery of such things as wheat, pork bellies, gold, and Treasury bills. And it also holds true for some of the newer futures, including those based on moves in popular stock indexes. *Margin* (cash down payment) requirements in the futures games are tiny, usually 5% of the total contract, compared with the 50% an investor has to put down for stocks. So even small moves in the prices of contracts can make—or erase—fortunes in minutes. (A 5% drop in a commodity's price can wipe out a contract holder. A 5% price rise, on the other hand, can enable a speculator to double the initial investment.) There are bona fide *hedgers* in the market who buy complementary contracts to cover their investments regardless of which way the market moves. But the majority of traders on any of the nine major U.S. futures exchanges are speculators. These are gunslingers who may be riding high one day and fall flat on their faces the next in a market that is no place for sissies. Despite the dangers, the opportunity for profits in futures is a powerful lure.

Commodity funds, perhaps the most cautious way to invest, continue to be popular with small investors even though their performance generally has been dismal. These funds, sometimes called pools, seem to offer a solution to the myriad of problems faced by the small speculator. For a relatively small investment, a limited partnership in a fund gives you the full-time trading expertise of a professional adviser, diversity in the number and kinds of contracts traded on your behalf, and limited liability in that, as is not true when you trade futures yourself, you can't lose more than your initial investment in a publicly registered fund. There's just one problem, however. For three out of the past four years, investors in public futures funds haven't made much money. Figure 84-1 gives an idea of performance of some of the larger funds.

Performance

Ordinarily, size is a mutual fund's primary strength. But in futures, commodity pools—like other traders in commodity markets—are limited in the size of trading positions they can take in any one market. That is, there are legal limits on how much of any given future a trader can buy. These limits sometimes force the funds to diversify more than they would like, even into relatively inactive markets, simply to stay fully invested. Because of their size, these funds also aren't noted for their agility. The relative slowness with which they respond to major market moves, in fact, has earned them the reputation of being "tortoises" of the futures markets.

As a rule, the funds tend to wait for clear trends before sticking their necks out too far. Most fund advisers buy and sell according to a trading system of their own devising based on price data fed into a computer-generated "trend model." The model tracks current price movements of particular contracts and compares them with how prices have behaved in the past. Weeks of data, however, may be required to add up to a trend. As a result, by the time a model clearly signals a "buy," for instance, the fund may already have missed a big share of the major market move. Says *Managed Account Reports* publisher Leon Rose: "The performance of these funds depends on the direction the economy goes. In general, these funds do well in inflationary periods and in bull markets, and poorly in down years." The funds also tend to perform best when the commodities markets are moving fairly broadly and steadily—either up or down—and less well when the markets are fluctuating more unpredictably.

Still, 1984 was the first time in four years that the funds' return beat the inflation rate. And over the past five years, they haven't done nearly as well as many other investments. Between December 31, 1979 and December 31, 1984, the funds ranked 13th out of 18 investments Rose examined in terms of total cumulative return (assuming any cash distributions were reinvested). The funds' cumulative gain for that period was 74.86%. By contrast, the S&P 500 reinvested returned 99.5% while equity-income funds (Number 1 on Rose's list) returned 124.07%. Even if the funds manage a strong finish in the next few years, they have a long way to go to make up

Figure 84-1
How Public Commodity Futures Pools Have Performed

Fund	Offering Firm	Trading Adviser	Date Started	Unit NAV at Start*	1982	1983	1984	1985
Aries Commodity Fund	A.G. Edward	Campbell & Co.; Futures Mgmt.	2/80	$1,000	+27.9	+ 7.1%	+47.7%	+22.4%
Chancellor Futures Fund	Prudential-Bache	Commodity Monitors	2/80	943	+ 4.6	− 5.2	+12.6	+29.2
Commodity Venture	Shearson Lehman Heinhold	Atlantic Assoc.	11/80	950	+25.0	− 8.4	+19.8	−12.5
Harvest Futures Fund I	Heinhold	Charles Curran	6/78	1,000	+24.5	+38.5	− 1.7	−10.6
Illinois Commodity Fund	Heinhold	Christopher Funk	1/78	975	+ 0.8	−21.7	+41.4	+24.0
Peavy Fund I	Dain Bosworth	Futures Mgmt.; Dunn Commodities	10/80	876	−36.1	−12.8	+64.7	+13.8
Resource Fund	Blyth Eastman	Milburn Partners	9/78	1,000	+33.4	−10.7	+10.0	+19.9
Thomson Financial Futures Partners I	Thomson McKinnon	Christopher Funk; Campbell & Co	3/82	994	+34.5	−47.9	+70.2	+83.6

*Net asset value of each unit when the fund began trading
Source: Managed Account Reports, 5513 Twin Knolls Rd, Suite 213, Columbia, MD 21045

ground they lost since the heady days of 1979-82. Back then, returns as high as 80% or 85% were common. But as inflation subsided, investors saw those gains fade away. For instance, Thompson Financial Futures Partners I, the top-performing fund in 1984, was up 70.2%. But the value of investors' units at the close of that year was $1,193, compared to a peak of $1,387 in October 1982.

How They Work

While futures funds resemble ordinary mutual funds in some respects, they differ in several important ways. To offer a public commodity fund, a brokerage sets up a limited partnership with the Federal Securities and Exchange Commission (SEC). The brokerage then functions as the pool's general partner, and investors are limited partners. The prospectus for, say, a $5 million fund, might provide for the sale of 5,000 limited-partnership units of $1,000 each. The minimum investment required is typically five units. If the investment is for an Individual Retirement Account, however, the minimum is usually $2,000 or $2,250.

The prospectus will tell you, among other things, who the brokerage has selected as the fund's trading adviser (some funds have more than one adviser). Trading advisers are generally independent outside firms that are supposed to be registered with the Commodity Futures Trading Commission (CFTC), the industry's chief federal regulator. Advisers are the ones who actually buy and sell contracts for the funds. In return, they get an annual fee and percentage of profits as an incentive. As a rule, trading profits are distributed to investors at the discretion of the general partner. Trading losses are subtracted from the fund's pool. This causes what is termed the "net asset value" or NAV of each unit to decline.

Private pools are also offered by some brokerages. Minimum investments in these funds are typically much higher than they are in public pools. There may be only a few dozen investors in a private pool and such funds needn't be registered with the SEC. Another variation, offshore funds organized outside the U.S. to invest in both domestic- and foreign-traded commodities, are extremely risky.

There are several other variations, including so-called "managed accounts." An investor usually needs $50,000 to open a managed account and must find his own trading adviser registered with the CFTC. The investor must then give the adviser legal authority to trade using his money. The managed-account adviser usually gets an incentive fee, but no commissions. With a "discretionary account," the trading adviser is an account executive or broker who gets commissions.

Advantages for Small Investors

Compared with these other forms of commodity investing, public funds are relatively pedestrian. Most strive for steady if slow profits rather than a quick killing. But because they offer certain advantages for small investors, the funds have grown rapidly. Besides the 85 funds trading in 1985, another nine funds are expected to be offered in 1986. That's up from just 16 in 1980. Total investment in the pools currently amounts to roughly $700 million, the lion's share of it from individuals. However, a growing number of pension funds are also using the pools to invest in futures. On the other hand, due to legal restrictions, relatively few mutual funds trade contracts.

The advantages the pool offers small investors are numerous. The initial investment in a public fund is far lower than the minimum that many brokers consider reasonable for trading commodities yourself: typically, an investor who wants to put $5,000 in futures needs about $50,000 in liquid assets backing his stake. In addition, using money from perhaps thousands of investors, a fund adviser can buy or sell a variety of contracts, reducing the risk of a disastrous loss in just one futures market. A fund also protects you from perhaps the biggest danger of commodity trading: the possibility of losing more than you invested. Because you can trade futures by putting up only a small percentage of the total value of a contract, a sharp price move in the wrong direction will not only wipe out your investment, but also leave you liable for the total price of the contract. In a fund, the general partner is responsible for making up that difference if the fund loses more than its equity.

In the event of heavy trading losses, however, most funds will self-liquidate. Over the period 1980-84, a total of 12 funds closed. In June 1985, three funds traded themselves into extinction—Global Futures Fund, Hutton Commodity Reserve Fund, and Western Capital Fund. This was the highest number of pools to go out of business in a single month since public funds first came on the investment scene in 1978.

The prospectus offers you an insight into how aggressively or how conservatively a fund will be managed. For instance, some funds allow only 30% or so of the pooled money to be used for futures trading; the rest is held in reserve against negative price fluctuations. While that kind of restriction limits investors' potential losses, it can also hamstring a fund's trading adviser and so limit everybody's potential profits. The prospectus will also give you a clue as to the fund manager's expertise, providing the firm's win/loss record for the past three years. Look hard at the adviser's worst showing and ask yourself if you could live with that. Most keep the funds invested in anywhere from 18 to 30 different kinds of contracts covering all commodity groups.

Some trading advisers, naturally, are better than others. Seek out funds whose advisers have kept them profitable despite difficult market conditions. Several monthly newsletters track fund performance. Among them are (despite its name) *Managed Account Reports*, which also includes *Futures Industry Newsletter*, 5513

Twin Knolls, Suite 213, Columbia, MD 21045, $225 a year (free sample available upon request); the *Norwood Index,* 6134 N. Milwaukee Ave., Chicago, IL 60646, $50; and *Commodity Traders Consumer Report,* 1731 Howe Ave., Suite 149, Sacramento, CA 95825, $150.

Costs Eat Up Profits

The main drawback of commodity funds is the fact that many of the costs of management are covered by the fund's investment pool. Many brokers pass on the entire cost of offering the fund to the public. Registering the fund with the SEC and the CFTC and issuing a prospectus can add up to anywhere from $250,000 to as much as $500,000. This means that the value of investors' units "takes a hit" even before the fund begins trading. Other fees make commodity funds less of a good deal for investors than typical mutual funds. For instance, the trading adviser for a commodity fund usually receives an annual fee of 4% of equity for his or her services, as well as a percentage of profits as an incentive. In comparison, mutual fund managers get between 0.5% to 0.75%. Commodity fund investors are also likely to pay more in commissions. The limited life of a futures contract and the fast-moving nature of the commodities markets require frequent trading. It isn't unusual for commissions to use up between 15% and 20% of a futures fund's average annual pool. Typically, all of that revenue goes to the general partners, who may collect anywhere from $25 to $75 for each "round-trip" trade (including both buy and sell orders).

Before you decide to dive into a commodity pool, do plenty of research on your own. Look carefully at the way these funds are set up, who runs them, and how particular funds compare with one another. A number of investors over the years have been victimized by scam-fund operators, so check the credentials of everybody connected with a pool before you ante up any cash.

The Sting

Since it is so profitable for brokerage firms to offer these funds, it pays even more than usual to know who you are doing business with. Stick to reputable firms that will still be around in case of problems; no fewer than 24 commodity firms disappeared during 1984. In March 1984, the collapse of Volume Investor Corp., a clearing firm for the New York Commodity Exchange (COMEX), shook the industry. The default of the company, which handled contracts for numerous other trading firms, could eventually cost its customers $3 million.

Be wary of private pools, where investors have been bilked for years by characters like Jerry David Dominelli and Bernard Striar. Both San Diego men recently pleaded guilty to fraud for running a variety of commodity-related scams going back decades. While fraudulent commodity-related deals can take several forms, the most common are "Ponzi" schemes. These are funds set up by slick operators who invariably keep most of the money they raise, but keep the scam going by occasionally paying out "dividends" as new investors are taken in.

Although the CFTC has been around since 1974, it has often been criticized for not being tough enough on the industry it oversees and for not really protecting investors. As a result, investors must largely fend for themselves. The Future Industry Association (FIA) is only now studying the idea of its member firms offering some type of private insurance to their customers. Such a plan might be funded by fees paid by the firms themselves, similar to the measure of protection afforded stock and bond investors through the Securities Investors Protection Corp. (SIPC).

While the public funds haven't had any problems with fraud, selecting one still calls for caution. In an issue of *Futures,* Robert Isaccson, a leading spokesman for several of the industry's self-regulatory groups, suggested examining these areas.

1. *Management.* Who are the fund's general partners? Are they isolated from the investor? Is their prime business commodities? Are they putting their own money in the trading program just like investors are?
2. *Track Record.* Ask for actual copies of trades or an audited statement from the trading adviser. Has the adviser ever had a loss large enough to cause disolution?
3. *Economics.* Are the general partners taking full advantage of certain arrangements that could save the fund money, like negotiated commissions? Is margin money intended to cover possible losses invested in a "safe" vehicle like Treasury bills?
4. *Service.* Do the general partners have the administrative capacity to provide daily and monthly equity statements and year-end tax work?

Several agencies can help you check the credentials of both the funds and their advisers. To see whether a fund is properly registered, you can call both the SEC, (202) 272-7540, and the CFTC, (202) 254-3067. Find out whether a foreign company is on the "foreign restricted list" by writing the SEC Office of Consumer Affairs, Washington, DC 10549. The National Futures Association (NFA) is headquartered in Chicago, (312) 781-1410. It can tell you whether an adviser is properly registered. If the adviser is registered, don't take this as an NFA endorsement; it merely means that the adviser does not have a criminal record. You can also check to see whether any complaints against an adviser have been filed with the SEC or the CFTC.

One of the most useful books for novice investors is *A Practical Guide to the Commodities Markets,* written by professional trader Ronald C. Spurga and available in many public libraries. Several other reasonably priced and not-too-technical books for novice commodity investors are just out and available in bookstores. Among them: *Understanding Futures,* by Robert W. Kolb ($11.95); *Getting Started in Commodities Futures Trading,* by Dr. Mark J. Powers ($12.95); and *Multiply Your Money,* by Merrill J. Oster ($14.95).

Convertible Bonds: An Alternative Equity Investment

Almost every stock market investor wants to make money when stock prices are rising and to *preserve* these gains when prices decline. To accomplish this goal, some investors turn to market timing. They invest in common stocks during "up" markets and in money market instruments during falling stock markets. The merits of this approach, however, are highly suspect. Hundreds of studies have shown that market timers tend to earn suboptimal returns after paying taxes and transaction costs.

If stock market timing cannot be successfully used to preserve profits during down markets, what is an investor to do? One answer is to *maintain* a portfolio consisting of both common stocks and money market instruments. For example, consider a portfolio which consists of 50% common stocks and 50% money market mutual funds. Suppose that during the year, common stocks rise by 30% and short term interest rates average 7%. The annual total rate of return for this portfolio is 18.5%. On the other hand, suppose stock prices fall by 30% during the year. In this case, the total portfolio return is *minus* 11.5%. Thus, this cash-hedged portfolio (in the sense that money market investments are used as protection against downturns) allows investors to participate in bull markets while mitigating the erosion of portfolio value during bear markets.

An Alternative

Still other investors attempt to protect themselves against losses during severe bear markets while allowing for gains during bull markets by investing in convertible bonds. A *convertible* bond can be exchanged for shares of the issuing company's common stock at the discretion of the bond holder. This involves a *conversion price* which determines the rate of exchange between the bonds and the underlying stock. When the price of the company's common stock rises above the conversion price, the price of the bond tends to move in tandem with the price of the stock. On the other hand, since these bonds also pay interest and have limited lives, their prices tend to behave like bond prices when the common stock price falls below the conversion price. Thus, a well diversified portfolio of convertible bonds allows investors to participate in rising stock markets while giving them a considerable degree of protection during severe bear markets.

Figure 85-1 illustrates the price action of a hypothetical convertible bond. The bond's *investment value,* shown as a horizontal line, is the price at which the bond would be expected to trade if it did not contain the conversion feature. The upward sloping line is the bond's *conversion value.* This is the bond's worth if it were exchanged for common stocks and is determined by multiplying the bond's conversion ratio by the current price of the stock. (The *conversion ratio* is the number of shares the holder would receive if one bond were exchanged for common stock.) For example, if the bond were convertible into 25 shares of common stock selling for $50 per share, the *conversion value* would be 25 x $50, or $1,250.

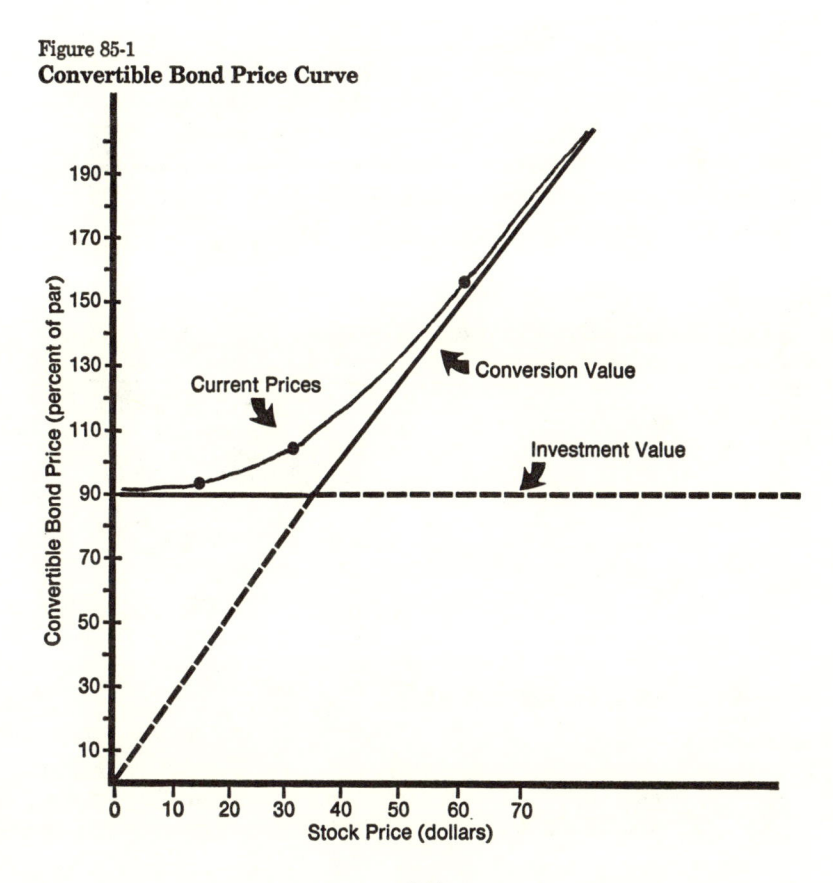

Figure 85-1
Convertible Bond Price Curve

Dollars and Sense

The curved line represents the expected price action of the convertible bond over a range of common stock prices. Note that the bond tends to sell at a premium above its conversion and investment value. The size of the premium varies with the price of the underlying common stock and with supply and demand conditions in the market.

Figure 85-2 illustrates the protective nature of a convertible bond. In this example, a hypothetical convertible bond has a 20-year maturity, a $1,000 par value, an 8% coupon interest rate and is convertible into 25 shares of common stock. The underlying common stock, which pays a cash dividend of $1, is currently selling at $30.

Suppose that an investor purchases 100 shares of common stock in this company for a total investment of $3,000. If after one year the stock price were to double, this investor would earn a $3,100 total return consisting of $3,000 capital appreciation and $100 in cash dividends. On the other hand, this investor would suffer a $1,400 loss after one year if the price of the stock declined by 50%. Thus, this investment strategy involves considerable risk.

Suppose that another investor, who was also bullish on the prospects for this company, made an equivalent dollar investment in the company's convertible bonds. Note that if the stock prices were to double after one year, this investor's portfolio would increase by $1,890 or by 63%. On the other hand, if stock prices were to fall by 50%, this investor would suffer only a 2.0% decline in portfolio value. That is, the investor in convertible bonds, in this instance, receives about two-thirds of the return obtained by the common

Figure 85-2
Risk/Reward Analysis: Common Stock Versus Convertible Bond

Change in stock price	$ 15	$ 30	$ 60
Estimated convertible price	$900	$1,000	$1,550
Strategy: Buy 100 shares of common stock			
Common stock gain or (loss)	$(1,500)	$ 0	$3,000
Plus dividends received	$ 100	$ 100	$ 100
total return ($)	$(1,400)	$ 100	$3,100
total return (%)	−46.7%	+3.3%	+103.3%
Strategy: Buy three convertible bonds			
Bond gain or (loss)	$ (300)	$ 0	$1,650
Plus interest received	$ 240	$ 240	$ 240
total return ($)	$ (60)	$ 240	$1,890
total return (%)	−2.0%	+8.0%	+63.0%

stock investor when the price of the stock climbs by 100%, but has eliminated nearly 95% of the loss incurred by the common stock investor if the price of the stock plummets. Thus, convertible bond investors can participate in stock market rallies while protecting themselves during market downturns.

The Convertible Bond Market

While investment in convertible bonds, at first glance, appears to be the ideal investment strategy for risk averse investors, implementation of the strategy does not come without its pitfalls. First, there isn't much trading in the convertible bond market, and spreads between bid and asked prices may be wide. As a result, an active trader may wind up paying excessive commission costs and conversion premiums which can erode investment returns. Thus, considerable care must be exercised when buying or selling in this market.

On the other hand, the lack of liquidity in this market offers a definite advantage to the individual investor. For example, when a large institutional holder decides to sell, it hopes that another institution is willing to buy at a price reasonably close to the current market price. If such a "swap" cannot be arranged, the price must be lowered to attract potential buyers. Smaller, individual investors gain by searching out the bargains created by institutions selling. Another attractive opportunity for individuals occurs in the trading of convertible bonds of small companies.

Figure 85-3
Risk/Reward Analysis: The Convertible Bond Hedge

An ABC Corporation convertible bond with an 8% coupon and exchangeable into 100 shares of common stock is currently selling at $1,100. A six-month put option on ABC common stock, at a price of $10, is currently trading at $1.00. The current share price of ABC common stock is $10.

	Current Price	Price in Six Months		
Common Stock	$ 10	$ 5	$ 10	$ 20
Convertible Bond	$1,100	$850	$1,100	$2,100
Put Option	$ 1	$ 5	0	0

Strategy: Buy 1 Bond and 1 Put

Profit (loss) on bond	$(250)	0	$1,000
Profit (loss) on put	400	$(100)	(100)
Interest received	40	40	40
total profit ($)	$ 190	$ (60)	$ 940
total return (%)	+15.8%	−5.0%	+78.3%

343

The Convertible Bond Hedge

Investors who want additional protection during bear markets may wish to consider hedging their convertible bond portfolios by purchasing put options on the underlying common stocks. (*Puts* are common stock options which allow the holder to sell shares of common stocks at a specified price for a specified period of time.) If the price of the underlying common stock falls below the option's price, the loss in stock price is covered by the put. Figure 85-3 on page 343 illustrates the rates of return that can be earned through this strategy. Note that profits are greatest when stock prices are volatile. Gains occur on large market swings up or down.

Finally, this strategy works best when a well diversified portfolio of convertible bonds of smaller equity capitalization firms is hedged by the purchase of index puts. The purchase of undervalued small firm convertible bonds hedged with index puts has been dubbed "super hedging" by Tom Noddings, the leading expert on convertible bond investment. The strategy is described in considerable detail in his excellent book *SuperHedging* (Probus Publishing, 1986.)

Bonds That Don't Make Interest Payments—On Purpose:
LIONs, TIGRs, CATS, and STRIPS

Back in 1982, Merrill Lynch was on the prowl for a new security that would appeal to fixed-income investors. It came up with TIGRs (Treasury Investment Growth Receipts). The brokerage giant created this odd creature by buying long-term Treasury bonds, removing the interest coupons from the principal portion of the bonds, and selling the two pieces separately.

The zero-coupon bonds were sold to investors at prices well below their face value ("deep discounts") and went like hotcakes. Other brokerage firms wasted no time copying the idea. Merrill Lynch's TIGRs were quickly followed by Salomon Brothers' CATS (Certificates of Accrual of Treasury Securities) and Lehman Brothers' LIONs (Lehman Investment Opportunity Notes).

In February 1985, Uncle Sam himself got in the game. The Treasury calls its own zero coupons STRIPS (for the mouthful: Separate Trading of Registered Interest and Principal of Securities). Initially, the government only offered the stripped version of 10-year and 30-year bonds. Since Uncle Sam's "zeros" are backed by the Treasury directly, they offer investors more safety than the broker-packaged certificates. The trade-off, as it usually is with securities carrying the full guarantee of the federal government, is a slightly lower yield.

Charm is Simplicity

One reason zeros are popular is that they are easy for investors to understand. For as little as $50, you can buy one and know with certainty that it will increase in value to a specific sum by the maturity date. Unlike garden variety full-coupon bonds, zeros don't pay annual interest. Instead, the total return comes from the fact that zeros are sold at prices below face value and increase to face value at maturity. That makes them useful financial-planning devices. Maturities typically range from as little as six months to as long as 30 years. Young parents, for instance, might buy a zero maturing about the time a child is scheduled to head off for college.

Zero coupons also eliminate the *reinvestment risk* interest-bearing bonds entail. This is a function of the *yield to maturity* on conventional bonds. Yield to maturity reflects both the periodic interest (coupon) paid on the bond and the rate at which those interest payments can be reinvested. If interest rates decline, so does the yield on reinvestment and, as a result, the yield to maturity. For example, say you buy a bond with a current yield of 14%. Suppose that after purchasing this bond, interest rates on investments fall to 12%. If rates stay at 12%, the actual yield to maturity on your bond will be 12.5% instead of 14%. On the other hand, if interest rates rise, so will the yield to maturity since you will be able to reinvest interest payments at higher rates.

Since zeros don't pay out periodic interest, there's no reinvestment risk. Instead, a zero's yield is determined by the discount from face value and the years to maturity. For example, on a five-year zero selling at $49.72, for each $100 face amount your dollar return would be the $50.28 difference between the cost of the bond and its redemption value of $100. That works out to a 14.48% yield to maturity.

Some Drawbacks

Despite their general appeal, zeros aren't well suited for every long-term investing need. One problem with these bonds is their unusual tax status. While investors don't receive a nickel in interest on a zero until the bond matures, the Internal Revenue Service requires that investors in zero-coupon bonds pay taxes each year on the so-called "imputed" interest—the increase in value even though the profit isn't realized until maturity. That means the investor must assume a net cash outflow (in the amount of taxes due) until the bonds mature.

To avoid this sticky problem, many investors use zeros to fund tax-sheltered investments like Individual Retirement Accounts and Keoghs. But when you're evaluating zeros for your IRA, first decide whether long-term fixed-income securities even belong in your portfolio. If they do, only then should you consider buying zeros. (Remember that historically only common stocks have consistently generated investment returns greater than the rate of inflation and thus increase wealth over the longer term.)

Another caveat: When interest rates are volatile, zeros are more risky than traditional bonds because interest on zero coupons is fixed. As a result, their market prices tend to rise and fall more dramatically as rates fluctuate. So the only way to ensure that you won't lose capital is to hold the zero coupon to maturity. (Actually, this is true with any bond.)

How safe are zeros? In the case of the government zeros sold by brokerage firms, the answer is: as safe as those brokers' banks. The zeros are actually certificates issued by the banks themselves—for TIGRs, it's Manufacturers Hanover, Morgan Guaranty for CATS. Acting as custodians, they hold the Treasury securities that brokers have "stripped" in a irrevocable trust until the bonds mature.

The Treasury's new STRIPS, however, are even safer because Uncle Sam eliminates the middleman. STRIPS have no coupons to begin with. Instead, the government itself divides the interest coupons from the bonds' principal. It then delivers the bonds directly to brokers and banks that sell them to the public. That, in turn, eases what has been up to now another drawback to zeros—sometimes excessive commission charges. Currently, a full-service broker might charge you about $5 to buy fewer than five bonds, in addition to commission fees of anywhere from 1.5% to as much as 5% of the price of the bonds. As more banks and brokerages compete for business in STRIPS, however, those fees will come down, probably to no more than 2%.

Zeros of Other Stripes

If the idea of locking in the guaranteed return of a zero-coupon bond has allure, LIONs, TIGRs, CATS, and STRIPS are far from your only choices. The array includes corporate zeros, mortgaged-backed and tax-exempt municipal zeros, and zero certificates of deposit. Corporate zeros are probably the most risky. (You're betting on a company's future ability to pay you and other bondholders perhaps as much as 30 years down the road.)

Hordes of companies have issued zeros in the past few years, locking themselves into some pretty heavy fixed interest costs. The vast majority of zeros can't be redeemed by their issuers before maturity—unlike most traditional bonds, which companies often can prepay within 5 to 10 years. The yield you receive, of course, depends on the level of risk of a default that you are willing to take. In addition, the longer you are willing to commit money, the higher your yield.

In a twist on the LIONs, TIGRs, and CATS idea, the brokerage firm of Kidder Peabody has created a zero backed by mortgage securities. These are securities issued by the Government National Mortgage Association (Ginnie Mae), Federal National Mortgage Association (Fannie Mae), and Federal Home Loan Mortgage Corporation (Freddie Mac). The Kidder zeros are called ABCs (for Agency Backed Compounded securities). These issues carry a higher yield than Treasury zeros, but like any mortgage-backed bond, the return isn't guaranteed. The securities underlying these zeros are backed by pools of mortgages on single-family homes. Therefore, there is a risk that homeowners will prepay their loans. If that happens, the bonds could be redeemed sooner than expected, with a loss of maturity.

An Income-and-Growth Hybrid

In zero tax-free municipals, the newest acronyms are GAINS (Growth and Income Securities) and FIGS (Future Income and Growth Securities). They're a cross between zeros and traditional, interest-paying bonds. Like regular zeros, investors buy them at a deep discount from face value. But instead of paying off at their full worth at maturity—typically 30 years—these bonds start paying interest after the first 10 or 15 years.

Some banks and savings and loans have begun offering what they call zero CDs, available either from them directly or through brokerage firms. Like other taxable zeros, they are designed primarily for IRAs, Keoghs, and other tax-shelterd accounts. Since the CDs are bank deposits, they are federally insured, up to a face value of $100,000.

If none of these strikes your fancy, Wall Street has more. For instance, E.F. Hutton has put together a high-yield unit trust that combines government zeros and "junk bonds"—bonds with a relatively high risk of default. Like an ordinary unit trust, it gives the investor a slice of a portfolio of bonds. The portfolio, which remains fixed for 10 years, contains 30% Treasury STRIPS and 70% junk bonds. Investors receive regular taxable payments which are generated entirely from the junk bonds. Hutton's first trust was offered in February 1985. Can similar tax-free concoctions be far behind? As long as investors are enamored of zeros, the financial community's creativity may be boundless.

How do you Take Your Municipals?

Unless you're a member of a cloistered religious order or on the Post Office blacklist, you're probably being bombarded with advertising for municipal bond trusts. These tax-exempt trusts are currently one of the hottest products on the retail investment circuit, and vendors are pushing them hard.

They've been easy to sell. For a couple of decades, people with moderate incomes have watched their tax brackets rise and their taxes outpace inflation. Investors began to realize that they would end up with more income if they bought tax-free municipal bonds than if they bought taxable issues even though the yield on the latter is higher. If they could buy municipals issued in the state they lived in, they also avoid state income taxes on the interest.

At the same time, the big institutional buyers—mostly banks and insurance companies—cut back their purchases of municipal bonds as their tax situations changed. Underwriters and stockbrokers shifted their selling efforts to the retail market. Result: individuals are now buying three times as many tax-exempt bonds as all other types of investors combined.

You might like to put together your own portfolio of municipal bonds, but most of us can't afford that. The basic sales lot is $25,000 of face value, so it takes about a quarter of a million dollars, in this one type of investment alone, to buy enough issues for even a minimal degree of diversification. The remaining possibilities are tax-free bond mutual *funds* and unit municipal bond *trusts*. Most investors are already familiar with the workings of mutual funds. If you're not, see the different Mutual Fund Doses covered in this book because the best way to understand the unit trusts is to compare them with mutual funds.

The accompanying figure presents a comparison of the investment features of a unit trust with those of municipal-bond mutual

Figure 87-1

Feature	Mutual Fund	Unit Trust
Portfolio Content	Actively managed, changing	Passively monitored, static
Income Volatility	Moderate	Low
Diversification	Broad	Moderate to narrow
Income Reinvestment	Automatic, if requested	Limited, nature of holding may change
Liquidity	High, at net asset value	Not guaranteed, at lower bid price if available
Costs	Sales charge, 0-8.5% Expenses, 0.5-1.5% per year	Sales charge, 3.5%-5.5% At resale or redemption, 1.5%-2% Expenses, 0.1-0.2% per year

funds. Both pass tax-exempt income through to their investors. But with that, the similarity ceases.

Trusts Versus Funds

Trusts are sponsored by brokerage firms. (Mutual funds are sponsored by investment counselors, insurance companies, or brokers.) The broker selects and purchases a portfolio of municipal bonds. A trust is created to hold the bonds on behalf of the individuals ("certificate holders") who buy shares, called units, of the trust. The bonds pay interest that is not subject to federal taxes. This interest is passed straight through to the certificate holders. Some trusts hold only bonds issued by a single state, providing income that is exempt from both federal and state taxes to certificate holders who live in the issuing state. Eventually, the issuers of the bonds repay the principal, which is then returned by the trust to the certificate holders. Once all the principal has been returned, the trust ends. (Most trusts are liquidated once bond repayments have reduced the remaining principal to a small fraction of its original size. The last bonds in the trust are then sold and the proceeds returned to the certificate holders.)

Portfolio Content Mutual funds are actively managed. That is, a professional portfolio manager is assigned to select, buy, and trade the bonds in the fund to achieve superior investment results. This is a complicated job. The returns available on municipal bonds vary with economic conditions in the issuing states or cities, with political changes, and with the source of income used to pay the interest on them, just to name a few of the factors. A bond fund manager is always looking for the best trade-offs between return and risk. Sometimes a manager is successful, sometimes not. The manager may increase the fund's return over that of an unmanaged portfolio—or reduce it. (Of course, if the manager's choices have negative results too often, he or she may wind up managing an unemployment check.) In any case, both the contents of the fund and its investment return will differ from that of an unmanaged portfolio, as a result of the manager's efforts.

When you by a unit trust, on the other hand, you can inspect the portfolio in advance—it's listed in the prospectus—and know that except under unusual circumstances, it will not change over the life of the trust. You lose the advantage of active professional management, but you gain two things. First, you know that if you hold on for the life of the trust, the bonds will mature and you will get back 100 cents for every dollar of face value you purchased (barring defaults). In contrast, when interest rates rise, the net asset value of a bond fund may remain continuously below the price you originally paid because interest and length to maturity are fixed. Second, you get certainty about the content of your portfolio. What you sees is what you gets.

A unit trust portfolio is not entirely ignored by its sponsor: if a bond appears to be in danger of default or if changes in tax laws threaten its exemption, the sponsor can sell it. (Note that bonds under threat of default or other trouble will drop sharply in price, and certificate holders will take a loss on that portion of the portfolio. One of the advantages of active portfolio management is the ability to move out of a dubious issue at the first hint of trouble.) However, defaults are rare.

Income Volatility Similarly, a unit trust's interest income flow is highly predictable. As long as the portfolio remains unchanged, the investor knows exactly how much income he has coming, and when. On the other hand, a mutual fund's interest income per share varies over time as the going rate in the market changes. Moreover, shareholders can add or withdraw money from a fund at any time, and the portfolio manager must buy or sell bonds to accommodate that cash flow. The timing of these purchases and sales can affect the overall yield from the fund. For most funds, the degree of volatility isn't too great, but income isn't perfectly predictable.

Diversification Many unit bond trusts contain fewer bond issues than the typical mutual fund. That means that the fortunes of any single issue will have a greater impact on the investor in a trust than on a fund shareholder. The fewer the issues, the greater the risk. Bond experts say that the lowest acceptable number of issues for safety is 8-10. I think that's cutting it pretty fine; most investors would sleep better with twice that number. But

Dollars and Sense

remember that diminishing returns set in eventually. After a point, there is little value gained from increasing diversification: a 20-bond portfolio is safer than a 10-bond one, but there is little benefit from adding another 10 or 20 issues to the original 20.

Trusts that specialize in the bonds of a single state are smaller and tend to hold fewer issues than do multistate portfolios. That's only to be expected, since the bonds have to be chosen from a smaller universe and are sold to a smaller group of potential investors. These single-state trusts achieve some diversification by holding various types of bonds: some from hospital projects, others that finance state college dormitories, some backed by tax revenues, and so forth. But there's no denying that such small portfolios, concentrated in single states, are riskier than larger trusts with a nationwide list of issues. The added risk is part of the price the investor pays for avoiding state as well as federal income tax.

Reinvestment Municipal bond mutual funds, like all funds, give their shareholders a wide range of reinvestment options. You can choose to take all your income as it is paid, or reinvest all or part in added shares of the fund, including fractional shares if the amount of income you reinvest doesn't cover a round number. The fund's manager combines all the income that shareholders reinvest and buys more bonds for the fund's portfolio.

This can't be done with a unit trust. Obviously, if earned income could be added to the trust, additional bonds would have to be purchased with it, and the composition of the trust's portfolio would change. The certificate holder is, therefore, faced with the job of finding a home for any income he or she wants to reinvest. The situation is compounded as bonds in the trust are redeemed by the issuer, because the investor then has the returned principal to reinvest as well. Trust sponsors do offer reinvestment options. Your money can sometimes be channeled automatically into another of the sponsor's unit trusts. It's a fair assumption that the new trust will resemble the old one as closely as possible, but it won't be identical. Other unit trusts permit reinvestment in a tax-free bond mutual fund run by the sponsor. This arrangement is tempting, since it has the advantage of convenience, but the investor should compare the sponsor's fund with competing funds to be sure it's the best available for his or her purposes.

Liquidity A unit trust is a long-term investment. The certificate holder gets no guarantee that he can sell his unit if for some reason he wants to get his money out before the trust ends. Nearly all sponsors maintain a secondary market for the units of their own trusts—that is, they buy units offered by current certificate holders and resell them to new investors—but they are not legally bound to do so, and can stop repurchasing at any time. Selling units is expensive. An investor may be able to sell shares through an organized securities market (a so-called "secondary market"), but this will usually result in the loss of some capital. If there is no secondary market, investors can redeem their units by returning them to the trust, but the cost may be even greater. In theory, high rates of redemption could force the trust to sell bonds, changing the portfolio. In fact, turnover is low and most investors in unit trusts intend to hold their units for the life of the trust. Most mutual funds, including bond funds, are also held as long-term investments. However, as is *not* true of unit trusts, if you invest in a tax-free bond fund, you have the comfort of knowing that you can always redeem your shares immediately at the current net asset value of the fund. (This is true in most cases. Some funds do have a so-called "exit charge" when you sell shares. Exit charges are relatively rare at this point, but are becoming more common. Check the prospectus carefully.)

Costs The cost ranges of funds and unit trusts overlap. All "no-load" funds (a "load" is a sales charge) are less expensive than unit trusts; you pay only a fee that covers annual operating expenses. The fee comes to about 1% of assets. However, a small investment in a load mutual fund, on which you might pay the maximum load or initial sales charge of 8.5%, is more costly than the 4% or so you might pay to get into a unit trust. (The sales charge on units bought in the secondary market may be higher than the charge on the initial offering.) Since unit trust portfolios are monitored, not managed, operating expenses are tiny—a fraction of a percent of assets.

A final cost of investing in unit trusts comes from the bid/offered spread. This is the difference between what a potential buyer is willing to pay (bid) and a seller is willing to accept (offered) for an issue, and determines resale prices. The spread is a result of the way the municipal bond market works. When you buy a stock, your broker goes into the market for you, gets you the best price he can, and then adds his commission based on the size of your investment. But municipal bonds carry no commissions. Brokers buy them wholesale and sell them to investors retail, like groceries, winter coats, or new cars. Moreover, the market for many issues is very thin (that is, the issues are seldom traded.). This makes for a volatile and uncertain market. On any given day, bond traders are offering for sale or are bidding to buy municipal issues. Naturally, bidders offer lower prices than sellers would like; sellers ask for higher prices than buyers want to pay. For a trade to take place, one or both parties have to give a little.

There is no central clearing house for these deals. But there is always a general range of recent bids for a given issue, and a general range of recent offers for the same issue. To value a unit trust, outside evaluators are hired to determine what the current bid and offered prices are for all the bonds in the trust (Standard & Poor's, among others, provides such a service.)

When an investor buys units, he pays a price based on the higher offered prices of the bonds in the portfolio, as determined by the evaluator. But when he sells or redeems his units, he gets a price based on the lower bid price. This spread is usually about 2% of the value of the bonds. Moreover, the evaluator's estimates of bid and offered prices are themselves questionable—the range of error has to be high, given the nature of the market, and it is hard for the investor in a unit trust to tell how good or how bad a deal he's getting.

With the costs of purchasing and selling totaling 5-8% of the overall investment, it should be clear that unit trusts are not appropriate for short-term investments or for speculative trading. Unfortunately, we have heard of some brokers pushing them for that purpose—which would greatly enrich the broker, but probably scalp the investor.

Making Your Choice

As with any investment, your choice between tax-free bond mutual funds and unit trusts boils down to two issues: your own circumstances and needs (for instance, your needs for liquidity or ability to hold them for the long term) and the terms of the specific fund or trust you're considering. The second point seems to be the one that gets skipped most often by unit trust buyers. Compared to a unit trust prospectus, the average mutual fund prospectus is light reading. So a number of investors we know have bought in, purely on a broker's recommendation, without really understanding what they were buying. But it makes no sense to plunge into this—or any other—investment vehicle unless you're willing to do the spadework required.

Investing In U.S. Savings Bonds

Uncle Sam's savings bonds have come out of the horse-and-buggy days when they paid less than you could get on your savings almost anywhere else. If you haven't compared them with what the banks are offering lately, look again. Buy U. S. Savings Bonds, once as exciting as watching grass grow, is suddenly where the action is. That's because while interest rates on other savings vehicles have tumbled, savings bond yields have held up well. These bonds, which are fully guaranteed by the U. S. government, now give people with as little as $25 the chance to earn as much, or more, on their money as someone with $5,000 to invest.

It wasn't always that way. Before 1982, savings bonds had a well-deserved reputation as being among the poorest places to save. Even when interest rates took off for the stratosphere, bonds didn't pay more than 9%. Finally, embarrassed into action, Congress in 1982 permitted the Treasury to index interest on newly issued savings bonds to the rate on five-year Treasury bonds. The rate on EE Series savings bonds is now recalculated every six months—at the beginning of November and May—to keep it at 85% of the average yield on five-year Treasuries for the *preceding* six months.

Because the rate on new savings bonds is indexed to older Treasury bonds, their yields look especially good when interest rates decline. Of course, the reverse is true when interest rates are rising. In addition, savings bonds hold allure for some investors because the interest income from these investments is exempt from both state and local taxes. And they may gain even more luster when you consider that federal income taxes on earned interest is deferred until the bonds are cashed in.

Paying Better Than Ever

The government's current ad campaign for savings bonds, which uses the slogan "Paying Better Than Ever," is designed to promote their competitiveness as an investment. The old slogan, "Take Stock in America," had been used since the 1960s to sell the bonds primarily on patriotism. And it worked up to a point—mainly with widows, school children, and people in the armed services—just a tiny segment of the general investing public. But even these investors eventually tired of seeing their savings steadily lose ground to inflation.

By the early 1980s, when market rates soared as high as 16%, many people holding savings bond were stuck with half that. Congress could no longer ignore the problem. Starting in 1979, legislators made several weak attempts to make the rate more competitive. By 1981, they had increased it to a high of 9% provided the bonds were held six years. The market-rate system was finally adopted in November 1982. As a result, EE Series bonds have gradually been losing their stodgy image and owners have earned decent returns.

Some Strings Attached

Of course, the bonds have disadvantages for some people. To get the current rate, you have to hold the bonds at least five years. Otherwise, the return is somewhat less, depending on when you cash them in. If you redeemed one of these bonds after four years, for example, the return would be 7%. After three years 6.5%, after two years 6%, and at the end of one year, just 5.5%.

In addition to the five-year holding period, you can't redeem the bonds at all within the first six months except in an emergency. If you must have the cash, you have to go to the considerable trouble of obtaining a special waiver from the government. Further, unlike other treasury securities, EE bonds can't be used as collateral for a loan. Saving bonds also must be registered in the owner's name, and ownership can't be transferred except under specific conditions, such as when the registered owner dies.

What's Old is New Again—Zeros

Ironically, good old savings bonds have always been based on what is currently a hot investment concept: zero-coupon bonds. Unlike traditional bonds, the "zeros" do not pay regular interest until maturity. However, when you buy any zero, you pay less than its stated (face) value. Your profit comes when the bonds are redeemed for full face value, plus interest. In the case of savings bonds, the purchase price is exactly half the face value. For example, the smallest available $50 bond costs $25 and the largest, which is a $10,000 bond, costs $5,000. In between, the denominations are $75, $100, $200, $500, $1,000 and $5,000.

You can buy—and redeem—savings bonds by walking into almost any commercial bank, as well as any Federal Reserve Bank. Or you can deal directly by mail with the Bureau of Public Debt,

Washington, D.C. 20226. As testimony to the bonds' newfound popularity with investors, over-the-counter purchases now account for more than half of all sales. Previously, most sales have been through payroll savings plans which many companies make available to their employees as an automatic investment vehicle.

While the Treasury touts the bonds as savings vehicles, they are also first-rate tax shelters. The big difference between savings bonds and other zeros is that, although interest is figured and compounded every six months, no federal tax is paid until the bond is redeemed. Zeros that Wall Street brokerages are pushing—including the so-called government "strips", which are Treasury bonds whose coupons have been removed—require investors to pay taxes on the accrued interest annually even though it isn't paid out.

Since savings-bond interest is credited only twice a year, the best time to redeem them is right after the rate change at the end of each six-month period. That means you should redeem them at the beginning of May or November. If you cash in your bonds in December, for example, you won't receive interest for that extra month. Depending on your tax situation, however, you might want to wait to redeem savings bonds until January to push the interest income into the next tax year.

Swapping EE Bonds for HH Bonds

As the federal tax picture now stands, the tax deferral already connected with savings bonds is reason enough to buy them in a child's name, say, to save for college. When the bonds are redeemed, the accumulated interest is taxed at the child's lower rate. Similarly, as long as other savings rates are down, EE bonds are also a good preretirement purchase. You can invest in the bonds now, when you're in a high tax bracket, and redeem them after retirement, when your bracket is probably lower.

When you are ready to retire or have already retired, it can also make sense to trade series EE bonds for series HH "current income" bonds. The only way to "purchase" HH bonds is by swapping the savings bonds you already have, including the older, lower-paying series E and series H bonds which the Treasury replaced with series EE and series HH bonds in 1980.

Series HH bonds are different from other savings bonds in a couple of important respects. For one, they pay a flat 7.5%; the rate doesn't "float." They also spin off a check for interest every six months. But that income is taxable. On the plus side, however, making the switch defers federal taxes for all the interest earned on the old bonds you traded in. When you eventually redeem your HH bonds, the taxable interest is the difference between their redemption value and what it cost you to buy the bonds.

Current-income HH bonds are sold in denominations of $500, $1,000, $5,000 and $10,000. You can switch into them by filling out the appropriate forms at any bank that sells savings bonds or at any Federal Reserve branch. You can also request the forms by mail from a branch office of the Bureau of Public Debt, 200 Third St., Parkersburg, W. VA 26101.

The government's helpful booklet, "50 Questions and Answers About Savings Bonds," explains in detail both swaps and how the market-interest system works. It's free from the Treasury's Savings Bond Division, Office of Public Affairs, Washington, D.C. 20226.

How to Earn Returns on Idle Cash

When professional investors have cash lying around that they don't yet want to commit to the stock or bond market, they stash it in what they call *cash equivalents*. These are short-term, low-risk securities that keep funds "at work" (earning interest) but easily available for longer-term investments when the time comes. Individuals need cash equivalents, too. Since they can't purchase most of the securities big investors use—most involve minimum purchases of $5,000-10,000 and active trading—they turn to bank accounts and money market mutual funds as cash equivalents. When people debate the merits of banks and funds, they often seem to suggest that you have to choose between them, and you'd better choose right! The fact is that many of us have both types of accounts, and more of us will continue to as time goes by. Each has features that make it particularly useful for some purposes. The trick is to keep the right amounts in the right places for the right reasons.

Individual Goals

These cash equivalents can help you accomplish three jobs within your total financial planning. They allow you to make the best use of the cash flow you spend, to efficiently and profitably transfer some of your cash flow to investment, and to hold some of your total capital in investments that are almost without risk. You can think of these as transaction accounts, accumulation accounts, and low-risk investments.

In selecting the right combination of bank and fund accounts, you'll have to make compromises among three benefits: *return on investment, convenience,* and *safety.* The rate of return on most cash equivalents can be determined with a little pencil pushing. But safety and convenience depend on your preferences.

Rates of Return

Anyone who tells you that "banks pay more than money market funds," or "funds pay more than banks" doesn't understand the actual rate of return. While either statement might be true *on average,* each type of vehicle pays a wide range of returns. The rate you end up with depends greatly on your choices of convenience and safety. You can't put your money in "The First Average National Bank" or "The Average Money Market Investors' Fund."

Comparing banks' and funds' rates of return is a little tricky. Funds charge management fees which are subtracted from the fund's earnings before the rate of return is calculated. Since these fees are calculated on total assets, all investors in the fund pay the same percentage. The reported return is the net amount investors actually got over the period shown after fees were paid.

Banks, on the other hand, may base both their rates and their fees on a variety of factors: account balances, number of transactions, etc. The net return depends on how you use your account and may differ from the return earned by other investors with the same kind of account. Get complete details from the bank before you figure your expected return. Also, remember to add into your return the value of extra services the bank may provide to depositors—a free checking account, for instance.

Convenience

If you use your cash equivalent account for transactions, you probably won't have a high average balance over the year. In that case, difference in rates of return, even fairly wide ones, won't have much of an effect on your earnings. Account provisions, such as minimum balance, minimum amount that can be withdrawn, number of monthly checks allowed, and so forth, will be more important to you. If you are using your account to build up savings balances for periodic investment, both rate of return and convenience have to be considered. You should probably check first with the institution through which you do most of your investing to see what kinds of accounts it has available. Most financial firms (including insurers and brokers as well as banks and fund managements) now offer cash equivalent investments and make transfers between the different accounts they offer as easy as possible.

After determining what conveniences are available, compare rates of return. You don't have to settle for a substandard return, but neither should you pass up an efficient transfer arrangement by reaching for the last hundredth of a point.

Safety

Over the entire range of investments, all short-term, highly liquid holdings are ranked as extremely conservative. That is, they involve relatively little risk. But there are still degrees of safety.

Investments guaranteed by the U.S. government are safest of all. These include all insured bank accounts and short-term Treasury securities. Some money market funds buy only securities issued by the U.S. government in order to provide this kind of safety. However, money market funds may put money to work with both United States and foreign banks and corporations. These nongovernment investments increase the risk of the fund. Risk is also affected by the average maturity of a fund's holdings. The longer the maturity, the more volatile is the price of security. All funds provide information on the assets they hold. This information is also available in summary form for all funds in publications of investment services such as Wiesenberger and Donoghue which can be found in many libraries.

As with all investments, cash equivalents involve a trade-off between risk and return. Quite simply, the higher the risk, the greater the potential return—and the potential for default. Funds that stick to Treasury issues and investments with very short maturities, while avoiding lower-rated or foreign issues, tend to return less than those with less risk-averse policies. The bad news is that it does take a bit of work to figure out which cash equivalent accounts are best suited to your purposes. The good news is that financial deregulation has resulted in such a range of possibilities that you can now have exactly what you need, just by taking the time to look for it.

Equity CDs—High Yield With a New Twist

Want an investment that provides a high yield along with the inflation hedge of real estate? Up until recently, the only way to get both was through real estate investment trusts or certain limited partnerships. But in 1984, a California-based savings and loan introduced a third alternative, the equity certificate of deposit (CD), which was enthusiastically received by the investment community. The stated yield (interest) and principal (face value) of the equity CD are guaranteed by the federal government, and it offers this bonus: a share in the market appreciation of properties financed with mortgages from the CD's proceeds. (Because they agree to share any potential profit from increased property values, borrowers obtaining mortgages financed by equity CDs pay lower interest rates.)

CrossLand Savings of New York, formerly Western Savings & Loan of Salt Lake City, was the second savings institution to offer the equity CDs, with its recent $50 million offering underwritten by Shearson Lehman/American Express. The CrossLand CD has a federally guaranteed 10% yield over an eight-year life. When the CDs mature, CrossLand will pay the holders additional "contingent interest" resulting from any rise in the value of the real estate. This bonus interest is dependent on market appreciation and is not guaranteed by the government. CrossLand offers two types of CDs: a coupon-bearing CD which is offered at par, or $1,000, and a zero-coupon CD which is priced at $460 and pays $1,000 at maturity. The coupon CD pays interest at regular intervals and is redeemed for its par (face) value at maturity. The zero-coupon CD pays no interest until maturity, but automatically compounds interest at a 10% rate so that it is redeemed for more than par. These new CDs initially sold at a rate of $1 million per day.

The *contingent interest* earned by the CD investors from property appreciation is calculated using a complex formula that allows CrossLand to increase the proportion of appreciation as property values rise. Figure 90-1 outlines the yields investors would receive

Figure 90-1
Equity CD Yields*

Annual property appreciation	0%	3.5%	5.0%	7.5%	10.0%	12.5%	15.0%
Yield to maturity on equity CDs	10%	13.5%	14.1%	15.2%	16.5%	17.3%	18.5%

*Based on equity CDs offered by CrossLand Savings of New York

from the CrossLand CDs from various levels of property appreciation.

As you can see, when property values rise sharply, the corresponding yields from the CDs do not rise as rapidly. However, if property values increase as little as 3.5%, holders of equity CDs would earn a respectable 13.5% rate of return. But the best part is that while upside potential (the amount to be gained from an increase in value) is great, all an investor can lose is contingent interest. The basic 10% interest rate and the principal are guaranteed by the government.

Drawbacks

While the new equity CDs sound like a great idea, there are drawbacks that have made some investment professionals skeptical. First, the broker fee charged on the sale of the new CDs is 6%—that's four times the fee charged by brokers for conventional CDs. And the guaranteed interest rate (on an equity CD) is slightly lower than what a depositor could earn on a conventional CD. Another catch is that if interest rates fall to a level that would make the CDs unprofitable to the savings and loan, issuing them can be terminated by returning the deposits plus any accrued interest. Finally, because the CD holder does not actually own the properties, the gain from the property appreciation is treated as ordinary income and is taxed accordingly.

But the biggest question now asked regarding the equity CDs concerns the savings and loan industry's underwriting capabilities. Not all institutions are in the position to enter the business of issuing commercial real estate loans. The Federal Home Loan Bank Board, the federal agency responsible for guaranteeing the equity CDs, foresaw such problems and limits the savings and loans that can issue the certificates.

The future of the popular, and sometimes controversial, new equity CDs will depend on performance. But in the meantime, those investors who venture into these untested grounds can rest assured that at least their principal, and the stated interest, are backed by Uncle Sam himself.

Investing in Gold and Precious Metals

When the United States took necessary actions against Libya, the repercussions of growing Middle East tensions were felt all the way to the financial market. Gold, in particular, was affected as other Middle East countries dumped their U.S. dollars and bought the precious metal. The price has dropped somewhat recently, but investors are now beginning to look once again at gold.

There is a surprisingly wide array of available investments in gold and other precious metals. These range from the highly conservative to the highly speculative, and include the outright purchase of bullion or coin, the purchase of common stock issued by a gold mining firm, the purchase or sale of futures contracts and options on such contracts, and the purchase of shares issued by precious metals mutual funds.

Bullion

Gold bullion, or bars, may be purchased from international dealers, brokerage houses, and most large banks. Increments of from one tenth of one ounce up to 400 ounces (a standard bar) are available, although purchases of less than five ounces carry a rather high "manufacturing charge." This is the cost your dealer incurs to have your gold put into bullion form (as either a bar or a wafer), which, of course, is passed along to you. Figure 91-1 lists typical manufacturing charges for varying bullion purchases.

In addition to the manufacturing charges, bullion investors must also pay brokerage commissions (although these tend to be relatively low) and, unless they feel comfortable stashing gold in their homes, storage costs as well.

Gold bullion comes in varying degrees of purity, from top-of-the-line bullion with a "fineness" of .9999 (which is considered pure) down to bullion with the lowest acceptable level of purity, a fineness

Figure 91-1
Bullion Manufacturing Costs

Amount of Bullion	Cost Per Ounce
1 oz.	$6.00
2 oz.	5.00
5 oz.	3.00
10 oz.	2.50
1 Kg.	2.00
100 oz.	1.00

Source: Cavelti, Peter C.; *New Profits in Gold, Silver & Strategic Metals;* McGraw-Hill, 1985.

of .9950. Wafers and bars of gold bullion carry their weight and fineness stamped right on them. In terms of trading, a 10 ounce bar with a fineness of .9999 is considered pure, so if gold is trading at $300 an ounce, this 10-ounce bar is classified as exactly 10 ounces of gold and is worth $3,000.

However, be careful if you're considering buying gold of lower purity level. The calculations are a bit different. For example, if you want to purchase a 10 ounce bar with a fineness of only .995, it will cost you less, obviously, than a 10 ounce bar of pure gold. To figure out the selling price, simply multiply the bar's fineness level by its weight to determine its "purity equivalent weight." In this case, it's .995 times 10 ounces, which is 9.95 ounces. Then multiply this result by the market price per ounce to determine the correct selling price. In this case, it's 9.95 ounces times $300/ounce, or $2,985.

When buying bullion, be sure to use leading dealers only, as they buy gold from refiners who are internationally recognized. This is important when you want to resell your gold, because if your gold's refiner is not recognized, your gold may have to be assayed (tested for fineness), which is an unnecessary expense.

Bullion Coins

Gold bullion may also be purchased in the form of coins. The Austrian Corona, the Hungarian Corona, the Mexican Peso, and the Russian Chervonetz were once the world's most popular gold coins. However, the amounts of gold in these coins varied. In recent years, they have been far outpaced by the South African Krugerrand, the Canadian Maple Leaf, and the Mexican Onza, which all contain a specified weight of pure gold.

Gold coins are more expensive than gold bullion. First, the dealer's (or bank's) premium on gold coins ranges between 2 and 8% and is incurred to cover the cost of minting and retailing the coins. Second, most states charge sales tax on bullion coins.

Gold Certificates

To avoid the problem of storing gold bullion, investors can purchase gold certificates and let the issuing institution worry about storage. However, the institution will charge a storage fee and, most likely, a transaction fee when the certificate is purchased. Because these fees range between 0.25 and 3%, it pays to shop around for the best deal. The top three dealers in the U.S. today are Deak-Perera, Citibank, and Republic National Bank.

Precious Metals Accounts

The increase in gold prices in the late 1970s, and the resulting pandemonium it caused in the gold market, led to another creative innovation by gold dealers—the gold passbook account. While such accounts served their purpose when the U.S. investing public was infected by the gold bug, the added conveniences they offer are hardly worth the extra cost at the present time. However, if the price of gold ever takes off as it did in its glory years of the 1970s, watch for gold accounts to proliferate once again.

Futures

The futures market allows buyers to purchase (and sellers to sell) a specific amount of a commodity at a set price on an agreed upon date in the future. Gold futures are used by two primary groups—industrial users and speculators. Industrial users (such as jewelers) are able to protect themselves from fluctuations in future gold prices by buying futures contracts. Thus, they are able to "lock in" gold prices and thereby reduce losses which could be caused by unfavorable future price fluctuations.

Because a futures contract can be purchased for a small fraction of its total value (known as "buying on margin"), for a relatively small investment speculators can get a piece of the futures action. In this market, small investments can be parlayed into millions of dollars.

But in this market, small investments can produce losses in the millions, as well.

Speculators have always dominated the gold futures market where, in 1983 alone, they accounted for 99% of all contracts traded. Futures trading should be undertaken only by those individuals with enough nerve and capital to accept the large associated risks.

Options

Gold options give the holder the right to buy or sell gold at a fixed price in the future. There are two types of options— calls and puts. When you buy a "call" option, you buy the right to *purchase* gold at a fixed price in the future. The price you pay for this privilege is called the *"premium,"* and the premium is the most you could lose if the market works against you.

When you buy a "put" option, you buy the right to *sell* gold at a fixed price in the future. Here, too, you pay a premium.

Buying options on gold futures is, therefore, less risky than buying futures outright, although the gains are usually much smaller, as well. However, entire books have been written on options strategies (which are beyond the scope of this chapter), and playing the gold options market successfully requires both expertise in options and a strong understanding of the precious metals market. Additionally, options should be thought of as short-term trading vehicles and not as long-term investments. Therefore, they require constant monitoring which many private investors find more time consuming than it is worth.

Gold Mining Stocks

Gold mining stocks offer another medium of investment in gold. Unlike gold bars or coins, mining stocks generally pay dividends, often quite high. It is important to differentiate between South African mining firms and their North American counterparts. South Africa boasts the largest gold mines in the world, and because of the size and quality of the deposits, South Africa mining firms are generally more profitable than those in North America. By law, South African firms must pay out their entire profits in the form of dividends, making their stocks quite attractive from a yield standpoint as well.

However, ongoing political turmoil in South Africa and anti-apartheid sentiments in the United States have made many South African investments much more questionable, not just from an ethical standpoint, but in terms of risk and return as well.

North American gold mining firms offer greater political and social stability, but because of their smaller size, lower deposit quality, and higher production costs, their profitability is somewhat limited.

Investing in gold mining shares is quite different from simply buying the precious metal. In addition to price changes in the precious metals market, mining share prices are affected by developments in the mining industry, government regulation, economic and political climate, and the status of the mining company issuing the shares. In other words, mining stock must be analyzed just like any other common stock, where earnings, growth rates, capitalization, and dividend policy all affect the current share price.

Beyond a purely fundamental financial analysis of the mining firm, investors must also consider a number of other factors specific to the mining process itself. Production costs, taxation, and the projected "life" of a mine are all important considerations. Adding to the complexities are the difficulties associated with any foreign investment, which include changes in currency exchange rates and in the political situation, different accounting standards, and timing of current information.

Precious Metals Mutual Funds

A much easier, and often less expensive, way to own mining stocks is by purchasing shares of one of the many mutual funds which specialize in that industry. Mutual funds offer professional management and diversification at a low cost. While many gold and precious metals funds charge a "load," or sales commission, on purchases, there are several good no-load funds which do not charge commissions. One of the most popular no-load funds is the United Services Gold Shares Fund (United Services Advisors, P.O. Box 29467, San Antonio, TX 78229; (800) 531-5777) which invests primarily in South African mining shares. The United Services group also offers the New Prospector fund which, in response to political and ethical factors, invests only in North American mining stocks.

Collectibles

Under the catchall phrase "collectibles," there are several different types of investments. Coins, medals, and jewelry are a few different types of collectible items which can be made from gold. Medals and jewelry are almost always worth more for their aesthetic appeal than for their gold content, and unless gold hits $800 an ounce again, melting down such pieces to get the gold won't pay.

Coins are valued not primarily because of their gold or silver content, but instead, for their rarity. As with many collectibles, a coin is judged on rarity, age, and appearance. This is quite complicated and requires a very high degree of knowledge. Investors who simply wish to buy precious metals should not consider rare coins.

Buying Gold on Margin

Most banks dealing in bullion offer lending programs through which investors can buy gold on margin, with minimum loan requirements usually starting at a hefty $50,000. This way, investors can buy more gold than they would have been able to afford otherwise. The bank loans the buyer up to, say, 50% of the dollar amount of gold he wishes to purchase, so he only has to come up with half the cost of the investment. The bank then keeps the gold as security against the loan.

Because of the effects of leverage in buying on a margin, if the price of gold rises, a buyer with $50,000 to invest who borrows another $50,000 from a bank to buy $100,000 worth of gold will earn a much better return on his original $50,000 than another buyer who simply buys gold with $50,000 of his own money. Sounds great? Not really, because leverage also works against buyers if the price of gold should decline.

What's worse is that if the buyer had borrowed the maximum percentage allowed by the lending bank, and the price of gold fell, the bank could demand more money as collateral. For example, assume the buyer's gold is originally worth $100,000 with 50% financed by the bank. Assume, then, that the price of gold falls so that his investment is now only worth $80,000. The bank, which had loaned $50,000 and required $100,000 in collateral, is now only holding $80,000 in collateral. It can demand an additional $20,000 cash from the buyer, and if the buyer can't come up with the cash, the bank can sell $20,000 of the buyer's gold—at the lower price—to bring the margin ratio back to 50%.

Not only are margin loans quite risky, but they are expensive as well. Most banks charge several points over the prime lending rate on margin loans, which is a hefty price to pay for assuming such high risks.

We have now covered the many different ways an investor can participate in the gold market. These are summarized in Figure 91-2. But we have done so without answering the question "*Should* investors participate in the gold market?" I feel that investors can almost always earn better returns in the stock market than by buying gold. However, there are some investors who simply *feel* better owning a little gold, so to them I give this advice: Gold is really only a good investment in the event of a worldwide economic collapse. So the best strategy is to commit 5% of your portfolio to gold, and pray that it goes down.

Figure 91-2
Gold Investments
The Pros and Cons

Type of Investment	Advantages	Disadvantages
Bullion	Less expensive than most other types of previous metals investment	Storage costs & risk
	Instant convertibility into cash	Pays no dividends
	Negotiable internationally	
	Prices widely quoted	
	Direct investment in precious metal	

Continued

Figure 91-2, Continued
Gold Investments
The Pros and Cons

Type of Investment	Advantages	Disadvantages
Bullion Coins	Relatively inexpensive	Storage cost & risk
	Instant convertibility into cash	Premiums are high
	Negotiable internationally	Sales tax
	Prices widely quoted	Pays no dividends
	Direct investment in precious metal	
Certificates	Inexpensive	Pays no dividends
	Highly liquid	Certificates must be registered
	No storage risk	
	No sales tax, in most cases	
	Bullion prices quoted widely	
Precious Metals Accounts	Convenience	Expensive
	Usually no storage risk	Restricted negotiability
	Transaction speed	Pays no dividends
Futures Contracts	Flexibility to assume a "long" position (betting the price will rise) or a "short" position (betting the price will fall)	Large risk-no limit to losses
	Leverage-buying on can be used. (A caveat here: leveraging can produce huge losses as well as gains, and entails a great degree of risk)	Investor is tied to certain contract and trading stipulations
	Liquidity	Delivery, if taken, is at an exchange warehouse
	Futures contract prices are widely quoted	
	No storage risk	

Continued

Figure 91-2, Continued
Gold Investments
The Pros and Cons

Type of Investment	Advantages	Disadvantages
Options	Investor can profit from declining prices as well as from rising prices	Requires good understanding of options markets
	Leverage may be used	Expensive
	Risks are more clearly defined	Contract sizes, maturity dates and trading hours are limited
	Option prices are widely quoted	
	No storage risk	
Stock Mining Company	Can earn dividend income	Knowledge of mining industry, individual firms, and precious metals required
	Highly liquid	
	Prices widely quoted	If shares are foreign companies, knowledge of international investment and rate risk is required
	Eligible for tax-deferred programs (IRAs, Keoghs, etc)	
		Share price fluctuations can be caused by more than just changes in price of precious metals
		Large minimum investment needed (100 shares) to avoid excessive brokerage costs
		Not a direct investment in precious metals

Continued

Figure 91-2, Continued
Gold Investments
The Pros and Cons

Type of Investment	Advantages	Disadvantages
Precious Metals Mutual Funds	Can earn dividend income Lost-cost diversification Low minimum investment Convenience Professional management Liquidity Prices widely quoted Eligible for tax-deferred programs	Load funds may charge up to 8.5% sales commission
Collectibles	Aesthetic appeal, historical significance, etc.	High cost Low liquidity Requires some knowledge.

Taken in part from: Cavelti, Peter C.; New Profits in Gold, Silver & Strategic Metals

Keeping Your Broker Honest

Preventing problems with your broker is often more important than solving them. Taking an intelligent interest in what your broker is doing for you is the best way to establish a good working relationship.

"Beware of your broker," said the headline in the business section of *Newsweek*, December 22, 1986. Below the headline were horror stories about investors who had been badly burned by their brokers. "Investors are left with a deck that's stacked against them," the story says.

But if you play your cards right, that doesn't have to be true. Your best protection against a dishonest broker is your own good sense—and constant vigilance. Managing your broker is like managing any other aspect of your investment program. You must think ahead about how to protect yourself and actually do what you have planned.

It's true that there are laws to protect defrauded investors, but you can only call on them after your investments have already been impaired. And none of them will replace any profits you may have lost. The Securities Investor Protection Commission, for instance, will make sure (up to a point) that you get back what's in your account if your broker goes bankrupt. But what you get back is the number of shares of stock without compensation for any loss of value while it was tied up in the reorganization. If you're an unsophisticated investor (as far as the law goes) and your broker has done you wrong, you may be able to get back what you paid in fees, taxes and interest—but nothing for loss of portfolio value. Securities fraud really is low-risk larceny.

So the thing to do, obviously, is to avoid problems rather than try to resolve them after they have happened. And the more you know, the less the incentive is for your broker to try to put one over on you.

The first thing to realize is that while a broker works for you, he is also working to feed himself and his dependents. This is a job with a built in conflict of interest. It is up to you to make sure that your own interests are properly protected.

Protecting yourself begins when you interview a new broker, and even before. Before you invest in a stock, you would read the annual report for that company, wouldn't you? Did you analyze the annual report of your brokerage firm the same way? Did you look for fudging in the footnotes? If it's publicly traded, did you find out how much stock management owns? How committed is it?

Once you're in the office, is the phone ringing so much your broker hardly has time to talk to you? He may be too busy to give you proper attention. On the other hand, if the phone doesn't ring at all, maybe all those noncallers know something you don't know.

Find out the philosophy of your broker and make sure it parallels your own. If you're an investor and he's a trader, go elsewhere. If you're 75 and he's recommending options, unless you're investing with gambling money, go elsewhere.

And once you find a broker you're comfortable with, for profits' sake, don't sign anything without reading it carefully first. There are all sorts of little surprises waiting in these contract documents. For instance, be sure you're not accidentally granting the broker the right to trade for you in certain situations unless you really want him to trade for you. We're not talking about an outright permission for discretionary trading; there are degrees of discretion—and you're wiser to keep them all to yourself.

Analyzing Recommendations

Once you've decided on a broker, how do you keep him honest? Begin by setting up a log, and in it record every conversation you have with your broker (so maybe sometimes you have to take notes on napkins—just make sure you transfer those notes to the log). This serves two purposes: you know what the broker said and you know what you said. Knowing you have to write down the entire conversation forces you to be more clear—and that helps the broker to serve you.

For instance, you want to sell some stock. The broker gives you the price at the last sale. So you order the sale—but by the time the trade reaches the floor, the price has dropped a point. Should he sell or not? To avoid confusion, you should have given him the price at which you'll sell, or told him to sell at market. Being clear from the start helps avoid problems later, say, when your account seems to be coming up short.

The fun part, though, is how you and the broker handle his recommendations to you. Be especially wary of new brokers trying to boost their business with products with which they are not familiar. Be equally wary of old brokers taking on new products—they may not know enough either.

Also, be aware that certain products, including tax-deferred annuities, carry higher commissions. Make sure you know the actual price and commission on whatever you buy.

Make sure when the broker is touting a new stock that he answers your questions promptly and directly. If he says, "It's in the prospectus," his recommendation isn't based on solid personal understanding of the stock.

Ask him where he's getting his information. Ask him about the management and the downside risk. Ask him how thin the market might be in an undertraded stock and how hard would it be for you to get your money back out if you need it.

Often the stock-of-the-week your broker is touting is part of an offering being underwritten by the brokerage firm he works for. Ask him whether he has any interest in the stock.

And, ask him whether he has a quota. Stranger things have happened.

Once in a while, a broker will cross that fine line between optimism about a stock and downright misrepresentation. True, you can get your money back under the Securities Act and state law if you've bought on the basis of false statements. But you don't want to worry about getting your money *back*—you don't want to *lose* it in the first place! So make sure you understand exactly what the broker is basing his recommendation on; this will help him make sure he understands as well.

If you decide not to accept a broker's recommendation, don't just forget about it. Track a couple of his recommendations over time to see how they perform. You may have missed a terrific opportunity by ignoring his advice. On the other hand, he may not be very good at picking stocks. And if he's not, and his recommendations don't do well, point this out from time to time to keep him up on the mark. (It's not necessary to be nasty, of course, but it's helpful that you pay attention to what he's saying and try to evaluate it thoroughly.)

As your broker gets to know you better, his recommendations should be more and more on target and more and more useful to you. The recommendations should be supportive of your overall investment strategy. And absolutely don't take any recommendations that you must act on *now*. No sound investment has to be acted on *right now*. If you take time to evaluate a stock carefully, you may occasionally miss a tick up in price. You will also miss a lot of ticks down. The bottom line is that if a company and its stock are sound, they'll be there after you've found out more about them. You don't have to buy every stock at its cheapest (good thing, because it's impossible). Your goal should be to buy at a price that will eventually make you money. Take your time and do it right.

When You Make a Trade

Sometimes you're going to be buying and selling stocks as well as evaluating recommendations. The way to make sure you are keeping your broker honest here is to hang on to those confirmation slips and compare them carefully to your monthly statement.

In particular, if you want to evaluate how well you're doing, watch the relation of equity to commissions. A number of years ago, securities lawyer Stuart Goldberg came up with the Goldberg Cost/Equity Maintenance Factor. The Goldberg Factor refers to the percentage of return on capital you need to pay your broker's commissions and other expenses.

To get the Goldberg Factor, you divide your average monthly equity into the commissions you pay for one year. If the average monthly equity is $50,000 and over a year you've paid $20,000 in commissions, you need an average rate of return of 40% just to pay your expenses. This is why I constantly remind the subscribers to my advisories that they should buy for the long term. The goal of an investment program is to improve your net worth, not your broker's.

The best way you can defend against churning (having your broker take you in and out of the market too often) is to *learn to say no*. Even if a recommendation sounds good, you can still say no for as long as it takes to evaluate the stock or other investment against your own financial goals properly.

Once you've bought a stock, remember that this is a business relationship—not a marriage. Don't let yourself get emotionally attached to a stock and don't listen if your broker wants you to stay with a stock that you feel is on a soaped slide. As with recommendations, ask him if his firm has an interest in the stock, or if he has. It's true that brokers usually don't discourage sales, but skepticism is appropriate when they do. Know your investments and know which ones shouldn't be in your portfolio any longer.

Don't let the broker talk you into investing too much in a single stock, either. Modern portfolio theory has shown that you need to hold a minimum of ten to twelve different stocks to adequately spread the risk.

Mistakes Will Happen

Yes indeed, things can go wrong without any real negligence or fraud. Paperwork can sometimes get delayed by volume. It's likely to get even more delayed if you're switching your account from one broker to another because it's human nature for a broker not to be in *too* big a hurry to release your account. Computers do make errors, although probably not as many as they're blamed for making. Your broker may occasionally get more enthusiastic or pessimistic about a stock than the stock really warrants. Just be sure it's honest mistakes and not your broker.

You can help keep your broker honest in some very simple ways: First, by being honest with your intentions and your goals. Second, by being clear with your orders and logging your conversations. Third, by reserving the right to make decisions yourself. Fourth, by monitoring the paperwork. And last, by getting all the facts *before* you make an investment decision and sticking to your investment program no matter how tempting a stock may look.

The law will help you, as stated before, to lock the stable door after the horse is gone and sometimes even get the horse back—although not necessarily in the same shape it left. You should really rely on your own judgement and not on the regulators to protect you in *advance*. Their job is primarily to make sure brokers are complying with the laws that regulate them.

If you do suspect foul play, don't let it continue. When things go wrong with a stock after you've held it for a long time or if you realize after an extended period that your broker is doing you wrong, the courts will look at your claims very skeptically. Judges and juries are all too familiar with human nature. They'll suspect you were hoping to make a killing for yourself and only cried wolf when things didn't continue to go your way. Proving that you're genuinely naive as an investor is no easy task. Unless there's been active deception, most investors cannot charge a broker with fraud.

So, to thine own self and thine own investment plan be true, secure your investment program as you'd secure any other asset you have. Don't take the relationship the broker has with you for granted.

I'm not suggesting that you become paranoid and accusatory. Just don't take anything on faith. Preventing problems with your broker is more important than solving them in many ways. Take an intelligent interest in what your broker is doing for you.

Commodities for the High-Risk Investor

Playing the commodities market is *not* an investment—it's speculation. If you want to play the game, you have to be willing to lose all the money you invest and sometimes even more. On the other hand, you can also be a big winner. In either case, you'll know where you stand within one day to six months. For the small investor interested in commodities, perhaps the most cautious way to start is by investing in *commodity funds*. See Dose 84.

Figure 93.1 is a sampling of the organized commodity exchanges and some of the commodities they handle. A complete listing can be found in the financial pages of large circulation newspapers.

Figure 93-1
Commodity Futures Fact Sheet

Commodity	Exchange	Trading Hours*	Contract Size	Minimum Fluctuation	Daily Limit Move	Five-Day Maximum Gain or Loss	Value of a One Cent Move
Cattle (Live)	CME	9:05–1:00	40,000 lbs	$.00025/lb.	1½c/lb.	$3000	$400
Cocoa	CSCE	8:30–2:00	10 Metric tons	$1.00/ton	$88/ton	$4400	10c
Coffee	CSCE	8:45–1:30	37,500 lbs	$.0001/lb.	4c/lb.	$7500	$375
Copper	COMEX	8:50–1:00	25,000 lbs	$.0005/lb.	5c/lb.	$6250	$250
Corn	CBOT	9:30–1:15	5,000 bu.	¼c/bu.	10c/lb.	$2500	$50
Cotton	NY COTTON	9:30–2:00	50,000 lbs	$.0001/lb.	2c/lb.	$5000	$500
Crude Oil/Lt.	NYMEX	9:30–3:30	1,000 bbl.	$.0001/bbl.	1c/bbl.	$50	$10
Gold	COMEX	9:00–2:30	100 troy oz.	$.10/tr. oz.	$25/tr. oz.	$12500	$1.00
Hogs (Live)	CME	9:10–1:00	30,000 lbs.	$.00025/lb.	1½c/lb.	$2250	$300
Lumber	CME	9:00–1:05	130,000 bd. ft.	$.10/bd. ft.	5c/bd. ft.	$32500	$1300
Oats	CBOT	9:30–1:15	5,000 bu.	6c/bu.	10c/bu.	$2500	$50
Orange Juice	NY COTTON	10:15–2:45	15,000 lbs	$.0005/lb.	5c/lb.	$3750	$150
Platinum	NYMEX	9:00–2:30	50 troy oz.	$.10/tr. oz.	$25/tr. oz.	$6250	$50c
Pork Bellies	CME	9:10–1:00	38,000 lbs	$.00025/lb.	2c/lb.	$3800	$380
Silver-New	CBOT	8:05–1:25	1,000 tr. oz.	$.0010/tr. oz.	50c/tr. oz.	$2500	$10
Soybeans	CBOT	9:30–1:15	5,000 bu.	¼c/bu.	30c/bu.	$7500	$50
Soybean Oil	CBOT	9:30–1:15	60,000 lbs	$.0001/lb.	1c/lb.	$3000	$600
Sugar	CSCE	10:00–1:43	112,000 lbs	$.0001/lb.	½c/lb.	$2800	$1120
Wheat	CBOT	9:30–1:15	5,000 bu.	¼c/bu.	20c/bu.	$5000	$50

*Central Standard (Daylight) Time
Exchanges:
CBOT—Chicago Board of Trade
CME—Chicago Mercantile Exchange
COMEX—Commodity Exchange, Inc.
NYMEX—N.Y. Mercantile Exchange
CSCE—N.Y. Coffee Sugar Cocoa Exchange
NY COTTON—N.Y. Cotton Exchange

One-Stop Shopping

It all came in one handsome gray envelope. Dignified maroon print on the front. It was addressed to "Resident." Curiosity got the better of me, and I opened it.

Inside, there were several highly respectable-looking gray and maroon sheets. The top sheet offered Resident a once-in-a-lifetime chance to buy into a certain real estate limited partnership. A brief paragraph described this fabulous deal: it offered safety of principal, current income, capital appreciation, and liquidity, and was suitable for individuals, endowments, charities, retirement plans, and educational trusts. Two hundred million dollars worth of this little item was available to Residents, if they would just send in for the prospectus.

What other investment marvels awaited me? I wondered. Flipping on to the next sheet....

"TERMITES?!" Lock's Pest Control, Member, National Pest Control Association, can handle Resident's bug problems. Cheap, too. This can't be happening, I thought. The termites got into this splendid and impressive business proposal by some horrible mistake. The next sheet...

"Retain your vital shape-giving tissues while you shed excess fat!" (This enterprise also offers a monthly newsletter.) The marketing of financial services is going through a wild and wooly period. What convinced that real estate partnership to do a joint mailing with the bug brigade, etc., we can't imagine. But may we suggest that you arrange your real estate partnerships, your mutual fund purchases, your mortgages, and all other financial transactions through the more conventional channels? Otherwise, the vital shape-giving tissues that pad out your wallet may suffer a horrible fate.

What is Money? Who Controls it?

The Federal Reserve Bank is the nation's money manager. And what the "Fed" says goes—as far as what money is, or isn't. As the nation's central bank, the Federal Reserve creates and manages our money. It wields tremendous power, placed in the hands of its governors, who are some of the smartest economists in the country. Yet to many professionals, as well as amateur investors, the Fed (as it is fondly known) remains an enigma.

One good reason is that the Fed keeps its operations largely secret. Yet the daily financial pages clearly show the central bank's ongoing struggle with its most important job: managing the amount of money in circulation. An unexpected jump in the so-called "M-1 (or basic) money supply" sends shock waves through the financial markets. And, a drop in the same figure reported by the Fed for the latest week causes rejoicing on Wall Street.

Arguing the relative importance of even small changes in the money supply—and what they reveal about the current course of the economy—keeps financial analysts in pocket change. So does the long-running debate among economists over how effectively the Fed can steer the economy by "fine-tuning" the money supply. At the heart of all this controversy lie two imponderables that the central bankers must live with. One is the knotty problem of answering our own deceptively simple question: What is Money?

The Fed is supposed to maintain the "right" level of money in circulation—enough to keep the economy growing, but not so much as to cause inflation. To do that, it must be able to accurately count the amount of money that is changing hands at any given time. One measure of the enormity of the task: cash (coins and currency) accounts for far less than 1% of the money supply. In the more than 75 years since the Fed was created in 1914, it still hasn't found a way to count everything else that might also be counted as money.

The other conundrum complicating the Fed's job of managing the nation's money is that monetary theory is just that—theory. In plain English, no one knows for certain how money works in the economy. So, the Fed can never say with any certainty what the money "supply" should be. The best the Fed can do is to analyze key indicators, such as unemployment, and decide whether it needs to "loosen" (allow the money supply to grow faster to speed up the economy) or "tighten" (restrict the money supply to slow the economy down).

If It Looks Like Money . . .

Defining just what is—and isn't—money has become considerably more difficult with the deregulation of the financial industry. Up until 1980, the Fed used five "Ms" (standing for money). They ranged from M-1 (coins, currency, and checking accounts at commercial banks) through M-5, which included all the other forms of cash in between plus interest-earning deposits at any kind of financial institution.

But the distinction between different kinds of financial institutions was blurring. In the mid-1970s, New England Savings and Loans found a way around the law that permitted only commercial banks to offer checking accounts, and the NOW account was born. Money market mutual funds came into their own and began offering check-writing privileges. Clearly, these new kinds of deposits didn't fit neatly into the five "Ms" that the Fed was using.

The Fed's solution was to come up with five new money measures, four of which are still used. Of those four, M-1, M-2, and M-3 are watched more closely by most economists than the largest, which is now called L. The differences between the various measures of money are astounding. For example, midway through 1985, M-1 stood at $581.5 billion, while M-2 amounted to $2.4 trillion, and M-3 to slightly more than $3 trillion. And a lot that could be counted as money isn't. Just one example: money you might have in an IRA or Keogh account at a financial institution or in a money market fund. Other forms of "near cash" that aren't counted include the unused credit line that may be available through your checking account or credit card, and the equity account that lets you spend against the appreciation on your home.

Where It Comes From

Yet at any given time, there is only a fixed amount of money in the U.S. economy. (See Figure 95-1.) The Fed alone can create more. That's despite the fact that the Treasury's presses run overtime to meet the growing demand for cold, hard cash. Currently, those presses turn out one sheet of 32 bills in denominations of from $1 to $100 (the largest printed today) at the rate of a sheet every

Figure 95-1
Currency in Circulation

Denomination	March 31, 1986 Total
$1	$ 3,590,269,312
2	714,875,086
5	4,835,050,285
10	11,075,994,880
20	52,994,775,420
50	22,926,520,700
100	81,274,480,200
500	153,623,000
1,000	178,201,000
5,000	1,815,000
10,000	3,480,000

two seconds—around the clock, seven days a week. That comes to roughly $32 billion a year.

The Treasury's Bureau of the Mint also turns out an increasing number of coins. Over the last 25 years, it has stepped up its production, from about 3 million coins in 1960 to more than 20 million a year. Worn-out money is returned to the Treasury. In an average year, nearly 20 billion coins alone—valued at well over $2 billion—pass through the Mint's processing units for recoinage.

But the Mint, and the Bureau of Engraving, which makes the bills, are merely money manufacturers. The Fed controls how much money is actually in circulation. It does that by speeding up—or slowing down—the rate at which new cash is available for spending through its open-market operations. Often misunderstood, these are essentially accounting transactions between the Fed—through its open-market trading desk in New York—and the 12 regional Federal Reserve Banks, and the Fed's 25 branches. The Fed creates new money with a simple bookkeeping entry. To do this, the Fed "trades" U.S. government securities—mainly treasury bills. Money is put in circulation if the Fed buys these "T-Bills," and are taken out of circulation through a sale. To buy, say, $1 million of Treasury bills, the Fed instantly credits the bond dealers' banks with $1 million of brand new reserves—money that literally didn't exist until that very moment. When the Fed wants to contract the money supply, the process works in reverse. It sells Treasury bills, wiping out an equivalent amount of old bank reserves.

The Fed's Other Powers

Ideally, the central bank tries to balance the amount of money available with the demand for it. When there is too much money around, relative to demand, Americans spend like there is no tomorrow (fearing prices will only go higher) and the result is inflation. When there is too little money available, relative to demand, more people put off purchases and the economy sinks into a recession. The Fed rarely has been able to strike a perfect balance for long. But aside from creating money and making it disappear, it uses several other powers granted by Congress to manage the money supply's impact on the economy.

One of those powers is the Fed's ability to set the basic interest rate, the *discount rate*. This is the rate charged when banks borrow from the Fed through its "discount window." By making it cheaper—or more expensive—for financial institutions to borrow money, the Fed strongly influences how much the public pays for a loan—the "price" of money is passed on to the consumer.

The Fed doesn't tinker with the discount rate often. A change, however, affects the financial markets because it reveals the Fed's current thinking on the state of the economy. A cut in the discount rate usually indicates that the Fed believes the economy is lagging and needs a boost. An increase in the discount rate typically means the Fed is concerned that the economy is overheating and needs to be cooled down.

In addition to the discount rate, the Fed also effectively controls the federal funds rate—the charge on loans that banks make to each other. Since that rate is usually lower than the discount rate, banks borrow 10 times as much in the federal funds market as they do from the Fed's discount window. So, while changes in the discount rate usually provide clues to future monetary policy, the federal funds rate is a far more sensitive barometer of the direction interest rates are headed.

Finally, the Fed also dictates how much banks must hold in reserve against possible withdrawals. The level of these so-called fractional, non-interest-bearing reserves is usually in the neighborhood of about 16 cents for each $1 of deposits. Even slight changes in the reserve requirement frees up—or contracts—the amount of money banks have for lending.

How the Fed Counts Money

Every Thursday after 3:30 p.m. (CST) the Federal Reserve Bank reports on the amount of money in circulation. This figure can usually be found in the financial section of most daily newspapers on Friday. Simply stated, the different forms of money are grouped into two liberal classifications: *M1, M2,* and *M-3*—money and near money; and *L*—longer-term liquid funds. Following is a detailed breakdown of each classification and its components. What it means to you is covered in "Why the Fed is Worth Watching," Dose 100.

M-1 Currency outside the Treasury, Federal Reserve Banks, and the vaults of commercial banks; travelers checks of nonbank issuers; demand deposits at all commercial banks other than those due to domestic banks, the U.S. government and foreign banks and official institutions less cash items in the process of collection and Federal Reserve float; other checkable deposits (OCD) consisting of negotiable order of withdrawal (NOW) and automatic transfer service (ATS) accounts at depository institutions, credit union share draft accounts, and demand deposits at thrift institutions.

M-2 = M-1, plus overnight (and continuing contract) repurchase agreements (RPs) issued by all commercial banks and overnight Eurodollars issued to U.S. residents by foreign branches of U.S. banks worldwide, money-market deposit accounts (MMDAs), savings and small-denomination time deposits (time deposits—excluding retail repurchase agreements in amounts of less than $100,000), and balances in both taxable and tax-exempt general purpose and broker/dealer money market mutual funds. Excludes individual retirement accounts (IRA) and Keogh balances at depository institutions and money market funds. Also excludes all balances held by U.S. commercial banks, money market funds (general purpose and broker/dealer), foreign governments and commercial banks, and the U.S. government.

Dollars and Sense

M-3 = M-2, plus large-denomination time deposits and term repurchase liabilities (in amounts of $100,000 or more) issued by commercial banks and thirft institutions; term Eurodollars held by U.S. residents at foreign branches of U.S. banks worldwide and at all banking offices in the United Kingdom and Canada, and balances in both taxable and tax-exempt institutions-only money market funds. Excludes amounts held by depository institutions, the U.S. government, money market funds, and foreign banks and official institutions.

L = M-3, plus the nonbank public holdings of U.S. savings bonds, short-term Treasury securities, commercial paper and bankers acceptances, net of money market fund holdings of these assets.

The Federal Dollar: Where it Comes From, Where it Goes

Balancing the federal budget, tax reform, spending cuts—we're all familiar with the key economic issues facing the federal government. What may not be as clear is where the money comes from—and where it goes. Following is $1 of federal revenue for fiscal 1987.

The *off-budget* items on the chart resulted from the Balanced Budget and Emergency Deficit Control Act of 1985. What this means is that receipts and outlays of the old-age and survivors insurance (OASI) and disability insurance (DI) programs are now *off-budget* and are exempt from any general budget limitations imposed by statute. In essence, these programs are protected.

The Federal Government Dollar
Fiscal Year 1987 Estimate

Where It Comes From ...

- Excise Taxes 4¢
- Corporation Income Taxes 9¢
- Other 4¢
- 21¢
- Social Insurance Receipts 9¢
- Borrowing 14¢
- Individual Income Taxes 39¢

Where It Goes ...

- 21¢
- National Defense 28¢
- Direct Benefit Payments for Individuals 20¢
- Net Interest 15¢
- Grants to States and Localities 10¢
- Other Federal Operations 6¢

Off-Budget ▨
On-Budget ☐

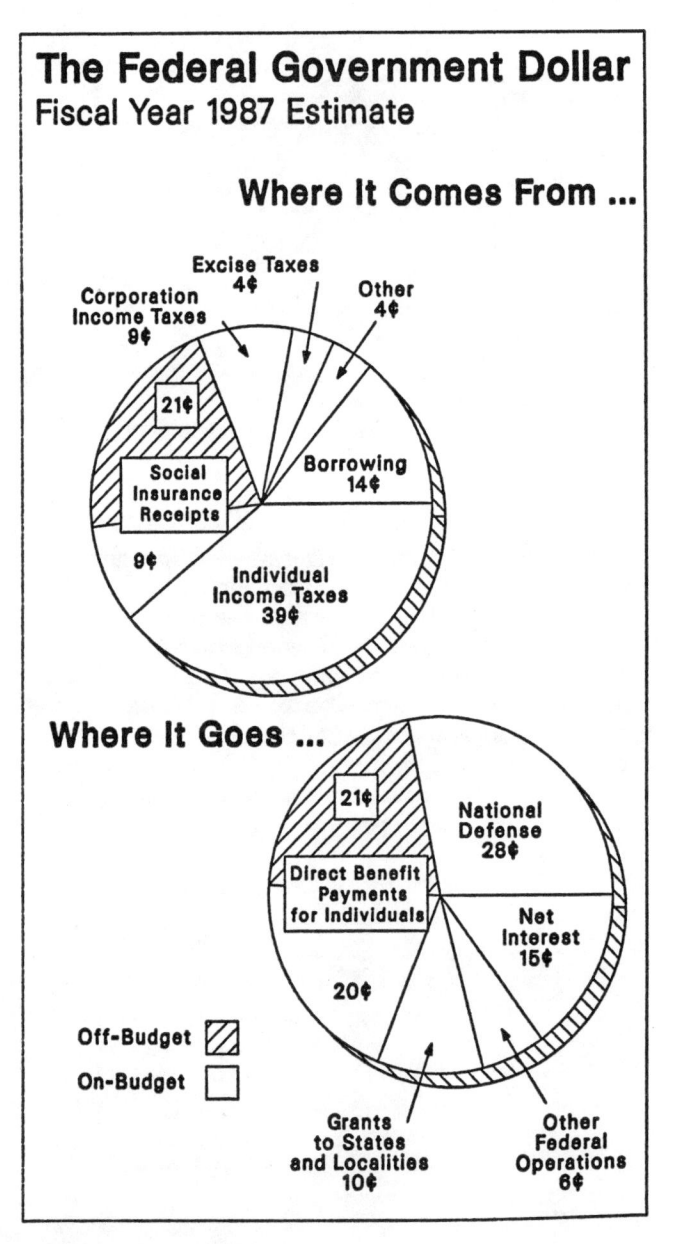

Source: U.S. Government Office
of Management and Budget
Washington, D.C. 20503

Uncle Sam's Big IOU

The federal debt now stands at over $2 trillion (that's 12 zeros) and is still growing. By 1985, it was nearly half as large as the gross national product (GNP)—the nation's total output of goods and services. This compares (not very favorably) to only one-third of the GNP just four short years earlier. (See Figure 98-1.)

What does the burgeoning federal debt really mean to the U.S. economy? Is it really the monster that it has been made to seem? The federal debt, like most economic issues, is a source of disagreement among economists, although at $2 trillion all would concede that it is a problem that should receive high priority from policymakers.

Who Owns the Federal Debt?

When the federal government spends more money than it receives, the resulting shortfall, or deficit, must be financed through borrowing. The government "borrows" when the Treasury issues interest-bearing securities and sells them to investors. These bonds comprise the national debt.

As a result, the national debt is "owned" by U.S. investors and private institutions, foreign investors, U.S. government agencies, and the Federal Reserve System, all of which hold the bonds. Figure 98-2 illustrates the breakdown of the debt during 1985. The lion's share, some 62%, was held by U.S. investors and U.S. financial institutions, such as commercial banks and insurance agencies. Foreign investors held about 12% of the total debt. Another 17% was held by government agencies, representing little more than an accounting transaction indicating that one government agency is making a loan to another. The Federal Reserve System held over 9% of the federal debt, which is an important determinant of the money supply in the United States.

Figure 98-1
GNP and Federal Debt
1968 – 1986

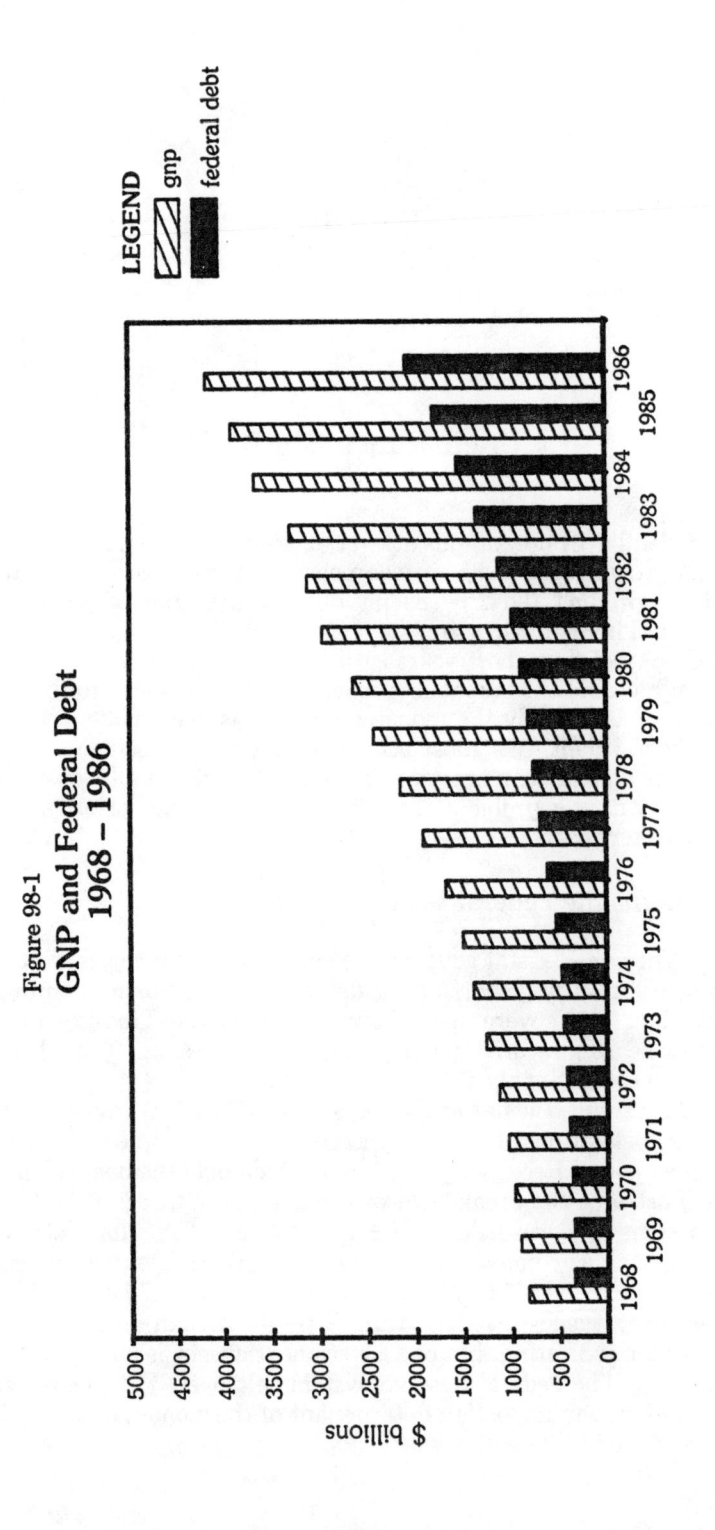

Figure 98-2
Uncle Sam's Creditors

As of September 30, 1985, the federal debt has reached a level of $1.8 trillion, twice its $900 billion level at the end of 1980. The following is a listing of who holds the federal IOUs.

	Amount Held ($ billions)	Percent of Total Debt
U.S. Government Agencies	$ 316.5	17.3%
Foreign investors	210.0	11.5
Commercial banks	197.0	10.8
Federal Reserve banks	169.7	9.3
State and local gov'ts.	165.0 *(e)*	9.0
Individuals	151.3	8.3
Insurance companies	84.0 *(e)*	4.6
Corporations	56.5	3.1
Money market funds	22.7	1.2
Other investors	454.8	24.9
	$1,827.5	100.0%

(e) estimate
Source: U.S. Treasury Bulletin

The Burden of Debt: An Ongoing Debate

Traditionally, there have been two schools of thought concerning the national debt and its burden on U.S. society. One side argues that future generations will pay for our fiscal overspending and inability to balance the federal budget. The federal debt expands each year that a deficit is run, and with annual deficits of $200 billion, the federal debt could be *twice* the size of the GNP in just 10 years. This side compares federal overspending to an uncontrolled buying spree with credit cards—eventually even more borrowing will be necessary just to cover interest payments. In the case of the federal government, this means that the interest payments on the debt could soon equal the annual deficit itself.

The second school of thought argues that because the vast majority of the debt is held domestically, the debt remains "in the family." That is, Treasury bonds represent not only a liability to the government, but also an asset to the bondholders. Therefore, this side claims, we will hand down an interest-bearing asset to future generations that will offset the tax burden associated with the interest payments on that asset.

The second argument hinges on the majority of the national debt being held domestically. But this premise was weakened when a strong U.S. dollar and high domestic interest rates attracted a flood of foreign investors who snapped up high-yielding government-backed securities. By 1985, more U.S. debt was held by overseas investors than vice versa. As a result, the United States joined the ranks of debtor nations.

Impact on Business

Chronic deficit spending and its accompanying swelling of the federal debt causes big worries, not the least of which are threats of soaring interest rates and more spiraling inflation.

One of the biggest risks posed by Uncle Sam's big IOU is that of slower economic growth. This occurs when the government absorbs too much of the credit available in the market (by selling large amounts of Treasury securities to the public), thereby "crowding out" other would-be borrowers. When businesses can't issue new debt to finance spending, business activity slows. This, of course, has a direct, and negative, impact on GNP.

Inflation Fears

The Treasury's seemingly insatiable appetite for credit is one reason why *real* U.S. interest rates have remained historically high. Although the general level of interest rates has dropped over the past year, the decrease has been due almost entirely to the drop in the inflation rate. The real (after inflation) cost of money still remains high.

Under the scenario of too-high interest rates and too-slow economic growth, the Federal Reserve could decide to increase the money supply to keep rates down and add fuel to the recovery. But such expansionary monetary policy could lead to more spiraling inflation.

Servicing the Debt

Growing federal debt means, of course, rising interest payments on that debt. One of the most unsettling thoughts plaguing economists lately is that if debt levels continue to rise at the present rate, interest payments alone could reach the proportions of the total deficit. In that case, more debt is required just to service the old debt.

Servicing the debt wasn't always a major concern. Over the period 1954-73, interest payments on the debt as a percentage of the GNP remained stable, hovering in the 1.5% range. But high interest rates and large budget deficits during the next 15 years pushed that ratio upward. By 1985, net interest payments reached $130 billion, or 3.2% of the total national output. (See Figure 98-3.) Even more disconcerting was the fact that over $20 billion of those interest payments went to foreign holders of Treasury securities.

However, the Congressional Budget Office and the Office of Management and Budget now agree that even without further bud-

Figure 98-3
Interest Payments on Federal Debt

	Net Interest Payment ($ billions)	GNP ($ billions)	Net Interest As Percent of GNP
1977	$ 29.9	$1,936	1.54%
1978	35.4	2,173	1.63
1979	42.6	2,452	1.74
1980	52.5	2,668	1.97
1981	68.7	2,986	2.30
1982	85.0	3,142	2.71
1983	89.8	3,321	2.70
1984	111.1	3,695	3.01
1985	129.4	3,937	3.24

Source: Treasury Bulletin

get cuts, the deficit will fall to $100 billion by 1991.

A word of caution: if economic growth is less than forecast, the $100 billion figure could be much higher. And even at $100 billion, the deficit could add $500 billion in new debt over the following five years. It appears that although the government has made some headway in managing the federal debt, it still has a long way to go.

What is the Consumer Price Index?

The "cost of living" has been a hot topic over the last decade. The media follow it avidly. We, in turn, use it as a measure of how well—or poorly—we're doing in financial terms: Are we keeping up, falling behind? Most often, a single measure is used to indicate changes in the cost of living: the Consumer Price Index (CPI) that reflects how much we, as consumers, have to pay for the things we buy. The CPI is a measure of the *average* change in the prices paid by *urban* consumers for a fixed "market basket" of goods and services, including most of the basics like food, clothing, housing, and transportation.

But the CPI is more than an indication of whether what we earn is keeping up with how much we have to spend. The CPI is widely used as a measure of inflation, and serves as an indicator of the effectiveness of government economic policy in controlling economic fluctuations. It is also used for economic analysis. Components of the CPI, such as the CPI series for food at home, are important as measures of price changes for segments of the consumers' budget, and are used to analyze such things as changing patterns of consumer demand.

Keeping Up with the Joneses

How often have we heard a union, group, or individual demand increases in pay or benefits that "reflect" the cost of living? Well, here's another place that the CPI comes in. For example, more than 8.5 million workers are covered by collective bargaining contracts that provide for increases in wages based on increases in the CPI. In addition to workers whose wages or pensions are adjusted according to changes in the CPI, the index now affects the income of more than 50 million persons, including almost 38 million social security beneficiaries, about 3.3 million retired military and Federal Civil Service employees and their survivors, and about 20 million food stamp recipients. National average payments for meals provided under the National School Lunch Act and the Child Nutrition Act are adjusted annually based on changes in the CPI "food away from home" category.

The Changing CPI

The Consumer Price Index was first calculated during World War I when rapid increases in prices made such an index essential for calculating cost-of-living adjustments in wages. At first, separate indexes were published for 32 cities. A national index, the U.S. city average, was begun in 1921.

The index was completely revised in 1953. Several revisions have been made since then. The most recent, in 1978, created *two* indexes. The first—the CPI-W—covered only wage earners and clerical workers, as did the original index. The second—the CPI-U—covered *all* urban consumers: professional and salaried workers, part-time workers, the self-employed, the unemployed, and retired people, in addition to wage earners and clerical workers. Obviously, it's a more broad measure.

The CPI underwent another revision in January 1987 which updated the "market basket" of goods and services used in computing the index. Such periodic revision is necessary because consumers change their purchasing patterns as a result of changes in: relative prices, real income, demographic characteristics, and personal tastes.

Who's Counted

The CPI is based on a sample of prices in seven major categories: food and beverages, housing, apparel and upkeep, transportation, medical care, entertainment, and other goods and services (e.g., tobacco products, personal care items, and educational expenses). Changes (increases or decreases) are measured against prices for the same items in a base period. Since it's impossible to know what every consumer spent on every purchase, statistical methods are used to obtain a representative sample of buying habits and costs.

The CPI is a *weighted* average. The weights reflect the importance of each item in terms of the average consumer's overall expenditures. As Figure 99-1 shows, the weights are the average of total expenditures that each category represents.

Prices for most goods and services used in calculating the index are collected in 85 urban areas across the country from about 24,000 establishments—grocery and department stores, hospitals, filling stations, and other types of stores and service establishments. The price of food, fuel, and a few other items are obtained every month in all 85 locations. Prices of most other goods and services are collected

Figure 99-1
Relative Importance (Weights) of Components in the Consumer Price Indexes

Expenditure Category	All Urban Consumers (CPI-U)	Urban Wage Earners & Clerical Workers (CPI-W)
Food and beverages	18.81%	20.48%
Housing	43.91	40.68
Apparel and upkeep	5.80	5.84
Transportation	18.03	20.23
Medical care	4.97	4.49
Entertainment	4.08	3.91
Other goods and services	4.40	4.37
Total	100.00	100.00

every month in the five largest urban areas and every other month in the remaining areas.

To calculate the overall index, price changes for the various items are averaged together and the weights applied. Monthly changes are expressed as percentages. Percent changes for 3- and 6-month periods are expressed as compound annual rates which involves projecting the current rate over 12 months. The monthly CPI is published the 20th and 25th of the month following the month in which the data are collected. (For example, the index for January is published in late February.) A summary and analysis of major price changes is also produced each month.

The CPI is not an exact measure. For one thing, it is based on a *sample,* so it doesn't completely reflect the behavior of all consumers. In addition, information provided by both purchasers and sellers may be inaccurate. While every effort is made to correct these errors, they do mean the CPI is not completely accurate. Finally, the CPI may not be directly applicable to questions about price movements for all specific groups. For example, the CPI-U represents the average movement of prices for the urban population. Rural populations aren't included. The CPI also doesn't provide information for any particular subgroup of the population like the aged.

Figure 99-2 shows how consumer prices have varied. During the 1950s, for example, the CPI increased at an annual rate of 2.2% while the decade of the 1970s was marked by sharp rises (7.4% annually). Since 1940, the CPI has risen at the average annual rate of 4.6%. During the last 46 years there have been only two periods during which the CPI actually declined (a drop of 1.8% in 1946 and a minuscule 0.5% decline during 1954). The largest annual price increases occurred in 1946 (18.2%), 1979 (13.3%), 1980 (12.4%), and 1974 (12.2%).

Figure 99-2
Consumer Price Variations

Ten-Year Period	Annual Increase in CPI	Total Increase for Decade
1940–1949	5.4%	68.5%
1950–1959	2.2	23.7
1960–1969	2.5	27.5
1970–1979	7.4	103.7
1980–1985	6.1	42.4

Why the Fed is Worth Watching

For all its muscle, the Fed seems unable to keep the economy from whipsawing every few years, from inflation to recession and back to inflation again. What role does the money supply play in this drama? That depends on which set of economists you talk to.

In one corner are those who believe that by "fine-tuning" the money supply (making discretionary increases and decreases), the Fed can control economic growth with considerable precision. In the other corner are the detractors. At the crux of their ongoing debate is the so-called "Quantity Theory of Money," also known as the "Equation of Exchange."

The equation looks like this: $MV = PQ$

Where: $M =$ Money supply.
$V =$ Velocity of money (the number of times $1 changes hands in a year).
$P =$ Average price level.
$Q =$ Total national output of goods and services.

The theory says that because $PQ = GNP$ (the gross national product—the value of the goods and services the country produces each year), and if the velocity of money is constant, then changes in the money supply have a direct impact on GNP. In other words, if the Fed wants the GNP to grow, it only has to make sure that the supply of money grows. If it wants to slow the growth of economic activity, it merely decreases the "Money Supply" (M). Moreover, the theory goes, by maintaining a steady grip on the money supply, the Fed can control the cost of money (interest rates). That accomplished, inflation will then take care of itself. Why? Proponents of this view say that the cost of money is a direct result of supply. At the beginning of an expansionary period, having too much around makes money cheap. But as inflation sets in, the cost of money rises—like everything else. Therefore, controlling the supply of money should enable the Fed to control its cost.

But the detractors contend that the Fed isn't that powerful. It is simply impossible, they say, for the central bankers to control money growth that closely. For that reason, their position is that the money supply should not be used for fine-tuning. Instead, it should merely be allowed to increase by the same annual rate as the potential growth in the GNP.

At the heart of this theory of money is that the Fed is something of a Monday morning quarterback. The monetarists contend that by the time the Fed steps in and takes action, it is too late—or it has become clear that action wasn't needed. This is because there is a lag between the time the Fed acts and when the results of its actions are felt. Therefore, the Fed really doesn't increase or decrease the money supply at the "correct" time. For example, the Fed may inject money into a sluggish economy to stimulate growth. But by the time that increase in the money supply takes hold, the economy may have already started expanding on its own. As a result, the injection of money, instead of correcting a recession, helps create an inflation.

Keynes and the Supply-Siders

Staunchly opposed to monetarists of any stripe are the modern-day disciples of the late English economist, John Maynard Keynes. To these economists, monetary policy—how the government creates and manages the nation's money—is less important than fiscal policy—how the government collects revenue and spends it. Keynesians argue that instead of tinkering with the money supply to try and speed up or slow down the economy, the government should make changes in federal taxes and its own spending. Essentially, they believe that the government should take a more activist approach to managing the economy.

Monetary policy is by necessity passive. The Fed creates money, but the money supply doesn't begin to grow until it changes hands. Moreover, it often takes months for changes in the money supply to have any real impact on the economy (the lag effect). On the other hand, changes in fiscal policy—the government altering its own borrowing or spending—can put more money to work much faster. Keynes would say that the government has to step in at times to keep the economy on an even keel. It was his opinion that because economies are not inherently stable, neither is the velocity of money. In other words, the rate at which the public borrows, spends, and invests varies over time. To keep the economy moving Keynes felt that the government has to sometimes get involved—to "prime the pump" by doing more borrowing and spending of its own, and the public would follow.

Dollars and Sense

Some of Keynes' ideas about fiscal policy helped shape the thinking of the Reagan administration's so-called "supply siders." These economists put forth a convincing argument that the solution to inflation was cutting taxes. Inflation had grown endemic in the U.S. economy, they contended, because Americans' demand for nearly everything exceeded their supply of money for getting it. Moreover, taxes had killed the incentive to work, save, and invest. The Reagan administration's tax cuts have indeed put more money in most Americans' pockets. And inflation has cooled. But as long as the federal budget deficit remains staggering, supply-side theory will be on trial.

Who's Protecting Your Money?

Unless you keep your cash under your mattress, this is a good question. The insurance provided by banks and brokerage firms is free, but it only goes so far. Insured money funds and bond investments are also protected only to a limited extent—and, in this case, you, the investor, get to pay for that protection.

Actually, the question of protection—how safe your investments are—traditionally hasn't been much of an issue. The financial world has been a bit like a saloon fight in a cowboy flick—grunts, punches, flying glass, but nobody hurt at the end. That's the way it's been the past few years for the banks where most of us put a large part of our savings and investments. Even official "failures," like that of giant Continental Illinois, have left individual investors unharmed.

But the financial world is becoming more volatile. New economic theories and government deregulation are leaving an impact on this once staid and stable industry. One result was an uproar in insurance annuities, which did some damage—though not a great deal. Life was tougher still for owners of bonds issued by Washington Public Power Supply Systems (WPPSS—bitterly pronounced "whoops!" by its investors). The utility defaulted, plunging bondholders into a welter of losses and lawsuits. Brokerage company failures, while uncommon, represent another risk to the investor.

This increasing turbulence exposes savers and investors to some risks. As a result, financial insurance has become an important safety valve for investors in today's high-pressure marketplace. So this is a good time to look at *how* you are protected and where you are *not* protected, if your bank or brokerage firm should fail. We'll also examine the new class of privately insured investments, including insured money market funds, bond funds, and bonds bundled into so-called "unit trusts."

Safe as Money in the Bank

Sadly, modern-day bank failures aren't usually front-page news anymore. There are hundreds of banks on the Federal Deposit Insurance Corp.'s "problem list" across the country. The FDIC is the U.S. government agency that insures your bank.

Should you fear for your savings or checking account? Probably not. The vast majority of the nation's 18,000 banks and savings and loans (S&Ls) are as sound as, well, as sound as a dollar. Still, they are grappling with problems at home and abroad.

With the deregulation of interest-rate ceilings, banks and S&Ls must now do battle for depositors' accounts by offering competitive rates. Meanwhile, the big banks have made loans to borrowers in certain Third World countries which poses a continuing threat of loss. A massive default by a Third World borrower is considered highly unlikely. But even if one were to occur, the federal government would stand ready to bail out many of the nation's largest banks. Such a crisis is almost unimaginable.

And your checking and savings accounts and certificates of deposit are almost certainly protected by federal deposit insurance, up to $100,000 in any one account. (Almost all banks and savings institutions are insured by either the FDIC or its counterpart, the Federal Savings and Loan Insurance Corp. There is a small number of financial institutions that don't participate in either agency, however. If you aren't sure about yours, by all means check.) Assuming your accounts are fully covered, in the event that your bank failed, you'd lose nothing. At worst, you might not have access to your funds for a week or so until the books are formally closed, and you might not get the interest that normally would have accrued during that short period.

Protecting Yourself

At least that was the situation up until now. But some politicians would like to cut federal deposit insurance to make your bank more cautious about how it lends and to whom. The idea is that with less federal insurance as protection, investors/savers will keep closer tabs on what "their" bank is doing. Under such scrutiny, prudent banks would thrive, while banks that make too many bad loans would wither and die a deserved death.

So far, any reduction in the federal deposit guarantee is merely talk. But there is some logic behind it. The measure was sparked by the massive, government-led $7.5 billion rescue of Continental Illinois. In that case, the FDIC made the unprecedented decision to guarantee all of Continental's deposits, even those above the usual $100,000 limit per account, largely because of the possible repercussions. The bank's customers included many substantial financial institutions, domestic and foreign.

But forewarned is forearmed: An FDIC official said the agency has no intention of guaranteeing all deposits in future bank failures. So, if your savings exceed the insured limit, distribute them in several accounts just to be safe. And even though your bank's quarterly and annual financial statements may sound like pretty dull reading, they might contain early warning signals. Among them: a high percentage of Third World loans, loans concentrated in any single industry, or loans to industries that are in serious trouble.

What If Your Broker Goes Broke?

So much for the state of your bank, what about your broker? A few small firms that hang out a shingle to buy and sell stocks fold every year. But the collapse of John Muir & Co. was a good example of what can happen to investors when a sizable brokerage house goes under. When Muir closed its doors in 1981, it was the first New York Stock Exchange member in eight years to be liquidated by Securities Investor Protection Corp. (SIPC).

A bit of background—the SIPC was created by Congress in 1970 in the aftermath of the so-called "go-go" era when the stock market was booming and scores of firms were buried by foul-ups and financial mismanagement. To offer investors some protection, SIPC was funded with about $217 million, collected by a levy on the firms' commission income. Since then, the level of funding has been increased to about $250 million via small annual assessments. Far more important, the agency also has a $1 billion line of credit with the U.S. Treasury. Currently, SIPC insurance is free to customers of more than 9,000 securities firms registered with the Securities and Exchange Commission. Check with SIPC to be sure your firm is covered. The agency's logo is supposed to be part of member firms' advertising.

Each account at a SIPC-member firm is insured for up to $500,000 in lost assets—lost, that is, through the failure of your brokerage firm. If your stocks go down while the firm remains intact, that's your problem. Of that $500,000, no more than $100,000 may be cash. A customer's cash, margin or short accounts are all considered one account for insurance purposes. So the small investor is almost always completely covered.

SIPC coverage is limited according to type of firms, lines of business, and amount. For instance, commodities accounts are not covered. However, SIPC coverage does extend to stock, bond, and money market mutual funds. When SIPC liquidates a bankrupt firm, the agency works with a trustee appointed by a federal bankruptcy judge. Depending on the circumstances, your account at the failed firm may be frozen for as long as a few weeks or even months. A booklet explaining how SIPC works in detail is available free from the agency, at 900 17th St., N.W., Washington, D.C. 20006.

Enter Some New Protectors

If you're willing to pay for it, you can also put your money in investments that, unlike stocks, bonds, or mutual funds, are also insured. These are not insured by any government agency, but rather by consortiums of some of the nation's biggest insurance companies. This new class of investments is in its infancy, but most of the growth so far has been in insured unit trusts. The trusts are sold by brokerage firms in typical minimums of $5,000. The insurance protects you if any of the issuers of bonds held by the trust default. You pay for the coverage in the form of slightly lower returns on your investment.

And finally, how about insuring your insurance? Check the financial strength of your insurers by consulting Best's Insurance Reports at your local library. Cross off any companies on your list that Best rates "A" or less. Then find out which states the remaining companies are licensed to do business in. New York and California, for instance, have some of the most stringent regulators. If you still have doubts, put your hard-earned cash elsewhere. And rest easy, knowing now exactly who's protecting your money.

Index

A

ABCs, see Agency Backed Compounded securities
Acadia, 82
Active Assets Money Trust, 188
Adjustable rate mortgages, 51, 57, 58
Advertising, 585
Advisers, financial, 192
Agency Backed Compounded securities, 347
Airline tickets, 122
Alarm systems, see Security systems
Alliance Capital Reserves, 190
American Arbitration Association, 62
American Council for an Energy-Efficient Economy, 70
American Council on Education, 126
American Express, 122, 219
American Institute for Economic Research, 87
American Movers Conference, 63
American Stock Exchange, 299
American Telephone & Telegraph, 221
Amortization, 53
Annual percentage rate, defined 57
Annuities, 84, 112, 254
Appliances, 70
Appraisals, 25
Appraisers Association of America, 26
Arbitration, 125
Art, 25, 308
Asset accounts, 40, 247
Asset-value investing, 208, 209
Audits, 22
Automated Government Money Trust, 189
Automobiles, 124
Averages, see Indexes

B

Balance sheets, personal, 2, 6
Baldwin-United, 84
Balloon loans, see Loans
Bank accounts, 253, 359, see also Certificates of Deposit
Bank Card Holders of America, 34, 45

Bank statements, 23
Bankers' acceptances, 178
Banks, 41, 108, 248, 249, 356, 402, see also Credit
Banz, Rolf, 298
Bathrooms, 69
Bear markets, 302, 341
Behavior sample, 195
A. M. Best Company, 255
Best's Insurance Reports, 404
Better Business Bureau, 124
Bills of lading, 63
Bond funds, 330, see also Mutual funds
Bond trusts, 202
Borrowing, see Leverage, Loans
Bonds, 100, 104, 238, 239, 244, 257, 291, 340, 345, see also Bond funds, Convertible bonds
Brokerage firms, 350, 401, 403, **see** also by name
Bull market, 302
Bureau of Public Debt, 356
Business Week, 257

C

CMA Money Fund, 185
CMA Tax-Exempt Fund, 186
Calls, see Options
Cap, defined, 58
Capital Preservation Fund, Inc., 189
Capitalization rate, see Discount
Cappiello, Frank, 241
Cars, 124
Cash, 359
Cash Equivalent Fund, 186
Cash equivalents, see Bank accounts, Money market funds
Cash management, 304
Cash Reserve Management, Inc., 186
Catalogs, 191
CATS, see Certificates of Accrual of Treasury Securities
Center for Auto Safety, 125
Certificate holders, 350
Certificates of Accrual of Treasury Securities, 345

405

Dollars and Sense

Certificates of deposit, 100, 104, 108, 239, 271, 348, 362, see also Bank accounts
Charitable deductions, 25
Chartists, 207
Checks, 23, 180, 248, 249, see also Bank accounts
Child Nutrition Act, 395
Chrysler Corporation, 124
Churning, 231
Citibank, 366
City Savings Bank, 48
Coins, 365, 368, see also Collectibles
Collectibles, 7, 9, 77, 368
College 45, see also Financial aid, Tuition
College Credit Card Corporation, 45
Commercial paper, 178
Commissions, 9, 157, 247, see also Fees
Commodities, 308, 310, 332, 378, 403, see also Futures
Commodities Futures Trading Commission, 335, 338
Commodity Traders Consumer Report, 337
Common stocks, see Stocks
Compatibility, with financial adviser, 197
Computer scholarship services, 131
Congressional Budget Office, 393
Constant ratio formulas, 282
Consultation fees, 9
Consumer Credit Protection Act, 42
Consumer Federation of America, 249
Consumer Financial Institute, 9
Consumer Price Index, 394
Contingent interest, 362
Continental Illinois Holding Corporation, 276, 402
Contrarians, 206
Conversion price, 340
Conversion ratio, 341
Convertible bonds, 340
Cooperative education, 130
Cooperative Education Opportunities, 130
Cost of living, 65, 394
Counselors, 16, 129
Credit, lines of, 35
Credit cards, 32, 35, 122, 248
Credit denial, 42

Credit instruments, see Money market
Credit reports, 41
Credit unions, 40
Crocker Bank, 37
"Curtain money," 60

D

DBL Cash Fund–Money Market Portfolio, 189
"Daddy Mac," 88
Daily Cash Accumulation Fund, Inc., 187
Daily Tax Free Fund, 190
Dean Witter/Sears Liquid Assets Fund, Inc., 186
Deak-Perera, 366
Debit cards, 248
Debt, 12, 43, see also Liability, National debt
Deductibles, 15, 64, see also Income taxes
Deferred annuities, see Annuities
Deficit spending, 391
Delaware Cash Reserves, 190
Depreciation, 28, 89
Dietz Algorithm, 234
Direct Marketing Association, 191
Discount brokers, 250
Discount rates, 18, 52, 58, 384
Discretionary accounts, 335
Diversification, 213, 269, 289, 351, see also Portfolio management
Dividends, 148, 291, 300, 367, see also Income taxes
Doctors, 16
Documents, 121, see also Recordkeeping
Dollar cost averaging, 270, 273, 284
Dominelli, Jerry David, 337
Donations, 25.
Donoghue's Money Fund Report, 168
Donoghue's Money Letter, 168
Donoghue's Mutual Fund Almanac, 179
Dow Jones Industrial Average, 222, see also Indexes
Dreyfus Liquid Assets, Inc., 185
Dreyfus Tax Exempt Money Market Fund, Inc., 187
Dun's Business Month, 257

E

Eastern Airlines, 274
Economic growth, 392

Index

Effective yield, 109, see also Yield
Efficient Market theory, 297
Electronic Realty Associates, 90
Employee benefits, 97, see also Pensions
Employee Relocation Council, 62
Energy costs, 70
Employment, 18, 129
Energy Guide Labels, 71
Equal Credit Opportunity Act, 44
Equal share purchasing, 274
Equation of exchange, 398
Equity capitalization, 300
Equity certificates of deposit, 362
Equity sharing, 88
Ethnicity, 130
Exchange privileges, 180
Executor, 7
Exemption, see Income taxes
Expenditures, averages, 3
Expense ratio, 143
Expense statement, 4
Extracurricular activities, 130

F

Fair Credit Reporting Act, 42
Family-Backed Mortgage Association, Inc., 89
Federal debt, 389
Federal deposit insurance, 253, 402
Federal Housing Administration, 326
Federal identification number, 31
Federated Master Trust, 187
Federal Reserve Banks, 178, 252, 356, 381, 385, 398
Federal Savings & Loan Insurance Corporation, 402
Federated Tax-Free Trust, 186
Federal Trade Commission, 124
Fees, 247, 363, see also Commissions
Fidelity Cash Reserves, 186
Fidelity Daily Income Trust, 187
Fidelity Money Market Trust— Domestic Portfolio, 190
Fidelity Tax-Exempt Money Market Fund, 187
FIGS, see Future Income and Growth Securities
Finance companies, 41
Financial aid, 128
Financial Analysts' Research Foundation, 212

Financial assets, see Investments and by name, e.g., Bonds
Financial planners, 3, 8, 192, 194
Fireplaces, 69
First National Bank of Chicago, 36
Fiscal policy, 399
Fisher, Philip A., 211
Forbes, 207
Ford Motor Co., 124
Forecasting, 311
Formula planning, 281
Fraud, 338
Front-end-load funds, 142, see also Mutual funds
Fund closings, 164
Fund Exchange Report, 168
Fundamental value, 208, 209
Fundline, 169
FundProbe, 170, 176
Funds, see by type, e.g., Mutual Funds
Future Income and Growth Securities, 348
Future Industry Association, 338
Futures, 366, see also Commodities
Futures Industry Newsletter, 336

G

GAINS, see Growth and Income Securities
Games, 307
General Motors Corporation, 124
Ginnie Mae, see Government National Mortgage Association
Global Futures Fund, 336
GNMA, see Government National Mortgage Association
Goals, 196
Gold, 215, 308, 364
Golden Retirement Annuity Mortgage Association, 90
Government bonds, 105, see also Bonds, Treasury bills
Government National Mortgage Association, 326
Graham, Benjamin, 243
"Grannie Mae," 88
Grants, see Financial Aid
Greenhouse, 69
Gross national product, 389, 398
Growth Fund Guide, 169
Growth and Income Securities, 348

407

Dollars and Sense

H

"Hard" assets, 308
Harris Bank, 38
Health insurance, see Insurance, health
Health maintenance organizations, 15
Hedging, 332, 340, 343
High pressure sales, 199
Hodgins, Roderic, 201
Home equity, 37
Home-buying, 68, 88, see also Real estate, Residence
Hospitals, 16
Human capital, 18, 260
E.F. Hutton, 9, 80, 348
Hutton AMA Cash Fund, 188
Hutton Commodity Reserve Fund, 336

I

IBM, 204
Ibbotson, Roger, 298
Imputed interest, 346
Income, 18, 43, 128, 351
Income splitting, 30
Income statement, 4
Income tax returns, 24
Income taxes, 9, 22, 28, 64, 81, 89, 98, 113, 143, 158, 346, 350, 355, see also Tax Shelters
Incorporation, 28
Inflation, 238, 394, see also Money supply
Inflation guard endorsement, 75
Inflation hedges, 307
Index rate, 51
Indexes, 58, 145, 228, 232, 283, 330, see also Consumer Price Index, Dow Jones Industrial Average
Individual retirement accounts, 13, 85, 100, 104, 108, 110, 114, 115, 118, 329, 335, see also Pensions
Institute of Certified Financial Planners, 9
Institutional investors, 297
Insurance, 239, 254, 401
Insurance, automobile, 7
Insurance, dental, 16
Insurance, disability, 7
Insurance, health, 15
Insurance, homeowners, 7, 63, 75
Insurance, life, 6, 7, 40, 78

Insurance, moving, 63
Insurance agents, 192
Intelligent Investor, 243
Interest, 33, 35, 51, 78, 345, 384, see also Mortgages, Savings, Yield
International Association of Financial Planners, 9
Interstate Commerce Commission, 62
Interviewing, 192
Investment objectives, 135, 144
Investment portfolios, see Portfolio Management
Investment risk, see Risk, Turnover
Investment strategies, 302, see also Portfolio Management
Investment Advisory Services, 168
Investment Company Act of 1940, 138
Investment Company Institute, 164
Isaccson, Robert, 338

J

Jewelry, see Collectibles
John Muir & Co., 403
Junk bonds, 348

K

Keogh plans, 13, 115, see also Pensions, Retirement
Kemper Money Market Fund, Inc., 186
Keynes, John Maynard, 399
Kidder Peabody, 347
Kirby, Robert G., 239
Kitchens, 69

L

Laboratory tests, 17
Lehman Investment Opportunity Notes, 345
"Lemon" laws, 124
Leverage, 13, 39
Liability, 29, 63
Liberty U.S. Government Securities Fund, 188
Limited partnerships, 335
Lindner, Kurt, 164
LIONS, see Lehman Investment Opportunity Notes
Liquid assets, 236, 270, 352, 360
Load, defined, 216
Load funds, 135

Index

Loans, 30, 38, 40, 114, 248, see also Financial Aid, Mortgages
Long-term treasury bills, see Treasury bills

M

MFS High Yield Municipal Bond Trust, 164
Mail-order loans, 40
Mail-order shopping, 191, 380
Managed Account Reports, 336
Managed accounts, 335
Manufacturers Hanover, 347
Margin, 40, 58, 332, 368
Market timing, 145, 304, 340
Market value nonfinancial assets, 1
Medals, see Collectibles
Media General Financial Weekly, 301
Merrill Lynch, 9, 82, 247, 345
Merrill Lynch Government Fund, 189
Merrill Lynch Ready Assets Trust, 185
Merrill Lynch Retirement Reserves Money Fund, 187
Metals, see Precious metals
Mining stocks, see Gold
Mistakes, 213
Momentum followers, 207
Monetarism, 398
Money, 307, explained, 381, 385
Money Fund Safety Ratings, 169
Money market, 177
Money market funds, 179, 182, 185, 230, 359
Money market instruments, 340
Money Market Trust, 189
Money supply, 385, 389, 398
Morgan Guaranty, 347
Mortgage checklist, 59
Mortgages, 47, 51, 57, 61, 89
Moving, 60
Municipal bonds, 322, 349
Municipal Fund for Temporary Investment, Inc., 188
Mutual Fund Forecaster, 169
Mutual Fund Investor, 169
Mutual Fund Letter, The, 170
Mutual Fund Management Systems, 170
Mutual Fund Specialist, 170
Mutual Fund Strategist, 171

Mutual funds, 100, 104, 135, 137, 144, 153, 155, 164, 175, 214, 238, 255, 270, 277, 300, 327, 332, 336, 349, 368

N

National Association of Securities Dealers, 83, Automated Quotation Service, 299, Composite, 229
National Commission on Student Financial Assistance, 128
National debt, 389
National Futures Association, 338
National Liquid Reserves, Inc., 190
National Scholarship Research Service, 131
National School Lunch Act, 395
Negative amortization, 53, defined, 58
Negotiable certificates of deposit, 178
Net asset value, 140
Net worth, computing, 1
New England Savings & Loan, 382
New York Commodity Exchange, 337
New York Stock Exchange, 218, 226, 299, Composite Index, 228
Noddings, Tom, 344
No-Load Funds, 171
No-Load Fund Indicator, 171
Non-taxable returns, see Returns, Tax shelters
Norwood Index, 337
NOW accounts, 249
Nuveen Tax-Exempt Money Market Fund, 187

O

Occupation, 43
Office of Management and Budget, 393
Offshore funds, 335
One-stop accounts, 247
Open-end funds, 139
Options, 366
Orthodontics, 16
Overdraft protection, 36, 248
Over-the-counter stocks, 229, see also Stocks

P

Paine Webber Cash Fund, Inc., 186
Paine Webber RMA Money Fund, Inc., 189

Dollars and Sense

Passports, 122
Penn Mutual, 164, 167
Pension funds, 336
Pension plans, 118, 261, see also Retirement
Performance, 149, 166, 214, 230
Performance Guide Publications, 171
Personal balance sheet, 2, 259
Personal property, donations, 25, see also Insurance, homeowners
Peter Dag Investment Letter, 171
Phoenix Money Market Services, 185
Planning guidelines, 3
Points, defined, 58, 218
"Ponzi" schemes, 338
Pools, 332, see also Commodities
Pope, Alan, 167
Portfolio management, 100, 104, 135, 140, 165, 211, 213, 230, 231, 253, 257, 262, 267, 269, 281, 327, 340, 350
Portfolio managers, 155, 182
Portfolio turnover rate, 140
Practical Guide to the Commodities Markets, 338
Precious metals, 364
Preferred Provider Organizations, 15
Premiums, 367
Prepayment risk, 328
Present value, 18
Price-earnings ratio, defined, 206, 220, 300
Price-to-price comparisons, 206
Price weighting, 224
Prime Investment Alert, 172
Productive tangibles, 308
Professionals, 6, 28
Profit-sharing plans, 111
Prospectuses, 137, 255, 336
Prudential-Bache, 9, 82
Prudential-Bache Government Securities Trust, 187
Public Utilities Commission, 62
Purchasing power, 238, 328
Puts, see Options

Q

Quantity theory of money, 398
Quotations, 218

R

Real estate, 27, 61, 89, 238, see also Home Equity

Recordkeeping, 22, 64, 121
Referrals, 192
Refinancing, 47
Regan, Donald T., 402
Reinvestments, 248, 346, 352
Related parties, 27
Relocation, see Moving
Remodeling, 68
Remodeling Contractor, 68
Repos, see Repurchase agreements
Repurchase agreements, 178
Republic National Bank, 366
Reserves, 384
Residence, 261
Retailers, 41
Retirement, 106, 117, 144, 274, see also Annuities, Individual Retirement Accounts, Pension Plans, Social Security
Return, 149, 153, 208, 300, 322, 333, 360, see also Performance, Yield
Reverse annuity mortgages, 89
Risk, 148, 177, 236, 245, 261, 266, 304, 327, 335, 378, see also Diversification, Portfolio Management
Risk-Adjusted Mutual Fund Performance Review, 172
Risk/reward analysis, 342
Room additions, 69
Rose, Leon, 333
Rosen, Kenneth, 89
Round lots, 218, 220
T. Rowe Price Prime Reserve Fund, Inc., 187
Royce Value Fund, 167
Rule of 72, 313
Runzheimer International, 65

S

Safe deposit boxes, 7
Safes, 7
Safety, 401, see also Risk
Sales charges, 247, see also Commissions, Fees
Salomon Brothers, 345
Savings, 94, 126, see also Bank accounts
Savings & Loans, 249, 402
Savings bonds, 355
Scholarship Search Service, 131
Scholarships, 126
Sears-Dean Witter, 9

Index

Securities, see Stocks, Bonds, Treasury bills, etc.
Securities and Exchange Commission Office of Consumer Affairs, 338
Securities Investor Protection Corp., 248, 338, 403
Security Pacific Bank, 37
Security Systems, 73
Separate Trading of Registered Interest and Principal of Securities, 345
Social Security, 22
Stocks, 206, 228, 230, 236, 238, 241, 244, 257, 266, 270, 296, 403, see also Mutual funds
Striar, Bernard, 337
STRIPS, see Separate Trading of Registered Interest and Principal of Securities
Subchapter S, 29
Superstocks, 241
Supply-siders, 399
Swimming pools, 69
Systems and Forecasts, 173

T

TRW Credit Data, 42
Tangibles, 307
Tax deferral, 30
Tax returns, see Income taxes
Taxable returns, see Return
Tax-exempt trusts, 349
Tax-exempt investments, 325, see also Tax shelters
Tax-Exempt Money Market Fund, Inc., 190
Tax-free dividends, 30
Tax-Free Instruments Trust, 190
Taxes, see Income taxes
Tax shelters, 357
"Teasers," 52
Telephone Switch Newsletter, 173
Temporary Investment Fund, 185
Term accounts, see Bank accounts
Term insurance, 79, see also Insurance, life
Thomas Cook, 122
Thomas McKinnon National Money Market Fund, 188
Thompson Financial Futures Partners I, 335
TIGR, see Treasury Investment Growth Receipts

Time Your Switch, 173
Title, 6, 7
Trading, 216, 240, 308, 335
TransUnion, 42
Travel, 121
Travelers checks, 122
Treasury bills, 105, 177, 251, 281, 285, 355, 361, 383
Treasury Investment Growth Receipts, 345
Trend following, 216
Trend models, 333
Trucks, 124
Trust for Short-Term Federal Securities, 181, 189
Trust for Short-Term U.S. Government Securities, 186
Trust for U.S. Treasury Obligations, 186
Trust Funds Liquid Assets Trust, 188, 190
Trusts, 31
Tuition, 126, see also Financial Aid
Turnover, 136, 145

U

Undergraduate Programs of Cooperative Education, 130
Union National Bank, 33
Unit Bond Trusts, 349, 401
United Mutual Fund Selector, 173
United Services Gold Shares Fund, 368
U.S. Savings Bonds, 355
U.S. Student Aid Funds, 130
U.S. Treasury Department, 383
Universal life insurance. 78
Utilities, 70

V

Value approach, 243
Value Line Investment Survey, 258, 301
Value weighting, 228
Values, common stock, 206
VanCaspel, Venita, 291
Vanguard Index Trust, 277, 285
Vanguard Money Market Trust, 188
Variable-rate bonds, 238
Variable-rate mortgages, 57
Variable ratio formulas, 282
Veterans Administration, 326
Volatility, defined, 145, 148

Dollars and Sense

Volcker, Paul, 400
Volume Investor Corp., 337

W

Wages, 92, see also Income
Wall Street Journal, 257
Warren, Gorham & Lamont, Inc., 174
Washington Public Power Supply System, 401
Wealth, see Net worth
Weber's Fund Advisor, 173
Webster Cash Reserve Fund, Inc., 189
Wellington's Worry-Free Investing, 174
Wells Fargo Bank, 32, 37, 38

Western Savings & Loan, 362
Western Capital Fund, 336
Whole life insurance, 40, 79
Wiesenberger Investment Companies Service, 135, 144, 173, 256
Wills, 6
Wilshire 5000 Equity, 229
Withholding, 20, see also Income taxes
Work-study grants, 130

Y

Yields, 140, 177, 180, 322, 325, 346, 355, 362

Z

Zero coupon bonds, 345, 356